MASTERPIECES OF THE MODERN THEATRE

A NINE VOLUME SET EDITED BY ROBERT W. CORRIGAN

CENTRAL EUROPEAN THEATRE / *The Game of Love* and *La Ronde* Schnitzler / *Electra* Hofmannsthal / *R.U.R.* Capek / *The Play's the Thing* Molnár

ENGLISH THEATRE / *The Importance of Being Earnest* Wilde / *Major Barbara* Shaw / *Loyalties* Galsworthy / *Dear Brutus* Barrie / *Enter Solly Gold* Kops

FRENCH THEATRE / *The Parisian Woman* Becque / *Christopher Columbus* de Ghelderode / *Electra* Giraudoux / *Eurydice (Legend of Lovers)* Anouilh / *Queen After Death* Montherlant / *Improvisation or The Shepherd's Chameleon* Ionesco

GERMAN THEATRE / *Woyzeck* Buechner / *Maria Magdalena* Hebbel / *The Weavers* Hauptmann / *The Marquis of Keith* Wedekind / *The Caucasian Chalk Circle* Brecht

IRISH THEATRE / *The Countess Cathleen* Yeats / *The Playboy of the Western World* and *Riders to the Sea* Synge / *The Silver Tassie* and *Cock-a-Doodle Dandy* O'Casey

ITALIAN THEATRE / *Six Characters in Search of an Author* and *The Pleasure of Honesty* Pirandello / *Crime on Goat Island* Betti / *Filumena Marturano* Filippo / *The Academy* and *The Return* Fratti

RUSSIAN THEATRE / *A Month in the Country* Turgenev / *Uncle Vanya* and *The Cherry Orchard* Chekhov / *The Lower Depths* Gorky / *The Bedbug* Mayakovsky

SCANDINAVIAN THEATRE / *Hedda Gabler* Ibsen / *Miss Julie* and *The Ghost Sonata* Strindberg / *The Difficult Hour* Lagerkvist / *The Defeat* Grieg / *Anna Sophie Hedwig* Abell

SPANISH THEATRE / *The Witches' Sabbath* Benavente / *The Cradle Song* Martínez-Sierra / *The Love of Don Perlimplín and Belisa in the Garden* Lorca / *The Dream Weaver* Buero Vallejo / *Death Thrust* Sastre

MASTERPIECES OF THE MODERN SPANISH THEATRE

Edited by ROBERT W. CORRIGAN

FIVE PLAYS

THE WITCHES' SABBATH

THE CRADLE SONG

THE LOVE OF DON PERLIMPLÍN AND BELISA IN THE GARDEN

THE DREAM WEAVER

DEATH THRUST

COLLIER BOOKS, *NEW YORK*

Library of Congress Catalog Card Number: 66-24431

First Printing

The Macmillan Company, New York

Printed in the United States of America

Grateful acknowledgment is hereby made to The Macmillan Compan
for permission to reprint material from *The Modern Theatre*, edite
by Robert W. Corrigan. Copyright © by Robert W. Corrigan, 196

CONTENTS

The Theatre and Repression in Spain 7

Introduction: Masters of the Modern Theatre 11

JACINTO BENAVENTE 33
Morality in the Theatre 37
THE WITCHES' SABBATH 51

ANTONIO BUERO VALLEJO 123
About Theatre 127
THE DREAM WEAVER 131

ALFONSO SASTRE 199
Drama and Society 201
DEATH THRUST 211

GREGORIO MARTÍNEZ SIERRA 275
An Introduction to the Plays of G. Martínez Sierra 279
THE CRADLE SONG 289

FEDERICO GARCÍA LORCA 351
The Authority of the Theatre 353
THE LOVE OF DON PERLIMPLÍN AND BELISA IN THE GARDEN 357

The Writers and Their Plays 381

Selected Bibliography 383

THE THEATRE AND REPRESSION IN SPAIN

by Robert W. Corrigan

EVEN THE MOST fragmentary study of the history of the Western theatre reveals that of all the arts the drama is certainly the most mercurial. Even in countries with strong theatrical traditions it has never consistently been either the dominant literary or popular mode of expression. True as this observation may be, however, no country has had a stronger theatrical history than Spain. The Greeks have had no theatre worth speaking of during the Christian era, but this phenomenon can be explained by both the poverty of the people and by their almost monomaniacal devotion to the past; the Irish playwrights have always tended to be assimilated by the London stage, although under the leadership of Yeats the Irish theatre movement did come into flower during the first part of this century; until the emergence of Pirandello just before World War I, Italy produced little drama of lasting value, but this was due more to the Italian people's love of opera and other nonliterary theatrical forms than it was to the absence of the dramatic impulse; and throughout the rest of Europe it has been a history of peaks and valleys. But such has not been the case in Spain.

Why the near absolute decline of a national theatre which in the sixteenth and seventeenth centuries was as vital as any in Europe? (Only the Elizabethan and Jacobean theatres of England even begin to be comparable.) What happened to the theatre that once claimed such illustrious and prolific practitioners as Lope de Vega, Tirso de Molina, Calderón, and Cervantes? Why, during the following four centuries, did only one playwright of comparable stature appear? These questions are even more puzzling when we remember the dramatic nature of Spanish life, or the Spaniards' love of flamenco music and dancing, and perhaps most important, their total involvement with the bullfight, certainly one of the most powerful and dramatic rituals still practiced in Western culture. But second thoughts provide some answers.

Immediately after the flowering of the Spanish Golden Age theatre the Inquisition planted its firmest roots in Spain. The Inquisition was hysterically puritanical, and one of the first moves made by its leaders was to close down the theatre—an institution they considered both licentious and idolatrous. The terrors of the Inquisition may have passed, but the power of the Spanish Catholic Church has persisted through the centuries; no church in modern Christendom has been so militantly puritanical. Thus what Torquemada began the clergy has maintained. But the decline of the Spanish theatre was not only a matter of repression. An equally important cause is to be found in the theatrical nature of those customs and entertainments which play such a significant part in the Spaniard's daily life. The histrionic appetites (not to mention other more aggressive ones) of her people have been more than adequately met by the bullfights regularly scheduled in every city and village in Spain. (What American entrepreneurs wouldn't give to have a theatre circuit in this country that even began to compare with the one set up for the Spanish bullfighters!) But the bullfight is not the only force that competes with the theatre. In addition to the *corrida*, the lives of the Spanish people are filled with countless other theatrical surrogates: the flamenco and the numerous religious processions to name but two. Who needs a theatre when almost every phase of daily life—for rich and poor alike—is filled with such direct forms of dramatic expression?

Still, one might expect that by the twentieth century Spain would have started catching up with the rest of the world. She did—almost—in the person of her one great modern dramatist, Federico García Lorca. Lorca, like Yeats, was in a position to initiate a theatrical renaissance. But, unlike his Irish counterpart, history was against him. Lorca was a great poet, a free spirit, and a natural born dramatist. As a child he wrote and produced puppet plays. In college he led what could almost be termed a revival movement in the Spanish theatre by taking a company of young actors to many of the cities and villages throughout the country. Soon writers, painters, and musicians of every description came to him with support. All the ingredients for resurgence were present. In the late 1920's Lorca came first to South America and then to the United States. Here he had a troubled time, but he learned much about the theatre and when he returned to his homeland he wrote his greatest plays—*Blood Wedding, Yerma,* and *The House of Bernarda Alba.* At last a great lyric poet had become a great dramatist, and with Lorca as the leader it looked as if the Spanish theatre was about to be reborn. But it was not to happen. The Spanish Revolution broke out; Lorca was killed by one of the "Black Squads" of Franco's Civil Guard; and the theatre has been caught in a stranglehold of censorship ever since.

There are signs that now as Franco approaches the end of his long reign, the Spanish theatre is beginning to stir again. But one hesitates to be very optimistic. For too long the playwright has been called upon to provide little more than an after-dinner divertissement for a satiated and dozing upper middle class. Those dramatists with serious ambitions still cannot, for the most part, be produced and are better known outside of Spain—particularly in Scandinavia—than they are at home. There is an "underground" theatre, and its leading writers—the recently deceased Casona, Buero Vallejo, and Sastre—are turning out plays that even the most charitable of evaluations must term wooden and derivative when compared with the achievements of other European dramatists. This does not mean that the current band of Spanish playwrights does not have considerable talent. The plays in this volume attest that they do, but until conditions change so that they can have their work regularly produced it will be impossible for them to develop a mastery of style and a theatrical medium which is uniquely their own.

During the past three centuries Spain's Golden Age has tarnished. The theatre can survive almost anything but repression, and this has been its fate in Spain. But, beginning in the early part of this century her theatre began to show signs of renewed life. The ascendency of Franco—and the concommitant death of Lorca—cut this revival short before it could reach maturity. Today, however, the tide is slowly beginning to turn: the government is getting nervous about its stringent censorship policies; the bullfight, as it becomes increasingly commercialized, is in decline and no longer appeals to the growing number of Spanish intellectuals; the church is gradually becoming more liberal in its attitudes. All this augurs well for the theatre, and fortunately there are a number of gifted playwrights ready to emerge to a position of international importance. It is hoped that this volume will not only indicate the jagged growth of the modern Spanish theatre, but will also—and more importantly—reveal intimations of a bright future.

New York City

MASTERS OF THE MODERN THEATRE

by Robert W. Corrigan

After visiting the United States in 1835, Alexis de Tocqueville described the kind of literature he believed an industrialized democratic society would produce. "I am persuaded," he wrote in *Democracy in America*, "that in the end democracy diverts the imagination from all that is external to man and fixes it on man alone. . . . It may be foreseen in like manner that poets living in democratic times will prefer the delineation of passions and ideas to that of persons and achievements. The language, the dress, and the daily actions of men in democracies are repugnant to conceptions of the ideal. . . . This forces the poet constantly to search below the external surface which is palpable to the senses, in order to read the inner soul. . . . The destinies of mankind, man himself taken aloof from his country, and his age, and standing in the presence of Nature and of God, with his passions, his doubts, his rare prosperities and inconceivable wretchedness, will become the chief, if not the sole theme of poetry." Any examination of the arts of the past century would seem to indicate that Tocqueville's prophecy has been fulfilled, and it is certainly clear that the theatre's general pattern of development during this time can be best described as a gradual but steady shift away from universal philosophical and social concerns toward the crises and conflicts of man's inner and private life. It is possible to discover foreshadowings of this change in direction and emphasis in the plays of the early nineteenth-century Romantics—Büchner, Hebbel, Kleist, Gogol, Musset—but it was not until Ibsen that the theatre's revolutionary break with the past becomes clearly discernible. In fact, Ibsen's career as a playwright to a large extent parallels both in form and theme the modern drama's increasing tendency to be more concerned with the conflicts of the individual's interior world than with the significance of his public deeds.

The causes of any revolution are always as difficult to untangle as its consequences are to assess, and any attempt on the part of the critic to describe them will inevitably result in oversimplification. But it is possible to discover certain basic changes in attitude which had been evolving in Europe since the time of Luther and had begun to crystallize in continental thought by the second half of the nineteenth century. And the works of the revolutionary playwrights—Ibsen, Strindberg, Chekhov, Shaw, and Hauptmann—were the first to express in the theatre certain of these radical shifts in the way man had come to think of nature, society, and himself. What follows is an attempt to set forth briefly some of the more important aspects of this revolution in the drama which Ibsen referred to as "a war to the knife with the past."

One of the dominant ideas of the modern *Weltanschauung* is the belief that it is impossible to know what the world is really like. Beginning with Luther's refusal to accept that there was any intelligible relationship between faith and works, the sacramental view of experience gradually disappeared. In rejecting the phenomenal world as an outward and visible manifestation of man's spiritual condition, Luther began a revolution in thought which, because of the achievements of science and technology in the past two hundred years, now makes it impossible for man to attach any objective value to the observations of his senses. This insistence on such a clear-cut division between the physical and the spiritual aspects of reality had a profound effect on the modern dramatist. Inevitably, it made him increasingly distrustful of his sensory responses to the "outside" world, and at the same time it tended to negate whatever belief he might have had in the objective validity of his subjective feelings and sensations. The modern artist no longer holds a mirror up to nature, at least not with any confidence; he can only stare at his own image. He becomes a voyeur to his own existence.

Probably no force in the nineteenth century did more to destroy man's belief in an established norm of human nature, and hence begin this process of internalization in the theatre, than the advent of psychology as a systematized field of study. In his book, *'Modernism' in the Modern Drama*, Joseph Wood Krutch argued that the basic issue confronting all the dramatists of the past one hundred years was the problem of "modernism." Briefly, modernism involves both the conviction and the practice that to be modern is to be, in many important ways, different from anyone who ever lived before. This does not mean that man has changed; human nature is the same, but man's way of looking at himself has changed in a way that is significantly new. It is this new view of man that creates the problem for the dramatist.

Good examples of this changed perception can be found in Ibsen's *Hedda Gabler* (1890) and Strindberg's *Miss Julie* (1888). Hedda and Julie have the distinction of being the first fully and consciously developed neurotic heroines in dramatic literature. By neurotic we mean that they are neither logical nor insane (in the sense of being random and unaccountable), but that the aims and motives of each of them have a secret personal logic of their own. The significant thing about both these characters is that they are motivated by the premise that there is a secret, and sometimes unconscious, world of aims and methods, a secret system of values, which is more important in human experience than rational ones. This approach to character is not, however, the same as the romantic attitude which affirms the superior validity of the nonrational. We need only read Strindberg's famous Preface to *Miss Julie* or Ibsen's working notes for *Hedda Gabler* to discover that they did not believe, as did the nineteenth-century Romantic poets, that the irrational was a supernatural and unknowable force; rather, in giving a detailed account of why their heroines behaved as they did, Ibsen and Strindberg insisted that neurotic behavior and mysterious events are always explainable in terms of natural causes. The significant difference is that neither of these characters can be explained or judged by a common standard; the actions of each dramatic character (and by extension, each human being) are explicable only in terms of that peculiar combination of forces, frustrations, and desires which is unique to himself.

For us living in the middle of the twentieth century there is nothing very new in these psychological ideas; but, coming when they did, they were quite revolutionary, and they have created problems for the playwright which have not yet been solved. By convincingly demonstrating that normal people are not as rational as they seem, and that abnormal people do not act in a random and unintelligible way, psychology has made it difficult, if not impossible, for the dramatist to present his characters in a direct way. In earlier times when it was believed that there was a sharp distinction between the sane and the insane, the irrational "aberrations" of human behavior were dramatically significant because they could be defined in terms of a commonly accepted standard of sane human conduct. It seems clear, for instance, that Shakespeare believed Lear on the heath to be insane, while it is equally clear that Macbeth at the witches' cauldron was not. But for the modern dramatist, deeds do not necessarily mean what they appear to mean, and in themselves they are not directly revelatory of the characters who commit them. Miss Julie, Hedda Gabler, and Kostya Treplev of Chekhovs' *The Sea Gull* are all suicides; but, unlike Othello's suicide, the meaning of each of their deaths cannot be clearly ascertained from the actions which preceded it. The plight of the modern dramatist in this regard becomes apparent when we realize that without Strindberg's *Preface* or Ibsen's Notebook we could never know for certain what, in each instance, the significance of the heroine's death really was. And the ambiguity of almost every interpretation of *The Sea Gull* is largely due to the fact that Chekhov never made the meaning of Treplev's suicide explicit.

All drama of the past is based upon the axiom "by their deeds shall ye know them." The significance of the dramatic hero was revealed by his deeds, and there was a direct relationship between the hero's overt acts and his inner spiritual condition. The significance of Oedipus, for instance, is revealed by his deeds, not by some explanation that he is suffering from an Oedipus complex; and there is a direct relationship between the act of tearing out his own eyes and his solving the riddle of the Sphinx. Even when a character commits a dissembling deed, it is to deceive the other characters in the play, not the spectators. Certainly one of the chief functions of the soliloquy in Elizabethan drama was to keep the audience continually informed as to what was going on. Hamlet may put an antic disposition on, but not before he tells the audience he is going to do so. However, during the nineteenth century, the drama began to reflect man's growing distrust in the ability of his senses to comprehend the true nature of reality. Appearances are no longer believed to be direct reflections of ideal reality, like the shadows on the wall of Plato's cave; rather they are thought of as a mask which hides or distorts reality. And by the time of Pirandello, particularly in such plays as *Right You Are, If You Think You*

Are (1916), *Six Characters in Search of an Author* (1921), and *The Mock Emperor* (*Enrico IV*) (1922), appearances not only do not express reality, they contradict it, and the meaning of these plays is not to be found in appearance or reality, but in the contradiction itself.

One of the great achievements of the Elizabethan dramatic form was its ability to express several levels of experience simultaneously. The world of Hamlet is both public and private, a world in which personal and familial relationships, fantasy and mystery, and political and psychological conflict coexist in a state of constant dramatic tension. One of the main reasons why the Elizabethan dramatic form works so successfully is that appearances can be taken at their face value. But when the dramatist begins to distrust the validity of his sensory perceptions it becomes difficult, if not impossible, for him to dramatize the complex totality of experience in a single form. Reality must be broken down into its component parts, and each part can only be expressed in a form peculiar to itself. Admitting the existence of individual differences in the work of each dramatist writing in any given period, it is nonetheless possible to describe with some accuracy the dramatic form employed by the playwrights of the Fifth-Century Greek theatre, the Elizabethan and Restoration theatres of England, and the French neoclassic theatre of the seventeenth century. But in discussing the modern theatre we must always speak of forms, for there is no single, dominant form in the serious theatre of the past hundred years. It is for this reason that the evolution of the drama since the time of Shakespeare has been so aptly described as a process of fragmentation.

It is very likely that every serious dramatist believes that it is his artistic duty to be true to his presuppositions about the real nature of the world in which he lives. However, once a playwright believes that the meaning of every human action is relative and intelligible only in terms of a unique and subsurface combination of forces, the dramatic events of the plot cease to have meaning in themselves, and they take on significance only as the secret motivations of the characters who participate in them are revealed. (The technique of earlier drama is just the reverse: the motivations of the characters are revealed by the events of the plot.) But how does the dramatist objectify the hidden and unconscious, and what happens to the theatre when he feels obligated to explain and probe into his characters' hidden lives? Explanation is always a dangerous business in the theatre (since the time of the ancient Greeks, exposition has always been the dramatist's most difficult problem), but the moment a playwright assumes that if he explains his characters he has written a play, that danger becomes mortal. All too often the writers of the modern theatre have forgotten that a dramatic situation requires not that we should *understand* a character but simply that we should *believe* in him. Dramatic action always leads to a judgment; it requires that something shall happen to and through the characters; something that is embodied in the events of which the characters are a part. Whenever the personality of the character, rather than the action of which the character should be a part, becomes the playwright's chief concern, dramatic process dissolves into explanation, and when that occurs, the range of the theatre is drastically reduced, if not unalterably damaged.

One has only to compare the plays of the mid-twentieth century to those of Ibsen, Shaw, or Strindberg to realize just how much the scope of the theatre has been narrowed. However, evidence of the gradual loss of belief in dramatic heroes, who needed no explaining, can initially be found in the sentimental bourgeois drama of the eighteenth century. For the first time a character was no longer noble, responsible, or morally significant, and was therefore dramatically interesting because of his birth, position, power, or wealth. As a result, the dramatist was obliged to justify both his choice of characters and the situations in which they are engaged. The Romantic drama of the eighteenth and nineteenth centuries resisted a break with the past, and attempted unsuccessfully to perpetuate the forms and figures of earlier times. Certainly, the revolt of Ibsen and his contemporaries in the last quarter of the nineteenth century was at least in some measure due to their conviction that the dramatic conflicts of the Romantic drama were inflated and without significance, and that the nobility of its characters was artificial and contrived. In rejecting the artificialities of Romanticism, the modernists changed the theatre in many ways; but for all their dissatisfaction with their predecessors they were unable to forestall the attrition of belief in the possibility of heroic characters who needed no explaining.

This was largely because, as a literary movement, nineteenth-century naturalism was so closely related to nineteenth-century biology. Darwin's theories of evolution (*The Origin of Species,* 1859) and the discovery of new genetic laws had convinced many writers that man's existence, including his personality, was a phenomenon which could be explained in terms of scientific laws. As a result, increasingly, man's complex biological needs rather than his capacity to make moral choices were thought to be his most significant characteristic. Once such a view was accepted, however, the exceptional man, who because of his position and power had the greatest freedom of choice, ceased to be the fullest embodiment, and therefore the best representative, of those conflicts and choices which most clearly define the human condition. Instead, the lives of the poor—where the role of natural necessity is most readily observable—became the playwright's most suitable subjects. The drama of the common man, then, did not happen by accident, nor did it evolve because some dramatist or group of dramatists wanted it to. Given the problem of creating in a world in which all human actions tend to be explained in terms of some kind of psychological or sociological cause and effect, a world in which the possibility of deliberative and moral choice is doubted if not rejected outright, it is difficult, if not impossible, for the playwright to fashion a character of traditional heroic stature.

There is an old saw about no man being a hero to his valet. Neither is he one to his psychoanalyst. Nor can he be one to a playwright who views his actions as behavioral phenomena explicable in terms of some kind of laws—scientific or other. Oedipus, for example, remains a hero of great stature so long as he is not suffering from an Oedipus complex. But once we learn to explain him in terms of repressed hopes and fears, traumatic childhood experience, or a vitamin deficiency in infancy, although he may remain interesting—he may, in fact, gain a new kind of interest, as Cocteau's *The Infernal Machine* attests—he loses stature. Or while, temporarily, we accept the Elizabethan attitude toward them, which of us can understand a Hamlet or a Lear? And which of us can forgive an Othello or a Macbeth? But it is precisely that they seem mysteriously beyond our powers of understanding, that they remain heroes for us. And it is a belief in a mysterious unknowable quality in men that substantiates man's sense of his own importance in the universe. However, if a playwright comes to believe that all human actions are in reality predictable behavioral responses, and his moral judgments of these actions can be dissolved by psychological understanding, how can he pattern a tragedy or create characters with stature? If there can be no possibility for an appraisal of personality as such, why should Hamlet's death be any more significant than that of Rosencrantz and Guildenstern?

But the problem does not end here. For once the dramatist dismisses the possibility of passing moral judgments on his characters' actions, he comes face to face with an even more frightening spectre: guilt—which has no form of expiation and thus turns into anxiety. It has long been known that art must ultimately always fail in its attempts to come to grips with the facts of death. Perhaps this is also true of anxiety. How can there be drama in an Age of Anxiety? What kind of play will be produced when the central conflict is between something and nothing? Many of the arts may be able to express the condition of anxiety (although even this may be highly questionable); but the theatre, because of the objective reality and irremovable presence of the living actor, and because the drama is essentially an embodiment of the conflict between at least two opposing recognizable and namable forces, is incapable of dealing with anxiety, or it does so to its own great peril. Beginning with the Watchman in the opening scene of the *Orestia* right on through the ghosts of Elsinore and the tormented heroes of Schiller and Kleist, the theater has always found a way to transform anxiety into fear; that is, give it a definite object. But when we come to such plays of Ibsen and Strindberg as *Ghosts, The Master Builder, There Are Crimes and Crimes,* and *The Ghost Sonata,* we discover that although this process of objectification is attempted, it is not totally successful. And when the transformation does not take place, the form and content of drama begin to change in uncontrollable ways, as some of the plays of Beckett and Ionesco, Pinter and Albee will attest. It is difficult enough to find a meaning for man in a world which views a return to nothingness as the ultimate reality, but it is next to impossible to create a dramatic "action" which can encompass the terror of being on the edge of the abyss. Kierkegaard, and more recently Paul Tillich, have declared that this threat of nothingness is the central anxiety of modern man. Many modern playwrights have sought to overcome the despair of this situation by maintainng that the only meaning of life is to be found in that death which is inevitable. But this is not an assertion which gives meaning to any of the particularities of life; in fact, it drains them of meaning. At best, it is a method of redeeming existence from meaningless anarchy by showing that the pattern of life is simple and imperturbable. But such a pattern, though it may appear to conquer chaos, is too abstract to live successfully in the theatre.

In life as we experience it, we are conscious of our physical natures, our social situation, and our unique psychic existence; and we live on all three of these levels simultaneously. For this reason it is impossible for us to act or make a choice without some element of human behavior—what we do out of physical necessity or because of social habit—playing a significant role in our decision. At the same time, because of the simultaneity of our being, it is impossible for us to understand completely the individuality of our actions. But in the theatre we see life as pure deed, that is life in which the arbitrariness of human behavior has been eliminated and in which the mysterious transformations of individuality have been fixed. Thus, in contrast to a person in life, who is recognized by the continuity of his being and finally can only be known through intuition, a character in a play is an identity who is defined by the coherence of his acts. For this reason the deeds of a dramatic action are always public, and the characters best suited to drama are men and women who, either by fate or choice, lead a public life and whose deeds are of public concern. This explains why traditionally kings, princes, and nobility have been the most suitable subjects for drama. But as the increasing dominance of the machine in modern life has gradually destroyed the direct relation between a man's intention and his deeds, public figures have ceased to be our most appropriate heroes because, as W. H. Auden points out, "the good and evil they do depends less upon their characters and intentions than upon the quantity of impersonal force at their disposal."

Our world, it would seem, has become almost too big for the playwright. Power is too impersonal, great deeds are collective achievements, and the great man is one who is capable of withstanding some of the pressures of a mass society and manages, somehow, to maintain a face and stance more or less his own. Compare, for example, the achievement of a Lindbergh (our last "lone" hero) to that of Colonel Glenn, who was interchangeable with five other astronauts. Or, how can the power of a Napoleon be envisioned today? In our times power is so enormous that it is barely visible and those who govern are little more than incidental and easily replaceable expressions of that power. Power is like an iceberg; the largest part is submerged in abstraction, anonymity, and bureaucracy. Government, like modern physics, has lost its physical reality and can be expressed only in statistics and formulae. Indeed, the true men of action in our time, those who transform the world, are not the statesmen and politicians, but the scientists. Unfortunately, their most significant actions are not suitable subjects for the theatre, because their deeds are concerned with things, not people, and are, therefore, speechless.

But what are the implications of this for the theatre? Who are the true representatives of a world whose heroes are nameless? As the Swiss playwright, Duerrenmatt, put it: "Any small-time crook, petty government official, or policeman better represents our world than a senator or president. Today art can only embrace victims if it can reach men at all; it can no longer come close to the mighty. Creon's secretaries close Antigone's case."

That there has been a shift in attitude toward the heroic is easily seen when we examine any one of the many modern adaptations of the Greek tragedies. For example, today most people find Anouilh's *Antigone* much more a reflection of their attitudes, and thus more immediately interesting than Sophocles' tragic working of the theme. The characters and the dilemma of their situation seem more human. Antigone is not a hard and almost inhuman girl, with such a monomaniacal fixity of purpose that she rejects all other feelings and desires. In the modern version she is, humanly, both weak and strong. She has a lover in Haemon, whom she rejects; but she is also a helpless little girl who runs to "Nanny" for comfort and strength; as she approaches death, she is afraid and seeks the consolations of even the most calloused of guards. Creon is not a blind and power-mad tyrant; he is a businessman king who is caught in the complex web of compromise and expediency which will not allow abstract moral principles to upset the business of government.

However, what the play gains in humanity it loses in tragic force. The sense of Antigone's aloneness and Creon's moral blindness, and of the inevitable destruction implicit in their conflict, has been softened. Anouilh's Antigone is not alone and unloved, and his Creon is not blind. We pity their situation in that they are two quite attractive people caught up in a situation which neither of them likes, but which they cannot control. They are victims in a disordered world which they have not created and which they have no moral obligation to correct. As the play ends, we are left with an ambiguity which allows for no reconciliation.

One of the most important functions of the hero, both in art and life, is to supply those images, values, and ethical standards which people aspire to and which they would like, if possible, to incorporate into their own lives. It would seem, however, that increasingly our modern industrialized society not only does not need heroes, but also actually suppresses or perverts our need of them. In their important book, *Industrialism and Industrial Man,* Kerr, Dunlop, Harbison, and Myers convincingly demonstrate that "like ideologies, the great personality—the one great figure around whom historians so frequently weave their story—began to seem less important. Instead of ideologies and dominant personalities, we became increasingly attentive to the inherent nature of the particular industrializing system and the basic strategy and forces at work within it." Only the system, then, is important, and it fills men's remaining need for heroes by promoting celebrities, those heroes of the surface who play their constantly shifting roles well.

Furthermore, specialization—the key operative principle of an industrial society—not only produces pluralism in our economic system, but also a pluralistic deviation of heroic types. However, when there are and can be so many heroic types—one cannot even begin to count all the heroes of the popular imagination—you begin to get a leveling: and with that leveling not only is the stature of heroism diminished, but the individual's sense of his own identity is actually invalidated.

Traditionally, the hero is always best described in terms of those forces which urge him to spiritual redemption. Maxwell Anderson once wrote that "from the point of view of the playwright, the essence of a tragedy, or even a serious play, is the spiritual awakening, or regeneration, of his hero." But the one thing that characterizes the hero of surfaces—and this is certainly in large measure due to industrialization and bureaucracy—is precisely the fact that he lacks the dimensions of spiritual awareness, personal morality, and social responsibility. Paul Tillich wrote in his *The Religious Situation* that "the fundamental value in ethics of a capitalistic society is economic efficiency—developed to the utmost degree of ruthless activity." Such an ethical standard is hardly conducive to the creation of great heroes in the drama.

That we live in an antiheroic age is a commonplace. Carlyle proclaimed its coming in the nineteenth century when he said "we shall either learn to know a hero . . . when we see him, or else go on to be forever governed by the unheroic." This transformation has occurred; we have accepted it; we are even used to it. Whatever nostalgia we may still occasionally feel is more than adequately taken care of by television. In the place of the hero we have the celebrity, that triumph of the ordinary. In our time, hero worship has become horizontal; indeed, we even look down to a "man like myself."

While the advent of psychology as a systematized field of study may have been the most powerful single force to shape the modern theatre, actually the process of internalization had begun much earlier. For instance, it is clear from Hebbel's essays on the drama that the despair of old Anton's "I don't understand the world any more" in the final scene of *Maria Magdalena* is much more than an expression of the age-old frustration of the parent who does not understand the behavior of his children. It also reflects his dimly understood but tremendously painful realization that it is no longer possible for him to comprehend what the world has become or to imagine what the future will be like. Until the Industrial Revolution, patterns of life were passed on from father to son with the confidence that these patterns would satisfy the needs and desires of each new generation. Such confidence was justified, for life changed so gradually and imperceptibly that when changes did occur they were easily assimilated into the shared life of the community. But by the middle of the nineteenth century the effects of the Industrial Revolution had begun to be felt on all levels of society. Technology, with its ever-increasing capacity to transform man's way of living, not only made the future so unpredictable that it soon became impossible for him to imagine what his life would be like twenty years hence, but in its singular concern with the individual's functional qualities technology tended to isolate him from his fellows and invalidate his spiritual values and metaphysical concerns. At the same time, the discoveries of the nineteenth century archeologists, and the ensuing interest in anthropology, tended to break down provincial and absolutist attitudes concerning human nature. Early anthropologists like Mannhardt, Robertson-Smith, Tylor, and the great James Frazer made it clear that human nature was not something fixed and unchanging, but only that kind of behavior exhibited in each culture. In fact, as early as 1860 scholars were demonstrating that human nature is so plastic that it can, as Frazer was later to point out in the Preface to the first edition of *The Golden Bough* (1890), "exhibit varieties of behavior which, in the animal Kingdom could only be exhibited by different species." Furthermore, by the middle of the century, democracy was finally beginning to be established both as a way of life and as a form of government. Today we tend to forget what a revolutionary idea democracy is and the shattering effects that it had upon the values of eighteenth- and nineteenth-century Europe. We also forget what Tocqueville told us long ago: "not only does democracy make every man forget his ancestors, but it hides his descendants and separates his contemporaries from him, it throws him back forever upon himself alone and threatens in the end to confine him entirely within the solitude of his own heart." In short, by the middle of the nineteenth century every established view of God, human nature, social organization, and the physical universe was beginning to be seriously challenged if not invalidated. And this revolutionary climate had a profound effect on the theatre.

Of all the Arts, theatre is the only one which has always concerned itself with human destinies. Dramatic action is historical in the sense that the perpetual present of each moment on the stage is created out of past events and is directed toward a definite, if yet unknown, future. In previous ages the destiny of any dramatic action was significant because the ever-changing events in the lives of dramatic heroes could be meaningfully related to eternity, that is, to some permanent value or idea such as Fate, the Gods, or Heaven and Hell, which transcends the human condition and which is believed in by the dramatist and/or his audience.

In the plays of Buechner and Hebbel we discover the first indications in the theatre of that sense of alienation both from God and Society which underscores the fact that man's belief in eternity had been shaken. And one of the most significant aspects of Ibsen's work (at least after *Peer Gynt,* 1867) is the fact that the realm of ultimate value has either disappeared or has become so mysterious that it has ceased to have dramatic relevance. In its place we find instead a belief in some form of social ideal or societal structure; first, as the agent of some unknown Destiny, and then as Destiny itself. But when Society begins to assume the role of Destiny, that is, is thought of as the determining force for good or evil in the lives of men, man cannot help but feel eventually that the meaning of his Destiny has been drastically reduced. For Society, as Robert Bolt writes in the preface to his *A Man For All Seasons,* "can only have as much idea as we have what we are about, for it has only our brains to think with. And the individual who tries to plot his position by reference to our society finds no fixed points, but only the vaunted absence of them—'freedom' and 'opportunity'; freedom for what, opportunity to do what, is nowhere indicated. The only positive he is given is 'get and spend' . . . and he did not need society to tell him that. In other words we are thrown back by our society upon ourselves, which of course sends us flying back to society with all the force of rebound."

Any mind capable of spiritual aspiration seeks in the actions of the dramatic hero that which affirms the vitality of the free will in any given situation. Man's free will may be defeated by the forces of Destiny—in fact, the great plays have always testified that the destroying forces of Destiny are as much a part of the hero's character as his free will; it may be paralyzed and thus incapable of action; it may be submerged by the battle in such a way as to become part of that Destiny; it may even turn out to be an illusion; but it must always be an active force if we are to believe that we are partaking in human greatness. Such a Destiny must be greater than an aggregate of human beings or an expression of social patterns.

Ironically, the revolt of Ibsen and Shaw against the conventional nineteenth-century drama was motivated by a desire to enlarge the range of Destiny in the theatre. In their attempts to present man in his total historical and social setting, they were rebelling against the narrow and private worlds that had been dominating the stage since the Restoration. But in spite of their efforts, nothing could change the fact that in the two hundred years since Shakespeare the world of the spirit had greatly diminished. The Ekdal's attic and Mrs. Warren's drawing room were not—and never could be—the same as Elsinore or Cleopatra's barge.

Nonetheless, the pioneers of the modern drama had revitalized the theatre precisely because they believed that significant social issues should be dealt with in the theatre. Thus for nearly three decades the theatre had a vitality of spirit and a forcefulness of manner which it had lacked for better than a century for the very reason that its context had been reduced. To the playwright writing at that time the human and social problems, which were the source materials of the naturalistic play, appeared capable of solution if only man and society would learn to use their common sense—which usually meant one of two things: the acceptance of a less rigid standard of social morality or the espousal of some form of socialism. But with the collapse of the established social order in the First World War, the validity of these too-easy solutions was impugned, and beginning with the plays of the early German Expressionists (written 1912–1916) the positive optimism of the Edwardian era gave way to a sense of bewilderment, exasperation, and defeatism, only occasionally tempered by the slim hope that the war had brought man to the threshold of a "New Age." The theatre reflects these changes from confidence to doubting and despair, from complacent faith in cherished values to an anxious questioning, from a rigorous, but rigid morality to the mystic evangelism, the fanatical polemics, and the frivolous apathy of a disintegrating world. These changes are most apparent in the Jekyll and Hyde theatre of the German Expressionists, whose nerve-shattered playwrights alternated between a militant idealism and grotesque nightmares. But one need only compare Shaw's *Heartbreak House* to *Major Barbara,* Pirandello's *Right You Are, If You Think You Are* to *Liola,* or Hauptmann's *Winter Ballad* to *The Weavers* to realize that the effects of the collapse of the old order were widespread and were reflected in the works of established writers as well as those of the new generation. Immediately after the war the theatre on the Continent was dominated by attitudes of emotionalism and cynicism, but these gradually gave way to feelings of frustration, futility, and despair and by the middle of the 1920's the serious drama of Europe had become almost totally introspective and psychological in its orientation.[1]

Obviously, this tendency toward paralyzing introspection has by no means been accepted by everyone writing for the theatre. In fact, a large segment of the modern theatre might be best described as a reaction against the despair and dehumanizing implications of the modernist position. These "resistance movements" have sought to discover the means, both formal and substantive, whereby the possibility and validity of selfhood and human integrity, personal responsibility, and morally significant judgments could be reasserted in the theatre. Some playwrights—especially Eliot, Fry, Betti, and Claudel—have turned to orthodox Christian belief to provide a metaphysical structure for their drama. Others, like Lorca and Synge, have written out of the traditions and value systems of premodern hieratic societies. Probably the largest group of all is composed of those dramatists who have sought to escape the deadly strictures of modernism by turning to classical mythology.

All of these writers shared one common and fundamental attitude: each of them was in some way rebelling against the conditions of the modern world. They were not only conscious of that lack of a sense of community which inevitably occurs in an increasingly democratic society; more important, they were aware of man's growing sense of his own isolation. The modern world, with its growing collectivism, paradoxically tends to throw man back upon himself, while at the same time it increasingly tends to destroy the individual's

[1] Because they were essentially isolated from the main currents of European history in the first two decades of the century, the Irish and American theatres were not immediately affected by the spreading paralysis which was transforming the rest of modern drama. But it is clear from O'Casey's *The Plow and the Stars* (1926) and *The Silver Tassie* (1927) that the Abbey Theatre could not withstand for long the theatre's introspective tendencies, and there was no serious American drama until O'Neill's plays were first produced right after the war. In the twenty years between *Beyond The Horizon* (1920) and *The Iceman Cometh* (1941) the American theatre repeated the continental cycle in its own terms, and by the beginning of the Second World War all of the Western Theatre had reached that No Man's Land between comedy and tragedy, between pathetic aspirations and ridiculous bewilderment, between never-beginning action and never-ending talk.

sense of his own selfhood. This creates an impasse which the modern dramatist, for the most part, has been unable to overcome.

Joseph Warren Beach, in analyzing the problems of modern fiction, describes the reaction of many writers to this condition in this way: "One of the hardest things for man to bear is spiritual isolation. The sense that he stands alone in the universe goes terribly against his gregarious instincts. He has an overpowering impulse to construct a system which will enable him to feel that he does not stand alone but is intimately associated with some force or group infinitely more powerful and significant than himself." It is clearly evident in the work of all those playwrights who have rebelled against modernism that they too are seeking to construct a system which will restore meaning to life and validity to art. In the end, however, they have not been completely successful, because they have all too often had to deny the realities of the modern world in the process. Furthermore, they have not accepted the wisdom of Brecht's statement that "when one sees that our world of today no longer fits into the drama, then it is merely that the drama no longer fits into the world." By insisting upon values that we may once have cherished, but which no longer in actuality exist, the playwrights of the resistance have not been able to revitalize the theatre or its audiences. And most important, they have not succeeded in stretching the imaginations of men in order that they might conquer that sense of isolation and despair which pervades the modern world. And this brings us to the playwrights of the mid-twentieth century.

In an age dominated by space orbits and telestars, the fear of nuclear war, the tension of cold war diplomacy, and the insecurity of a defense economy, our greatest uncertainty is whether or not in the midst of epochal disorder, man has any good chance, to borrow Faulkner's phrase, of prevailing; and if he does, what kind of man will prevail.

This uncertainty has had a profound effect on our theatre, and if there is one thing that characterizes the work of almost all of our serious playwrights of the last two decades it is that their plays express the contemporary theatre's tremendous concern to find a metaphor for universal modern man as he lives on the brink of disaster—a metaphor that expresses the inalienable part of every man, that irreducible part of each of us which exists after all the differences have been stripped away, and which is beyond and beneath all that is social, political, economic, religious, and ideological. In short, they are searching for a metaphor of man left face-to-face with himself.

Such an idea of the theatre has tremendous implications for the drama, and we are just now becoming aware of them. First of all, it abolishes the traditional linear plot because our contemporary playwrights are not interested in presenting an action in any Aristotelian sense, but are, rather, dramatizing a condition. Whenever one asks what the central action of a Beckett, Ionesco, or Pinter play is, he comes a cropper; "action" for the contemporary playwright is an artificial concept. He is concerned with showing life as it is, and in life there is no central action, there are only people, and the only thing that is basic to each individual is the ontological solitude of his being. The dramatist's only concern is to create in his plays a situation which will reveal the private drama that each man has inside himself and which is enacted every day in the random, apparently meaningless, and undramatic events of our common routine. "History," said Stephen Daedalus, "is a nightmare from which I must awake." The rapidity of historical change and the apparent powerlessness of the individual to affect Collective History has led in the theatre to a retreat from history. Instead of tracing the history of an individual who is born, grows old, and dies, many modern playwrights have devoted their attention to the timeless passionate moments of life, to states of being. They want to express the paradox, the contradiction, and the incompleteness of experience. They are attempting to suggest the raggedness, the confusion, the complexity of motivation, the "discontinuous continuity," and the basic ambiguity of all human behavior. They are, in short, pursuing to their fullest and most logical conclusions the premises of modernism. The writers of the contemporary theatre are facing the "facts of life." If the dramatic meaning of their plays is that drama is no longer possible, they would contend that any other meaning would be artificial, illusory, false; if the dialogue in their plays consists of meaningless clichés and stereotyped phrases, they would insist that this is the way we talk; if their characters are constantly changing their personalities, these playwrights would point out that no one today is really consistent or truly integrated. If the people in their plays seem to be helpless puppets without any will of their own, they would argue that we are all passively at the mercy of blind fate and meaningless circumstance. They call their theatre "Anti-Theatre," and this they insist is the true theatre of our times. If they are correct, so be it! Then history has again followed its own inexorable laws. The very forces which gave life and strength to the modern theatre have caused its decline and death.

But the theatre is always dying, and with equal regularity, like the phoenix, it is resurrected. No one can say with certainty what its new form will be, but that there will be a future seems certain. First, largely because of the development of college and university theatre programs in this country and the large increase in the number of professional repertory theatres here and abroad, there are more people who have experienced good theatre than ever before. And this enlarged audience wants and needs theatre; it will not be satisfied for long with the maimed rites of psychological and moral cliché, or impassioned Jeremiads from prophets of doom, or the meandering contemplations of writers who are morbidly consumed in introspection and self-analysis. Fortunately, there are audiences who want and need the theatre, and they go to the theatre in the hopeful anticipation that the stage will be capable of accommodating all of the terrible-wonderful emotions and insoluble dilemmas of our shared life together. This demand bid made by our audiences for a drama that deals with the significant issues and concerns of our public life will, I believe, force our playwrights to open up new frontiers in the drama, and thus extend the boundaries of the theatre. The second great hope of the theatre is that, in spite of the overriding temper of despair and the current dominance of anti-theatricality, our playwrights still find human action significant, still find it necessary to write plays, and in the very act of writing attest to the miracle of life that contemporary despair would deny. We live in one of the most dramatic ages in the history of mankind, and if the past is any kind of reliable guide to what the future of the Theatre will be, we have good reason to believe that the Theatre of tomorrow can be as dramatic as the world in which we live today.

MASTERPIECES OF THE MODERN SPANISH THEATRE

JACINTO BENAVENTE

1866–1954

JACINTO BENAVENTE was remarkably energetic and versatile in contending with the new forces in the theatre, in literature, and in Spanish society. He wrote an incredible number of plays of every sort imaginable—social criticism, fantasies, peasant dramas, puppet plays, commedia dell'arte. He was very much a man of the theatre, beginning with some youthful adventures in a circus and proceeding into acting, theatre management, dramatic and literary criticism and translation. He approved of the sound fiscal qualities of Molière and Shakespeare and was himself no less a businessman. He was a member of the Spanish Academy and was awarded the Nobel Prize in 1922.

Benavente's accomplishments seem a bit mild in comparison with other playwrights of his time. Indeed, considering the tradition to which he was heir, it is sometimes difficult to believe that this dramatist was really a Spanish writer. There is a striking cosmopolitan air and an ironic, almost cynical tone to many of his plays which comes across even in the tableaux-structured, semi-fantastic setting of plays such as *Witches' Sabbath*. In this play (as in many of his dramas, notably *Señora Ana* and *The Passion Flower*), Benavente introduced the powerfully willful character of Imperia. She is one of many of Benavente's attractive female characters. Each of them embodies noble aspirations in spite of her involvement in ignoble situations. Benavente has drawn them subtly, frequently making them cerebral like the Yerma of Garcia Lorca and always as passionate. Finally, in Acacia, the silently seething girl-bride of *The Passion Flower*, probably his best-known play, Benavente's psychological portraiture reached a finesse almost equal to Ibsen's.

Benavente's way with dialogue contributed to his influence in the Spanish theatre. His language is quick, clear, and at times even epigrammatic. But he also had strong moralizing tendencies, with the result that in practically every play Benavente has a "mouthpiece."

Today Benavente seems hopelessly dated, but it should be remembered that he was the first dramatist to introduce the techniques of continental naturalism to the near-moribund Spanish theatre. And his *Witches' Sabbath*, although considered a minor achievement during his lifetime, is now thought to be his most significant play. In it he combines the concerns of the still-new twentieth century with the spirit and themes of old-world Spain.

MORALITY IN THE THEATRE[1]

by Jacinto Benavente

Translated by William I. Oliver

IT WOULD BE impudent of me to solicit your good will. God willing, I am as sure of it as I am of these . . . what shall I call them . . . anything but lessons . . . that I am about to deliver. They are not even lectures. They are devoid of anything which transcends toward the doctoral or pedagogical. I am neither a professor nor a teacher but a student always—and a poor one at that—of books and of life. Always at the mercy of encounters, I am more concerned with the roads I travel than in coming to some definite destination. For isn't the best way to arrive at the truth actually to surrender all practical objectives? Whenever we set out deliberately to seek out a truth, premeditatively, we do so because we seek a truth that is to our own advantage and profit. The man who is in need of a certain truth is in danger of accepting the first lie that satisfies him and then of building upon it a whole philosophy which will permit him to live as he pleases. Only when we are unmindful of all practical objectives, when any truth whatever is good, as any amusement will serve the merrymaker, only then does truth reveal itself to us in all of its indifference. The first condition of truth is that it be true even if it is of no use to us, even though it harm us. However, nothing is more difficult than accepting a truth that hurts us or contradicts us—and this in spite of the fact that, as the English put it, truth is precisely what is true and not what one finds convenient to preach as though it were so. But there are so few who look for truth disinterestedly,

1 Published in Spanish as "La Moral En El Teatro." Used by permission of Aguilar, S. A. de Ediciones, Madrid, and of the translator.

with a remote interest that is exempt of practical intentions!

We want useful truths. When science gives us a truth, immediately we ask, "What's it for?" And from art (if it is true art it will be even more disinterested than science since as it searches out its truth it avoids calling it truth and names it beauty) . . . and from art we also demand utilitarianism. It must serve sometimes to entertain our spirits and at others perhaps only our sense. On other occasions we demand of art that it pass for teaching or a morality immediately applicable to our lives. We seek an art in which the artist says all there is and in which our own conscience is mute—our own conscience! The very grounds where art constructs its morality! It is not the artist but we ourselves who should discover this morality within us.

Art is very like one of those trick mirrors that reduces the size of things in its image, consequently giving us a clearer picture. Reality seems more intense and affects us more profoundly when reflected by the arts. Of course the soul of the artist is not always a clean and clear mirror—it is, more often than not, like rippling water which imparts a trembling to the image. The emotion of the artist is also a form of life which brings an added liveliness to his image. This image is not reality itself, it possesses something ideal. But if this ideal, by existing, has become a fact—is it not also a reality? Art then is, on the one hand, an objective reality and, on the other hand, a subjective reality. On the one hand. . . . No! Enough handy dualisms, let us examine the perfect unity of the whole: body and soul, form and content. Who will ever master them? Even the spiritualists require actual mediums to evoke the spirits. To materialize the spiritual until it becomes palpable, to spiritualize the material until it becomes invisible—that is the whole secret of art.

From this fusion of the external reality of the world with the internal reality of the artist's soul surges the ideal and from the ideal the morality of art. For according to Fouillée, if morality consists in man living by the highest ideal conceived by him, then the very perception of this ideal is already a force determining his conduct. Again, as Fouillée puts it, if seeing is knowing, to know is to be able to act. Anyone who has found a truth, no matter how disinterestedly he searched for it, will soon try to apply it to his own advantage.

But just what is this ideal truth that we see in art? Is it always a moral truth? The problem of morality in art, like all social problems, is fundamentally a religious problem. Either we believe or we don't—or we wish to believe even though we don't. If we believe with profound religious faith, then, of course, our ideal is in the next life and our morality has no other purpose but to achieve the eternal blessing of heaven. If we have no religious belief, if we expect neither punishments nor rewards after death, we can believe in the possibility of the future happiness of man on this earth provided each of us sacrifices his personal egoism for the collective good. If we believe that life is (as it may well be, judging solely by what we see of it) something which has revealed the whole truth when we know that we were born and that we are to die, that life is a matter of inescapable pain and joys stolen from sorrow, an egoistic struggle against the egoism of other men and the egoism of society—then, also, without believing in anything fundamental, we can believe through egoism, in the need to believe in something—founding, as it were, our belief in that very need.

Moral opportunists, we label the unknown as X and solve the moral problem by moving from an occult morality to one of necessity. We will accept the effect without preoccupying ourselves with its cause—in a word, we turn necessity into virtue. It's very well not to believe in anything, but one must live as though one did. The official religion in all countires can be defined in the following: think whatever you wish, believe or no as you choose, but do what the rest of us do.

Art may be moral or immoral or amoral, as the case may be, since to contradict the morality of the moment or to lack it produces the same social effect. The morality of art may be religious or philosophical. We do not say that it can be a scientific morality for science has not been able to discover the reason of life, and morality, properly speaking, consists in determining that very reason. If science were to pause at some truth or other and consider it as the solution and supreme reason of our lives, it would already become a philosophical truth, an applied truth. Darwin and his disciples and, later, Nietzsche, that great romantic of Darwinism, wished to detain truth in its path in order to fix it permanently in practical philosophy. They speak to us of life as a struggle of the individual against the species and, sometimes, the struggle of one species against another, a selective process, continuous warfare, constant discord. Yes, all that is science, because it is an aspect of the truth. But is it the whole truth? Newton used to say, we poor men of knowledge are like children "playing on the seashore diverting ourselves now and then finding a smoother pebble or a prettier shell than ordinary, whilst the great ocean of truth lies all undiscovered before us."

Biology and natural history, to the best of my knowledge, tell us that life is a struggle for existence. Could it not also be that war for the sake of peace and discord for the sake of accord are also struggles for existence? The gestures of love, carefully observed, really look more like a combat; all love has about it the physical and spiritual quality of an invasion. Who knows if, when they are seen from very far and on high, combats don't resemble the embraces of love and if in the clash of armor there is not something which sounds like the smack of kisses! If the inquiry of science is infinite, why detain it when it speaks to us of eternal misery and sorrow? If science stops when it sees no more than this, art must push on. The truth of art is not the reality seen by the eyes; its truth is, as Tennyson said, behind the veil, behind all veils, and beyond all kindness and shadow.

However, if art can appear to be amoral, denying the scientific grounds of all morality, it cannot be so absolutely simply because it cannot be antisocial—and this no matter how opposed it may appear to the prevailing social state. It cannot be antisocial, because art is before all else a communication through intelligence and feeling first between reality and the conscience of the artist, and, next, through the manifestation of the communication, between the conscience of the artist and that of his public.

Actors and audience alike find that our reason and our emotion are insufficient to deal with life. We need to know about one another, we need to share our sensations and thoughts. Our journey through life would be a dismal one without companions. When we achieve that state of mental superiority in which, as they say, better alone than poorly befriended; when we are able to move through the spectacle of life as solitary travelers, preferring solitude and satisfied with our own emotions—when we have achieved this, let us not forget that we have managed to do this by first having learned and gathered from social encounters experiences, emotions, lessons—culture, in short. If Robinson Crusoe was able to survive alone and on his own on his desert island it was because he had first learned among men and in society all that would stand him in good stead in his solitary life. In other words, in his very separation from society, it was, none-theless, society which saved and protected his life.

No, art cannot be antisocial because it is the product of society itself. As I have said it may appear to be antisocial, as in the case of revolutionary art, opposed to the prevailing social order. We are all of us either conservatives or liberals, not necessarily in the political sense, but in the broader sense of finding ourselves well disposed toward things as they are or of impatiently seeking something better, of being believers in human will and the evolution of man. As an expression of these two opposed tendencies there will always be a con-servative art, an official art, and a free and impulsive art which will place its ideals in a more perfect social state.

Conservative art may be religious when its religion is that of the state. Otherwise religious art would be the most rev-olutionary of all since it places its ideals above all the other interests of the world and neither society, state, power, nor family can take precedence to its divine ideals. This art will have as its sole inspiration and conscience the religious doc-trine of its church. Conservative art in its relationships with the state will be the firm support of the establishment. Its conscience will be the authority of the state, the conscience of the city.

Liberal art, the truly romantic art, will have no conscience other than that of the individual artist. Its ideal will be that of rebellion. It is a dangerous art, the constant worry of the legislator. For, except when the individual conscience con-forms with the social conscience . . . is one to allow this art to disturb society in the cause of artistic freedom? On the other hand, are the legislator and the ruler ever so certain of the truth that they can oppose the free growth of another ideal? All of today's conservatives conserve institutions and laws based upon ideals which were once liberal, revolution-ary, and the enemies of a former social order.

Just how much freedom may the state allow to the arts? I believe that art should be granted all possible freedom or, as Barrés puts it, it should be granted all license except against love. But we have already stated that art cannot be antisocial because its very essence is spiritual communication, sympathy, in another word, love. Even when art is most pessimistic, corrosive, when it attacks everything and has remedies for nothing, when it tells us that everything is evil, it is indicating that its ideal is goodness. The conscience of the artist has the absolute right to manifest itself in all its truth. It can tell us that all is evil, pain, and death, it can tell us that we should destroy society, the world, and scatter the very seeds of life. Saying this would be antisocial if the social conscience upon hearing it failed to react with greater energy in its own defense. If this is not the case, if the society accepts its sentence, then it was a rotten organism and the artistic cautery merely consumed dead flesh, it did not scar the living.

"Not that which goeth into the mouth defileth a man," says the Scripture, "but that which cometh out of the mouth." Art can be antisocial only in the midst of a decadent and decomposing society. Otherwise that pessimistic and apparently corrosive art will be far healthier for the strong society than that other art of sugared optimism, so well attuned to things as they are. An art which pretends to no improvements or corrections and goes about cavorting and exclaiming idiotically, "Joy and happiness! Life is gay and all's well with the world!" This is indeed the art of stagnancy which claims only to give to putrefaction the appearance of a preserve seasoned with the salt of humor and the spice of sensuality. This art is nothing less than spiritual pornography. All is well because I am happy and nothing needs improving because I am comfortable. This art is truly antisocial, for it forgets in its self-centeredness the pain of others and pursues personal pleasure. It does not see, it does not wish to see, it does not remember ever having seen—it does not know how to take its soundings in the depths of human sorrow.

Nor is it necessary to return from the levels of hell as did the Florentine poet with mortal pallor on his face. It is enough to feel in one's soul the sympathy of pain! A child goes by, crippled, propped up between crutches, pale and with lusterless eyes. Let us never say that those who can look upon this sadness of life with indifference are happy. No. They are pitiful, very pitiful!

And it isn't that one should curse life because of suffering. On the contrary, pain ought to confirm us as veteran fighters in our resolution to overcome it. Yet to what spiritual heights one must climb in order not to doubt everything, in order not to curse and blaspheme, in order to understand finally, though we may never explain it, how that blot of sorrow upon the life of a child might be necessary to the final harmony of all.

If conservative art is the optimistic one that never disturbs, that never moves us to pity, blessed be art that's free, the art of the gutter and the rebel which tells us as it offends and wounds us to wake up, struggle, and live! And let us reject that art which says, "Sleep on in your placid dream. Don't even think about dying. Whatever for? You're dead already."

What I have said about art in general applies as well to the theatre in so far as it is an art. What I said about the influence of art upon society obviously applies to the theatre. The theatre, like all art and perhaps more than all others is a matter of communication and sympathy. The playwright tells us a fable which he has invented and the spectator comes prompted by curiosity to hear it. For as Ariosto says: "This desire is in everyone's heart: to know other people's business." But in this case the spectator comes in groups. In matters of spiritual mathematics the sum *public* is not the same as the total number of spectators. The conscience and, even more, the understanding of a crowd is something very different from the conscience and understanding of any one of its members: it is a social conscience composed of a mutual respect for social hypocrisies. Though each of us is sure that the rest are not as good as ourselves, out of fear that the others might think us their equals, we endeavor to appear better than we actually are. We each have a suit of moral clothing to wear about the house, often a rather loose-fitting thing, and then we have another, a second dressier suit that we don when we attend the theatre. The man who has spent all day organizing a business deal of doubtful pulchritude, the man who has amassed great riches without the least hesitation of a scruple—when at the play, this man lets a tear come to his eye as the young hero inveighs against money and simultaneously embraces his honest poverty and the heroine. The man who tries to marry his daughter to the highest bidder becomes incensed against the father of the play who opposes a love match between his daughter and the hero. When at the theatre, the indulgent husband applauds the pistol shot that avenges the honor of the wronged husband upon the stage.

On certain occasions in French prisons the prisoners are shown theatrical presentations. It is reported that never has a play awakened such a keen moral fervor, never has a traitor been rebuked with more indignation, nor has virtue triumphed more resoundingly than amid this audience of delinquents and criminals.

Who has not been approached with propositions to commit some dishonorable business? And no matter how our honesty is aroused, if the proponent is well spoken and personable, we will hear him through to the end without qualms. And only after having heard him out, and then with the greatest tact we give him to understand that he has made a mistake. A little later as we recount the event to an intimate friend we exclaim indignantly, "You can imagine! I never let him finish! Propose such a thing to me?!" Later, if by chance we happen to repeat the story to a group, we exclaim with even greater indignation, "Just imagine! Propose such a thing to me? I didn't even let him begin to speak before I'd thrown him down the stairs!" The gathering unanimously praises our conduct but not, however, without each of them remarking to himself, "What good business propositions some people get!" This is the way we are to ourselves, man to man, and in groups. And so we live on deceiving one another, deceiving even ourselves.

Being thus we, nevertheless, demand sincerity of art and truth and reality from the theatre. For this reason the influence of the theatre is virtually nil. A play is more a thing impelled than a thing compelling. The playwright who preaches the most can be certain that he will be heard only when he preaches to those who need no convincing. Of course, this is true of all preachers: religious, political, or sociological. The priest preaches in church to the catholics, the socialist to the socialists in his group, the anarchist to his companions at their meeting hall. In this way one avoids disagreements and controversy.

Upon occasion a playwright fancies himself a leader of the masses because a play of his awakens a clamor that was already awaiting an opportunity of release. A playwright's skill like that of the orator consists in detecting with great subtlety the moment in which many people are thinking the same thing but no one dares to utter his thoughts. Thus Marc Antony at the burial of Caesar was able to perceive, under the apparent support by the Roman people of Caesar's assassins, the true feelings that Caesar's death had aroused, feelings which awaited one lone voice to awaken them into thousands of cries. For this very reason, because theatre does only convince the converted, the convinced, it can help rulers and sociologists to regulate the pulse of public opinion at key moments. Thus in Greece the governing artists turned the theatre into a civico-religious spectacle. The Catholic Church, master psychologist and expert on multitudes that she is, in her early stages took advantage of the theatre. If it did not enliven the theatre it at least restrained the defection of the faithful from its religious ceremonies. As was natural, the laudable desire to attract ever larger numbers of believers awakened a keen competition between the various churches and guilds. When religious topics were found to be too tame they turned to the profane and aimed themselves headlong at danger. For the devil, who is always lurking about, offended no doubt by the thankless role invariably assigned him in these devout performances, took his revenge by insinuating himself into the very fiber of the works through bawdy songs and suggestive dances—and to a degree that would scandalize any audience in spite of the fact that we today are supposed to be shockproof.

From this partnership of the religious and the profane, in which the devil was altogether triumphant, was born the popular theatre of the more advanced nations of Europe. It retained a religious nature only in so far as licentiousness did not become intolerable or in cases where the authority of the church was not strong enough to appropriate the religious fervor of the artist. So it is that in Spain the *autos Sacramentales* endured for quite some time under the patronage of the church. In some towns and country places a few of these religious works have survived to this very day in all the ingenuousness of their original presentation.

Wherever civil power is confused with the theocratic one, as was true in most of Europe during the sixteenth and seventeenth centuries, the theatre must take very special care to avoid crossing the church as did Don Quixote and Sancho. The theatre, the school and mirror of manners and convention, limits itself to being a mirror since its didactic role proves dangerous. Furthermore, it is a mirror in which convention and manners are reflected, not as they are in reality, but as social opinion would have them appear. The great Spanish theatre of the seventeenth century has absolutely no reality to it beyond that of the false idealism imposed on it by a social conscience. It has no conscience other than the authority of the church reinforced by the monarchical power.

Was that society the thing we see represented in its drama? Certainly not. Neither was honor so rigorously defended, nor were the ladies as discreet or audacious, nor were marriages arranged as readily, nor were their servants as familiar with their masters, nor were all the ladies maternal orphans, nor were there so many duels—in short, nothing was true. In moments of honesty the playwrights themselves joke about these falsehoods, indicating that life was one thing and the theatre quite another. It is enough proof for one to notice the different portrait of the times that we find in the novels of the period; these were more concerned with reality by virtue of addressing themselves to the less falsified conscience of the individual reader. This remains true even though many of the novels borrowed turns from the theatre to adorn reality, yet even so they never succeeded in falsifying reality to the degree encountered in the plays.

The systematic elimination from the ancient Spanish theatre of a figure of such social importance as the mother has been discussed at great length. Without any real basis it has been argued that this omission was due to the respect and veneration inspired by the figure of the mother in such chivalrous times and that her representation in farces and plays would have been considered indecorous. I say that this is without basis for the character is not altogether absent from the drama of the period. The Queen Doña María, mother of Ferdinand IV, suffered nothing in being represented in *La pudencia en la mujer* by Tirso de Molina. The figure of the mother appears in various plays by Lope de Vega—those that come to mind are *La testigo enamorada, La dama melindrosa,* and *De fuera vendra.* If indeed it was respect and awe which detained these authors from employing the figure of the mother, Lope certainly shared little of it with them in these plays. It would be hard to find plays modern or ancient in which a mother comes off more ridiculously or is spoken to by her daughters with less love and respect. To be sure Lope knew how to compensate and then some for these slights when he wrote the mother of *El testimonio vengado* who, when hearing her own son accuse and malign her both as mother and queen, makes no rebuke but replies out of her mother's love in terms worthy of Shakespeare, "I grieve, my son, only because God must punish you."

The classical Spanish theatre, as I have said, is one of

false idealism, constructed upon a lack of social conscience which was the major determinant of our decadence. All life, all social life based upon deception cannot endure. It is possible, perhaps, to live by deceiving the rest of the world but never by deceiving oneself. Life will surprise us in the end with the truth of our lives which is always what we have earnestly wished them to be. Our deeds respond always to our true sentiments. The trouble is that in order to know when we have acted according to our will we must first realize that all human determination appears first in what we pretend to believe; second, in what we believe we believe; and, finally in what we really do believe. And it is here, on this last level, where one must search for the truth—both personal and public. Inquire into the causes of those actions of the sort that we call involuntary, our forgettings, our misunderstandings—you will always find at the root of the deed a firm desire to forget or to misunderstand. How often we exclaim "How could I have done this? I didn't want to!" Ah! What you didn't want was to see what you wanted—that is quite another matter and therefore it will always catch you by surprise. That's why nations are surprised by their catastrophes and their downfalls. "How did we come to this?" . . . By living without truth and without a conscience.

Nations of America, heed the example of Europe whose terrible hour came and could ask only "Was all our civilization no more than this ferocity?" And it was so. Our civilization was kneaded through with greed, pride, militarism, and the desire to make commerce of anything and without conscience. This was the truth beneath our most beautiful aspects, and in the end the truth gave birth to its monster and appalled the world. Theatre today enjoys the greatest freedom. It can tell us how we are and how we should be. The spectator is the only authority which can oppose the liberties of the playwright. Never more than today has the theatre revealed itself in its two universal tendencies: conservative and liberal. The one, pleasant, optimistic, flatterer of the bourgeois audience; the other, restless, belligerent, popular, or aristocratic—for, as the world goes nowadays, to be aristocratic is to be a revolutionary. This theatre needs a new public, it needs to address itself to the future. The future happens to be the people, and the children; children and people come to the same thing, for together they are the future and their evolution takes precedence over all concerns. This is the future life and to talk of the future life is to talk of eternity.

For these reasons the responsibility of the playwright is greater today than ever before. The theatre is a representation of society, its manners and its conscience. May it not react upon these manners and this conscience through the representation of a higher morality aimed at determining a more perfect social state? Or must we deny the influence of art and the theatre in particular; believing that its only social value lies in being an entertainment, one of the amenities of life? We must say as did the comedian Regnard about the moralizing playwrights of his time: "Because of four miserable verses that you may have written you believe you have defined man and rebuilt Paris." And to say Paris is to mean the world.

However, even though we are fatalists let us be so in the manner of a certain fellow who was very convinced that all that happens in this world cannot but happen because, as the Mohammedans say, "it is written." But he, in spite of his belief, lived his life complaining angrily at every step and endeavoring to put things in better order. When someone would ask, "Why lose your temper if you believe that all that happens must happen because *it is written?*" He would answer more annoyed than ever, "Because it is also written that I should be indignant." The fellow was right. Let us always be among those who indignate even though we become angry fatalistically. For it may be written that there should always be noble spirits who do not believe in or accept resignedly the fate of evil and pain without struggling against them with the fatal energy of will that can, perhaps, do nothing. But . . . I can do! I can! The will made fertile by love gave birth to the world and all that is. And the spirit will triumph by virtue of will and love—the spirit of God which is in each of us and seeks in each of us the perfection which must be God himself.

"Man is God's partner," according to Seneca. By partners we mean His collaborator. In whom can God manifest himself to better advantage than in his most perfect work? The history of God is the history of man. In the beginning, for the man of natural instincts, there existed only a God of vengeance; later man conceived of a just God; later, a God of mercy, a God who out of love makes himself man, and being all power and knowledge refuses to judge man until he has suffered the whole of human sorrow. A lovely truth for the believer—and for the disbeliever, what a lovely symbol of the truth! To sigh out as he died upon the cross "My God, why hast thou forsaken me?" There are those who doubt that God could have made himself man. But there is no one who can doubt that at that moment, crucified for loving all the pains of the flesh, and the sorrows of the soul, man made himself God. Upon this death of the crucified God, man-God, or God-man, there began to dawn the spirit which leads men in the path of our redemption and our eternity: love.

You may say that it is still dawning and the day has yet to come. There is no need to despair. Life is war and struggle is the nature of our spirit. The blood that reddens the earth paints the dawn of heaven with a rosy light. What do centuries mean within the dawning of the spirit if day will break for eternity?

THE WITCHES' SABBATH

by JACINTO BENAVENTE

1903

THE WITCHES' SABBATH[1]

Translated by William I. Oliver

CAST OF CHARACTERS

(in order of appearance)

READER
PRINCESS ETELVINA
LADY SEYMOUR
COUNTESS RINALDI
LEONARDO
PRINCE MICHAEL
PRINCE FLORENCIO
HARRY LUCENTI
THE DUKE OF SUAVIA
EDITH
THE PREFECT OF POLICE (*the Signore*)
IMPERIA
MR. JACOB
ARTIST
RUHU-SAHIB
WAITER
SERVANTS, SAILORS, GAMBLERS
ESTHER
JULIETTE
JENNY
TOBACCO
CORNAC
ROSINA
PEPITA
LELIA
NUNU
TOMMY
DONINA
ZAIDA
CECCO
GAETANO
HER MAJESTY
PIETRO
DEPUTY

[1] Published in Spanish as LAS BRUJAS DEL DOMINGO. Used by permission of the translator.

PROLOGUE

READER. *The Witches' Sabbath.* Sea, sky, and earth are lovingly joined in joy. Light, wave, mountain, and fern seem to laugh with the freshness of a new-born world ignorant of sorrow and death. Enchanted corner of the earth! Only gods and heroes, nymphs and fauns should people you; and love and wisdom alone should rule within your shore. Theocritus and Virgil captured your soul. And if in our sorry time a poet has turned to you to elevate his melancholy, it was Shelley, the believer in eternal harmony of Beauty, Truth, and Good . . . Shelley, who refused to limit the infinite and worshiped God in all things . . . who worshiped with the same passionate litany of the saintly poet of Assisi, the universal lover, who greeted all creatures with a song of love: Brother Sun, Brother Sea, Brother Birds, Brother Wolf . . . all . . . all brothers!

And now, into this enchanted corner of the world, comes man. It is the fashionable winter season. Men have chosen their earthly paradise well . . . for paradise it would be . . . if it weren't for the fact that men flee the cold but bring the chill of their lives with them; they flee their lives and their lives pursue them. All their paths lead to Dante's inferno whose portals are inscribed:

> Through me is the way to the city of woe.
> Through me is the way to eternal sorrow.
> Through me is the way of the lost
>
> (*Per me si va nella città dolente;*
> *per me si va nell eterno dolore;*
> *per me si va trà la perdutta gente.*)

ACT ONE

[*A hall in a sumptuous villa.*

The PRINCESS ETELVINA, LADY SEYMOUR, *the* COUNTESS RINALDI, LEONARDO, PRINCE MICHAEL, PRINCE FLORENCIO, LORD SEYMOUR, HARRY LUCENTI, *and the* DUKE OF SUAVIA *are seated about the room.* EDITH *plays upon the lute while* LADY SEYMOUR *and* LEONARDO *listen to the music.* PRINCESS ETELVINA, PRINCE MICHAEL, LORD SEYMOUR, *and the* DUKE OF SUAVIA *take tea.* PRINCE FLORENCIO, *the* COUNTESS RINALDI, *and* HARRY LUCENTI *examine a number of etchings and engravings, while conversing animatedly. A servant hands a telegram to* PRINCE MICHAEL.]

ETELVINA. News from Suavia?

PRINCE MICHAEL. Great news . . . [*To* PRINCESS ETELVINA.] You should be the first to announce it. Here, read . . .

DUKE. Is it serious? . . . The music!

[*There is an imposing silence.*]

ETELVINA. How wonderful! Listen, my son. Her Imperial Highness has given birth to a boy, a prince and heir.

MICHAEL. Long live the Prince!

ALL. Long live the Prince!

PRINCE FLORENCIO [*as he takes the telegram*]. At last! . . . after seven princesses—a prince! The empire has haunted me long enough. It's become my disease. Now I'll be able to recover my health.

LADY SEYMOUR. You're taking it all quite cheerfully, I must say!

RINALDI. You don't lose a throne every day.

ETELVINA [*to* PRINCE MICHAEL]. We mustn't be late. See that our best wishes and congratulations are sent at once.

PRINCE FLORENCIO. Not that anyone will believe them. I am always misunderstood. The Empress suggested an absence from court because she was afraid I was in too much of a hurry to become Emperor. Now that the future of my august cousin is linked to mine, there is more reason than ever to keep me out of Suavia. Besides, I've got enough to do leading my own life.

ETELVINA. So it seems, judging from the little you care for it.

FLORENCIO. Now that it's mine, now that it belongs to me completely . . . I just might, in the long run, come to like life. I'm free! . . . no longer heir to the throne, the center of all that hope, ambition . . . and hatred. And my seven cousins, the princesses, dreaming all this time of becoming imperial consorts . . . well, it won't matter to them now what I do.

ETELVINA. Don't talk that way . . . always flippant.

DUKE. Your Highness, many of us placed our faith in you. We fought side by side with your father. We were present at your birth. The Prince is a baby, the Emperor is old, and there is unrest throughout the empire.

MICHAEL. True; but it doesn't solve matters.

FLORENCIO [*to* PRINCE MICHAEL]. My dear uncle, you're still young. You will be regent just as you would have been in my case. Because, I swear to you, the empire would have fallen on your shoulders . . . it would have come to you anyway . . . my reign would have been short.

ETELVINA. Who knows? Life may have meant something to you then. Now? . . . However, you seem happy.

FLORENCIO. Very. And you? Remember Daudet's *Kings in Exile*? Are you less fond of me now that I'm no king?

ETELVINA. Oh you mad, ungrateful boy! All I want is for you to be happy.

LADY SEYMOUR. What a coincidence. Edith was just playing the national anthem of your lost empire. It's rather original.

FLORENCIO. On the lute! How dreary. It's a march full of trumpets and drums, makes no sense without flashing swords and shining armor. The whole warlike soul of our country is in that song. And, believe it or not, they say it was written by a foreign monk for the funeral of some poet or other.

DUKE. That's a silly myth.

LADY SEYMOUR. Oh how sweet, a monk and a poet . . .

LEONARDO. Tennyson may have written a poem now and then that . . .

LADY SEYMOUR. Tennyson was a great poet! *He* was a gentleman received by the best people!

HARRY LUCENTI [*to* LEONARDO]. Lady Seymour wants to put me in my place. She'll never forgive the Prince for inviting me.

LEONARDO. You're the scandal of England.

HARRY. Take any great lady you like, look through her *secrétaire* and, next to her lover's letters, you'll find a volume of my poems. Look on her drawing room table and you'll find the *Bible* and a book by Kipling.

LEONARDO. Your great lady who sees her respectable husband at dinner sitting at the head of the table . . .

HARRY. And after dinner finds him beneath the table.

LEONARDO. I told you that joke yesterday and you found it in bad taste.

HARRY. Still do when it's told by a foreigner. You think it's easy to stop being English? England banished me like Byron . . .

LEONARDO. But you haven't banished England.

RINALDI. Byron? You know, *he* doesn't strike me as being immoral. When I was a little girl I learned English reading Byron.

LEONARDO. Hadn't you anything better to do than to learn English by reading Byron?

RINALDI. Italian women aren't like Lady Seymour; we're not afraid of rubbing shoulders with banished poets.

LEONARDO. The countess is shockproof. . . . You've been cured of shyness.

RINALDI. Not cured . . . I'm convalescing. That's why I come here every winter.

LEONARDO. Always alone.

RINALDI. My husband won't come.

LEONARDO. I take it his cure is complete.

ETELVINA. I suppose Suavia is ablaze with celebration now.

DUKE. The court, the officials . . . yes. But the people . . . they love Prince Florencio. They would never forget that he's the son of the invincible liberator, your husband, who's venerated through all Suavia.

ETELVINA. That's so. But you know how they've tried to discredit him these last few years.

DUKE. Well, what young man of twenty could stand up under such continuous censure?

MICHAEL. If Florencio had been different . . . I don't want to upset you, he's your only son, I know how you love him . . . but if his conduct . . .

ETELVINA. What can you tell me I don't already know. I've shed tears a-plenty. His health is all that matters to me now. It should improve here.

MICHAEL. Here? You arrived two days ago and already the Prefect of Police has warned me that the Prince has been seen at very dangerous places.

ETELVINA. Dear God!

MICHAEL. The Prefect is a man of the world. They call him the Signore. This little principality pays him well to keep the peace and to cast a net of respectability over the doings of this very dangerous cosmopolis.

ETELVINA. And you say Florencio . . .

MICHAEL. Don't worry. The Signore has assigned a detail of secret agents to follow him and protect him . . . if necessary. But just the same it's shameful.

ETELVINA. Yes it is. You can pity me. All we needed was for him to strike up a friendship with this poet Lucenti . . . half-English, half-Italian . . . evil man, utterly without morals. Lord and Lady Seymour were scandalized to find him here.

MICHAEL. Really? But I thought . . . Pardon me a moment. . . . My lady, I've just been told that you are offended by the presence of Harry Lucenti.

LADY SEYMOUR. Quite right. No one should receive that man.

MICHAEL. I beg your pardon. But I thought I saw you talking to him last night at the casino.

LADY SEYMOUR. Oh, yes, often! But never in front of my husband.

MICHAEL. Yet I've often seen your husband talking to him.

LADY SEYMOUR. Certainly . . . but not in my presence.

MICHAEL. English propriety is more complicated than I imagined.

LADY SEYMOUR. It's a matter of respectability.

RINALDI [*to* LEONARDO]. I'm not in a mood for you to be jolly at my expense. I'm very sad, very sad . . . you've no idea how sad!

LEONARDO. And you're dying to tell me.

RINALDI. Artists are such dangerous confidants. You never keep secrets.

LEONARDO. I'm a sculptor. In order for my art to reveal your secrets . . . well! Incidentally, you'd make a wonderful Juno.

RINALDI. The other day it was Minerva.

LEONARDO. Tomorrow it may be Venus. There's a time for everything!

RINALDI. As models go, you could do worse.

LEONARDO. I don't doubt it!

RINALDI. Take into consideration I'm not wearing a corset. Just a little support *à la grècque*.

LEONARDO. Now you're encroaching on my domain. Only spiritual confidences if you please!

RINALDI. Why do you suppose I'm here tonight?

LEONARDO. How should I know? Probably because you were invited to dinner by Prince Michael, like the rest of us, to celebrate the joyous arrival of his sister-in-law, the Princess Alexandra Etelvina, and her august son, Prince Florencio, the late prospective emperor.

RINALDI. Invited? On the contrary, I came because I was not invited.

LEONARDO. What?

RINALDI. Apparently I'm considered *déclasée*. Oh, it's my own fault; in Paris I was presented to the Prince officially by the Italian ambassador. But here, where there's no etiquette, where one comes for pleasure, for a change of life . . . the Casino, the races, the gun club are as neutral as the country itself. Well, one day I happened to meet the prince at one of these places with . . . with his . . .

LEONARDO. With Imperia.

RINALDI. Well, I wasn't going to cut him! That's absurd! I'm no Lady Seymour who's afraid of being seen with a talented fellow countryman and artist like Harry Lucenti.

LEONARDO. It *is* silly.

RINALDI. In Italy art and beauty are sacred. It was a pope who said of Benvenuto Cellini, that such artists were above the law. I didn't hesitate to meet the Prince's "lady friend"; I wouldn't dream of denying myself the parties at her villa. Nor would I dream of leaving the parties here . . . when she makes her appearance late in the evening and only the inner circle stays on. That's the best part of these parties. However, the Prince has taken my condescension for abdication. That's why I had to come here without an invitation. Naturally, he hasn't let on, but the Princess was as cold as ice.

LEONARDO. They say she's very strict and surrounds herself with dragons of virtue.

RINALDI. . . . *and* ugliness . . . like that little lady in waiting, daughter of the Duke of Suavia. A sentimental little thing that the Princess—in spite of all her strictness—keeps at her side to induce Prince Florencio to amuse himself at home and stop scandalizing the court.

LEONARDO. Poor Prince! He's very handsome, a patron of the arts, but indefatigable in his pursuit of beauty.

RINALDI. Over zealous! Wasn't he Imperia's lover before the Uncle?

LEONARDO. So they say.

RINALDI. And after you?

LEONARDO. I was never her lover; she was my model—no more. She took her name from my statue. Prince Florencio met her at my studio in Rome.

RINALDI. . . . and promptly stole away . . . your model. You see, I take you at your word. It was after that when you fell ill.

LEONARDO. Malaria.

RINALDI. Changed your life completely . . . sent your art into a decline. Didn't you shatter a magnificent block of marble you were saving for a colossal sculpture? *The Triumph of Life,* wasn't it? Supposed to be a work of genius, the first in a series—certainly not the last. Italy might have boasted of two Leonardos.

LEONARDO. Leonardo! You don't know how that name's haunted me. My father loved beauty and worshiped the great artists . . . so he called me Leonardo. A name that forced me to dream great dreams! But one can't realize a great ideal until it's broken into little bits. There's proof! From that block of Carrara, which I meant to be my masterpiece, I carved the thousand and one figurines that you've seen . . . first at the expositions and in the windows, then after in the parlors and boudoirs of the fashionable: pretty, charming . . . people like them, they sell well. Instead of a blaze of inspiration in one gigantic work—a little spark of art in each of a thousand trinkets. Instead of a heroic monument that addressed the soul of the people—a paper weight, or a knicknack for a lampstand. And people assume that I am fulfilling my ideal. By my works they will judge me. They see the grains of sand and will never know that a mountain was pulverized to create them.

RINALDI. But suppose one's ideal is love?

LEONARDO. You have the secret. Break the block of your dream and content yourself with figurines. Then love each one as you would have loved the master dream.

RINALDI. Loving many is not the same as loving much. Take your case. You broke the marble, but have you forgotten your model, your Imperia? You wouldn't come here if it weren't for her.

LEONARDO. We're all here for a reason.

RINALDI. Which we keep to ourselves. One thing certain, we're all running away from life, from that public existence forced on us by position and the world. That's why we all scurry to this little cove of promiscuity where everything is known and no one knows anything. Tonight, for instance, the Princess is making us behave and we're bored to death . . . wishing our bodies could follow our thoughts.

LEONARDO. We go through life as shadows of ourselves. We think we know the people we see, but we can't see their souls.

FLORENCIO [*to* HARRY LUCENTI]. I'll leave with Mother, I don't want her to worry about me. When she retires, I'll tell her I'm going to bed. I'll see you later. Those people will be there, won't they?

HARRY. We'll pick them up at the theatre. You haven't seen Mr. Jacob's new theatre, have you? A splendid music hall-circus, in the worst possible taste, but amusing. However, it lacks the atmosphere of the old puppet theatre down by the wharf with its sailors and stevedores gaping at some fine lady on the prowl for adventure. But Cecco's tavern is still intact with its old clientele and a few improvements. Cecco gives the foreigners their money's worth, a whole show: native dances, knife fight, and police raid, all of it rehearsed and directed by Cecco . . . reality itself.

FLORENCIO. We can have supper there with the people from Jacob's. I'll find it more amusing than those monotonous *restaurants de nuit.*

HARRY. Oh, it's much more fun. We can have the performance canceled tonight, since we're in on the secret.

[*They continue talking.*]

RINALDI [*to* LEONARDO]. I suppose you're right. I should have known you were a friend. But your intimacy with Prince Michael made me doubt you. As it happens, my husband is free to return to Suavia as ambassador, but just the same, I wouldn't want these people to know a thing. Otherwise I'd be forced to talk to the Prefect.

LEONARDO. The Signore? Don't be foolish. This place would be a paradise if it weren't for him. In order to earn his pay, every winter he assembles here the most exotic collection of criminals to be found anywhere in the world. However, don't worry, leave the matter to me. You say he works at the music hall? . . . an acrobat, a beautiful brute of a man?

RINALDI. A brute . . . but wonderful. You're an artist so you understand everything.

LEONARDO. And he's blackmailing you?

RINALDI. I've already paid 5000 francs.

LEONARDO. That's terrible! You've been too soft . . . twice.

RINALDI. You won't tell, will you?

LEONARDO. No, I won't tell. . . . Though, I already knew about it. So don't imagine that everyone heard it from me . . . because I've already heard it from everyone.

RINALDI. You mean it's out . . . already?

LEONARDO. Don't bother. The same thing happened to Lady Seymour with one of her grooms, and, you see, there she stands wrapped in the Union Jack scarcely deigning to speak to you all evening long. Did you ever notice how people cut us sometimes, not because of what they know about us, but rather, because of what they think we know about them.

RINALDI. Exactly. That's why one should never hold anything back. We must reveal everything, and not out of malice, but in order to encourage tolerance and humility, and so that we'll see that we're all made of the same clay. Virtue, after all, is composed of vices—the ones we don't possess. If it had been a virtue not to eat apples, and if I had been Eve, we'd still be in the garden of Eden. I can't abide apples. But by the same token, I wouldn't dream of complaining about those who do eat apples. They must have a reason.

LEONARDO. There's a reason for everything—even madness.

ETELVINA [*rising*]. We'll go now, it's late. [*To* PRINCE MICHAEL.] You'll lunch with us tomorrow?

MICHAEL. Of course. And we'll write to the Emperor.

DUKE [*to the servant*]. Her Highness' carriage. Gentlemen, Her Highness retires.

ETELVINA. Goodnight. It's been a pleasure to see my old friends again. My lady . . . you are as dear to me as ever.

LADY SEYMOUR. You honor me, Your Highness.

ETELVINA. Countess . . . [*To* LEONARDO.] My favorite artist, I have placed your works all about my house. You must work very hard. Your new style is enchanting. Like the old masters, you don't seem to find it beneath you to beautify useful objects. Gentlemen.

FLORENCIO [*to* HARRY]. Don't be late.

HARRY. I'll beat you there. So long.

FLORENCIO. My dear uncle, goodnight.

MICHAEL. Take care of yourself . . . for your mother's sake.

FLORENCIO. You see how it is . . . I'm staying home tonight.

ETELVINA. He's promised me.

[PRINCESS ETELVINA, PRINCE FLORENCIO, EDITH, *and the* DUKE OF SUAVIA *leave, accompanied by* PRINCE MICHAEL.]

RINALDI. The Princess is remarkably well preserved.

LEONARDO. She still looks young.

LADY SEYMOUR. She's a saint and so charitable!

RINALDI. She's very popular in Suavia.

LEONARDO. *Her* good deeds were more embarrassing to the court than her son's bad deeds. That's why they were advised to travel.

LORD SEYMOUR. I'm not up on foreign affairs.

LEONARDO. I was talking to myself, my lord . . . it's an artistic quirk.

LORD SEYMOUR. Bad habit. [*To* LADY SEYMOUR.] Let me take you . . . where are you spending the *soirée*?

LADY SEYMOUR. Villa Miranda. There's to be chamber music. Utterly charming!

MICHAEL [*returning*]. The Princess was delighted to see you again.

LADY SEYMOUR. When she's present everything is pleasant. I'll see you soon, Your Highness. You *have* received an invitation to my concert.

MICHAEL. Only a true artist such as yourself could arrange such a concert.

[LORD *and* LADY SEYMOUR *say goodnight and are escorted out by* PRINCE MICHAEL.]

RINALDI. You see? She didn't invite me either. Well, I don't care. I don't need her invitation.

LEONARDO. With or without one, you'll go anyway.

RINALDI. Rest assured.

HARRY. Beware of pushing an Englishwoman too far . . . the risk is too great.

RINALDI. I'll arrive on the arm of one of her grooms.

HARRY. You shouldn't talk about such things.

RINALDI. How can you defend hypocritical society after . . . after it made you its victim?

HARRY. I'm not complaining. I go my way, they go theirs. I scandalized England, but the world was large.

RINALDI. So now you scandalize the world.

HARRY. The world's stupid. If one had to live to suit the world . . . Do you try to please the world?

LEONARDO. The Countess does and loves every minute of it.

RINALDI. I worry a great deal about the things people say.

LEONARDO. It shows.

RINALDI. I'm not joking.

LEONARDO. Seriously, now . . . it's obvious, because if you *didn't* worry about gossip . . . well!

HARRY. Prince Florencio is waiting for me.

RINALDI. He seems to be a great friend of yours. Had he become emperor, he would have made you his . . .

HARRY. You were going to say "fool" weren't you?

RINALDI. You're too sad for a fool.

HARRY. English fools are that way, they might pass for diplomats.

LEONARDO. All fools are sad . . . and laughter is the most efficient gravedigger. We cry over whatever lives, what hurts, what lingers in our memory—when we laugh at something: love, faith, hope, a memory . . . it's dead. Shakespeare's fools are the most tragic figures in his tragedies. Hamlet is dwarfed by the gravediggers who laugh and sing among the graves. Their spades dig into the earth and out pops poor Yorick still laughing through a horrible smirk of bone. All things die . . . except laughter. What's life, forever renewing itself, but the laughter of love as it conquers death.

RINALDI. But death is the end of everything . . . and after . . .

HARRY. After death, hell. Fortunately you Italians have a lovely Inferno. I can see you now, Countess, in the same circle with Francesca . . . always in the best society.

RINALDI. Don't joke. I have faith and I hope to be saved.

LEONARDO. Why not? The life of a saint is usually divided into two parts . . . you're still in the first.

RINALDI. Change the subject. If you only knew the nights I've jumped out of bed screaming, terrified, because I dreamed I was dying. Sometimes in broad daylight, on one of those holidays all sunshine and fun, in the middle of a crowd of gay people, I think to myself, "In a few years they'll all be gone, they'll be dead!" And I want to scream at them, warn them of the danger! Then, suddenly, a shroud of silence, a shadow . . . drops over me . . . it's horrible. I've been to the doctors . . .

LEONARDO. What do they prescribe?

RINALDI. I'm told to amuse myself . . . and always to sleep with the light on and somebody near.

LEONARDO. A pleasant treatment. Shouldn't be too difficult to follow.

[PRINCE MICHAEL *and the* SIGNORE *enter*.]

SIGNORE. Gentlemen! Ah, the Countess! It's been a long time, Countess . . . but I haven't forgotten you.

RINALDI. The Prefect is very kind, the more so since we always seem to meet under rather disagreeable circumstances. Our last encounter was when my jewels were stolen.

SIGNORE. Now, now . . . you shouldn't complain of me. Do you remember when you heard subterranean rumblings in your villa . . . and the time that famous gigolo tried to make you sing to the tune of some very interesting letters?

RINALDI. Forgeries.

SIGNORE. And those anonymous notes everyone received revealing such horrors about your private life . . . ? I am always at your service and ready to protect you.

RINALDI. Thank you, Signore . . . [*Whispering to* LEONARDO.] I can never remember the man's name!

LEONARDO. Since everyone knows he doesn't use his real name, they call him the Signore and avoid confusion.

MICHAEL. I had no idea the Countess was such a good client.

SIGNORE. One of the best! The theft of the jewels: a trick to make people think they were real. They were pastes and she valued them at three million francs. The anonymous notes she wrote herself so that she could play the martyr.

MICHAEL. Charming woman.

SIGNORE. But dangerous.

RINALDI [*to* LEONARDO]. I don't like the Signore. He always greets me so mysteriously, as though he were doing me a favor to keep my secrets.

LEONARDO. Take care. I'm told he's planning to publish his memoirs.

RINALDI. Good gracious! I'll have to buy up the whole edition! Will you come with me.

LEONARDO. All right.

RINALDI. You're not going to wait for Imperia?

LEONARDO. No. We'll leave as soon as you wish.

RINALDI. Your Highness, thank you for your kind invitation.

MICHAEL. Leaving so soon? Imperia should be here any minute now that the inner circle is assembled.

RINALDI. I've decided to be less intimate. I thought there was only a garden and gate between your villa and Imperia's. However, I see that you've put up an insuperable wall.

MICHAEL. Don't be vindictive. It wasn't my fault. Princess Etelvina admits few into her friendship.

RINALDI. A wise woman. I'll try my best to follow her example. Good evening, Your Highness.

HARRY. I'll be going too, Your Highness.

MICHAEL. You diabolical poet . . . like Virgil, a guide to hell. Take care of Prince Florencio, his health is poor.

HARRY. I'll watch over him as though I were Your Highness. You stole his mistress—for his own good. I'll do as much whenever I get the chance.

MICHAEL. Good evening.

[THE COUNTESS, LEONARDO, *and* HARRY *go out.*]

MICHAEL. To what do I owe this honor, Signore?

SIGNORE. It's rather difficult . . . and believe me, it's all out of concern for Your Highness' interests . . . that I'm forced to intrude so annoyingly.

MICHAEL. Oh, you don't annoy me, not at all.

SIGNORE. Well, *I* find it annoying. You must know that Suavia regards the presence here of you two princes, possible heirs to the throne, with a certain alarm.

MICHAEL. Alarm which is no longer justified. You haven't heard the news. Here, read.

SIGNORE. An heir! What a relief! That is, I'm sorry for you . . . but I am relieved.

MICHAEL. Don't worry about me, and be sad or rejoice, as you choose.

SIGNORE. Then I'll rejoice. They feared some sort of conspiracy and I was assigned to watch the two of you. Of course, as far as I'm concerned, knowing you as I do, acquainted with the kind of life you lead here . . .

MICHAEL. Conspiracy! I would conspire my life long to *avoid* being Emperor! Do you think I'd exchange my freedom for an empire?

SIGNORE. Enough! Please! I wouldn't have told you unless I'd been sure. But the government of Suavia thrives on conspiracies. One day, assassination, the next day, revolution. Last season they forced us to spy on a Belgian suspected of anarchy who lived in the most unusual fashion in a wooden lean-to he built himself. He was visited by the strangest and most ragged crew of people! We felt sure we'd discovered a political hot-bed, so we raided the place. It turned out to be a cinema studio! . . . Ah yes but you should see the films! Such views! I had him arrested for pornography. . . . Incidentally, I still have the films. If you ever want to arrange a curious entertainment for your friends, I'll be delighted to lend them to you.

MICHAEL. Thank you, no. You might raid my villa . . . thinking it was another conspiracy.

SIGNORE. In my entire career I have never committed a single indiscretion.

MICHAEL. You must know a great deal.

SIGNORE. I hold the clues to so many unsolved mysteries . . . Most people look at life as they look at the theatre: all they see is the stage while the real drama is going on in the wings.

MICHAEL. Which reminds me. Prince Florencio . . .

SIGNORE. Never out of our sight . . . though somewhat difficult to follow. That English poet knows more dives and such people! He'd make a good policeman.

MICHAEL. You're one of a kind, sir!

SIGNORE. Inimitable! Although everything looks calm on the surface, I'd hate to think of this tower of Babel without me. The difficult trick in my profession is not to find out other people's business . . . rather, it's to keep myself from discovering that which is not my business. Your Highness, at your service . . . and forgive me for . . . for having had to suspect you.

MICHAEL. I forgive you.

[THE SIGNORE *leaves. During the last of this scene* IMPERIA *has been descending the staircase of the hall.*]

MICHAEL. Imperia! How are you? Haven't seen you all day . . . not a spare moment.

IMPERIA. I also had guests.

MICHAEL. So I see.

IMPERIA. You're wrong. You know very well I dress for myself. I like to see myself this way. Your friends didn't wait for me.

MICHAEL. They all had something to do this evening. The Countess was furious with me because I didn't invite her.

IMPERIA. So . . . she invited herself. Good for her. Wherever Lady Seymour and Harry Lucenti are welcome, the Countess could scarcely be out of place. Your hypocrisy is appalling.

MICHAEL. As far as Lady Seymour is concerned, people talk but know nothing. As for the poet, he's a friend of Prince Florencio, and an artist.

IMPERIA. The Countess is also an artist . . . in her way.

MICHAEL. She's mad. Her latest is to fall in love with an acrobat. It's not enough for her to go to the circus every night, she goes backstage and mingles with the performers.

IMPERIA. I know, I've seen her there several times.

MICHAEL. You? You go to the circus?

IMPERIA. I haven't missed a performance these last four nights.

MICHAEL. You said nothing about it.

IMPERIA. You didn't ask.

MICHAEL. What is this fad?

IMPERIA. No fad. I go to see my daughter.

MICHAEL. Daughter? What daughter? I didn't know . . .

IMPERIA. You never asked me that either. What *do* you know about my life? . . . What others have told you? They know nothing. . . . What I have chosen to tell you? . . . Yes. . . . For I'll never lie to you.

MICHAEL. And that daughter?

IMPERIA. The child of the only man I ever loved.

MICHAEL. Thanks.

IMPERIA. I still love him and will . . . forever!

MICHAEL. Where is he?

IMPERIA. In prison for life . . . reprieved from a death sentence.

MICHAEL. How romantic!

IMPERIA. He robbed a man in Rome and killed him. He'd gone three days without food. The malaria had driven the artists out of Rome and we models weren't making any money.

MICHAEL. Were you living with him?

IMPERIA. No. He lived with his mother. I lived at home with my parents, my brothers and sisters, and my daughter. My father had a house by the river . . . half-tavern, half-theatre. We all worked there. During the day we modeled; at night we danced tarantellas and sang Neopolitan songs in the theatre. Leonardo paid my father five hundred lire to let me come and live with him.

MICHAEL. Imperia, that's horrible!

IMPERIA. It's true. What could my father do? We had to live.

MICHAEL. And your daughter . . . how old is she?

IMPERIA. Fourteen. I was fifteen when she was born.

MICHAEL. Where has she been all this time?

IMPERIA. My parents.

MICHAEL. Didn't you ever want her with you?

IMPERIA. Why? I sent her money, she wanted for nothing. She was better off. I did want to go back . . . many times . . . but to bring her . . .

MICHAEL. And now?

IMPERIA. They wrote me that she'd fallen in love.

MICHAEL. At fourteen? Precocious!

IMPERIA. Not in Italy. We are not like you. She fell in love with a young boy who danced in my father's theatre. Eloped with him.

MICHAEL. Marvelous!

IMPERIA. Now they're here dancing in Mr. Jacob's new theatre. Donina . . . she's called Donina just as I was at home, is the star of the troupe. Not pretty but she's attractive . . . as I was . . . as I would have been. The boy is handsome, well built, *bello, bello!* A face like a Madonna's angel, bu they say he's a scamp. The women fight over him an Donina is jealous. Oh, how jealous! As jealous as I woul have been.

MICHAEL. Imperia, you shock me! You allow this? You . .

IMPERIA. Allow what? Allow my daughter to love a man, t be happy loving him, and to suffer for him? That's life. asked her, "Do you want to come and live with me in villa that's *bella, bella* . . . and wear clothes like these?" Sh doesn't want to. It's natural. She doesn't love me.

MICHAEL. Doesn't love her mother? That's terrible!

IMPERIA. It's the truth. Why should she love me? I left he when she was two years old. All she knew was that I wa far away and that I sent her presents and kisses . . . b mail. My brothers must have told her all kinds of horr ble things about me . . . my parents too. Nothing I ser *them* would ever seem enough.

MICHAEL. How can one live this way?

IMPERIA. Why not, if we love each other? Hurt one of us an the whole family would come together for revenge. W don't forgive our enemies, ever. But you people . . . where your love? You don't insult one another . . . that's true . . you never resort to blows. No one falls in love with you children and offers to buy them for five hundred lire. Wit your sort, nothing is quite what it seems to be: what yo say, what you feel. With us it's all truth . . . that's why seems worse.

MICHAEL. Perhaps you're right. In *our* lives we face trut so seldom!

IMPERIA. I'll be leaving now. I'm going to see my daughte

MICHAEL. I'd like to see her too. Meet me there.

IMPERIA. But don't let yourself be seen.

MICHAEL. Why?

IMPERIA. She knows I'm living with a prince and she im agines him a prince out of a fairy book . . . *bello, bello.*

MICHAEL. And you don't want to disillusion her. That's kin of you.

IMPERIA. It's the truth. She's . . . she's just as I used to b All she understands is love . . . like his. Youth, happines and joy!

CURTAIN

ACT TWO

[*A café-greenroom, backstage of the music hall, decorated to resemble a fantastic grotto. Tables and chairs at either side. Ladies and gentlemen sit at the tables smoking and drinking. Waiters come and go. Upstage, a gypsy orchestra.* MR. JACOB *is talking to an* ARTIST. RUHU-SAHIB *sits at the table and drinks enormously.*]

JACOB [*to* ARTIST]. But this! What do you think of this? Allow me. Here is the best perspective.

ARTIST. Wonderful! Magic!

JACOB. It's simply a must . . . eh? What do you say? Allow me. Another perspective.

ARTIST. Wonderful! Magic!

JACOB. My own idea . . . and believe me, it didn't just come to me all of a sudden! You don't get ideas like this every day. The whole place turned into a grotto! . . . a haven for the tired body and the imagination dazzled by the spectacle of the stage. There's nothing like it in all Europe . . . or America, for that matter! It's the most magnificent music hall anywhere in the world! I've sunk four million francs into this place. You can quote me in your article.

ARTIST. My article? Oh, but Mr. Jacob! I'm not a reporter.

JACOB. What! Aren't you the man from *The Vaudeville Courier* of Milan or the one from the Genoa *Managers' Monitor*?

ARTIST. I didn't say . . .

JACOB. But the card I got in the office . . .

ARTIST. Not mine . . . a . . . a mistake. I'm an artist, a performer, a famous one. I've got a wonderful proposition.

JACOB. Proposition?

ARTIST. Yes! me! . . . I've got some great reviews . . .

JACOB. You made me waste two whole hours showing you my theatre just for this! *Andante al diavolo! Morte de un cane! Mais fichez-moi la paix toute de suite!* Waste my time! My precious time!

ARTIST. But, Mr. Jacob! Mr. Jacob!

[MR. JACOB *stalks off followed by the* ARTIST.]

RUHU-SAHIB [*calling a* WAITER]. Is first part finish?

WAITER. Just. Don't you see the people coming out?

RUHU. Take this bottle, bring other bottle. I pay. No charge to the *Madame*.

WAITER. The *Madame* says she won't foot your bill any longer. You should have heard the row she made yesterday!

RUHU. I tol' you . . . dis bottle I pay myself! Bring other bottle! And shut up or I break you head!

WAITER. All right, all right!

ESTHER. Look at the Elephant boy.

JULIETTE. A rare one, he is.

ESTHER. A real gem.

JULIETTE. But not for my collection, thank you—he'd be one too many.

[*Enter* JENNY *and* TOBACCO.]

ESTHER. Oh, here's Tobacco. I like that little nigger clown, he looks like a monkey.

JULIETTE. Is she his wife?

ESTHER. That's right. She's English and you know what? They're actually married! They love each other, though. They must—they've got seven kids.

JULIETTE. Blondes?

ESTHER. Not yet. They all came out like daddy. My but it's dead tonight!

JULIETTE. Nobody here but women.

JENNY [*to* TOBACCO]. Did you go to the bank?

TOBACCO. Sure. [*Jotting something into a pocket book.*] Let me figure this out. Five thousand francs in Turkish—if I can sell them like last week . . . we'll clear a hundred francs.

JENNY. Not bad!

TOBACCO. I might get a new costume for the act.

JENNY. What for? Why do you want to throw your money away? You don't have to wear silk to play the clown.

TOBACCO. The Russian has a new costume every night.

JENNY. And the audience doesn't laugh a bit more because of it. To be an artist like you . . . the Russian would have to. . . . Mr. Jacob's an idiot paying him six thousand francs!

TOBACCO. Mr. Jacob thinks it's too much to pay me ten thousand. He's looking for a chance to kick me out. But the people, the public . . . they won't laugh at anyone but Tobacco. There's only one Tobacco in the whole world! . . . But now he's putting the Russian in the second half of the bill, the good spot, and he's moved me into the third spot of the first half. And, you know what, the people come early to see me . . . and, what's more, they leave early to miss the Russian. It's the audience who pays the artist, not the manager . . . and it's the audience who sets the wage, not the artist.

JENNY. Mr. Jacob is a crook. He thinks he's back at the old puppet theatre.

[CORNAC *runs on.*]

CORNAC. Mr. Ruhu! Mr. Ruhu! Hurry, please! Nero lost his temper, and he's broken a bar of his cage! He won't let us put his shawl on him!

RUHU. I'm coming . . . coming! Nero . . . He's hot. Too hot! Give him beer. I want beer too! Waiter!

CORNAC. The *Madame* doesn't like the elephants to drink beer!

RUHU. *Madame* no like nothing . . . no pay for nothing! I pay for beer. Bottle for me and barrel for elephants!

[MR. JACOB *enters.*]

JACOB. Ruhu, Ruhu! One of the elephants is upset; he's made a mess of his cage . . . a two hundred franc mess! And what's worse . . . now he won't perform!

RUHU. He work, he work. Poor animal! Nice animal! You don understand him!

JACOB. If you don't go and do something with . . .

RUHU. Don hurry . . . wait! Nero no do nothing. I know him, he no do nothing. Of seven elephants Nero is sweet one!

JACOB. And don't drink so much. The audience notices how you are . . . and so do the elephants.

RUHU. How I am? An? I know how perform. I know. You an idiot to say things like that. I drink, drink . . . but I know what I drink.

JACOB. *Ma andante al diavolo! Bribón del infierno!*

[ROSINA *and* PEPITA *detain* MR. JACOB.]

ROSINA. Mr. Jacob, are you angry?

JACOB. That savage of a Hindu! After costing me twelve thousand francs plus the food for his animals . . . and don't the little beasts eat, though! . . . and the public doesn't care anymore—see them once and you've had it! A fine deal I got! Ha! Business? People see the audience and look at me and say, "Ah, Mr. Jacob! Fortune smiles on you! A theatre full of people, enormous receipts, the *maximum tous les soirs* . . ." But they don't know what goes on backstage. They don't know what artists are like! They don't know anything about management and business . . . !

ROSINA. You shouldn't be angry, Mr. Jacob . . . especially now when I'm going to ask you a favor.

JACOB. Favors, always favors!

ROSINA. It's for my friend . . .

PEPITA. *Monsieur* . . .

ROSINA. If you'd be nice enough to let her have a pass for the season . . . you'll do it, won't you?

JACOB. You mean to say that a girl like that can't get someone to pay her way?

ROSINA. Well, Mr. Jacob, if it wasn't for us, who'd come here?

JACOB. On the contrary, you've driven away all the respectable people, all the . . .

ROSINA. Ta-ta-ta-ta, enough! When have you had more princes hanging about the place? Come on, be a sweetie.

JACOB. Well, since you recommend her . . . Drop by the office later. But . . . ah . . . tell her to be a little more careful with her *toilette*.

ROSINA. She just got in and her baggage hasn't caught up with her. But don't worry, I'll put her under my wing.

JACOB. And where does your little friend come from?

ROSINA. Marseilles.

JACOB. Oh, dear me! Marseilles! Tell her not to say she's from Marseilles! That's bad billing.

ROSINA. Naturally. But since she doesn't have a Parisian style, she's thinking of making her debut as a Spaniard.

JACOB. The Spanish type is *passé* . . . but it's better than Marseilles. The important thing is to be a personality, to be unique. She's got a certain something about the face. Well directed, she might just make it. Although it's difficult, there're so many of you. But . . . don't give up hope! Good luck, my dears, good luck. I've got to rush now.

ROSINA. Thank you, Mr. Jacob.

PEPITA. Thanks.

[PRINCE FLORENCIO *and* HARRY LUCENTI *have come on some moments before and are now at one of the tables.*]

ROSINA. I told you he was a darling. Oh, look! A prince! The Prince of Suavia!

PEPITA. Do you get a lot of princes?

ROSINA. Real ones? . . . very few.

[*They go out talking.*]

JACOB [*to the* PRINCE]. Your Highness! What an honor! . . . both for me and my theatre! At your service. *Monsieur!* It almost slipped my mind: next week we're to have some new and sensational attractions. One number alone is costing me twenty thousand francs! Business is becoming more difficult by the day! . . . Your Highness. [*He backs away bowing.*]

HARRY. The amazing Mr. Jacob.

FLORENCIO. He must have a gay old time of it with his artists.

[MR. JACOB *crosses to* JENNY, *who is busy knitting.*]

JACOB. Madame Jenny, why must we always quarrel?

JENNY. What now?

JACOB. Is this a place to knit booties?

JENNY. Oh! Well, I do as I please! I'm knitting for my babies. Is there anything wrong with that?

JACOB. Why don't you cook your meals here?

JENNY. I suppose it's all right to do . . . to do what some others do here.

JACOB. It's all my fault for allowing the artists to mix with the public.

TOBACCO. Is he talking to me?

JENNY. It's plain you don't know how to deal with artists.

JACOB. I'm not used to dealing with artists?

TOBACCO. No, you're not! And this isn't a theatre or a circus, it's a whore house!

JENNY [*pointing to the streetwalkers*]. Those are the artists *you* want.

JACOB. If people weren't looking . . .

TOBACCO. What if they are? You wait . . . wait! [*Squaring off. Several people pull them apart.*]

SOME. Mr. Jacob!

OTHERS. Tobacco! Messieurs!

[CORNAC *runs in.*]

CORNAC. Mr. Ruhu, Nero is breaking up everything! He's trying to get out.

RUHU. Go'way, go'way. Leave me alone. [*He drinks and saunters off. The bell rings.*]

JACOB. I mustn't waste time! My sacred time! . . . The curtain's going up. . . . Idiots!

TOBACCO. I won't spend another day in this place, not one day . . . I swear!

[MADAME LELIA *enters carrying a large handbag.*]

LELIA. Tobacco, what's the matter? Mr. Jacob giving you trouble? Doesn't surprise me. He's a crude, indecent fellow! Good evening, Madame Jenny. How are the children?

JENNY. Too healthy! They eat and break more than we can make.

LELIA. Strength and health are the key to success—they'll make it all back, don't worry.

TOBACCO. You're right there! They're going to be great acrobats—better than the Sheffers!

JENNY. And your baby, Madame Lelia?

LELIA. Fussy, very fussy. I've had to wean him. What with my work on the high wire . . . well I just couldn't go on breast feeding him. Didn't feel comfortable up there!

JENNY. I raised my seven on a bottle. Artists can't do it any other way. Start them off on solids as soon as you can.

LELIA. What was Mr. Jacob's trouble?

JENNY. He got angry because I was knitting here. I was making a little sweater for Alex.

LELIA. He got angry at me the other night because he didn't like this hat! Said it wasn't fit to be seen! And it cost me fifteen francs at the Paris Exposition! Honestly, artists and decent people are out of place here!

TOBACCO. This is no theatre, believe me! Not even a circus! When you've worked for Wulf's of *Berlin*, *Rentz* in Vienna, and *Corradini* in Rome . . . Those are real circuses! Artists are artists in places like that!

LELIA. Those were the old days. But now it's all the same. All you need to be an artist nowadays is some sort of electrical gadget . . . a trick . . . while we real artists have to work for peanuts. Take my husband, when it comes to contortions, he's a genius!

TOBACCO. You can't beat him.

LELIA. I'm not bragging, mind you, but on the high wire I'm as good as they come . . . better! I do a forward leap with a pirouette and a flim-flam! I'm the only woman in Europe who can!

TOBACCO. And that's the god's truth!

JENNY. The second bill just started.

LELIA. Going to watch it?

JENNY. I want to catch the Russian. My husband needs to learn some new tricks.

LELIA. Is it possible? Mr. Tobacco? Oh, you're joking!

TOBACCO. I know . . . but Mr. Jacob finds the Russian very funny.

LELIA. I'm waiting for my husband. Kiss the kiddies for me.

JENNY. You do the same, Madame Lelia.

[TOBACCO *and* JENNY *leave*. NUNU *and* TOMMY *enter*.]

TOMMY [*pointing at the* PRINCE]. There they are.

NUNU. I told you they'd be here. The Prince doesn't like to stand in the wings.

TOMMY. Shall we go over?

NUNU. Wait till they call, you know the Prince. Let's sit here. Have something . . . on me. [*They sit*.]

TOMMY. . . . We going to eat there tonight?

NUNU. That's right.

TOMMY. And Donina?

NUNU. Donina's a fool. She doesn't want to come. Always jealous because I kid around with the other girls.

TOMMY. Why doesn't she play around too?

NUNU. If she only would! . . . or just for once, with the Prince. We'd make a fortune!

TOMMY. Why don't you force her?

NUNU. Force her? You don't know her very well, do you? She wouldn't come. But she *will* come out of jealousy. Tell her I'm there with another woman and she'd come even if it were hell itself.

TOMMY. Does the Prince really like Donina?

NUNU. How should I know! He's got a whim. . . . I'm fed up with her and I need money, lots of it, in order to get out of this rotten life and become a decent person. The Prince is a little queer, like a lot of those great people, he doesn't know what he wants.

TOMMY. You can say that again! You hear what happened to Fred with the Countess? She gave him all kinds of jewels and lots of money, and now that she's tired of him, she claims he blackmailed her and she's going to the police.

NUNU. The police! He's a fool if he lets her get away with it. I swear if I manage to hook the Prince, *he* won't go to the police.

TOMMY. Why not?

NUNU. Donina is a minor, you fool, she's under age! I know the law. And the Prince can't afford a scandal. You see?

TOMMY. I don't know. If I were a prince I'd do whatever I damned well pleased.

NUNU. So would I. But these people are funny that way . . . they want to have a good time but they want it kept secret . . . and that costs money.

TOMMY. But you better watch out. Even though it doesn't look that way, these people always have someone around taking care of them.

NUNU. Not this one. There's a certain interest in seeing him in some kind of scandal. The police told me about it. They saw me with him, you know, and . . . well, it seems that back in his country he has a large group of followers who want to make him Emperor. That's why he was sent away.

TOMMY. So now you're a conspirator!

NUNU. So what? I want money . . . that's all we can get out of this. He can be Emperor for all I care. I just want to get out of here, go home, and marry the girl I really love, a real decent girl! Her father wouldn't have me. Said I was no good . . . but when he sees me with money, when I'm somebody . . .

TOMMY. And so Donina isn't . . .

NUNU. Donina loves *me* . . . I let her, like the rest of them. These theatre women are good for only one thing: *hors d'œuvres* for the nobility.

TOMMY. I thought you loved her, that you were happy.

NUNU. I get by . . . but I keep my eye on the future. Don't you?

TOMMY. You're right there! But I'm tied to the woman and kid . . . so why keep an eye on the future?

NUNU. Maybe not for you, but for your boy, then. You want him to have it better than you did, don't you?

TOMMY. Sure.

NUNU. Well, there you are.

ESTHER. Which one is the Prince?

JULIETTE. The younger one, the silent one. He never talks. Look at those two. [*She points to* ROSINA *and* PEPITA *who had seated themselves at the* PRINCE'S *table some moments earlier.*] Aren't they set up, though! Well . . . they're certainly taking a chance.

ESTHER. Why does the Prince come here?

JULIETTE. For the performers. His private secretary—that's that Englishman who's always with him—well, he organizes some very unusual late suppers . . . or so they say . . . in a sort of dive where only the worst people go.

[ROSINA *and* PEPITA, *who have been talking to the* PRINCE, *excuse themselves and leave.*]

ESTHER. They're trying so hard to look bored! And, look, the men are laughing at them!

JULIETTE. Wait till they come by, I'll give them an earful . . . just watch.

ESTHER. Don't make a scene or Mr. Jacob will take our pass away.

FLORENCIO. Oh, Harry, I'm bored tonight, I'm bored! What have you invented for me?

HARRY. A march on Suavia, crown you emperor, and then declare war on the whole world . . .

FLORENCIO. Be quiet . . . you imperialist poet.

HARRY. Why not? I'm an emperor myself. Remember what Hamlet says? "I could be bounded in a nutshell, and count myself king of infinite space."

FLORENCIO. But his dreams made him unhappy.

HARRY. Mine don't. Within my nutshell I'm emperor of myself and I'm at war with the world. I am an island . . . an impregnable island . . . more difficult to storm than those of my own country.

FLORENCIO. How do you do it?

HARRY. I make myself hated. Love and kindness are to blame for all our weakness, our compromise, and cowardice. Because of love, we credit others with virtues they don't possess . . . and then we, in turn, are obliged to pretend virtues that *we* don't possess.

FLORENCIO. Paradox. But you haven't made me hate you.

HARRY. Not yet. I've never told you the truth.

FLORENCIO. Just because you haven't felt like it. You can, you know.

HARRY. The truth? You are the worst possible excuse for a Prince. You're ridiculous and rotten to the marrow.

FLORENCIO. Bah! Pass me the whiskey.

HARRY. The truth, Florencio, the truth? Your scandals, your vices! You want to scandalize the world and end up shocking only the old ladies in waiting at the court. Your bacchanalias are no more than restaurant parties at five hundred francs a throw. Little escapades of a college boy who's read three or four bad novels . . . that's the hell into which you descend with ill-disguised fear and trembling. Hail Emperor, Heliogabalus, child of the sun!

FLORENCIO. Are you through? A few truths like that won't make me hate you. The times are too puny to produce a Nero or Heliogabalus . . . or a Shakespeare for that matter. Although you have written some sonnets very like his and there's one, to be sure, that's copied from a seventeenth-century Italian.

HARRY [*outraged*]. That's a lie! I steal from no one. Those are rumors, gossip made up by people who are jealous! I proved that the Italian sonnet was a forgery. They made it up to annoy me. I've proved it and they won't believe me. Only an idiot would say that . . . and if you say it, that's what you are.

FLORENCIO [*laughing*]. You see, my dear Harry, truth stings a poet sooner than an Emperor.

HARRY. Idiot!

[*The* PRINCE *rises and starts toward* NUNU *and* TOMMY.]

FLORENCIO. Come on, Harry dear, and arrange me something diabolical, something big, something more than five-hundred-francs-worth. Hello, Nunu . . . Tommy.

NUNU. Your Highness.

FLORENCIO. Sit down. Put your hats on. Have you gone on yet?

NUNU. No, our number is almost at the end. We were waiting for you.

FLORENCIO. Will everyone be there? . . . your Donina?

NUNU. Donina . . .

FLORENCIO. There, you see! It's you who don't want her to come. I thought so. . . . and you trying to palm yourself off as a cynic! You and your *piccola* Donina. I don't give a damn! You're in love with her and want to keep her to yourself.

NUNU. Oh no, no, Your Highness! She's the one who's in love with me. You know that. [*Noticing a ring on the* PRINCE'S *finger.*] Excuse me . . . may I . . . what a lovely ring!

FLORENCIO. You like jewels?

NUNU. Like them?

FLORENCIO [*noticing one of* NUNU'S *rings*]. Yes . . . I see you do.

NUNU. It's only glass. At night under the lights, it'll do . . . when you can't afford anything better. What stone is that?

FLORENCIO. A ruby. This one's an opal.

TOMMY. They're bad luck.

FLORENCIO. Not for me. Think you're brave enough to wear it? [*Tosses him the ring.*]

TOMMY. Try me! [*Puts on the ring.*] Thanks, Your Highness. I'm just sorry that I won't be able to wear it long. You know how it is with us . . . a hard time and . . . well, that'll be my bad luck.

NUNU [*offended*]. So Tommy is your friend now.

FLORENCIO. And you are not. I have no present for you. We are enemies.

NUNU. But if I have a surprise for you tonight?

FLORENCIO. Then I'll have a ring for you which will make your friends die with envy . . .

NUNU. A pretty one?

FLORENCIO. . . . and some other things I know you like.

[*The* PRINCE *takes out a gold cigarette case and offers cigarettes.*]

NUNU. Another one! Gold too! They're all gold! But this one has jewels on it! Is that your name?

FLORENCIO. No . . . just some English verse. Nunu, it's yours.

NUNU. Your Highness!

FLORENCIO. I insist.

NUNU. Ah, lovely! Look Tommy! Diamonds and these . . . these are like yours.

TOMMY. Rubies.

NUNU. And you say they're verses? [*He reads.*] "Oh you the master-mistress." I can't make out the rest.

HARRY. That's just as well.

NUNU. Here come Donina and Zaida.

HARRY. The one who claims she's an Arab?

NUNU. But it's true. She's from Constantina in Algiers. She's a Jewess. Used to do oriental dances until her manager turned her over to us. She passes for Neapolitan.

FLORENCIO. I thought she was.

NUNU. But she's a whiner, that one, always crying, cries over everything.

FLORENCIO. And . . . ah . . . who takes care of *her*?

NUNU. No one. She likes me, I can tell. But she's such friends with Donina that when I make a pass she goes wild! Loves Donina blindly . . . protects her like a lioness.

HARRY. At this rate, it won't be long before the three of you'll be loving one another all the way round.

NUNU. No! I tell you, she's as innocent as a baby!

FLORENCIO. Doesn't surprise me, living with the likes of you. We'll see you later on. Will you go straight from here?

NUNU. In costume, just as you arranged it.

FLORENCIO. Will they *all* be there?

NUNU. All. I'll show you I'm your friend.

FLORENCIO. So long. Come along, Harry. [*He sees* IMPERIA *who has entered some moments before with* DONINA *and* ZAIDA.] Ah, Imperia! You see that, Harry?

[NUNU *and* TOMMY *go over to the women.* DONINA *gets up and argues with* NUNU *somewhat apart from the others.*]

HARRY. Yes, and I know what brings her here: an old friendship with Donina's mother. They were in the same troupe. She heard the girl was here and came to see her . . . and keeps coming to see her. That's the *official* truth.

FLORENCIO. I'm sure my uncle doesn't know that his lady-friend goes to such places. He'd think it improper. It's my duty to let him know!

HARRY. But of course! It's one's duty to tell everything that might be the least bit annoying.

[*The* PRINCE *and* HARRY *go out.*]

NUNU [*to* DONINA]. You saw who I was talking to?

ONINA. And I also saw you in the wings. Do you think I'm blind? There was nobody left but that Japanese woman! . . . and while her husband was out there doing his act . . . Furthermore, I know there's to be a big party tonight, and that you've left me out of it.

UNU. No we haven't, you're invited.

ONINA. I am, eh? To my face . . . What really makes me angry is not your playing around with the girls, laughing, hugging, and kissing them . . . it's the way you let others do it to me! You stand there and laugh!

UNU. You're silly. [*He takes out the case and lights a cigarette.*]

ONINA. What's that? Who gave it to you? What's this say here?

UNU. Ha, ha, ha!

ONINA [*throws the case to the ground and stamps on it furiously*]. There! Look! It doesn't say anything now. It's nothing! I'd do the same to you or to anyone who . . .

UNU [*threatening her*]. Donina! What are you doing? Look! I swear I . . .

MPERIA AND ZAIDA [*coming between them*]. All right, Nunu!

UNU. If we weren't here . . .

ONINA. That's right, hit me! Kill me! Anything's better than this!

AIDA [*her arms around* DONINA]. Donina! My poor Donina!

UNU. Come on, Tommy, let's get dressed. Come on! She'll be there tonight. [NUNU *and* TOMMY *go out.*]

AIDA. Don't cry . . . all these people . . . they mustn't see you . . .

ONINA. What do I care!

MPERIA. Now, will you come with me?

ONINA. No, no! I'll stick to him even if he kills me! He wasn't always like this. He loved me very much. Oh, he went with the other girls, I know, but I was always his Donina, the first, the only one he really cared for. I suppose I was even proud that they all wanted him . . . and that after he kicked them over, he would come back to me . . . always me . . . he couldn't forget me. But it's changed now . . . he means to hurt me. It's not just that he deceives me . . . it's that he wants me to know about it. It's those men. Ever since they came . . .

AIDA. Nunu was bad sometimes . . . but now he's all bad. I used to love him but Donina wasn't jealous. She knew

I liked him because of her . . . I loved him from the heart. I was like a sister to both of them. Donina knows that. But it's true, Nunu has changed. He doesn't clown for us any more . . . and he used to be so happy. When he was happy there was laughter everywhere.

DONINA. That's the truth! Oh, we were so happy! We used to laugh, and sing and dance for hours, for the joy of it without getting tired, without even caring that we had to sing and dance in the theatre for an audience.

DONINA. We were very happy.

ZAIDA. And we would have been, we three, always.

DONINA. It's those men, those awful men, that whey-faced prince who can turn your blood to ice with one look.

IMPERIA. Yes, the Prince! I know him well. He's happy only when he is corrupting or torturing someone.

DONINA. But I'll go with them tonight. He wants me to.

IMPERIA. No, don't! Live for the man you love, the one you chose, the one who's like you. Live as best you can, the joy, the sorrow . . . You see, I'm not trying to meddle. But the Prince is another matter. Never go near him! If you do, all you'll find is hate, misery, and shame. He dresses his women in rags and then tortures them. He surrounds himself with poor wretched beggars, tempts them with money . . . and then there's nothing so vile they won't perform for him. He gives young girls to repulsive old men and he makes young healthy boys go to diseased, old whores. He buys daughters from their parents and sisters from their brothers. His parties are carnivals in hell. In Suavia, on nights when it was so cold the ground was covered with ice, he would roam the streets and round up all the homeless. Then he would lead his retinue of half-starved beggars to the morgue . . . where they stored the bodies of the suicides, of the murdered, of the ones who died in the streets of hunger or cold. They died in swarms in the winter: men, women, little children. It was horrible! He would scatter gold coins over the corpses. It was awful . . . the scrabble of that horde, mad at the sight of gold! A coin would fall on an open wound and a hundred hands would lunge for it. They pushed and shoved and trampled the bodies underfoot. . . . And he? He didn't even laugh. He stared, he looked on . . . just as the devil must look upon the evil committed by those who are hungry when they're provoked by men with no hearts. That's your Prince, the pale prince who makes your blood run cold.

DONINA. Then I didn't hate him for nothing. If Nunu sees him again he'll see no more of me.

IMPERIA. Will you come to me?

DONINA. No. Not without him. I said he'd see no more of me because I'll kill myself. It's the only way I could leave him.

IMPERIA. So it's love . . . in life or death. That's that!

ZAIDA. Donina, they're playing the music for the act before ours. Let's not be late.

DONINA. You're right . . . sing and dance! . . . But he won't go tonight, he won't go! Are you coming in to see me?

IMPERIA. Yes.

DONINA. So long. Kiss me. [*Points to* ZAIDA.] Kiss her too.

ZAIDA. I love you very much, ma'am. I love everyone who likes Donina.

[ZAIDA *and* DONINA *leave. The* COUNTESS RINALDI *and* LEONARDO *enter.*]

LEONARDO. It doesn't make sense. I no sooner rescue you from one danger, as you so aptly put it, than I find you talking to Ruhu-Sahib, the elephant trainer.

RINALDI. Do you mean to say that you think I . . . ? With an Indian? A savage? I was simply inquiring about his elephants. I think they're fascinating. Oh, but these people lead such interesting lives . . . much more exciting than ours. What would you say if, suddenly, I decided to join a circus? What people would think?

LEONARDO. They'd think you were settling down . . . it's far from the wildest thing you've done.

RINALDI. To tell you the truth, this monotonous life of ours . . . what a bore!

LEONARDO. I dare say, if you suppress the "monotony" of *your* life, you *would* be bored.

RINALDI. My! Well, come on, treat me to some ice cream. The tutti-frutti is delicious.

LEONARDO. With pleasure . . . Ah! Imperia. You see?

RINALDI. I do . . . and I've seen her here before.

LEONARDO. Strange. Here alone and in that gown too.

RINALDI. She always dresses regally. She too plays at being the artist now and then . . . but not exactly in my line.

LEONARDO. I don't understand.

RINALDI. How innocent! You should know your own mod better than I do! Incidentally, when you met her, wha was she like? I've heard so many stories!

LEONARDO. I met her in Rome. She was one of that flock o models that hangs around the *Piazza di Spagna*. Donin that was her name, was a common little thing . . . poo with that poverty of the big city which is more than jus hunger for bread, it's the hunger for all the joys of life As a model she was so plain she had to beg to call atten tion to herself. The painters saw nothing in her. Neithe did I. Then one day she begged me for some mone There was nothing weak or whimpering in her voice. was strong and demanded attention. We talked and a she spoke her face changed, her eyes looked different, an her body too. She was no longer the poor little model, sh was a work of art . . . she was my statue, Imperia, the on that made me famous. Remember? It was she, with he bare feet, tattered skirt, half naked . . . as though she ha just climbed a high rock with great effort and much pai . . . And there on the top she sank exhausted on a thron her face glowing with a strange look . . . the smile of tr umphant life . . . *or* the smile of death that leads us all t rest. It's a long time since I've seen the statue. My feelin about art has changed, but I'm sure there's somethin there: a daring use of materials, a granite pedestal, marbl figure, the throne of gilded bronze . . . it shone like gol

RINALDI. And what does the statue mean?

LEONARDO. How should I know? The artist tries to spea through his works, but the works speak for themselve The statue shows . . . what you see . . . woman, Imperia a wretched woman who climbs up over the rocks, her bod torn and bruised, until she reaches a throne. It may mea something more. The power of this world conquered a last by the poor and the wretched. I don't know! The effo of man to turn his dream into fact . . . Who hasn't dreame of a throne? . . . a throne for our will, our vanity, ou love.

RINALDI. How long did these "relations" of yours last?

LEONARDO. No time at all. The same breath that blew lif into my statue breathed a new spirit into Donina. Th statue came to life . . . *she* became Imperia. Prince Flo encio met her in my studio about the time I was finishin the statue. She was still the poor, ragged Donina with that hungry look about the face . . . and you know the Prince's tastes. One morning she said goodby. "Girl where are you going?" I asked. "To Suavia," she answered, "to become Empress." And you know, I couldn't laugh. She spoke with such conviction I couldn't protest. That little girl could have been an Empress.

RINALDI. Does she still cling to her dream?

LEONARDO. I can't say. I've heard that the Prince Florencio abused her; that she tried to kill him: that she was sent out of Suavia; that, in Paris, she took up with Prince Michael; and that she has led a very peaceful and profitable existence ever since.

RINALDI. Prince Michael is the richest prince in Suavia.

LEONARDO. And as prodigal as an ancient king.

RINALDI. What power can rule the world better than money? Imperia's dreams of empire have been reduced, it seems, to this rather practical reality. Wasn't the throne of your statue a golden one?

LEONARDO. It was . . . but because *light* is golden and it was a throne of light, of hope . . . the ideal.

[IMPERIA *rises and comes over to greet them.*]

IMPERIA. Countess! Leonardo! Didn't you see me?

RINALDI. Why, no. I'm sorry. . . .

IMPERIA. You were talking about me.

RINALDI. You mean to say you heard?

IMPERIA. No, but I could guess . . . you kept looking over at me. I suppose you were remarking on my presence here.

RINALDI. Not at all. We are here too.

LEONARDO. And it would be difficult to explain her own presence here.

RINALDI. Difficult? Nothing of the sort! We are all here for the same thing more or less. Here we meet and talk openly . . . even though tomorrow we may let it appear that we never met at all.

IMPERIA. It's our souls that meet . . . like witches. When I was a little girl there was an old woman that lived near our house. She was poor, and very old . . . lived alone, and seemed to be a very good person. She cleaned her house, tended her garden, fed the pigeons, mended her clothes . . . very busy all day long. A peaceful and settled life she had.

But people claimed she was a witch and that every Saturday on the stroke of midnight she would fly off to her witches' lair, and would worship the devil with the other witches. This much is true, however: one Sunday morning they found the old woman dead in an open field far away from home. There was a dagger stuck in her heart. They never found the murderer, nor the motive for the murder, nor the reason why the woman was in that faraway place when everyone had seen her the night before locking her door as usual. When they brought the body back, the door was still locked.

RINALDI. You mean to say . . . ? Oh, but then one would have to believe in witches!

IMPERIA. Not that kind . . . no. But the most peaceful life has its witches' sabbath when our souls fly off to their secret haunts. We put up with days and days of boredom for that one hour of possession. Our souls fly away, some to their dreams, others to vice, and some others to love . . . toward anything so long as it is far from our lives, our real lives.

RINALDI. You're right. And here we are in our witches' den. Welcome, sister!

IMPERIA. Sister, brother! How do you fly this evening? . . toward good or evil?

LEONARDO. I go where life dissolves into a dream.

RINALDI. And I fly to the kingdom of love where death is not allowed.

LEONARDO. And you, Imperia?

IMPERIA. I'm searching for myself. I'm looking for a Donina . . . poor, ignorant Donina . . . Donina in love. Your statue showed me how beautiful I was, and that beauty will make my dream come true.

LEONARDO. And that is?

IMPERIA. To get rich. Money is power. It makes all things possible: good, evil, justice, or revenge.

RINALDI. The show is over and we're about to be invaded.

LEONARDO. It's time to go.

RINALDI. Look . . . the Indian! Really, aren't you interested in seeing him tame those elephants?

LEONARDO. No, but I am interested in seeing how one tames an animal tamer. Shall we join him?

RINALDI. Now don't be rude. It's perfectly clear you don't know how to behave in these affairs.

LEONARDO. As you wish. I shall simply chaperone.

[ZAIDA *enters in tears. She goes to* IMPERIA *and puts her arms around her.*]

ZAIDA. Oh, Ma'am! Don't you know? Donina. . . .

IMPERIA. What?

ZAIDA. She's mad! She wouldn't listen to me. After all you told her, she's letting Nunu take her with all those people . . . to the Prince.

IMPERIA. Nunu sold her to him! You know where they are, don't you?

ZAIDA. They went off in costume . . . yes I know. I don't know the name but I know the place.

IMPERIA. Come!

ZAIDA. Yes, let's . . . but not like that! You don't know these people!

IMPERIA. Who cares what I've got on! They're my people too, my kind . . . they'll know me. I'm going to stop that man! I'll revenge a thousand crimes with one blow. Come! Good evening, Countess . . . Leonardo.

RINALDI. Where are you going, Imperia?

LEONARDO. Goodnight, Imperia.

IMPERIA. I'm going off. It's the witches' sabbath . . . and I must fly to meet some others.

[*The café is full of people. The gypsy orchestra begins to play.*]

CURTAIN

ACT THREE

[CECCO'S *tavern at night. Sailors and toughs of all sorts sit about in groups gambling and drinking.* CECCO *and* GAETANO *move about pouring wine and waiting tables.* HER MAJESTY, *an old crone, sits at one of the tables nodding sleepily.* PIETRO *is among the patrons.*]

THIRD SAILOR. Push that money this way! Wine! It's on me.
GAETANO. Coming.
SECOND SAILOR. Let's stop.
THIRD SAILOR. Let me be!
SECOND SAILOR. All right, then I'll take my money out . . . and it's a lot!
THIRD SAILOR. For Chris' sake, take it! I'm tired of hearing you.
SECOND SAILOR. No. If you're going to go on . . .
FIRST SAILOR. Are you playing or aren't you?
THIRD SAILOR. Yes. Here goes. All of it!
GAETANO [*to* CECCO]. Where are they from? I don't know them.
CECCO. Off a yacht that came in this morning. They're wearing its colors. How's it going?
GAETANO. They've got money all right, but they're not taking any chances.
CECCO. So I see. But no trouble tonight, eh! Let'em have fun but don't fleece them. If you do they'll set up a howl. . . . They'll be back tomorrow.
GAETANO. I'll break up the game if you want.
CECCO. No. Won't do to have it empty either. So long as they don't make trouble . . .

[*The* DEPUTY *enters.*]

DEPUTY. Good evening, Cecco.
CECCO. Good evening. Anything new?

DEPUTY. No. We saw the Prince come in.

CECCO. Yes, he's here.

DEPUTY. Who's with him?

CECCO. I don't know all of them. The Englishman, the circus crowd.

DEPUTY [*referring to a list*]. Let's see if I've got them all . . . you check me. The Englishman, Nunu and Tommy, of the Neapolitan troupe; Donina, Celeste, Teresina, of the same troupe; Dick and Fred, jockeys for the Duke of Zealand, and two English girls . . . Any more?

CECCO. No. That's it.

DEPUTY. If something happens, we're outside.

CECCO. I know. I'll send something out in a bit. It's cold tonight.

DEPUTY. There's a fog. See you later, Cecco . . . And these people?

CECCO. The usual.

DEPUTY. Those sailors?

CECCO. From the yacht that came in this morning. Haven't you seen it?

DEPUTY. I know about it. So long.

FIRST SAILOR. Big things on tonight? Lots of important people. All right for us to stick around?

CECCO. Just keep your eyes open and your mouth shut.

ONE OF THE DRINKERS [*going to* HER MAJESTY *and nudging her*]. Hey you, why aren't you invited to the party?

CECCO. Leave the old thing alone, she isn't bothering anyone.

DRINKER. The Prince ought to have asked you in. Maybe he didn't recognize you. You should have said "Your Highness, we're equals you and I. I was queen once! They still call me Your Majesty."

[*Several laugh and call her name, "Her Majesty."*]

HER MAJESTY. You dogs!

CECCO. I said to leave her alone! Don't pay any attention to them, Majesty.

MAJESTY. I? I don't see them, I don't hear them! They're far, far away.

THIRD SAILOR. She crazy?

PIETRO. No . . . it's just that at this time of day she's always . . .

CECCO. She's telling the truth though. I know because I've

heard it from people who knew her then. She was beautiful once . . . mistress of some king or other. She's had coaches, and diamonds, and palaces . . .

THIRD SAILOR. Ah . . . probably all made up.

DRINKER. I don't care how old she is or how much she's changed . . . it's not possible. I don't believe it.

THIRD SAILOR. To tell the truth, just looking at her . . .

DRINKER. Come on, tell your story. Now, what king was it? And where were all those palaces?

PIETRO. Come on, granny, tell your story. So this guy was a king, eh?

CECCO. Let her be!

MAJESTY. You dogs! You scum! What could I tell you? You believe only what you see. See me now? Well, I was beautiful once. Paintings of my face and statues of my body are kept in palaces and museums! If I took you and pointed to them and said, "Here I am!" you wouldn't believe me. I've been loved by lots of men, big men, important men, wise men . . . even a king! . . . One word from me and he would have kicked over his crown. See me now? Well this old body of mine has worn gowns embroidered with enough pearls to buy a whole kingdom! In one day I'd spend more on flowers than I'd need now to last me the rest of my life! You don't believe me? What's left of it all, eh? Well, come here . . . [*She takes off a pair of woolen mittens.*] These hands are left. Hands that've never done a single stroke of work. A queen's hands. Many men have kissed these hands and considered it a privilege. They're my last vanity. I may go hungry, but I've always got money for mittens. Look at them! They're the hands of a queen, aren't they!

PIETRO. It's true.

DRINKER. I guess people can still kiss your hands, if nothing else.

MAJESTY. You could become the richest man on earth, you could conquer the whole world, proclaim yourself king of everything! . . . and your children's children would never have hands like these.

PIETRO. They look as though they've been well greased with vice.

DRINKER. They look as though they could have held on to something more than their whiteness. If you were telling the truth, you wouldn't be here now.

MAJESTY. These hands can't hold anything. Treasure spilled into them like water falling into the shell of a fountain . . . only to spatter away again.

DRINKER. You must have been a great one for charities.

PIETRO. . . . and good works.

MAJESTY. Good, evil, I don't know! People came to me . . . poor people, bad people . . . all the same to me. If one stops to think! Those people who refuse a beggar money because it may be spent on wine . . . why, the devil laughs at them! You share your joy with joy. Some need wine more than bread. No one eats flowers but the earth gives them just the same. The heart that doesn't give flowers is dry.

PETRO. Well said.

DRINKER. Well, what do you know!

CECCO. I told you she wasn't crazy. Now, buy her a drink.

PIETRO. Give her whatever she wants.

MAJESTY. All the same to me.

THIRD SAILOR. Champagne! Nothing less for Her Majesty!

DRINKER. Champagne, champagne . . . come on . . . here's the money.

PIETRO. Do you *have* any champagne?

CECCO. Tonight we do. I'll bring some if you're not joking.

DRINKER. Since the prince won't treat you, we will.

MAJESTY. The Prince of Suavia? I knew the Emperor when he was heir apparent. I saw him once in a military review . . . on his white horse he cut such a proud figure! I also knew Princess Etelvina, the mother of this prince. She was a little girl then. I wouldn't know what she looked like now.

CECCO. The champagne! Hold out your glasses.

PIETRO. To Her Majesty! A toast. . . . Do you still want to live a long time?

MAJESTY. Why not, God willing?

PIETRO. To your health, then.

MAJESTY. . . . And to yours and your happiness too . . . for you have lots of time. Well, what do you know! It *is* champagne!

CECCO. What did you expect?

MAJESTY. I thought you were joking. It's been ages since I've had any. God bless you. Another glass! Ah, it's a gay wine . . . and this isn't bad, Cecco. I know.

PIETRO. You're not the only majesty here tonight . . . look.

[IMPERIA *and* ZAIDA *appear at the door.*]

IMPERIA. Is this it?
ZAIDA. Yes, ma'am. Aren't you afraid?
IMPERIA. Why? I grew up in a place like this. Come on.
PIETRO [*pointing at* IMPERIA]. This seems to be a night for royalty.
CECCO. Shut up.
PIETRO. Your Majesty, were your dresses like that?
DRINKER. Do you know that queen?
MAJESTY. Queen? . . . She's no more a queen than I was! No, I don't know her. The one's I knew are dead or ancient.
IMPERIA. Where's the Prince? Don't lie to me. I know he was coming here and I know who is with him.
CECCO. Was he expecting you? They haven't told me . . .
IMPERIA. No, he's not expecting me. One moment. [*She writes a note on a little paper.*] Give him this and bring me his answer at once.
CECCO. All right. Do you want to sit down?
IMPERIA. No. Isn't there some other place where we can wait?
CECCO. A little hole upstairs.
IMPERIA. Hurry. Go.
CECCO. Don't be afraid . . . they're nice people. [*Leaves.*]
IMPERIA. I'm not afraid.
ZAIDA. I wish I hadn't told you.
IMPERIA. Why? You think I'm scared, don't you? The place, the people . . . they're not strange to me. It's I who seem strange.
PIETRO [*to* HER MAJESTY]. Why don't you offer her a drink . . . among equals . . .
DRINKER. It's up to you to do the honors.
MAJESTY [*she staggers and laughs drunkenly*]. All right, all right! [*Offering a glass to* IMPERIA.] Madam.
ZAIDA [*frightened*]. Oh!
IMPERIA. Don't be afraid. Woman, what do you want?
MAJESTY. Your Majesty . . . I too am a majesty . . . Don't you know me?
PIETRO. Don't be afraid of her. She's just a little touched.
MAJESTY. I'm holding a party in my palace and I offer you a glass of champagne. Go ahead, drink, it's not poisoned.

Why should I hurt you . . . you can't hurt me. I'm happy. Who can take my happiness away from me? But be careful! Not everybody is like me. Some people are bad. I know. They've done me enough harm! But I? I've never hurt anyone! Anyone! That's why I'm happy. That's the happiness they can't steal from me.

ZAIDA. Signora, I'm afraid.

IMPERIA. And I am not. On the contrary, I like her mad rambling. There's something prophetic about it. Here woman, take this. [*She gives her money.*]

MAJESTY. Gold! You see? [*Throws the coins.*] Well, then, more champagne! Champagne!

PIETRO. Save it, save it! You'll need it.

MAJESTY. No, I don't need anything. It's for you. More champagne. [*She falls senseless.* HARRY LUCENTI *enters.*]

HARRY. Imperia!

IMPERIA. And the Prince?

HARRY. He's sent me to offer you my arm and his invitation to join us . . . now that you've come this far.

IMPERIA. Does he know why I'm here?

HARRY. Jealousy?

IMPERIA. Of whom?

HARRY. We've seen you at the circus.

IMPERIA. You're probably accusing me of something monstrous . . . something truly worthy of you and the Prince.

HARRY. Something amusing, certainly. The Prince will be delighted to see you. My arm . . .

IMPERIA. Take me in. [*A scream is heard.*] What's that?

CECCO [*runs on*]. What's happened?

HARRY. Who screamed?

CECCO [*closing the door*]. Quiet! Stand still all of you! Stay right where you are! [*He runs off.*]

DRINKER. What is it?

[TOMMY *and* CECCO *come back supporting the* PRINCE. CELESTE, TERESINA, *the two* JOCKEYS, NUNU, *and* DONINA *follow, all of them showing great fear.*]

DRINKER. What's that?

CECCO. The Prince!

IMPERIA. Blood!

HARRY. Is he wounded?

SAILORS AND OTHERS. Let's get out of here! What's going on here? Out! Get out of here!

CECCO [*to* GAETANO]. Lock the door! Nobody leaves!

[GAETANO *draws a knife and locks the door.*]

PIETRO. Get out of the way! Or else . . .

[*Several draw their knives.*]

CECCO. Do you want the police to arrest all of us?! Now, be quiet!

NUNU [*to* DONINA, *furiously*]. You did it! You! Now we're really lost!

DONINA. Yes I did it . . . for you, you scum.

IMPERIA. You?

DONINA. He sold me! You know that? . . . You dog!

CELESTE. Well, are you going to let him die like this?

CECCO. Whatever happens, no one leaves!

HARRY. No bleeding. Bad sign. He won't come to.

CECCO. The police are just across the street. They must have heard the shouts. If they come we've got to open up. Easy does it! The blood! [*He spills some wine.*] That takes care of that. You surround him . . . and hold him up! And you, sing and dance! Where's the harmonica? The police! Quick . . . or we're all lost!

[*They perform.*]

DONINA. My God, my God!

NUNU [*shoving her*]. Dance! Didn't you hear the man?

[DONINA, NUNU, ZAIDA, *and* TOMMY *dance a tarantella. The* DEPUTY *enters.*]

DEPUTY. What's the matter?

CECCO. Nothing . . . see?

DEPUTY. We heard shouts.

CECCO. It's the party. They don't know what they're doing any more. They're having a fine time. The Prince can hardly stand up. Look at him. We shut the doors to keep the people out. Want a drink?

DEPUTY. No thanks. Goodnight.

CECCO. Goodnight. [*Never taking his eyes off the people in the tavern.*] Go on! Keep it up!

[*The women who were sitting next to the* PRINCE *move away in panic and the* PRINCE *rolls under the table.*]

CELESTE. He's dead!

TERESINA. Oh!

[*There is great confusion. All want to leave.*]

CECCO. You've ruined me! What'll we do now? No one leave this room.

NUNU [*threatening him*]. We're all leaving.

CECCO. It's no use. The police have your names. They'd pic you up in no time. If we get out of this at all we'll get o of it together.

IMPERIA. Harry, take him to my house . . . in the coach. It the best way. They mustn't find him here. We'll think something . . . Will you do it?

HARRY. All right.

CECCO. You going to take him away? Good. But later. We' got to wait. There are still people in the street at this hou I'll draw off the police, then you start leaving . . . one two at a time . . . But be careful!

PIETRO. And the first one who tells . . . !

DRINKER. We know what's good for us. We know.

CECCO. And you, keep singing and dancing! Damn it!

DONINA [*falling exhausted*]. I can't any more! Kill me if yo want but I can't dance any more.

CECCO [*going up to* HER MAJESTY]. This one's seen nothi and the others will say nothing.

HARRY [*by the* PRINCE]. He's dead . . . cold already.

IMPERIA. Yes. Dead . . . dead! How horrible.

CURTAIN

ACT FOUR

A room in IMPERIA'S *villa.* IMPERIA *finishes writing a letter and gives it to a servant.* COUNTESS RINALDI'S *voice is heard outside.*]

RINALDI. She is always at home to me, I assure you! No . . . don't bother!

[IMPERIA *jumps up and hurries to meet the* COUNTESS.]

IMPERIA. Countess!

RINALDI. Surprised you, didn't I? The doorman, the servants . . . they weren't going to let me in. Told me you were resting. But I just had to see you so I trod them all underfoot. You'll forgive me, I'm sure. I know you're alone now because I ran into Prince Michael over by the Princess's villa . . . no doubt going to pay her a visit.

IMPERIA. No doubt. Did you talk to him?

RINALDI. No. He was driving a coach and I was on foot. I walk a lot you know . . . to wear down those beastly nerves of mine. We nodded but no more. Well . . . what *about* last night? How was *your* witches' sabbath?

IMPERIA. Last night?

RINALDI. Oh, now you're being mean! Loving you the way I do, how *could* you keep secrets from me. If you only were more . . . well, it would be fun sometimes to exchange impressions or adventures . . . so to speak. . . . Even though I've decided to turn over a new leaf. Oh, yes! The follies of yesteryear have come to an end. I've had the most wonderful good luck! I've found a man who's going to be my salvation. If I'd only met him at the beginning of my career! When I think of all those worthless men for whom I've compromised my good name and sacrificed my peace of mind! Oh!

IMPERIA. His name?

RINALDI. He's not the kind of man a woman like myself ha the misfortune of meeting on every streetcorner. He's primitive spirit, a simple soul . . . Oh, you know him!

IMPERIA. I do?

RINALDI. Well, you've seen the seven elephants at the circus haven't you?

IMPERIA. Countess!

RINALDI. Well . . . it's the tamer. . . . You're not laughing are you?

IMPERIA. You just told me you were through with follie

RINALDI. Surely you don't think this is a folly? . . . It's ju that you don't know my plans yet.

IMPERIA. Then for goodness sake tell them to me. And let hope that they're the most fantastic extravagances, th strangest foolishnesses . . . Dreams, fantasies, anything tha will ward off the truth that haunts us. . . . Oh, if you onl knew! Some dreams, horrible nightmares, smack so of th truth they escape from sleep and invade our life . . . I'v dreamed, I'm certain I've dreamed something which seem now actually to have seen and heard . . . somethin which I know can't be, can't possibly have been. That why I want you to tell me fantastic things, strange drean . . . insanity. I want to be so confused I won't know whe I'm dreaming among ghosts or walking among the livin

RINALDI. All my plans are quite sane! I want to put my a fairs in order and devote myself to the management of n estate. Because it just so happens that I have a wonderf opportunity for a brilliant speculation that will triple n investment in a year!

IMPERIA. Oh, how happy I am you came! You've drive every thought I had right out of my head!

RINALDI. Well, if you think it's a joke . . . well, it's not! I a very serious matter! Ruhu, his name is Ruhu, you kno . . . it's an Oriental name . . . well, Ruhu is not the re Ruhu!

IMPERIA. I don't follow.

RINALDI. Oh, no! The real Ruhu-Sahib was the previous ow er and elephant-tamer. The present one was just his sistant, that's all. Now . . . when the real Ruhu died, widow, an Englishwoman, inherited the seven elephants. she proposed to the assistant that he take the old Ruh place . . . on salary . . . but it turned out to be an infamo exploitation! While he risks his life every day for a miserable wage, she, the widow, the owner, collects a fabulous amount of money! . . . Well what do you think? Don't the exploited have a right to protest the exploiters? Poor Ruhu unburdened himself to me with tears in his eyes. "Oh," he said to me, "if the elephants were only mine; if only I had one hundred thousand francs, if I could only find a partner . . ."

MPERIA. Not another word! I know! You were touched. You're going to buy the elephants and join the circus!

RINALDI. Not I! Don't be ridiculous! I buy them, he works them, and I get fifty percent of the profits! . . . My dear, you have no idea how much that amounts to! Twelve thousand francs a month! A twelve month contract! Seven trained elephants at a hundred thousand francs! It's the opportunity of a lifetime! Really, you've no idea what elephants cost now-a-days! And these are Indian elephants! The very best! You can tell them by the ears and the trunks.

MPERIA. I can see you've studied the matter. It's a very serious business.

RINALDI. Well I should think so! What better way to invest one hundred thousand francs? That's why I came to see you so early in the morning. At the moment I don't seem to be able to lay my hands on such a large sum of money. My account at the *Crédit* is only about sixty to seventy thousand. But that's only a matter of fifteen days or so. I know that any of my friends would gladly . . . but I wanted to prove to you how much affection and confidence I have . . .

MPERIA. I wish I could answer in kind . . . but at the moment, I can't. I don't even know if I could lay my hands on so much money.

INALDI. So much? How can you call that "so much"?

MPERIA. I can tell you definitely this afternoon. Believe me.

INALDI. This afternoon? I'm afraid you're putting me off. I know for a fact that Prince Michael can not possibly deny you anything! And I'm speaking to you as a friend. Don't forget that your friendship has cost me many other friendships . . . not that they matter, of course.

MPERIA. As I say, I'll give you an answer this afternoon.

[*A servant enters.*]

SERVANT. His Highness.

[PRINCE MICHAEL *enters*.]

MICHAEL. Countess! [*To* IMPERIA.] How are you?

IMPERIA. Well. The Countess tells me she passed you by th
Princess's villa. Were you there?

MICHAEL. Yes, I was going to have lunch there. But don
you know?

IMPERIA. What?

MICHAEL. I'll tell you later. I . . . ah, I couldn't go to th
circus last night as I'd planned. A new telegram fro
Suavia. I had to go to the Duke.

IMPERIA. What's happened?

MICHAEL. Nothing.

RINALDI. Your Highness . . . I can see you want to talk
Imperia in private.

MICHAEL. Nothing pressing.

RINALDI. Since I do without invitations when they're wit
held, I certainly do not need them to prompt my exit whe
my presence might prove embarrassing. Till later Yo
Highness. . . . My dear, I'll stay home all afternoon un
I have your reply.

MICHAEL. How much did her visit cost this time?

IMPERIA. You know her well.

MICHAEL. I admit she compensates by being very amusin
Her latest adventure is always worth something. Leonar
gave me the story. You must know about it by now. Som
thing at the circus. And your Donina . . . Did you see h
last night? As you see, I'm not jealous. I believe whatev
you say.

IMPERIA. Why shouldn't you? You've been kind and genero
to me . . . your loyalty deserves mine. You never tried
hold me by means of money. At the very beginning, y
gave me enough to set me free. "I want no slaves," y
said. And when you set me free, you enslaved my gra
tude.

MICHAEL. Forever? You are restless, ambitious, you have b
dreams. I, on the other hand, I want one day to be no d
ferent from the next. Let all my days fuse into one so
single day, calm and undisturbed. But the threat of emp
has fallen on me once more . . . The new Prince is dyi

IMPERIA. Dying?

MICHAEL. He had only a breath or two of life in him when he was born. They telegraphed again just a few hours after the announcement of his birth. The Emperor wishes Florencio and his mother to return to court. He wants to effect a reconciliation. He may even be thinking of abdicating. He's tired and the people threaten to revolt. Despotism's no longer possible in our time. . . . And now I'm threatened by Florencio's poor health . . . Close to the throne once more.

IMPERIA. Very close . . . Prince Florencio is the only thing that stands between you. Have you see him today?

MICHAEL. No. I was over at the villa . . . would have had lunch there but his poor mother is half crazy with worry. Florencio's been out all night . . . hasn't come home yet.

IMPERIA. Don't they know . . .

MICHAEL. Nothing's gone wrong, I'm sure. He probably woke up in some dive or other and doesn't want to be seen coming out . . . I've notified the Prefect.

IMPERIA. You say his mother . . .

MICHAEL. He'll be the death of her. She just can't get used to it all. He keeps her in constant anxiety. Today she was more upset than usual. She told me that at midnight she woke up suddenly in a fright . . . she thought she heard a scream.

IMPERIA. At midnight?

MICHAEL. She takes it as some kind of omen. To tell the truth, I was upset by it myself . . . although I'm certain nothing's happened. We would have known. The police watch him at all times. It's impossible . . . I haven't seen Harry Lucenti either. However, the Signore is coming to give me a report any minute now.

IMPERIA. Do you know where he was?

MICHAEL. They know where he was and who was with him. I tell you it's impossible that . . . You don't think something's happened to him, do you?

IMPERIA. That scream his mother heard . . . do you believe that our souls can call one another across a great distance? . . . He must have thought of her and then screamed, "Mother!" . . . and his mother heard the scream.

MICHAEL. What are you talking about, Imperia? You're not making sense.

IMPERIA. I say *if* something's happened to him . . . one shoul be prepared for the worst.

[*A* SERVANT *enters.*]

SERVANT. The Prefect wishes to see Your Highness.

MICHAEL. At once. We'll know soon enough . . .

[*The* PRINCE *leaves.* IMPERIA *listens at the door.* HARRY LUCENTI *appears at another door. He is pale and is still wearing his evening clothes. He appears to be somewhat drunk.*]

IMPERIA. Who is it? Oh! Why are you here? Don't leave hin

HARRY. He won't try to get away. I heard talking. Have the found out?

IMPERIA. No. They're searching but they'll know soo enough. Any moment now. Now get back there. The mustn't see you. And don't leave him alone.

HARRY. He's hidden under a piece of brocade . . . a prope shroud for an Emperor. What petty little death! As insignif cant as his life. . . . Ludwig of Bavaria was the last re king.

IMPERIA. Oh, for God's sake, shut up! I don't want to hea you! I don't want to see you! You were two of a kind. H deserved the death he got, no matter who killed him.

HARRY. Then you think it was the hand of God, eh? Don talk nonsense, Imperia. There's many a sinner who's die in bed an old man blessed and lamented by his children.

[LEONARDO *enters.*]

IMPERIA. Leonardo! What kept you so long?

LEONARDO. I just received your letter. Ah, Harry! What a you doing here?

HARRY. Imperia will tell you. . . . I? I am performing a sa duty which gives me little to do but much to think abou . . . Mum's the word! [*He goes out.*]

IMPERIA. After so many years I really haven't the fainte idea what you think of me . . . what memories of me yo have kept. I do know that in important moments of m life, when my heart speaks out, I have always thought you as a true friend. Was I wrong?

LEONARDO. No. We parted without struggle or hate. You love life and you wanted to make my statue come true. I ra away from life and took refuge in my thoughts. Reality came between us. Why have you sent for me?

IMPERIA. To destroy the reality that's taking hold of my life, our life. Your idea, our dream, Imperia's throne . . . it seems so near! It's not inherited . . . the poor never inherit thrones, but we have the strength to make them topple. We also have the intelligence to rule from behind a throne. Do you remember? I said to you, "I'm going to Suavia to become an empress." Well, I am no empress but I rule the heart of an emperor. I know him . . . he's mine. I know it! He can't live without me. What do you say? Am I your Imperia, your work of art? Your soul fired mine. I'm your dreams made fact!

LEONARDO. Yes . . . my Imperia . . . my love . . . my only love. Live for me and triumph for me. I've never done more than dream.

IMPERIA. I'll triumph. But first I've got to destroy the facts, I've got to destroy reality. The heir apparent of Suavia is dying. The old Emperor plans to abdicate.

LEONARDO. Then Prince Florencio.

IMPERIA. Florencio is dead.

LEONARDO. Dead?

IMPERIA. He was murdered last night in my presence. . . . No. I killed him myself.

LEONARDO. You? What are you talking about? You're mad!

IMPERIA. Yes, I did it. I! Or, rather, my daughter, Donina . . . it's the same thing. She was trying to protect her youth and innocence . . . her love. All of us who fell to that man were revenged. You don't believe me? Look. His dagger . . . like everything he owned, a work of art: stiletto beautifully engraved, the handle of gold and jewels. They say that, between threats and caresses, he was trying to bribe her with it. "Would you really dare to kill me?" he asked. "A kiss and it's yours." He offered her the handle as though it were a jewel. When Donina felt him kiss her, she sank the knife in his heart. No, no I'm not raving, they are just echoes from a witches' sabbath. . . . Remember? When we parted last night I said, "It's the witches' sabbath." Well its ghosts have followed me back into life. They're here. Do you want to see him? He's over there. Harry Lucenti is watching over the corpse.

LEONARDO. But this can't be! It hasn't happened. It's all a dream, a nightmare.

IMPERIA. I thought so too. When I came back, I managed to forget everything. A moment ago I was joking and laughing with the Countess and it all seemed so remote . . . a nightmare from another world, from our witches' cave. But it's true, Leonardo, it's real.

LEONARDO. Then what are you waiting for? If they know that you . . .

IMPERIA. I'm not afraid. I'll fight and I'll win. I'm not afraid of ghosts. They'll be here soon. They may even know now . . . You see, I'm calm. They won't say a word.

LEONARDO. No, you're trembling. What are you staring at?

IMPERIA. No, no, I'm all right! Be quiet! They're here.

LEONARDO. They must know.

IMPERIA. If they don't, I'll tell them myself.

[*The* PRINCE *and the* SIGNORE *enter*.]

MICHAEL. Imperia, the Prefect wishes to speak with you. Oh, Leonardo, forgive me, I didn't see you.

LEONARDO. Your Highness.

MICHAEL [*to the* SIGNORE]. If you want to speak to her alone, Leonardo and I can . . .

IMPERIA. No, I want him to stay for the interrogation. I assume the Signore does want to examine me.

LEONARDO. So it seems.

IMPERIA. I prefer to answer in the presence of my friends. Alone . . . and the authority of the Prefect would turn me into a coward.

MICHAEL. Unfortunately, the probability that something serious has happened to Prince Florencio increases by the moment. He hasn't been seen all morning and it's impossible to determine his whereabouts.

SIGNORE. It's known that he was at Cecco's tavern last night. Here is a list of the people who were there . . . of all of them. Look it over. Is there anyone missing?

IMPERIA. No.

MICHAEL. Your name is on the list.

IMPERIA. Proof that the Signore's police serve him well.

SIGNORE. Then it may also be true that the Prince left the tavern some time before dawn, a bit drunk it seems and, supported by Harry Lucenti and the owner of the tavern, he was helped into your carriage and driven to your house. You returned soon after in the company of a young girl from the circus, a certain Donina, a person you must know well, since it isn't the first time you've been seen together.

MICHAEL. The Signore knows who Donina is and of your relationship.

SIGNORE. I know everything. With the exception of the persons that are in your house, all those who were with the Prince are under arrest . . . a precautionary measure. It is a very delicate matter. The least indiscretion might compromise certain persons of quality who can not be treated like ordinary criminals. I question you as a friend. Those who were with the Prince swear he left the tavern at the same time you did . . . as I said. Are we dealing with a lovers' adventure? A political intrigue? *Is* Prince Florencio here at this moment?

IMPERIA. Prince Florencio is here. I brought him here . . . but I brought him home dead.

MICHAEL. Dead!

SIGNORE. Dead!

IMPERIA. Yes. Florencio committed suicide.

SIGNORE. What did you say?

MICHAEL. It can't be.

LEONARDO. What are you trying . . . ?

IMPERIA [*definitely*]. He has committed suicide! In spite of everything you know, in spite of anything you see . . . this will be the truth!

SIGNORE. Who'd believe it? There's nothing to indicate . . .

MICHAEL. Come, let's . . .

IMPERIA. No! Hear me out. He was murdered. That's the truth as I know it, as I saw it, and as I heard it. But no one can be held responsible for his death. If you try to investigate, to pursue and punish; if you try to expose the truth . . . then the truth will be lost forever in the lies, gossip, and filth which will link us all to this very crime. All of us, from those poor people whose miserable faces still proclaim the degeneracy of that hideous Prince to the Emperor of Suavia who could very well have hired an assassin to free the crown of such an heir.

MICHAEL. Preposterous!

SIGNORE. Madam!

IMPERIA. Yes, I was there, your mistress, the mistress to the heir of the throne! No one knows why I was there. I can implicate myself and involve all of you. The Prince had followers in Suavia. A halo of martyrdom would certainly flatter his memory. Now if you want to disenchant these followers by proclaiming the truth, then go ahead . . . talk about his death! Talk, talk, talk! I too know how to talk. You will have to describe the life of your dear Prince, tell the world about his crimes, his vices. You'll have to stain his memory and then the contempt and hatred of the world will seek you out as surely and impartially as it will seek out the Prince's partners in filth.

[*A* SERVANT *enters.*]

SERVANT. Your Highness.
MICHAEL. Yes?

[*The* DUKE OF SUAVIA *enters.*]

DUKE. Your Highness, the Princess has found out her son is here. She wants to see him. We couldn't prevent her . . .
MICHAEL. No! Take her away! Well, come on!

[PRINCE MICHAEL, *the* SIGNORE, *and the* DUKE *go out.*]

LEONARDO. Do you think they'll tell the truth?
IMPERIA. No. They're afraid. Truth frightens them. Don't you see, I know what his life really was, his intrigues, his crime, his perversion. They won't tell. It's my silence for theirs. The Prince was not murdered. No one is to blame for his death. It was a nightmare. You see! I can destroy reality! I can conquer fact. When one loves, facts retreat like frightened ghosts.
DONINA [*outside*]. Let me go! Let me through! [*Entering.*] Mother! Mother!
LEONARDO. Your daughter?
IMPERIA. Yes, my daughter. Why are you running, child? You're trembling.
DONINA. Help me! Hide me! They're coming to get me. I don't care if I die . . . so long as they don't look at me or talk to me. I won't say anything.
IMPERIA. Leonardo, take her away. Take her far away.
LEONARDO. We couldn't leave here without being seen.
DONINA. They can kill me, I don't care! It's just that I saw him again! I'll never stop seeing him!
IMPERIA. You . . . ?

DONINA. Yes! I woke up shaking with fear. I had to get away so I ran out without thinking . . . and I saw him, I saw him, I'll never stop seeing him! . . . Oh! I'm losing my mind!

IMPERIA. Be quiet! . . . Leonardo, listen.

LEONARDO. It's the Princess. She's crying.

IMPERIA. No, don't listen . . . it's nothing.

DONINA. Yes, she's crying! His mother is crying! I can hear her! Listen. Closer, closer, closer!

LEONARDO. They're coming here. Surely they won't let her . . .

IMPERIA. Wait! They're passing by . . . Come, now let's go. Let's leave.

DONINA. Listen to her cry! "My boy! My son!"

IMPERIA. Let's get out of here! Come . . .

DONINA. No! I'll hear her always: "My boy! My son!"

IMPERIA. I can't stand it any longer. They weren't ghosts, Leonardo, we can't destroy reality after all. It seeps back into our lives and overcomes us. That mother crying for her boy, and my daughter half dead with fear and remorse . . . they've torn my heart apart. I give up . . . come what may.

LEONARDO. No, Imperia. You're strong. Don't throw your life away. Fight! Win!

IMPERIA. No, no, leave me, forget me. . . . But save my daughter, save my daughter.

CURTAIN

ACT FIVE

[*A garden in* IMPERIA'S *villa.* DONINA *is modeling for* LEONARDO. NUNU *strolls about restlessly.*]

LEONARDO. That's all for today, Donina.

DONINA. I'm not tired. Don't stop because . . .

LEONARDO. Oh, I know you're strong and that I no longer have to worry about your health. It's not the model who's tired this time . . . it's the artist. Who could work on a day like this? We pray for weather like this on our holidays, but when nature really volunteers it, we should put aside all work. Work today? Don't even think of it! To enjoy a day like this just let yourself drink in the light, and breathe in the air, and the odors of the land and the sea. . . . You're sad, Donina. Why are you always sad?

NUNU. She's afraid she's going to die.

LEONARDO. The doctors say you've recovered. You're lucky. And now that you are well again, you want to die! Believe me, Donina, you're really very fortunate, Donina.

DONINA. I know I am . . . that's why I'm afraid.

NUNU. Can you see Prince Michael's yacht from here?

LEONARDO. Yes. That one over there. It came in this morning.

DONINA. Why did Prince Michael come back? I heard he'd gone off to be Emperor.

LEONARDO. Don't ask me. Donina, we shouldn't bother about anything. Suavia is very far away.

DONINA. Too near, you mean.

NUNU. Why don't we go boating again? We're not going to spend the whole afternoon here, are we?

DONINA. Are you bored?

NUNU. No, but the sea air will do you good. We never go out.

DONINA. It's so beautiful . . .

NUNU. . . . and so boring . . . like a prison.

DONINA. Prison?

LEONARDO [*sotto voce to* NUNU]. You're a bad actor, Nunu.
NUNU. I can't take it any longer.

[IMPERIA *enters.*]

IMPERIA. You've stopped early today. Isn't Donina feeling well?

DONINA. No. It was Leonardo's idea.

LEONARDO. Yes, it's my fault . . . always lazy . . . but we're almost finished.

DONINA. It looks just like me!

IMPERIA. I don't want to see it until it's finished. Does she remind you of me when I was your model?

LEONARDO. No. A line here and there but the expression is different. There was more life in you. Donina could never climb rocks and reach a throne.

IMPERIA. Why should she? No, I want you to copy the sweet sadness of her face . . . copy it! . . . don't bother expressing any ideas. My statue was meant to astound the world, it was meant to be a masterpiece. This statue is for me alone. Use your art and cheat death of as much of that life as you can . . . it's the only way we can save any of it.

LEONARDO. I said *I* was tired just now, but it was Donina. She frightened me. Her color, her heavy breathing! There's no hope.

IMPERIA. They say that those who die this way never know they're dying. But Donina talks of nothing else! She knows it's coming. She's waiting for it.

LEONARDO. That's not so. It's an invalid's trick. . . . She knows it's a bad sign to pretend she'll live forever so she pretends that she's dying . . . but she doesn't really believe it.

[DONINA *laughs.*]

IMPERIA. She's laughing, she's gay! She's happy! What are you doing, Donina?

DONINA. Picking flowers . . . roses . . . for you. Aren't they your favorites? I was laughing because Nunu told me a story about some roses. It wasn't a nice story, but it was very funny . . . like all his stories. It was about the rose garden in a convent. Well once the devil came to the convent and hung a little demon on each bush. They were as pink as the roses . . . so pink they looked like cupids or little angels. When the nuns saw them they thought they were in mortal sin and, so as not to give themselves away, they took them and hid them in their cells. But the little demons got away and jumped and ran about and did all kinds of naughty things. They sang in the choir, danced to the organ music, rang the bells, and finally . . . no! I can't tell you that part. It's very funny but I'm embarrassed. Nunu, you tell them so they can laugh too.

NUNU. Don't be silly. Come pick some more roses.

IMPERIA. Yes, laugh, Donina, laugh. Oh, Leonardo, why do we waste our life in dreams and schemes? This is the real life . . . something that springs from our heart and our womb. The laughter of a child is the only proof of the value of our own lives.

LEONARDO. I take it you're not going to Suavia. Prince Michael came back for you alone and will now go back alone to rule his Empire.

IMPERIA. He swears that, without me, he won't accept the crown. Threatens to sail away and end his days in some unknown country. He's a quiet soul . . . his energy is all mine.

LEONARDO. And you?

IMPERIA. While my daughter is alive, I stay here.

LEONARDO. That won't be for long.

IMPERIA. I've never wanted to stop time the way I do now. On a day like this it seems she could never die. It seems impossible that we go through life like ghosts merely glancing at the earth, sea, and sky as we pass through. . . . Oh! they seem to scream their eternity and announce our death! If it's true, then life is a cruel joke! There must be something in us that's bigger, more permanent . . . than that earth and sea and sky!

LEONARDO. But what is there about us that deserves immortality? What we are? What we pretend to be? What we loved and how? What we dreamed? What *is* our real life?

[DONINA *and* NUNU *return with an armful of roses.*]

DONINA. Look at the roses! All colors! Bring them here, Nunu. We've cut every rose in the garden but it doesn't matter. The bushes will be heavy with them again tomorrow.

IMPERIA. No other flower can compare with them.

LEONARDO. And how they remind one of life! All the colors of flesh: red as blood; red as burning lips; amber ones with a touch of carmine, like a Titian nude; these opulent ones, like goddesses by Rubens . . . and these, bloodless and pale, like the hands of a Virgin.

DONINA. And these pale yellow like wax, like the dead.

LEONARDO. That's enough, Donina. No. They're all alive, not a one of them speaks of death. Look how they live. Upside down, like this, they're like little ladies . . . the petals make the skirt. Look at this one . . . a Madame Pompadour with rose petal panniers; the stem, her waist; these two leaves, the full sleeves . . . there's something missing. Ah! A petal will do . . . and now we have a little head. Place it on the slender neck of my little marquise . . . those lovely necks that seemed to taper for the guillotine, as the poet said. Ha! And this one looks like a Spanish Infanta with her large farthingale. And this velvet crimson is a superb Dogaressa of Venice. Don't they look like women?

DONINA. You're right! How sweet! See how they look like women, Nunu? No! Don't look. You can't resist a woman in any form. I'd tear them apart first! Here, duck! [*She throws some roses at him.*]

NUNU. A battle of flowers . . . look out! [*He throws roses at her.*]

DONINA. Look out yourself!

[*They run out throwing roses and laughing.*]

IMPERIA. It can't be death. She's happy.

LEONARDO. A deceptive happiness. You know its price.

IMPERIA. I know, but Donina couldn't live without him . . . in spite of it all. I forced him to come here by frightening him and by convincing him that it's to his advantage. I manage to keep him under control, sentenced to act the lover. The little wretch tried to run away, but I threatened to have him taken to Suavia to stand trial for Prince Florencio's murder. He believed me. I don't care if it is a lie! Donina has forgiven him. She is happy thinking he loves her more than ever. It's worth it all if she dies happy. Without my deceit, she would have died long ago out of her mind with sorrow and remorse . . . and the sting of his treachery.

LEONARDO. Do you think Nunu will be able to act his part much longer?

IMPERIA. I'm not counting on his virtue, it's his fear I trust . . . and his greed. I'll see that *they* are kept alive.

LEONARDO. Countess Rinaldi's coach has stopped at the garden gate.

IMPERIA. Probably to find out if I'm going to Suavia. She must have seen the Prince's yacht. Tell her I'm out, get rid of her as soon as possible. I can't stand that woman!

LEONARDO. Why, pray tell? She's just another ghost going through life . . . a tireless huntress of ideals . . .

[IMPERIA *leaves. The* COUNTESS *enters.*]

RINALDI. Leonardo!

LEONARDO. My dear Countess! Have they told you Imperia is not in?

RINALDI. I haven't asked. No one so much as crossed my path and I was sure I would stumble across someone . . . especially now that Imperia is living *en famille*. I hear that you are one of the closest relatives.

LEONARDO. As always . . . but only as an artist.

RINALDI. We all run full circle . . . if we live long enough. But be careful. Prince Michael has come back too . . . in spite of heavens only knows what!

LEONARDO. In spite of it? He never meant to do anything else.

RINALDI. It seemed that, after Prince Florencio's . . . suicide . . . you see how I respect the official truth.

LEONARDO. It's the only truth . . . after all, we live by it.

RINALDI. It's a pity that people prefer the likely lie. Amazing how no one could explain the suicide . . .

LEONARDO. Ask the Signore . . .

RINALDI. Much good that would do. A crime of that sort would have frightened the aristocratic clientele that spends so much of its money here. No one dies here, no one is killed here . . . unless it's in an extremely agreeable fashion. We die of joy, and we kill ourselves to avoid inconveniencing others. In short, we're agreed to believe everything . . . tales of a witches' sabbath . . . like Lady Seymour's. You've heard?

LEONARDO. Another suicide?

RINALDI. Not quite. I saw her with her arm in a sling . . . she tripped getting in or out of her automobile. Last year it was a bruise over the eyebrow . . . a fall from a horse. These accidents always coincide with her husband's departure on a long trip, trips which last two or three months . . . long enough for the wounds to heal.

LEONARDO. Both physically and morally . . . right?

RINALDI. I stick to the official truth.

LEONARDO. Long may it reign. I find you looking very healthy and in fine color . . . but there's a certain austerity of dress . . . ?

RINALDI. A new leaf—a new life! I was almost vanquished by neurasthenia, but my physican prescribed a frightfully severe regimen. "You simply must control those nerves of yours," he said. "Remember, neurasthenia is no longer in fashion. The reign of nerves is at an end and the renaissance of muscle is at hand!"

LEONARDO. You'll be the Michael Angelo of this Renaissance.

RINALDI. Fortunately, I made the change with no trouble at all. Heaven has put me on the true path of salvation.

LEONARDO. Without elephants?

RINALDI. Don't remind me! I've thrust all those mad escapades behind me. Well, just picture it: on one of my hygienic hikes through the countryside I stopped, by chance, at the door of a Franciscan monastery. It occurred to me, suddenly, that I'd like to go in. A pale-faced friar with a long bushy beard was preaching. And what a sermon! Oh, how he talked of love! . . . human and divine.

LEONARDO. I dare say *you* could have preached a better sermon on the former.

RINALDI. Don't make fun of me. He's made a new woman out of me. I go to hear him every afternoon. He's a second Saint Francis. I've taken it upon myself to restore the monastery and am planning a series of benefits . . .

LEONARDO. Oh, the poor saint. Saint Anthony had it easy!

RINALDI. Now, don't you talk like that. You don't even know him.

LEONARDO. But I know you.

RINALDI. I accept the judgment of the world, it's a well-deserved penance. I wish people would judge me even more harshly! . . . In order to accomplish my mission, I am soliciting from door to door. Of course I can count on you and Imperia. You *will* send me one of your works for the auction at my little kermess.

LEONARDO. With pleasure. Something appropriate . . . a Magdalen! But would you prefer her before or after conversion?

RINALDI. Just see to it that she's got lots of clothes!

LEONARDO. That would be *before* conversion. Afterwards, well you can imagine how she wandered about in the wilderness. I suppose you'll be following her example soon enough . . . with the possible exception of the wilderness setting.

[DONINA *enters chasing* NUNU.]

DONINA. Don't run any more! Give me that letter! Give it to me or . . .

NUNU [*seeing the* COUNTESS]. Be quiet! Can't you see! . . . How many times have I got to tell you?

DONINA. Oh! "How-many-times" yourself!

NUNU. Be quiet!

RINALDI [*to* LEONARDO]. Don't explain . . . these are Imperia's protégés! Daphnis and Chloë? Paul and Virginia? This villa has become a veritable garden of love!

LEONARDO. Profane love. It's not for you.

RINALDI. You'll tell Imperia why I called?

LEONARDO. I will proclaim your conversion.

RINALDI. But only as an introduction . . . afterwards, tell her I'm counting on her for . . .

LEONARDO. Don't worry.

RINALDI. They're interesting, these love birds. They're children, of course . . . How old is the boy?

LEONARDO. A good age, Countess . . . a very good age!

[*The* COUNTESS *and* LEONARDO *leave.*]

DONINA. Give me that letter. Give it here!

NUNU. That's right, scream, cry, and stamp your feet so everyone will know, so I'll be blamed if you get worse. I told you it's to Tommy. Look! What do you want me to say!

DONINA. For Tommy? That's what the envelope says, but you can put another letter inside. You can make an arrangement with . . . If there's nothing important in it why did you have to hide to write it. You would have told me. Can't I know what you said to Tommy?

NUNU. It would serve you right.

DONINA. Very well, give me the letter.

NUNU. Let go! Let go!

DONINA. Oh! I can't stand it! . . . Oh, God, I can't breathe!

NUNU. Now you see!

DONINA. My God!

LEONARDO [*as he enters*]. What's this? What's happened to Donina?

DONINA. Nothing . . . nothing.

NUNU. She's crazy. Tried to read a letter I'd written to a friend. I mean, a fellow can't do anything! Just because you give me everything I want, you're not paying me, you know. If it weren't because . . .

DONINA. Pay? If it weren't for what? What do you mean?

LEONARDO. Nunu! Why torture Donina?

DONINA. He's my only happiness, that's why. I've given my life for him . . . my soul! I'm dying for him and . . . I killed for him. I've lost my soul for him.

LEONARDO. Donina! [*Aside to* NUNU.] What have you done! Couldn't you wait, you wretch?

NUNU. Wait! I've waited long enough. I can't stand it any longer. Enough! You want to read the letter? You want to know what I said to my friend? Well, then read! Read!

DONINA [*taking the letter*]. Ah!

NUNU. Read! It's not my fault.

LEONARDO. What does it say?

DONINA. Oh, God! [*She faints.*]

LEONARDO. What have you done? . . . Donina! Donina!

DONINA. Leave me, go away. I want to die. It was all a lie!

IMPERIA. What's happened? That letter! What's in it?

DONINA. Leave me alone. Leave me.

IMPERIA. Oh! You've killed her! You've killed her!

NUNU. It's not my fault. She wanted it this way. I've had all I can take of this! I want my freedom!

IMPERIA. Your freedom? You forget what I can do to you, you dog. I thought that if I paid a good price I could make your soul what I wanted . . . good or evil. But it wasn't the life you lead that made you bad, it was your own heart. You're a shadow of Prince Florencio! You're hell-ridden souls, the two of you! . . . incapable of love *or* pity.

DONINA. Let him go! Let him go! Why did you make him lie to me? And why did you do it, Nunu? You're free, Nunu, I forgive you. You won't have to wait for me to die in order to collect your pay. . . . Give him what's coming to him. He lied well. But I know the truth now. I'm dying. That's the only truth he ever told me.

IMPERIA. You wrote that letter on purpose so she would see it. You know how to murder with clean hands.

NUNU. That's a lie! She . . .

IMPERIA. Get out! Go away! . . . Before Donina begs me to forgive you. Get out! Go!

NUNU. Just like that?

LEONARDO. Don't worry, you'll get your money.

[NUNU *and* LEONARDO *leave*.]

DONINA. Why did you lie to me? If my whole life was a lie, how can I go on living?

IMPERIA. Donina!

DONINA. My life is a nuisance to both of us. They're waiting for you. That Prince and his damned Empire, that Empire of ice. There's his yacht: white, with pale white-faced sailors . . . come to take you to the empire you've always wanted.

IMPERIA. No, Donina. I'll stay here with you, always . . . that ship will sail away like a white ghost. And I'll stay here! Our love for each other will be our only truth. And I'll stay with you forever, for always.

DONINA. Waiting for me to die . . . as he did?

IMPERIA. No, Donina! You're my whole life!

DONINA. I'll be the one to sail away . . . like a white ghost. Without knowing it, I'll go away forever like a ghost that passed through your life.

IMPERIA. No, Donina, no! Child of my heart, of my only love! Our lives may disappear like ghosts . . . all, all! But what the heart has lived . . . that will remain.

[*Enter* LEONARDO *and* PRINCE MICHAEL.]

LEONARDO. Imperia . . . the Prince.

IMPERIA. Ah! Why are you here?

MICHAEL. You didn't answer. I waited all day.

DONINA. He's coming for you.

IMPERIA. I won't go.

DONINA. I know the truth! I'll kill myself if you go on lying . . . staying here to watch me die when.

IMPERIA. What are you saying?

DONINA. Promise me you won't wait . . . that you'll go today. I swear I'll kill myself before I'll get in your way. Will you go?

IMPERIA. I'll go. Today. And now you rest here, Donina. Leonardo, help her.

LEONARDO. Donina!

DONINA. No, it's nothing. I'm all right now. I know what it is, now.

MICHAEL [*as they move off*]. Will you really come?

IMPERIA. Yes.

MICHAEL. I wouldn't go back without you.

IMPERIA. Would you have renounced the throne?

MICHAEL. Certainly. It's difficult enough to govern my own life peacefully . . . what would it be to rule an Empire? Millions of people trying to be happy and expecting their happiness to be guaranteed by my laws, my wise laws.

IMPERIA. Don't talk like that! What a coward! Would you give up your divine right? Those millions you talked about will never get happiness through you . . . or anyone else, for that matter! We can't bring happiness even to the ones we love the most! Death and pain are invincible; but the effort to conquer them is what makes us equal to God. You know nothing of life. Good and evil have no clear meaning for you. But they do for me. I've fought enough in my time to make up for several lifetimes of struggle! I was so low, so worthless . . . like the clay Leonardo used for his statue. Poverty, shame, hatred, cruelty, injustice . . . I've suffered all of it. But I'm strong now, I have power, and in the name of justice I can do good as easily as evil. But I happen to want the good! I want all the poor and the oppressed of your Empire to know your love . . . so that your Empire may become a glory among nations, and that your name and mine will be well remembered. Love! Justice! Oh! I heard a moan! . . . Leonardo!

LEONARDO. It wasn't a moan. She's resting. She's asleep.

IMPERIA. No, she called me. I heard her.

LEONARDO. She's not calling you. It's another name. Well, to each his love! Her love was all feeling and flesh and it claimed her life . . . *your* love is a thing of strength and will. Go, Imperia, go.

IMPERIA. No, I can't. I mustn't leave her. My child, my baby!

MICHAEL. Bring her with you.

LEONARDO. Her death is inevitable. I'll stay with her.

IMPERIA. No. She's still alive. I can't leave.

LEONARDO. Your Highness, leave her for a moment. I promise you she'll come.

MICHAEL. Imperia, if you don't come before tonight, my boat will sail without me. It will carry my abdication. And, in the morning, I'll be back to you and our old life. The

Empire of Suavia will be lost to you . . . like a dream. [*He goes out.*]

IMPERIA. Leonardo! What should I do? I'm your ideal! Give me your will.

LEONARDO. Your life is your own! Your will is your own! Can't you see where they lead?

IMPERIA. My life is your ideal, your dream! I'll go . . . I'll go. But my daughter? Is she sleeping?

LEONARDO. You'll lose your courage.

IMPERIA. No. I want to look at her.

LEONARDO. If you do, you'll stay here, Imperia! You'll never leave! [IMPERIA *goes into the house and then comes back.*] Imperia.

IMPERIA. She's asleep. I kissed her forehead. She didn't wake up.

LEONARDO. You kissed her?

IMPERIA. I should go, shouldn't I?

LEONARDO. Yes! And conquer. It is the ideal that triumphs. But tell me . . . when you kissed the child . . .

IMPERIA. What do you want to know?

LEONARDO. Was she . . .

IMPERIA. She was dead. Her death won't hold me back. Does that surprise you?

LEONARDO. You are a wonderful person. You frighten me and I admire you.

IMPERIA. In order to do something great we must destroy reality and push aside its ghosts that get in our way. We must pursue our only truth down its path of our dreams, toward perfection where our souls fly about in their witches' sabbath. Some fly toward evil losing themselves in the fog . . . others toward good to live forever as spirits of light and love. Goodby, Leonardo.

LEONARDO. Goodby, Imperia.

IMPERIA. Your soul is as great as your ideal . . . and you embraced me with your soul.

CURTAIN

ANTONIO BUERO VALLEJO

1916–

ANTONIO BUERO VALLEJO is, together with Alfonso Sastre, the leading dramatist presently writing in Spain. Born in Guadalajara, his first ambition was to be a painter. When the Spanish Civil War broke out he joined the Republican Army and shortly thereafter was captured and taken to prison, where he remained for the next six years. Upon his release, he took up his painting again and also began to write plays and movie scripts. In 1949 he burst onto the theatrical scene when his first two plays won Spain's most coveted drama prizes. The full length *Story of a Staircase* (*Historia de una escalera*) was awarded the Lope de Vega Prize. It is a play with an American 1930's quality to it and is reminiscent of Elmer Rice's *Street Scene* and Sidney Kingsley's *Dead End*. *Words in the Sand* (*Palabras en la arena*), which has similar social overtones, won the Quintero Prize for the best new one-act play.

Since 1949 there has been a tremendous leap in Buero Vallejo's range and style. His more recent plays have a symbolic depth and an imaginative power which most of his Spanish contemporaries have been unable to achieve. *The Dream Weaver* is certainly the most interesting of these plays. It is a retelling of Ulysses' homecoming which has been infused with a rich fantasy and expressed in vigorous language. Much like his French contemporaries, Buero Vallejo uses the Homeric legend to comment on conditions in his own time. Penelope is symbolic of the beleaguered people of Spain who must endure the ravages of false suitors while they await the return of the true husbandman. Her efforts, which on the surface appear so futile, are revealed to be, in fact, an increasingly virulent movement of passive resistance.

The most important Spanish critics consider Buero Vallejo their nation's top-ranking playwright. This may very well be true, but the fact that he is not at all popular with audiences reflects the dilemma facing the contemporary Spanish theatre. Their best writers are rejected (if not actually harassed) by a government which pretty much controls the theatre. As a result, playwrights like Buero Vallejo are denied an opportunity for continued production, and hence the optimum conditions for artistic growth. In spite of this, he continues to work, and if and when the situation changes, Antonio Buero Vallejo is sure to be in the vanguard of the new theatre of Spain.

ABOUT THEATRE[1]

by Antonio Buero Vallejo

Translated by William I. Oliver

THE PLAYWRIGHT's first duty is the question of reality. However, one must really make a question of it, for it is not yet answered. The theatre must lean upon what is known, but it must also explore the unknown. Therefore it cannot be entirely "solutionist"; it must always be to some extent problematical.

The most ideologically affirmative theatre will contribute nothing to effective progress if it does not allow for the possibility of answering its most essential questions upon entirely new or different grounds.

In the presence of the great field of the unknown, the playwright, like all artists, has the right and the duty to venture his personal intuitions.

When it is considered as a simple instrument for the transformation of real life, the theatre can become the dead appendage of old ideologies and it will lose rather than gain the strength of action. When considered exclusively as an intuitive form of perception or as contemplation of reality, the theatre can fall prey to arbitrariness and dehumanization. Great drama, like all great art, overcomes this last dilemma and becomes a form of active contemplation. But every playwright has a right to make mistakes. In activities which are as subject to intuitive processes as are the arts, errors are necessary and no roads of exploration should be barred.

When one recommends realism one is advocating a healthy proposition, but it is a proposition that has no unequivocal formula. What was not realistic yesterday manages to become

[1] "Sobre el Teatro" is used here by permission of the author and the translator.

so today; what today we brand as unrealistic may become realistic tomorrow.

If theatre, as a social function, had no other purpose than to adapt to its age, all exceptions would be negative and realism would require no more than its successive and changing definitions in order to be historically true. However, one of the most positive modes of social action is to push ahead. To see further than others is one of the most profound ways of acting in favor, not only of the future, but of contemporary society as well—and this in spite of the fact that the various social strata may consider this vision to be antisocial and an evasion of reality. In so far as art is concerned, there is no guaranteeing that the sociologist or the critic will see further than the artist.

The temptation of the doctrinaire is to impose restraints upon works that surge forward.

If social problems were to suffer upon the stage an exclusively didactic treatment based upon generalized rationalizations, the resulting works would be sociology, they would not be social drama. When social problems are fleshed in singular conflicts and concrete human beings then there may be a social drama.

Between the didactic, which leans upon that portion of reality that has supposedly been rationalized, and the poetic, which appears within that portion not rationalized—one must establish a careful balance. And if the poetic is indeed authentic, then it is so light that it will not take much of the didactic to tip the scales.

A play which can be advantageously supplanted by an explication of its content is a bad play.

If a play does not suggest a great deal more than what it states explicitly it is dead. The implicit is not an error of deficiency but the virtue of plenitude.

Certain plays in which problems are implicitly stated are far more positive and valuable for society than others which are explicitly social. There are plays in which the problem is implicit that are far more vigorous metaphysical statements than other plays which are explicitly metaphysical. There are . . . etc.

Ever since the Greeks, the theatre has aroused our emotions and sought to make the spectator identify with the action of the play. Ever since the Greeks, the theatre has prompted critical or objective thought and the alienation of the spectator from the action of the play. To favor one or the other of these two aspects is to see only one of the theatre's faces. Great plays, however, present to us both of these faces no matter how they may be polemically related by their authors to one tendency or the other.

The very same thing occurs in great acting: if the actor builds his performance upon emotion he will eventually encounter reflection; if he builds upon reflection he will come to emotion.

The *esperpento* of Valle-Inclan is good because it is not absolute.

Every valuable theatrical discovery has its lesser antecedents. This is true even in the case of popular theatre. However, not all lesser discoveries prove valuable.

Tragedy is not pessimistic. Tragedy never flourishes when people believe in the infallible force of destiny but rather when, consciously or unconsciously, people begin to doubt it. Tragedy explores the ways in which human failings *disguise themselves* as destiny.

"Durch Leiden Freude," said Beethoven. "Through sorrow to joy." This is the ultimate meaning of tragedy. This is the final significance of *The Eumenides* by Aeschylus. All tragedy postulates liberating Eumenides even though they end as *Agamemnon.*

The theatre works like a pair of glasses for the nearsighted who want to see more clearly. However, not all of the nearsighted care to see what they should, and not all suffer the same degree of myopia, while some others have far keener eyesight than the playwright. Hence the difficulty of writing for any audience.

No poetics is strong enough to prevail against a play which reforms. When a play confirms itself by surviving, it is the play that judges and modifies the principles.

No poetics is poetical. Poetry is to be found in the play and not in the rules. This is what the doctrinaire forgets.

The present sketch of a poetics is worth nothing against the great plays which contradict it. But if it implies more than it states, it is perhaps worth something.

THE DREAM WEAVER

by ANTONIO BUERO VALLEJO

1952

THE DREAM WEAVER[1]

Translated by William I. Oliver

CAST OF CHARACTERS
(in order of appearance)

DIONE, *a slave girl*
1ST SLAVE GIRL
2ND SLAVE GIRL
3RD SLAVE GIRL
4TH SLAVE GIRL
EURICLEA, *the nurse*
PENELOPE, *the queen*
TELEMACHUS, *her son*
THE STRANGER
ANTINOUS, *a suitor for the queen's hand*
EURYMACHUS, *a suitor for the queen's hand*
PISANDER, *a suitor for the queen's hand*
LEOCRITES, *a suitor for the queen's hand*
AMPHION, *a suitor for the queen's hand*
EUMAEUS, *the swineherd*
PHILETAS, *the shepherd*

[1] LA TEJEDORA DE SUENOS is used here by permission of the author and the translator.

ACT ONE

[*A gallery in the palace of* ULYSSES, *king of Ithaca . . . now the palace of* PENELOPE. *It is a high gallery overlooking the ceremonial court. In the foreground and running the length of the stage are three steps or levels. Up Center is the queen's weaving room, a spacious chamber the foundations of which rest, supposedly, in the court below. Its doorway, carved in bas-reliefs, faces front onto the gallery. There are stone arches to either side of this door and also at Stage Right and Left. A balustrade extends between the arches immediately to the sides of the queen's room. One can look down from this balustrade into the court below. Hung from crossbars between the arches that face the court are large curtains that fall to the floor and prevent the persons in the gallery from looking into the courtyard. The arch at Right has no door and leads to the gyneceum; in the arch at Left, there is a door of wood and bronze which closes off the women's quarters from the rest of the palace. This door is now open. The gallery is, therefore, the first of the women's chambers. There are torches in the columns of the arches. To the Left of the door leading into the queen's chamber hangs* ULYSSES' *quiver and immense bow. The vault of the sky seen above the curtains is already dark, but the last fires of sunset flicker through the openings between the curtains. The interior of the queen's chamber is also alight with the setting sun which shines in through a big window which overlooks the court. This window is scarcely visible because the queen's large loom, on which she is weaving* LAERTES' *shroud, blocks our view of the room. All we see through the open door of the chamber is a portion of the back of the loom and, to its Left, a high bronze candelabrum, its candles unlit.*

The Queen sits weaving and hidden from view by the cloth on the loom. Standing by the doorway, motionless, facing front, her head high, is the old nurse, EURICLEA. *She is blind. Seated here and there along the steps are five slave women who wind yarn from skeins of various colors. These skeins are taken from and stored in a pair of shallow baskets on the floor. The slave at Left and on the highest step or level is* DIONE. *She holds a skein while the* 4TH SLAVE WOMAN, *seated lower and to her right, winds the yarn. As they work they intone a crude poetic chant without melody.*]

CHORUS [*in clear and pleasant voices*].

Penelope, star that shines in the palace,
may Gods smile on her while she works
and reward her sleeplessness with favor . . .
Golden spider of our good fortune.

Ruled by the wisdom of Ulysses, her husband
her vassals enjoy her vigilant peace.
Working her loom to honor this house
designer of beauties, richness, and joy.

[*They fall silent.* PENELOPE'S *soft laughter issues from the room. It is a penetrating laughter, musical, mysterious, full of deep but restrained joy. The* SLAVE WOMEN *listen and then make quick and confidential remarks in a mocking tone.*]

DIONE. The widow is laughing again! [*She continues to stare at the* QUEEN'S *chamber while the others talk.*]

1ST SLAVE [*the one farthest Right*]. She'll be moaning soon . . .

2ND SLAVE. If she would only moan for the wasted fire wood!

3RD SLAVE. Or the slaughtered sheep.

4TH SLAVE. And the looted palace or the poverty that haunts us.

EURICLEA. Silence! The queen is weaving.

[*They fall silent and continue their work. The expression on* DIONE'S *face changes and, while the others watch in fear, she takes a ball of red wool and crosses cautiously to the queen's chamber.* EURICLEA *senses her approach.*]

Who is coming?

[DIONE *is close to the door and she tries to peek in. The nurse stops her.*]

Dione, isn't it?

DIONE [*innocently, after a wink at the others, while giving* EURICLEA *the ball of yarn*]. Euriclea, here is some blue yarn.

EURICLEA. The queen hasn't asked for it. [*She feels the yarn.*] And this isn't blue . . . it's red.

[*The* SLAVE WOMEN *murmur in amazement.*]

DIONE. It's blue, Nurse . . .

EURICLEA. To your place, liar! I know you.

[*She pushes her. Angrily,* DIONE *snatches the ball of yarn from the* NURSE'S *hand and returns to her place amid the giggles of the others.*]

DIONE [*angrily, after picking up the skein*]. What are you laughing at?

[*They avoid her look.*]

4TH SLAVE [*changing the subject*]. What I say is that if the queen really cared about the misery and poverty here in the palace, she would have remarried long ago. If she moans it's because of her husband's death.

3RD SLAVE. Then why does she laugh?

4TH SLAVE. That too is for Ulysses . . . when she remembers him as a young man. What do you think, Dione?

DIONE. You are all foolish. [*Teasing them.*] Why does Penelope moan? Why does Penelope laugh?

[PENELOPE'S *sweet laughter is heard once more. They listen.* DIONE *mimics her.*]

Hi, hi, hi! For Ulysses. Bah!

1ST SLAVE. Sh! Euriclea will hear you . . .

DIONE [*raising her voice tauntingly*]. That one? She's not only blind, she's deaf!

3RD SLAVE [*frightened*]. But she can see and hear with her hands . . .

[*They look with fear at* EURICLEA *who stands still. Pause.*]

1ST SLAVE. Well, I think the queen is still waiting for Ulysses to come back.

DIONE. Don't be stupid. She knows as well as you that she's a widow. The whole country calls her "the widow"! [*Confidentially.*] Listen. I know why the queen laughs and why she moans. And I know what it is she's weaving into that shroud.

2ND SLAVE. You don't know anything.

DIONE. I know all about it!

2ND SLAVE [*raising her voice*]. Don't look so mysterious. You know just as much as we do . . . nothing!

DIONE [*very loud*]. Everything!

EURICLEA. Silence!

[DIONE *looks at her with a look of a trapped animal.*]

Go on with your chant. [*Imperiously.*] Well, what are you waiting for?

1ST SLAVE. Yes, Nurse.

[*She begins the chant and the others join in.* DIONE *remains silent, her eyes lowered. Then, later, she looks at the queen's chamber with increasing concentration.*]

CHORUS [*chanting*]:

Queen of all and of our hearts,
we lovingly wind and spin for your hands.
Artemis blesses your chastity;
Helen herself becomes jealous
at the thought of your radiant beauty.

[*A brief pause. Softly, full of languid and infinite pain,* PENELOPE'S *lament issues from the chamber.*]

DIONE. There, she moaned!

3RD SLAVE [*bored*]. What of it! She always does.

DIONE. But not like you! Or you! . . . You moan at night, sometimes, when the suitors come to amuse themselves with you. She moans in solitude!

2ND SLAVE [*wickedly*]. Not all the suitors amuse themselves with the slave girls.

[*They suppress their giggles.*]

1ST SLAVE. Amphion is very chaste. No one has managed to move him.

[DIONE *rises in anger.*]

2ND SLAVE [*cuttingly*]. Nor is the queen the only woman who sighs alone.

[*The giggles burst into laughter.*]

DIONE [*rushing at her*]. Bitch!

[*She hits her and throws her to the ground. The rest scream and try to pull them apart. The distaffs and skeins tumble down the steps.* EURICLEA *comes forward, her hands extended.*]

EURICLEA. Silence! The queen is weaving and mustn't be disturbed. [*She tries vainly to separate them.*] Gods in heaven, what trouble! You'll be punished for this! Dione, you're going to be whipped! You're to blame for this! [PENELOPE'S *voice is heard, hard and angry.*]

PENELOPE. Euriclea!

[*The* NURSE *halts and stands frightened. The* SLAVE WOMEN *quickly gather up their skeins and balls of yarn. Pause.* PENELOPE *comes to the door of her chamber and looks disdainfully at the women. Though no longer young, she is still beautiful. Her full and graceful body draws itself up majestically. The expression of her features seems torn between a smiling pride and a timid anxiety. She is now very serious.*]

You seem to forget, Euriclea, that while I am weaving you should not move from the door.

EURICLEA. Forgive, my lady. The slave women . . .

PENELOPE [*conclusively*]. Do not leave the door. [*A brief pause.*] I suppose that the slaves were quarreling over some nonsense . . . little beasts that they are . . . that's so, isn't it?

[*All but* DIONE *lower their heads.*]

SLAVE WOMEN. Yes, my lady.

PENELOPE. I can understand how you'd weary of chanting the rhapsody. The old palace bard who composed it in my honor was not very gifted, poor fellow. But I was weaving in peace until your voices made me get up. [*She steps forward and stares at* DIONE, *saying*:] Don't let it happen again.

[*They all look at* DIONE.]

DIONE [*braving it out*]. Forgive us, lady. We become tired after dark because we can't see to do our work. We become restless and, sometimes, we relax by having little chats.

EURICLEA. That's why you are ordered to chant.

DIONE [*quickly, to* PENELOPE]. It's just that we also hear your laughter and your laments and . . .

PENELOPE [*hard*]. What?

DIONE [*prudently*]. You too become weary, lady.

PENELOPE [*after looking at her for a moment*]. Your tongue is too long for a slave. Don't forget it.

DIONE. No, my lady.

PENELOPE. And don't answer back! [*Pause.*] Withdraw.

[*The* SLAVE WOMEN *gather their things and, after bowing, they leave silently at right.* PENELOPE *crosses left and peeks through the curtains into the court below. She remarks with a note of happiness in her voice.*]

My suitors have finished dining and the servants are eating what they've left. There's hunger in the house.

EURICLEA. Lady, let me punish Dione.

PENELOPE [*without turning*]. No. [*She laughs softly.*] The shepherd, Philetas, told me there's only one flock left. Those men have devoured the rest.

EURICLEA. Why do you never let me punish Dione?

PENELOPE [*turns smiling*]. Because my son Telemachus would feel sorry for her and love her all the more. You know that only too well, Nurse. [*A short pause.*] When I gave him permission to make a journey in search of his father . . . I did not do it simply to free him from the jibes of the suitors. Nor did I do it in order that he should find my husband. No. Ulysses could find his way back alone . . . whenever he wanted to [*Short pause.*] But I had to get him away from Dione. And you see . . . it did no good at all. He hates me now, I know . . .

EURICLEA. Lady!

PENELOPE. He hates me because he knows what I think of that little vixen. And if I punished her . . . he'd hate me even more. [*She sighs.*] It's hard to be a mother, Euriclea . . . [*Darkly.*] . . . and even more difficult to be queen.

EURICLEA. You can say, my lady, I'm just an ordinary woman . . .

PENELOPE. Like myself. What can we do? This palace, which yesterday belonged to Ulysses, is falling into ruin because it's in the hands of a weak woman . . . and a blind one.

EURICLEA [*sadly*]. Yes. I've been blind for thirty years now . . . and it's twenty years since . . .

PENELOPE. Since I became a widow.

EURICLEA. Lady!

PENELOPE. Say it! They all do.

EURICLEA [*gently*]. I was going to say that it's been twenty years since Ulysses went off to the Trojan War. [*Short pause.*] I'm blind, my lady, and almost deaf. But I can hear the Gods who surround us. I hear the steps of the avenging Furies as they tread up and down these stairs. [*She points Left.*] I'm blind and that's why you place me at the door. So that no one, not even I, can see what figures and shapes you are weaving in there. Blind . . . deaf . . . I scarcely live . . . except for you. [*A sudden change.*] And that's why I know you well. You're as strong and as crafty as your husband. Cunning, very cunning with the suitors, and you know it! And very hard on the whims of your son. What does it matter to you if Telemachus loves Dione? Let me punish her!

PENELOPE. You'll not punish Dione.

EURICLEA. Why?

PENELOPE. Because I say so. Because of Telemachus.

EURICLEA. You're right. I'm blind. The darkness closes in on me and I can't understand you. I don't know you.

[PENELOPE *stares at her.*]

All I know is that you laugh and moan as you weave.

[*The* QUEEN *approaches her slowly.*]

PENELOPE. What else?

EURICLEA. This much. I know that when some new misfortune comes upon us . . . when they bring you word that our cattle are almost gone or that they have to water what little wine is left, or that those bandits have stolen your jewels, then . . .

PENELOPE [*at her side*]. Then?

EURICLEA. Then you don't moan. You laugh.

PENELOPE [*withdrawing*]. That's not true.

EURICLEA. You just did! I heard you laugh just now when you saw the servants in the court below.

PENELOPE [*ironically*]. Your poor ears hear all kinds of things. The laughter of the Gods . . . the footfall of the Furies on the stairway.

[EURICLEA'S *silence makes her turn.*]

What's the matter?

EURICLEA [*trembling*]. Just like now, my lady . . . the Furies are coming up . . . and vengeance comes with them. Don't you hear them? They're coming! [*She points left and turns toward the door. After listening for a moment* PENELOPE *advances to the door.*]

PENELOPE [*smiling*]. Be calm, Nurse. It's only Telemachus.

[TELEMACHUS *enters as his mother finishes speaking. He is an adolescent, tormented by his desire for maturity, and embittered by the jests of the suitors and* DIONE'S *coldness.*]

TELEMACHUS. . . . and a stranger, Mother, whom I want you to meet.

[*The* STRANGER *follows him in. He is an old beggar with gray hair and a fugitive glance. He is strong but stooped and leans upon a large walking stick. He bows in silence before the queen.*]

PENELOPE [*to* TELEMACHUS, *somewhat puzzled and haughty*]. Why?

TELEMACHUS [*triumphantly*]. Because he brings news of my father. Ulysses will be here soon! This fellow has seen him.

PENELOPE [*after gazing at the* STRANGER *she speaks in a cold tone*]. He's not the first.

TELEMACHUS [*almost hostile*]. And what if he isn't! You don't want to believe! But this time you'll be convinced.

PENELOPE. Don't be a child. Is it true that you bring word from abroad?

STRANGER [*bowing*]. It is, Your Highness.

PENELOPE. The palace is poor and, no matter how good, I couldn't reward you for your tidings.

TELEMACHUS. He doesn't seek any. Eumaeus, the swineherd, and the shepherd, Philetas, share their food with him. That's all he asks.

PENELOPE. You be quiet. [*To the* STRANGER.] When did you arrive?

STRANGER. I landed on your shores yesterday, Your Highness. Philetas gave me shelter for the night.

PENELOPE. Where are you from?

STRANGER. I fought in the Trojan War with the Acheans. I've just come from Sparta, from the palace of Menelaus and Helen.

PENELOPE. What!

STRANGER. Yes, my Queen . . . and it was there I saw your husband.

TELEMACHUS. Do you hear that, Mother! He saw him with his own eyes.

PENELOPE [*cautiously*]. In Sparta?

STRANGER. He was there when I was there . . . safe and sound from all his adventures . . . but sad. Menelaus and Ulysses were both sad. It was a time for mourning in the palace.

PENELOPE [*with unusual eagerness*]. Who died? Helen?

STRANGER. No. But she was not sad. She's not given to melancholy.

PENELOPE. Who then?

STRANGER. Agamemnon. A messenger came to Menelaus with news that his brother Agamemnon had been assassinated upon his return from Troy.

PENELOPE. Assassinated?

STRANGER. Yes, by his wife, Clytemnestra . . . and her lover. After that, Ulysses used to wander about the beach alone, every afternoon. I approached him and spoke to him several times.

TELEMACHUS. Tell my mother what he said!

STRANGER [*hesitating*]. I told you not knowing who you were. Don't force me to tell the queen.

PENELOPE. Is it so awful?

STRANGER. It's not for your ears . . .

PENELOPE. Am I to be the last one to know of it? Out with it.

STRANGER. Well . . . Ulysses wanted to sail for home two moons later. But he told me that, after hearing what happened to Agamemnon on his return, he had reconsidered his own departure. [*There is a long silence.*]

PENELOPE. Euriclea, go away. You too, Telemachus.

[EURICLEA *retires hesitatingly, right.*]

TELEMACHUS [*somewhat embarrassed by the enthusiasm with which he has followed the* STRANGER'S *tale*]. Forgive me, Mother. I thought you should know.

PENELOPE [*measures him with her gaze*]. Go away.

[TELEMACHUS *lowers his head and starts out right.*]

Telemachus!

[*He stops. She points to the door left.*] That way.

TELEMACHUS [*annoyed*]. Yes, Mother.

PENELOPE. Sit there. [*She indicates the steps. The* STRANGER *obeys her and sits on the first step at left. She paces up and down above him looking at him stealthily and avoids his glances.*] You don't have a truthful face. You've told me something unpleasant, but how do I know it isn't a clever trick to make me believe you.

STRANGER [*shrugging*]. No one believes a beggar.

PENELOPE [*ironically*]. I wonder why? [*Brief pause.*] You say you've seen Ulysses?

STRANGER. I left him in Sparta.

PENELOPE. Was that a long time ago?

STRANGER. Four years.

PENELOPE. Hm . . . I don't know whether to believe you or not. You're the third who claims to have seen him, but he doesn't return.

STRANGER. I've already told you . . .

PENELOPE. Silence. It may be that he hasn't decided to return. It may be that his bones have been bleaching in the sun for twenty years. You aren't the one to convince me of either of these things. [*Pause. She stops, observing him from above.*] Is it true, at least, that you were in Sparta?

STRANGER [*sighing*]. I was in Sparta and I saw Ulysses.

PENELOPE [*with assumed casualness*]. And Helen? Did you see her?

STRANGER. I saw her. Your husband used to say to me that, in spite of it all, Menelaus was lucky enough to rescue his wife and . . .

PENELOPE [*who is sitting very close to him, although on a higher step and almost behind him*]. How is Helen?

[*He looks at her.*]

What are you thinking? Answer me.

STRANGER. Is it Ulysses you want to know about . . . or Helen?

PENELOPE. About Ulysses, of course. But Helen . . . how is she?

STRANGER. Always gay . . . as I said.

PENELOPE. That's to be expected. A woman capable of stirring up a war couldn't possibly be serious . . . or, for that matter, a dreamer. Happy, she's happy like a contented little animal . . . isn't that so?

STRANGER [*amazed*]. Do you know her?

PENELOPE [*with a sarcastic smile*]. I've never seen her. Is she old?

STRANGER. Would it please you if she were?

PENELOPE. Why do you say that? It's a simple question. She must be more . . . more than forty. And then, living that life of constant dissipation . . .

STRANGER. And if I told you that she is still beautiful?

PENELOPE. Is that so?

STRANGER. Very beautiful. When she passes by even an old man's heart beats fast with desire. Her husband has eyes for her alone and . . . always forgives her everything.

PENELOPE [*with disdain*]. That poor man . . .

STRANGER. You were the one to say it, not I. The humble should not criticize kings. But Helen is so beautiful that one can understand how . . . even something like a Trojan War could take place for her. I'm just an old warrior . . . when I took a wife I couldn't be very particular. She was an ugly, slow-witted little creature. Just the same I was happy with her because one should be content with one's lot. [*Short pause.*] Well . . . I've been jealous of Menelaus, and Paris, and all the men who've possessed Helen. I saw her in Sparta . . . and I've come to understand rape and crime and, for the first time, I've wished that I had power and wealth in order to possess that woman.

PENELOPE [*unable to hide her displeasure, she rises and steps toward her chamber*]. Enough!

STRANGER [*quickly*]. Of course faithfulness is better than beauty. No doubt about it. Helen is just a loose woman and a dangerous one.

PENELOPE. You're presumptuous. Forget your little stratagems. [*Quoting him.*] And don't criticize kings . . . or queens. Now go away.

[*The* STRANGER *rises.*]

STRANGER. Forgive an old man who must beg for a living. . . .

PENELOPE [*with a warm smile*]. Is that your excuse? You've lied to me about everything, haven't you? If you admit it, I'll forgive you.

STRANGER. I've told you nothing but the truth, Your Highness.

PENELOPE [*once more cold*]. Get out.

STRANGER [*grumbling*]. You've got to lie. [*He moves toward the door.*] I go hungry because I don't know how. It's a sad life.

[*Laughter and voices are heard in the courtyard.* TELEMACHUS' *voice is distinct and is heard shouting several times. The* STRANGER *stops short.*]

TELEMACHUS' VOICE. Leave me alone! Leave me alone!

PENELOPE [*commanding*]. See what's happening.

STRANGER [*looking through the curtain*]. Five men. Your son among them, angry . . . They have him pinned down. They want to tie him up.

[PENELOPE *becomes alarmed.*]

No, I'm wrong . . . one of the five wants to defend him but can't . . .

PENELOPE [*with sudden warmth*]. That's Amphion.

STRANGER [*looking at her*]. Amphion it is . . . [*He looks back through the curtains.*] It looks like a joke, they're all laughing . . . all but Amphion.

ANTINOUS' VOICE. We want to see Penelope.

PISANDER'S VOICE. And see what she's weaving!

VOICES OF THE OTHERS. That's right!

[PENELOPE *quickly closes the door to her chamber, turns the key, and puts the key away.*]

STRANGER [*in a tone of humble reproof*]. I'm no thief.

PENELOPE [*surprised and upset*]. What?

STRANGER. We poor are well acquainted with that gesture. In my case, however, it isn't necessary.

PENELOPE. Learn one thing, Stranger, while you are here . . . no one but me enters that room.

STRANGER [*innocently*]. Why?

PENELOPE [*witheringly*]. Don't ask!

[*She goes out Right. The noises in the courtyard have died down. The* STRANGER *approaches the queen's chamber and examines the door. Suddenly, he crosses to Down Right and waits, smiling and submissive. The suitors enter at Left:* ANTINOUS, EURYMACHUS, PISAN-

DER, *and* LEOCRITES. *Behind them, melancholy and calm, is* AMPHION, *the fifth suitor. As soon as they enter they halt and look at the* STRANGER, *who greets them. Then* ANTINOUS, *a handsome and arrogant young man who is now completely drunk, crosses to the* STRANGER. *With all the solemnity of a drunk, he puts his hand on the* STRANGER'S *shoulder.* AMPHION *breaks away from the group and leans against the corner of the queen's chamber.*]

ANTINOUS. Don't move . . . understand? And don't shout!

STRANGER. As you wish.

ANTINOUS. Don't move and don't shout.

STRANGER. As you say.

ANTINOUS. That's it. No movement at all . . . at all. And no shouting. That's how we left Telemachus. [*To the rest.*] Isn't that so, friends? [*To the* STRANGER.] But alive! Oh, yes! We're not cruel. We've promised Penelope. If anyone bothers . . . Tie him up and gag him, that's all. Agreed?

STRANGER. Agreed.

ANTINOUS. Because we're really very, very good and we love the queen. And her slightest wish is law! [*Threateningly.*] And if you don't obey her . . .

STRANGER [*protesting*]. But I do obey her . . .

ANTINOUS [*wagging his finger threateningly*]. Well, that's good. [*Short pause.*] Come to think of it, who are you?

STRANGER. For that matter, who are you?

[LEOCRITES, *who has been eating a bunch of grapes, guffaws.*]

ANTINOUS. And what are you laughing about? [*Meaning the* STRANGER.] Who is he?

PISANDER [*a cynic*]. An old busybody who asks too many questions.

STRANGER. I'm a poor man who begs for his bread. I arrived yesterday after surviving many misfortunes. A pittance and I'll serve you well. I can do many things.

ANTINOUS. Can you open doors?

STRANGER. If I'm allowed to share . . . which door?

ANTINOUS. That one. [*He points to the queen's chamber.*]

STRANGER. That belongs to the queen. Why do you want to open it?

EURYMACHUS [*a subtle hypocrite. He approaches the*

STRANGER *and speaks softly*.]. Listen, you lousy filth, take care how you treat us. Don't ask so many questions. You are talking to kings.

STRANGER [*shrugging apologetically*]. I should have known from your majestic carriage. But you are so young . . .

ANTINOUS. Just because you're an old gray-beard don't think you can treat us like children. Want us to put a gag on you?

PISANDER. He sounds just like my father. Come on, let's tie him up!

LEOCRITES. All these old scarecrows look down on us because they were at Troy and we weren't. They've got no cause to give themselves airs. [*He throws away the grape stem and wipes his hands on his tunic*.]

STRANGER. No doubt, no doubt. I too was at Troy and, you see . . . I'm nobody now.

ANTINOUS. That's the way to talk.

STRANGER. And you say you are kings?

ANTINOUS [*proudly*]. We will be. I am Antinous, son of the king of Eupiter.

LEOCRITES. I'm Leocrites, son of Evander.

EURYMACHUS. We're all princes of the Islands of Ithaca.

AMPHION [*simply*]. But we are not kings. Ulysses was our king.

ANTINOUS. The humble one has spoken!

PISANDER. Who remembers Ulysses?

EURYMACHUS. Quiet, my friends. Amphion says we are not kings . . . because he isn't a king. Since he has no lands or subjects, he hopes to become our king by marrying Penelope.

PISANDER. Enough. Another tyrant like Ulysses. We want no more tyrants.

ANTINOUS [*to the* STRANGER]. Death to the tyrants!

PISANDER [*advancing*]. Stop shouting and win your bet. I seem to recall that we had some purpose in coming up here.

ANTINOUS. All right, all right! You think I'm going to back down? [*He shoves the* STRANGER *aside and crosses to the door of the queen's chamber. They all move toward the door*.]

PISANDER. Don't trust your brute strength, Antinous, it's a strong door.

ANTINOUS. We'll see!

[AMPHION *glides calmly to the door and stands, with his arms crossed, beneath the lintel.*]

AMPHION. No, Antinous. We shouldn't open it.
ANTINOUS. Why? Because you say so?
AMPHION [*calmly*]. Because Penelope doesn't wish it.
ANTINOUS. And who is Penelope?
AMPHION. The woman whose wishes are law. You said it yourself.
EURYMACHUS [*intervening*]. Listen, Amphion, do you want to marry her?
AMPHION. As much as all of you.
EURYMACHUS [*indicating the chamber*]. Then don't you realize that until she finishes weaving that shroud she'll not marry any of us?
AMPHION. What of it?
LEOCRITES. We haven't seen her working today.
AMPHION. But she has worked.
ANTINOUS. I don't care! I want to see the shroud.
AMPHION. Call her so that she can show it to you here, as usual.
ANTINOUS. No. I'm tired of seeing that the shroud doesn't grow. I want to see it more closely. Move out of the way!
AMPHION [*angrily*]. Get out of here!
PISANDER. You're going to lose your bet.

[*Goaded,* ANTINOUS *grapples with* AMPHION, *trying to shove him aside.* AMPHION *pushes him away with such violence that he staggers.*]

AMPHION. Don't fight with me now. You can't even hold yourself up.
ANTINOUS [*red with anger*]. Look at him! He won't join us in our games! He won't drink! . . . But he's as anxious as any of us to force Penelope to decide. Hypocrite! I'm going to . . . [*He is so dizzy that two of them must hold him up.*]
AMPHION. Take him away and let him sleep.
EURYMACHUS. Not without seeing the queen.
PISANDER. And the slave girls . . . you're forgetting the slave girls.
LEOCRITES. I, for one, wasn't forgetting them! But Amphion, as you know, hasn't much appetite for . . . that kind of thing.

AMPHION [*violent*]. Leocrites!
LEOCRITES [*crossing toward him provokingly*]. What?

[*They all approach* AMPHION.]

Come, Amphion is calling us.
PISANDER. What?
EURYMACHUS. What do you want from Leocrites?
ANTINOUS [*still held up by* EURYMACHUS]. From all of us!

[*Short pause.* AMPHION *stares at them disdainfully. They come a little closer, threateningly. The* STRANGER, *who has remained down stage, crosses in toward them.*]

STRANGER [*casually*]. Are you too the son of a king, Amphion?
PISANDER [*bursting into a loud guffaw*]. Ha!
LEOCRITES [*laughing*]. The old man asked the question!
EURYMACHUS [*chuckling*]. He's joined our side. He knows what he's doing.

[*They all look at the* STRANGER *who smiles docilely. The group breaks up quickly. The danger that threatened* AMPHION *is past. The* STRANGER *steps in and faces him. The rest make way for him and look on with amusement.*]

AMPHION. Don't mock me, old man.
STRANGER. I didn't mean to. But you haven't named your father.
AMPHION [*bitterly*]. What business is it of yours? I'm nobody, an orphan without home or riches . . . another unfortunate like yourself.
PISANDER. I'll tell you. His father was king of Dulichaeon.
EURYMACHUS [*ironically*]. No. Say it as he does! His father was Nisos Aretiadon, a faithful vassal of Ulysses, his most devoted servant, and his best friend.

[*A silence.*]

STRANGER. I saw him fight. He was a great leader.
AMPHION [*bitterly*]. Spare me your flattery, wretch, I can't reward you.

[*The suitors smile jeeringly and the* STRANGER *shrugs his gesture of excuse.* TELEMACHUS *has appeared at the door left, his face contorted with rage.*]

TELEMACHUS. Amphion!

[*They all turn and stare at him.*]

ANTINOUS. Oh! Someone's gone and untied the cockerel!

[TELEMACHUS *crosses until he stands facing* AMPHION.]

TELEMACHUS. How many times do I have to tell you not to defend me. I know what you hope to gain by it. But I swear that I'll give my mother away to one of these thieves before I'll give her to you!
PISANDER. But for the insult, bravo!
AMPHION. Why do you hate me? I'm not to blame for your troubles.
TELEMACHUS [*angrily*]. What do you mean?
AMPHION [*softly*]. I didn't mean to upset you.
TELEMACHUS. But you have!
ANTINOUS. Scratch him, rooster, scratch him!
AMPHION. Don't set him against me.
PISANDER. Hit him!
AMPHION. Don't do it, Telemachus.
TELEMACHUS. I think I will!
LEOCRITES. Go on, rooster, peck him! He won't mind.
EURYMACHUS. Then maybe Dione will pay attention to you.
AMPHION. Eurymachus, that's enough!

[*He scarcely has time to turn and grab* TELEMACHUS' *wrist. After a moment, he forces the fist down.* TELEMACHUS *cannot suppress a gasp of pain.* PENELOPE *enters Right in time to hear it. Upon seeing her,* AMPHION *releases* TELEMACHUS *who clutches his bruised arm.* PENELOPE *advances a few steps, followed by* EURICLEA *and the* SLAVE WOMEN. *The suitors back away to the Left. The queen halts.* EURICLEA *and the slaves form in a close group to her Right.* AMPHION *remains by her chamber. The* STRANGER *stands at his Left,* TELEMACHUS *joins him. The sun has long since set and pale moonlight now lights the scene. A pause. Finally* EURYMACHUS *steps forward prepared to speak.*]

PENELOPE. No, don't speak to me. I know what you seek. As you can see, I bring them to you myself. In this way I can at least pretend that I command here.
EURYMACHUS. And you do command . . .

PENELOPE. Silence. [*Brief pause.*] You're drunk . . . like yesterday . . . like every day. That's how you vie for my hand . . . seeing who can drink the most.

PISANDER [*without breaking away from the group of suitors at Left*]. Wine is sacred, Penelope.

PENELOPE. Enough! I don't want to hear you. Spare me your sodden voices. [*Indicating the* SLAVE WOMEN.] Here they are. Well, what are you waiting for?

EURYMACHUS. That's not why we came, Your Highness.

PENELOPE. Why then?

EURYMACHUS. We didn't see you work on the shroud today.

PENELOPE [*sarcastically*]. My! You're in a hurry, aren't you? The palace is becoming poor isn't it?

EURYMACHUS. Because of us, it's true. But it's in your power to end this.

PENELOPE. I repeat what I said to you four years ago. My dear Ulysses' father is old and I will marry no one until I have woven him a shroud worthy of a hero.

EURYMACHUS. You've said it yourself, Penelope . . . we've been waiting for four years!

PENELOPE [*drily*]. You see me work all day long. I can do no more.

EURYMACHUS. Perhaps you could . . . if you wanted to.

[*Short pause.*]

PENELOPE [*flatly*]. What do you mean?

EURYMACHUS. We have sometimes seen a light here . . . at night.

PENELOPE [*quickly*]. When I can't sleep . . . I come here and breathe the pure early-morning air . . . it makes me sleepy.

EURYMACHUS. You could then . . . work at night as well.

[*Long pause.*]

PENELOPE. It's easy to say that. I spend hours at the loom, I grow weak and lose my sleep . . . because of you. And you demand more of me!

EURYMACHUS. We beg more of you. [*Pause.*]

PENELOPE. Do you want me to start tonight?

EURYMACHUS. Why not?

PENELOPE. I'll do it. But, of course, you know I'll need help. . . . Leave the slave women with me.

[*The suitors look at each other, unable to make up their minds. She laughs. Suddenly,* LEOCRITES *crosses over and grabs the* 2ND SLAVE *by the arm.*]

LEOCRITES [*as he returns to stage Left with her*]. Weave some other night.

[PISANDER *follows* LEOCRITES' *example with the* 1ST SLAVE *as he says*:]

PISANDER. Yes, Queen, some other night.

[PENELOPE *continues laughing.* ANTINOUS *crosses and takes the* 3RD SLAVE.]

PENELOPE [*as* ANTINOUS *returns to his place*]. Kill another pig tonight! Drink another skin-full of wine. There is still some left! [*She laughs.*]

EURYMACHUS [*with a sigh*]. Forgive them. They are very impatient.

PENELOPE [*hard*]. Take yours!

[EURYMACHUS *holds out his hand and the* 4TH SLAVE, *timid, her head down, passes beneath the reproving glance of the queen and crosses to him.*]

PISANDER. May the Gods watch over your sleep, Your Highness. [*He begins to move off.*]

ANTINOUS [*chiming in foolishly*]. And don't be jealous . . . they're just slave women . . .

PENELOPE [*contemptuously*]. Jealous? Go on, take them away. Instruct them. Teach them . . . a new rhapsody to sing to me while I work.

EURYMACHUS [*puzzled*]. A new rhapsody?

PENELOPE [*laughing*]. Why not? In that way you can help me to weave. It would be a pleasant way of spending your nights . . . with them. The rhapsody they chant now is crude and ugly. They become bored. [*Accusingly.*] They begin talking about other things and neglect their work.

[*The* SLAVE WOMEN *exchange glances of embarrassment.*]

ANTINOUS [*not aware that she is joking*]. Writing poetry is such low work.

PENELOPE. And, of course, you're so high and noble. Very well, don't do it. Now, go away!

[*The* SUITORS *salute her and leave with the slave women.*]

EURYMACHUS [*before leaving, in a kind tone*]. We'll leave them for you one of these nights so you can work. I promise you. [*He leaves with his slave woman. Pause.*]

STRANGER. I'll compose your rhapsody, my Queen. I think I know what you need.

PENELOPE [*surprised*]. You?

STRANGER. Men in my position must know how to do everything.

PENELOPE. We shall see . . . now, you may go.

STRANGER. Since I don't know the way to Eumaeus' hut, I was waiting . . .

PENELOPE. Telemachus.

[TELEMACHUS *had gone over to* DIONE *the minute she was left alone and has been pleading with her in whispers. She has paid no attention to him. His mother's voice startles him.*]

PENELOPE. Go lead the stranger to Eumaeus' hut. [TELEMACHUS *hesitates.*] Why are you waiting?

TELEMACHUS [*sullenly*]. I'm going, Mother. I'm always going . . . [*Crosses the stage.*]

STRANGER [*bowing before he leaves with* TELEMACHUS.] My thanks for your hospitality, Queen. May the night be kind to you.

[*He leaves with* TELEMACHUS. *Pause.* PENELOPE *goes toward* AMPHION *and then turns back to* DIONE, *looking from one to the other.*]

PENELOPE [*daring*]. You may take her . . . Only Dione is left.

[*Hopefully,* DIONE *advances a few steps and waits anxiously.*]

AMPHION. No, my Queen. I prefer to devote my nights to the low work of the poet . . . thinking of you.

PENELOPE [*triumphant*]. Get back to the women's quarters, Dione. [*The* SLAVE *does so with a gesture of disappointment.* PENELOPE *turns back to* AMPHION *smiling and flattered.*] All your nights?

AMPHION. Every night of my life, Your Highness. You asked them for something in jest . . . but I could see how you suffered wishing they were otherwise. [*The* QUEEN *holds her hands out to him.*] I'll compose your rhapsody.

[*He kisses her hands and leaves rapidly. A pause.* PENELOPE *closes her eyes and passes the backs of her hands over her cheeks in a gesture that is half emotion, half dream. Later she turns to* EURICLEA *who is hunched over, still, as though stunned.*]

PENELOPE [*surprised*]. What's the matter? [She *crosses to her and grabs her arms.*] What's wrong with you?

EURICLEA. I'm afraid!

PENELOPE. Because they spoke of the light they see here at night? They're not very clever. They don't investigate anything. [*She turns to her chamber and takes out the key.*]

EURICLEA. My lady . . . what do you weave into Laertes' shroud?

PENELOPE [*softly*]. Things.

EURICLEA. What things?

PENELOPE [*a note of warning in her voice*]. Euriclea!

EURICLEA. I only want to help you, Penelope. Why do you laugh and cry as you weave? [*A short pause.*]

PENELOPE [*she lowers her head*]. Ulysses is late. [*With sudden resolution she opens the door. Exalted.*] He waits, waits too long. He can wait forever!

EURICLEA. Madam!

PENELOPE. Widow! Why don't you call me widow? That mad widow who weaves her cloth while the country goes to rack and ruin! She's a madwoman who prefers her memories to a sensible betrothal, isn't that so?

EURICLEA. I never said that . . .

PENELOPE. But it's been said by others and you agree. It hasn't been so long since you told me that not even Artemis herself would condemn me if I were to take a new husband.

EURICLEA [*with fear*]. I say that no longer, my lady. No, no, not now! I said so then because the palace was being stripped, but . . .

PENELOPE. And what of it? I'm not to blame. If the Achaean army has been bleeding itself to death for years . . . what does it matter if we shed the blood of a few flocks of sheep? If we are forced to give up our husbands while we're still young and if we are forced to assume all the responsibilities of the household [*With infinite hatred.*] . . .

and all because some fool stole a little whore from another fool . . . who is to blame for all these miseries? Answer me!

EURICLEA. They made him leave. Don't blame Ulysses.

PENELOPE. Who's talking of Ulysses! It's Helen! That little trollop, that whore! Twenty years ago she took it into her head to smile at a man who was not her husband . . . and off went all the chieftains of Greece! There was nothing we could do to stop them.

EURICLEA. Agamemnon threatened them and they had to go . . .

PENELOPE. And on his return, his own wife killed him! She revenged us all.

EURICLEA [*horrified*]. But you wouldn't do a thing like that?

PENELOPE. No. [*With sad irony.*] I'm the faithful Penelope . . . the prudent wife of the not less prudent Ulysses. If he came back we'd all have prudence enough, and to spare. Don't worry. [*She approaches the bow that hangs on the side of the door and looks at it.*] No. I wouldn't kill him. [*She turns back.*] Do you think he'll return, Nurse? [*She shakes her head sadly while she waits for the* NURSE'S *reply*].

EURICLEA [*hesitatingly*]. I don't know.

PENELOPE [*touching the bow*]. His bow reminds me of him. It's strong and supple . . . just as he was. It was with this bow that he won me. In order to avoid quarrels, my father organized a contest for my suitors. Oh yes, Nurse, I had suitors then too. They were twenty of the most handsome princes in the realm. My father said, "He who draws this bow and hits the mark will win her." And Ulysses won. There were stronger than he . . . but this bow will not be mastered by strength alone. It requires skillful hands. [*Pause.*] My good fortune turned out to be somewhat bitter. [*Sighs.*] Well, to work. Close the door. [*She pushes the* NURSE *gently toward the door at Left.* EURICLEA *crosses and throws the bolt as the* QUEEN *watches.*]

EURICLEA [*upon returning*]. Penelope, if they knew that you'd been cheating them for years . . . Penelope, don't unweave the cloth tonight!

PENELOPE [*somberly*]. I have to. [*Short pause.*]

EURICLEA. Are you going to light the candles?

PENELOPE. No. I can see the threads by the moonlight.

EURICLEA. That's good. They mustn't suspect.

PENELOPE [*with pain*]. That's not it, Euriclea. I don't want to see the figures I'm unweaving. [*She is about to enter the chamber when she is again arrested by the almost paralyzed attitude of the* NURSE.] What is the matter tonight? [*She approaches her.*] What! Crying! You . . . crying? You?

EURICLEA. I haven't wept in twenty years . . . fate must be crying through my dead eyes.

[*In a kind way,* PENELOPE *leads her to the door of the chamber and places her at her post, where she was at the opening of the act.*]

PENELOPE [*sadly*]. While life weeps from mine, Euriclea . . . the life I never lived. [*Not yet ready to enter her chamber.*] Because my whole life has been one everlasting unraveling. Weave and dream . . . and then to wake up at night, to awaken from the weaving and the dreaming . . . unraveling! [*A sudden change.*] Damn, damn Helen! May the Gods destroy her!

[*The* NURSE *falls to her knees crying pitifully and in silence.*]

CURTAIN

ACT TWO

[*It is night. The curtains between the arches are still drawn. The door to the chamber is closed. The stage is empty and lit by moonlight. The door at Left creaks open and* EURYMACHUS *enters cautiously with the* STRANGER, *who no longer carries his walking stick. When they have made sure that there is no one about they run to the door of the* QUEEN'S *chamber.*]

EURYMACHUS. It's always locked.

STRANGER. Women love secrets.

EURYMACHUS. Bah! The designs that only Death can look upon! Nonsense!

STRANGER. Exactly. Women's nonsense.

EURYMACHUS. Where will you hide?

STRANGER. Leave that to me. I have my plan.

EURYMACHUS. What a fox you've become! Where's your lair?

STRANGER. Where would you hide?

EURYMACHUS [*looking about*]. In the hall of the women's quarters.

STRANGER. A bad place.

EURYMACHUS. I see no other.

STRANGER. There's another.

EURYMACHUS. Where?

STRANGER. That's simple, look. [*He crosses to the balustrade at Left and pulls the curtain nearest the* QUEEN'S *chamber.*] See. The torches from the courtyard don't shine this far.

EURYMACHUS. And?

STRANGER. I'll be in the gallery and yet I won't. [*He straddles the balustrade, his back against the side of the* QUEEN'S *chamber.*] I'll hide myself with the curtain. [*He hides and reappears.*] What do you think?

EURYMACHUS. They'll notice your legs.

STRANGER. When necessary I'll hold on to the outside border of the balustrade. [*He draws up his legs and does so.*]

EURYMACHUS. You'll fall.

STRANGER. No. I'm still strong. [*He jumps back into the gallery.*]

EURYMACHUS. What if someone draws the curtain?

STRANGER. That's a risk I must take.

EURYMACHUS. Perfect. [*Slapping him on the back.*] We'll pay you well for this.

STRANGER. Thanks. Now, leave me alone. The women will be here any moment.

EURYMACHUS. Once more, now . . . keep your eyes open and tell us everything you see.

STRANGER. I mean to.

EURYMACHUS. We'll play a trick tonight. Since opening doors is one of your skills, be ready to open that door when you hear us coming up the stairs.

STRANGER. Well, now! This is something new.

EURYMACHUS. I thought of it just now when I saw where you were hiding. This door opens easily, all you have to do is to pull the bolt. If our first plan fails, jump out quickly and open the door.

STRANGER. What plan?

EURYMACHUS. Don't ask so many questions, you'll see soon enough. If it fails, we'll tap at the door and you let us in. Agreed?

STRANGER. Agreed.

EURYMACHUS. Well, I leave you then . . . [*Starts out.*]

STRANGER. Be still! [EURYMACHUS *stops and looks at him. The* STRANGER *peeks through the curtains.*] Telemachus has just come into the courtyard. Hurry.

EURYMACHUS. A keen ear.

STRANGER. That's my trade.

EURYMACHUS. Hide!

[*He leaves. The* STRANGER *looks out through the curtains. Suddenly he turns and listens.* DIONE *enters at Right, looking backwards as she walks. She crosses to the queen's chamber and rattles the door violently. The* STRANGER *ducks and, presently, crosses to his hiding place.* TELEMACHUS *enters Left. He watches* DIONE *and then runs to her side.* DIONE *utters a little scream.*]

TELEMACHUS. Dione! [*He embraces her passionately.*]

DIONE [*struggling with him*]. Leave me alone!

TELEMACHUS. No, I can't. I can't!

DIONE [*angry. Hitting him*]. You can't? Well, why not?

TELEMACHUS. Because I love you . . .

DIONE. Well, I don't love you . . . and you know it. Now let go of me! [*She gives him a violent shove and breaks loose.*] You're not even able to hold on to a woman!

TELEMACHUS [*panting*]. What were you doing at that door?

DIONE. Does it matter to you?

TELEMACHUS [*grabbing her by the arm*]. What did you want in there?

DIONE. Let go! [*She breaks away once more.*]

TELEMACHUS. There's nothing in there . . . only the shroud.

DIONE. And something else!

TELEMACHUS. Something else?

DIONE. Yes! The figures in the shroud.

TELEMACHUS. Bah! Female nonsense.

DIONE. Nonsense? Then why does she laugh and sigh when she's weaving? And why does she moan at night [*Stressing the words.*] . . . when she unravels?

TELEMACHUS. What?

DIONE. Didn't you know? [*Short pause.*]

TELEMACHUS. If it's true, you should keep it to yourself. Because it means that . . . she is putting off the suitors . . . to give my father time to return.

DIONE. Idiot! It's just a question of indecision. She's a poor woman who doesn't know how to be queen. And she's afraid of love. Her laughter and her moaning fool no one! They mean love!

TELEMACHUS. Dione!

DIONE. Oh, but I'll force her to make up her mind. I'll force her to stop dreaming and make her pick the man she loves. You look away! . . . You're as weak as she is. You don't like to face the truth, you'd rather dream, as your mother does . . . only you dream of the impossible return of a dead man.

TELEMACHUS. My father lives!

DIONE. He's dead and *she* knows only too well. It's not Ulysses *she* dreams of . . . no. You know who she dreams of . . . it's Amphion!

TELEMACHUS [*confused*]. You . . . you love Amphion.

DIONE. What of it?

TELEMACHUS. I don't understand . . . why you want my mother to choose him.

DIONE [*scornfully*]. What do you know about anything?

[*Short pause.*]

TELEMACHUS [*exploding*]. What kind of snake are you? What are you plotting? [*She laughs. His tone changes.*] All right, don't tell me anything . . . but take pity. I can't live without you. Someday this palace will be mine. I'm the prince. Tomorrow it will all be yours, if you want it.

DIONE [*laughing*]. I am higher than that.

TELEMACHUS [*grabbing her brutally*]. You'll be mine whether you like it or not! Mine!

DIONE. Let go!

TELEMACHUS. Mine!

DIONE. You're nothing! I laugh at you! [*She struggles.*] Let me go!

[AMPHION *enters at Left. When he sees them he halts.* DIONE *breaks away and runs to him.*] Amphion! [*She flings her arms around his neck and glances back at* TELEMACHUS *out of the corner of her eyes.*]

AMPHION. It's very late, Telemachus. You should be sleeping.

TELEMACHUS. Don't play father with me! I have one father, one only! And he's alive!

AMPHION. Your mother will be here soon . . . she won't like finding you here.

TELEMACHUS [*clenching his fists*]. We'll meet again tonight! By all the Gods, I promise you! [*He leaves quickly at Left.*]

DIONE [*weeping*]. Thanks, my Lord. [*She tries to kneel.*]

AMPHION [*preventing her*]. Get up.

DIONE. He hounds me all the time. He's a beastly, repulsive little boy. I can't love him. But he's threatened you! I don't want him to harm you . . . because of me. [*Putting her arms around him.*]

AMPHION [*coolly as he breaks away from her*]. He won't hurt me. And now, please, tell Penelope I'm here. I must speak with her.

[DIONE *steps back a few steps and looks at him with curiosity.*]

DIONE. Yes . . . you're right. You must force her.

AMPHION. What do you mean?

DIONE. She doesn't know how to be queen. She lets them squander away her riches while she hides away in there . . . [*She points to the chamber.*] . . . to dream. [*A pause. She moves toward* AMPHION, *feline.*] To dream of you, Amphion. [AMPHION *is startled.*] Yes, Amphion. Yes. It's you she loves. But she hasn't the courage to elect you. She thinks of you during the day when she's weaving . . . and at night, too . . . when she unravels.

[AMPHION *is, once more, surprised. A short pause.*]

AMPHION. Why do you tell me this?

DIONE. I want to serve you.

AMPHION [*doubtful*]. I don't believe you. If the queen had loved me, as you say, she would have chosen me.

DIONE. She's uncertain, she doesn't dare. She's a coward. [*Brief pause.*] This palace needs a man to set it to rights. A little courage and you'll be that man.

AMPHION [*utterly confused*]. But she hasn't chosen me.

DIONE [*exasperated*]. I know she hasn't! You've got to make up her mind for her! Her heart has ripened . . . just for you.

AMPHION [*backing away instinctively and distrustful*]. I don't understand your game.

DIONE. You know that . . . I love you, don't you? [*She approaches him.*] I'll tell you my little game. Because I love you and I know that you're sensible. I'll tell you. [*She takes a few more steps until she is standing close to him.*] This house also needs a woman to manage it. She doesn't know how and Euriclea's old. I'm a slave . . . I'm your slave body and soul. I'd give you anything you asked of me! Everything! [AMPHION *moves slightly.*] I know! I know that she's the one you love. That's why you should take her, such as she is . . . [*With increasing scorn.*] . . . weak at heart and incapable of managing the affairs of the palace . . . a dreamer. Let her be your delight, the woman that's worshiped but from whom nothing is expected. . . . But you should be the man of the house and you'll need a real woman to stand by your side. I am the only one who can be the true mistress of this house . . . once you are its master. [AMPHION *turns his back to her with a vague gesture.*] Now do you understand my little game? Well, then there's only one more thing for me to say. [*Emphati-*

cally.] Our game should be played soon . . . if there's to be anything left for us to rule.

AMPHION [*facing her*]. Those last words destroyed everything. [*Smiling.*] You're careless.

DIONE. How like a man! You're blind! Don't you understand? I don't want to be cautious . . . with you. [*She approaches him, frightened, and in a movement of surrender.*]

AMPHION. You are deceiving yourself. If you ever saw yourself as you are you couldn't stand living with yourself.

DIONE [*moving away angrily*]. I hate you!

AMPHION. Not really. It's just spite. [PENELOPE *appears at Right.*] Go tell your mistress I'm here.

PENELOPE [*coming on*]. That won't be necessary. What were you doing here Dione?

DIONE [*looking from one to the other, she spits out her words*]. Spying! I came to see if the door would open so that I could look at the figures on the shroud.

PENELOPE. Dione!

DIONE. Beat me! Have me punished at once! [*Short pause.*]

PENELOPE. Get inside. . . . And tell Euriclea and the rest of them to come to work . . . but not right away.

DIONE [*desperate*]. Punish me!

PENELOPE [*calmly*]. Go inside. [*With a moan of impotence,* DIONE *runs off Right. Pause.*] It's strange . . . I came out hoping to find you here . . . I don't know why. And here you are . . . [*Short pause.*] . . . with Dione.

AMPHION. Beware of that woman, Your Highness.

PENELOPE. She is insolent, often, but I don't want to punish her. It's not important.

AMPHION. Your Highness is too kind.

PENELOPE. Your Highness, Your Highness! Call me by name. I am just a simple woman. The queen of Ithaca, yes, but what is Ithaca? A poor and dismembered kingdom. I'm nobody. I no longer rule . . . not even among my slaves . . . and not even in there, when I'm weaving, do I rule . . . over myself.

AMPHION [*hesitatingly*]. Are you going to unravel tonight?

PENELOPE [*surprised*]. What?

AMPHION. Don't ask me to tell you how I learned of it. Accusations disgust me. But if it's true, be careful. I've come to warn you. They're plotting against you. Perhaps even tonight. They haven't gone to bed yet.

PENELOPE. I suspected as much. They left the slave women with me tonight. They won't surprise me . . . I'll lock the door.

AMPHION. Then, you do unweave.

PENELOPE. It's a trick . . . a trick to discourage the suitors . . . [*Then anxiously.*] . . . the other suitors, Amphion.

AMPHION [*coolly*]. Isn't it easier to have done with it?

PENELOPE [*warmly*]. Do you want me to?

AMPHION. I will always want what you want . . . Penelope.

PENELOPE. What a lovely phrase.

AMPHION [*annoyed*]. I meant it!

PENELOPE. And almost feminine. Something I'd like to say myself. It has such a pleasant sound. . . . Eurymachus, I will always want . . . No. I doesn't go with Eurymachus. [*Thinking.*] Nor with Antinous, nor with . . . No, no.

AMPHION. Penelope . . .

PENELOPE. Please, be still. Let me see . . . Amphion, I will always want what you want . . . [*She waits, looking at him out of the corners of her eyes.*]

AMPHION [*bitterly*]. A moving phrase which is, nonetheless, insincere.

PENELOPE [*hurt*]. If you say so . . .

AMPHION [*the words burst out*]. It couldn't be sincere! Don't be cruel, don't play games with me. What have I done to you?

PENELOPE. Amphion!

AMPHION. You could choose but you don't choose. You could finish the shroud but you unravel it at night. It appears that you love none of us. I'm a man, I can reason things out. If you can choose but prefer to mock us and discourage us . . .

PENELOPE [*coldly*]. Are you, too, discouraged?

AMPHION [*bitterly*]. I'll wait, without hope, as long as you wish.

PENELOPE. I thank you. But didn't you tell me that you were a man and knew how to reason? What else do you think?

AMPHION [*slowly*]. That if you can choose but prefer to deceive us with that shroud . . . there's only one explanation.

PENELOPE. Which is?

AMPHION. That you love Ulysses and mean to wait for him the rest of your life.

PENELOPE. How well you men think! There's no doubt! Perfect reasoning! You amaze me!

AMPHION. I didn't mean to anger you.

PENELOPE [*violently*]. You're leaving tomorrow, aren't you?

AMPHION [*alarmed*]. Why?

PENELOPE. To follow your line of reason . . . you know that I deceive you by unweaving. Your hopes are destroyed. I love Ulysses and you're too good to take me by force. Your reason should advise you to leave the field of battle.

AMPHION. I won't go!

PENELOPE [*ironically*]. Why not?

AMPHION. Because . . . because . . . Oh, enough! [*He turns to go.*]

PENELOPE. Wait! [*Cowed by the tone of her voice, he halts and looks at her.*] Not yet. [*Gently.*] I'm ten years older than you. You remind me of a little boy whose favorite toy has been broken . . . the toy of reason. We women don't know how to reason . . . but we dream. And now I should tell you of the dreams I have in there . . . many things. You should know them.

AMPHION. I?

PENELOPE [*somewhat impatiently*]. Yes, you. [*Then, once more, in a kindly tone.*] You. . . . Come closer. [AMPHION *does so.*] Helen stole our husbands. Because of that . . . that sow, we honest women have become widows, condemned to weaving and winding our lives away in our cold homes. We were condemned to die of shame and anger because the men . . . reasoned . . . and decided that, in order to avenge the honor of a poor idiot called Menelaus, it was necessary to spill blood in a war that lasted ten years. [*Pause.*] That's what I thought. But when you came to sue for my hand. Oh, how free I breathed! While thirty young chieftains, now old or dead, were leading our armies in Troy . . . because of Helen . . . thirty young chieftains, sons, many of them, of the other thirty, came to contend for me. For me, Penelope! Not for Helen, no! But for Penelope! [*Pause.*] That was my consolation prize . . . my little Trojan War. I came to life again. I had to make this war of mine last as long as it could, by whatever means I could think of. This war healed my wounded pride, it confirmed my own existence in a way that I hadn't known . . . since Ulysses won me from the other nineteen princes, many years ago.

AMPHION. Penelope . . .

PENELOPE. You see, you see I confess everything to you. That's why I began the shroud: because I was still waiting for Ulysses . . . yes. But above all because I wanted to hear your fights; because I, an honest woman, wanted to feel a little like Helen and see you down in that courtyard fighting for me. Because I wanted to convince myself that, if there were men capable of leaving us like a poor slave, there were others willing to worship us like a young and beautiful queen. [*Pause.*] Because I didn't want you to leave and because I didn't want to choose either. That's why I began the shroud. [*A somber pause.*] Twenty-five of you have already left. They were the most impatient, the ones who came to win a rich kingdom by marrying its queen. When they saw the signs of poverty they gave up. [*Bitterly.*] They didn't love me! [*Short pause.*] And four of those that are left do not love me either. But they're stubborn. They compete with one another to see which one backs down first and gives up the prize: a kingdom without riches and a woman . . . who . . . is growing old.

AMPHION. They couldn't be thinking that.

PENELOPE. Why? Because you don't? I assure you they do. They think of it. You are the only one . . . who doesn't entertain himself with the slave girls, because you are the only one who thinks of me as being young. But I'm not young, Amphion . . .

AMPHION. You are the most beautiful and the best of all women.

PENELOPE [*melancholy*]. And I'm not good either. You should know that, after what I've told you.

AMPHION. I see nothing evil in it.

PENELOPE. Really? You understand it and forgive . . . you alone. [*Lowering her voice.*] It's because of you that I make the others wait.

AMPHION [*pleading*]. Penelope, don't make me believe that . . .

PENELOPE. Be still! I don't know how to reason and ideas have a way of escaping me. While we weave and sew, we women think without rhyme or reason. And, at the high pitch of our work, excited without thinking, we put into our embroidery and our weaving some of the things that we dream of. [*Short pause.*] For four years I've told myself . . . Helen has beaten me. My Trojan War is repugnant. They don't want me, nor are they capable of fighting for me. The ones who remain are the least ambitious of all. They would be satisfied with the crumbs. They'd turn this kingdom into a colony and take me off to their islands.

There's only one who loves me, only one who would accept poverty at my side. Only that orphan boy would stay here with me. He's not in a hurry . . . because, where the others see me older than I am, he finds me forever young. [*Changing her tone.*] But if I choose him . . . the one who stands alone who has no followers to defend him . . . they'd kill him!

AMPHION. Penelope! [*He tries to embrace her.*]

PENELOPE [*backs away and holds him at arm's length*]. So I scheme and scheme in there . . . trying to think of the necessary stratagem, the effective trick that will save his life. Since he is so gentle and peaceloving that he can't fight against them . . . I decided to let them rob me of everything. That's why I unweave every night. A widow who no longer thinks of Ulysses . . . [AMPHION *kneels and kisses her hands.*] . . . because I don't know how to reason!

[AMPHION *puts his arms around her legs.*]

AMPHION. Forgive me, my Queen.

PENELOPE. No, no! Leave me. Get up. [*She breaks away and goes upstage close to the* STRANGER'S *hiding place.* AMPHION *rises.*] They're upset because I won't show them the figures on the shroud. I pretend that only Death can look upon those figures. Nevertheless, they're not so frightening, nor are they very clear. However, they are much too intimate. So much so that only someone . . . very close to me . . . could tell what they were and what they meant. Made as they are in the heat of my weaver's anguish . . . they're like myself. They're . . . my dreams. My dreams which I must unravel at night in order that, someday, I may realize them. [*She looks at him meaningfully.*] That's why I'm ashamed of showing them. It would be like showing myself naked . . . [*She lowers her head.*] If you wish, I . . . I'll show them to you. [*Short pause.*] But, no, no don't ask me! [*Flirting.*] No, Amphion, you shouldn't ask me! [*She waits for him to ask her.* AMPHION *approaches her, respectfully, his eyes downcast.*]

AMPHION. No. I have no right. [PENELOPE *is unable to disguise her disappointment.*] I don't deserve such intimacy. [*He kneels and kisses her tunic.*]

PENELOPE [*sadly, stroking his hair*]. You deserve it all . . . all.

AMPHION. I'm weak and a coward, you're right. Misfortune and being an orphan have made me what I am. I didn't dare to believe . . . Nor was I able to think of a way to rid you of those four. Now I must bear the shame of hearing what you have done for me. Forgive me. I can only fight with my fists, in the open . . .

PENELOPE. Because you're good . . . better than I am.

AMPHION. I'll challenge them!

PENELOPE. No! I don't want them to harm you. Let things take their course . . . and don't feel ashamed. You've brought me back to life.

AMPHION. Penelope!

PENELOPE. Sh! The slave women. [*They move apart.* EURICLEA *and the* SLAVES *enter carrying their baskets of yarn, skeins, and distaffs. Next to* EURICLEA *is the* 1ST SLAVE *carrying a burning taper. When* PENELOPE *speaks again it is in her imperious manner.*] Euriclea, light the chamber . . . and you, sit down.

[*The* SLAVES *seat themselves on the steps and arrange their things.* EURICLEA *opens the chamber with the key, which is now in her possession; she takes the taper from the* 1ST SLAVE, *enters the chamber, finds the candelabrum, and lights it. During this the* 1ST SLAVE *joins the others. When* EURICLEA *is done, she comes to the side of the door and takes her place. Meanwhile:*]

AMPHION. Do you want me to stay and defend you? It may be necessary.

PENELOPE. I'll manage.

AMPHION. I don't feel easy about it. [*He goes to the curtains near the place where the* STRANGER *is hidden.* PENELOPE *follows him.* DIONE, *who is seated at Left, never takes her eyes off of them.*] No, they'd see me from here because of the moon. [*He goes to the other side of the chamber which is darker.* PENELOPE *follows him with concern.* AMPHION *parts the curtain at Right. He is hidden by the shadow of the queen's chamber.*] They are in the courtyard and are looking in this direction. [*He turns back.*] Let me stay!

PENELOPE [*gently*]. It can't be. They'd hate you more than ever.

[AMPHION *starts out Left with* PENELOPE *at his side. Before going he tries to kiss her hands but she stops him, indicating with a glance that they are not alone.* DIONE *pretends not to look.*]

AMPHION [*solicitously*]. Keep the door locked.

PENELOPE. I will. [AMPHION *goes out and* PENELOPE *watches him from the door as he descends the stairs.*]

DIONE [*rises and approaches the* QUEEN]. Shall I close the door? [*Her manner is humble, as though she were asking forgiveness for her former impertinence.*]

PENELOPE [*thoughtfully*]. That's not necessary . . . I'll do it.

[*Stung,* DIONE *returns to her place.*]

EURICLEA. The room is ready, Penelope. [*The* QUEEN *closes the door and sighs then crosses slowly to the chamber. When she comes to* EURICLEA, PENELOPE *puts a hand on her shoulder as though she meant to say something.* EURICLEA *turns expectantly.* PENELOPE *lets her hand drop and starts to go through the door.*] Do you need yarn, my Lady?

PENELOPE [*undecided, she looks at the* SLAVE WOMEN]. No, not yet. For the time being . . . let them sing something for me. [*A short pause. Unable to make herself enter the room.*] I don't know what's wrong with me . . . I should be happy . . . instead I feel a deep sadness.

EURICLEA. It's the night.

PENELOPE. That must be it. [*She goes in and sits behind the loom.*]

EURICLEA [*to herself*]. It's the night. The night lends itself to deceit and horror . . . I too am sad. It's fitting to be sad at night, the Gods want it that way. [*Pause.*]

PENELOPE [*inside, moaning*]. Oh, Nurse . . .

EURICLEA. Patience, my lamb, patience.

[*The* SLAVES *who had been still now stir about to abate their fears. Finally they burst out.*]

3RD SLAVE. Nurse, I'm afraid.

4TH SLAVE. Nurse, doesn't the queen want some green wool?

1ST SLAVE. And some yellow wool, too, Nurse?

EURICLEA [*harshly*]. Be quiet. You heard her say she didn't want any.

2ND SLAVE. I'm afraid.

PENELOPE'S VOICE. Tell them to sing.

EURICLEA. The rhapsody?

PENELOPE'S VOICE. No, something else. The words of the rhapsody wouldn't be appropriate tonight. Let them sing the song without words.

2ND SLAVE. Oh, no! That's worse.

EURICLEA. Silence! Begin at once. [*Frightened, the* SLAVES *look at one another and begin humming quaveringly. There is a pause after the opening during which we hear* PENELOPE'S *moan once more. The song is resumed and continues sad and plaintive and more and more quaveringly.* DIONE *rises quietly and crosses to the door Left. The* SLAVE WOMEN *look at her with fear, the song goes out of tune, and almost dies out.*] What's wrong? [DIONE *gestures for them to say nothing.*]

2ND SLAVE. Nothing, Nurse . . .

4TH SLAVE [*almost in tears*]. Nothing . . .

PENELOPE'S VOICE. Euriclea, why have they stopped singing?

[DIONE *freezes.*]

EURICLEA. I don't know, Lady.

PENELOPE'S VOICE. Is there something wrong?

EURICLEA [*hesitantly*]. I don't think so, my Lady.

PENELOPE. Is the door locked?

EURICLEA [*anxiously*]. You locked it yourself, didn't you?

PENELOPE [*reassured*]. Yes, of course. Tell them to continue.

EURICLEA [*to the* SLAVES]. Continue. [DIONE *makes violent gestures of affirmation. The song is quaveringly resumed. Keeping an eye on* EURICLEA *who seems restless,* DIONE *draws the bolt and opens the door noiselessly. The song has become more strident and haunting as though the* SLAVE WOMEN, *drawn on by its rhythm, had no other means of expressing their fear.* DIONE *returns to her place immediately and joins in the singing. The singing takes on a darker quality. It is no less anguished than before but it now seems to be suspenseful as well.* EURICLEA'S *ragged voice cuts through the song.*] Lady!

PENELOPE'S VOICE [*wearily*]. Don't bother me . . .

EURICLEA. My Lady! The Furies! They're coming . . . I hear them!

PENELOPE'S VOICE. Be still and they won't bother us! [*Pause. The four* SUITORS *enter at Left, tiptoeing, and signaling the* SLAVES *not to give them away. Protected by the loud singing, the* SUITORS *cross toward* EURICLEA. *The song reaches its peak and stops, suddenly, as the* SUITORS *come near the* NURSE.]

EURICLEA. You've stopped again? What's the matter? What is it? [*She moves like a blind animal that senses danger.*

Her features contract. Before she can scream, ANTINOUS *and* EURYMACHUS *grab her and cover her mouth. The* SLAVE WOMEN *jump up in terror and gather in a group at Down Right.* DIONE, *however, remains standing in her place. The* SUITORS *come to the door and look in. After a while they look at each other and nod as though agreeing upon a verdict.*]

PENELOPE'S VOICE. Euriclea, why have they stopped singing? Are they frightened again?

EURYMACHUS. Don't unweave any more, Penelope.

[PENELOPE *screams, snuffs the candelabrum and comes to the door. The* STRANGER *crawls out of his hiding place and moves down stage.* ANTINOUS *and* EURYMACHUS *release* EURICLEA, *who crosses sobbing to the door Left.*]

PENELOPE [*blocking the door to the chamber with her arms*]. Stay out!

ANTINOUS. So you were cheating us, eh?

EURYMACHUS. Your little game is over, my Queen.

PENELOPE. Don't come in!

PISANDER. Why should we? We've already seen you unweaving. At that rate you'd never finish.

LEOCRITES. You're still waiting for Ulysses.

EURYMACHUS. Come, admit that you've been unraveling.

ANTINOUS. And cheating us.

PENELOPE. I admit everything . . . but stay out of here!

EURYMACHUS. That's not necessary, Queen. You've lost your game.

[PENELOPE *closes the door with the key which had been in the lock and which she now hides rapidly.*]

PENELOPE. Yes. I've lost my game. What of it?

PISANDER. He who loses must pay.

PENELOPE. And what must I pay?

EURICLEA [*from the balustrade at Left*]. Lady! I hear swords in the courtyard!

PENELOPE. What? [*Followed by the* SUITORS, *she goes to the balustrade and draws the curtains. The* SUITORS *draw the curtains all the way and look down.*] Telemachus! Amphion! [*This time she calls him.*] Amphion!

TELEMACHUS [*from a distance*]. Don't run away, you coward!

[PENELOPE *turns and faces the door and waits anxiously. The* SUITORS *return to the center of the stage.*]

PISANDER [*to* EURYMACHUS]. It would have been nice if Telemachus had . . . [*He makes a gesture of skewering with a sword.*] . . . eh?

EURYMACHUS. The two of them, the two of them.

[AMPHION *enters panting, sword in hand.* TELEMACHUS, *in the same fashion, follows close on his heels.*]

AMPHION. Forgive me, Queen. He provoked me.

TELEMACHUS. Coward! [*He strikes and* AMPHION *parries with his sword.*]

PENELOPE. Drop those swords! [AMPHION *does so.*] Did you hear me, Telemachus? [TELEMACHUS *throws his sword down with an angry gesture.*] How well you protect me! The two of you! . . . How clever you've been, gentlemen! And ladies! You women . . . betraying me and opening the door. You, Euriclea, who can make out footsteps that aren't even real . . . caught . . . caught like a little stupid and gagged. [*To* TELEMACHUS.] You . . . picking fights . . . I don't want to know what unmentionable motives you had! [*To* AMPHION.] And you . . . while the others set their trap for me . . . amused yourself trying to kill my son!

AMPHION. I would never have killed him.

PENELOPE. Be quiet. Quiet all of you, or I'll throw myself into the courtyard . . . and end, once and for all, the disgraceful life you force upon me.

TELEMACHUS. Mother, I . . .

PENELOPE. I . . . I can't stand to listen to you. Your voices, your faces, all this misery . . . you're destroying me. It's all one horrible gloom . . .

ANTINOUS. Queen, we . . .

PENELOPE. Out of here! Out! You and you! All of you! [*She crosses Right in a wild passion. She turns with a scream that ends in sobbing.*] Out! Leave me alone!

EURYMACHUS. We are going, Your Highness. [*Short pause.*] As soon as we come to a definite decision about your marriage.

LEOCRITES. Then you won't have to jump into the courtyard.

ANTINOUS. What you need is a man. You should choose among us now.

PISANDER. Just as though you'd finished the shroud. [*Pause.*]
PENELOPE [*gloomily*]. Leave me alone.
LEOCRITES. No. You've got to choose.
PENELOPE. Now?
ANTINOUS. Yes. Now.

[PENELOPE *steps forward looking at them. Her look of despair begins to give way to one of craftiness.*]

PENELOPE. What will the rejected suitors do then?
ANTINOUS. Go away. [*Crowing.*] If, for example, you chose me . . .
PISANDER. Ah? Easy, easy!
LEOCRITES. Hold your tongue!
PENELOPE [*slowly*]. I'm thinking of it . . . yes. Perhaps I'll elect you, Antinous. [ANTINOUS *swells with insolent pride. The other suitors prick up their ears and close in.*] But look at them! You know what they're like . . . those faces bode no good. I'm not so sure they'd forgive you . . . for my choice. [*The* SUITORS *look at each other and, instinctively, form in a group, leaving* ANTINOUS *by himself, facing* PENELOPE.] Perhaps they'd kill you.
ANTINOUS [*looking at them distrustfully*]. Kill me?
PENELOPE. In order to make me choose again. [*The* SUITORS *speak in low voices glancing sideways at* ANTINOUS.] Nevertheless, yes. I think I almost . . . almost . . . prefer Antinous.

[*Pause.* ANTINOUS *takes a step toward her as though to plead with her. He turns back to the others and takes* PISANDER *by the arm and looks into his eyes. He does the same to* LEOCRITES.]

EURYMACHUS. Nonsense. [*To* PENELOPE.] Penelope, your solution is too bloody. We've got to find another.
PENELOPE [*exalted*]. Then fight for me! If you're men, fight for me!
EURYMACHUS. That amounts to the same thing. [*Rejecting it.*] It won't do.
PENELOPE. I want to make my choice! You can't stop me! Antinous, you're the one I choose. Don't let them tear my kingdom away from you.
ANTINOUS [*flaring up at the others*]. There, now you know. The queen has chosen me! And I tell you . . .
EURYMACHUS [*taking him by the arm*]. Shut up, you idiot!

[*He whispers in* ANTINOUS' *ear in the presence of the other two who seem to agree to this.* ANTINOUS *lowers his head and then steps away without looking at* PENELOPE.] Antinous declines your election, Your Highness. Have you something else to propose? Something else that will not be a new choice. We all reject that.

AMPHION [*stepping forward*]. I will accept Penelope's choice if she will do me such honor.

PENELOPE [*quickly*]. No! No, no. Eurymachus is right. I should not choose.

EURYMACHUS [*smiling*]. So then . . . ?

PENELOPE. I . . . I don't know. I don't know what to do.

STRANGER [*stepping forward*]. If you will allow me . . .

[*They all turn to him.*]

PENELOPE [*haughty*]. What are you doing here?

STRANGER. I couldn't sleep. I heard shouts and came up with the rest of them. I'm a poor old beggar, but I'm old and I know something about life. If you will allow me to suggest something . . . [*Short pause.*]

PENELOPE. Speak.

STRANGER. Something that would spare . . . the others . . . the shame of not being elected. [*He halts suddenly.*] Provided, of course, that they all agree to accept the judgment.

EURYMACHUS. Have done with it.

STRANGER. In a moment. If the queen agrees to it as well . . . the best way out would be to hold a contest.

LEOCRITES. A contest?

STRANGER. The winner would marry the queen.

ANTINOUS. What kind of a contest?

STRANGER. Oh, I can't say . . . Something that would satisfy the queen. For example . . . something to do with that bow . . .

TELEMACHUS [*excitedly*]. That's it! My father's bow! You'll never master it, he's the only one who can draw it! He's as strong as an oak! Say yes, Mother! With the bow!

STRANGER [*approaching the bow*]. Truly a bow fit for a God! But these young men are strong. It's hard to believe that there isn't one among them who can draw it.

TELEMACHUS. Agree to it, Mother. Twelve rings in the air, in a row, and shoot an arrow straight through the center of them as Father did.

[PENELOPE *approaches the bow and touches it. She looks at the bow thoughtfully and, then, rubs her hand over the wood and looks sadly at* AMPHION.]

ANTINOUS. I can do that. If Penelope agrees to it, I'll accept the contest.
PENELOPE. If I could only know . . . if I could only remember . . .
PISANDER. I'll draw that bow on the first try.
TELEMACHUS. Accept it, Mother.
EURYMACHUS. Very well, we're all agreed on it, aren't we?
LEOCRITES. I'd like to see first if . . . [*He walks toward the bow.*]
ANTINOUS. Don't touch it! Do you accept?
LEOCRITES. I accept.
EURYMACHUS. And you Amphion?
AMPHION. If she wishes it . . . yes.

[*They all look at the* QUEEN *and wait.*]

PENELOPE [*disconcerted*]. All right . . . I . . . agree.
STRANGER. Not even Helen has been so well contested.
ANTINOUS. Or by better men. I'll win!
PISANDER [*very pleased*]. When will we hold the contest?
TELEMACHUS [*very pleased*]. Today at noon. I'll make the preparations myself.
EURYMACHUS. Does the Queen agree?
PENELOPE. Isn't that rather soon? It's already dawn . . .
ANTINOUS. That doesn't matter, we'll sleep until it's time.
LEOCRITES. The sooner the better.
PENELOPE [*irresolutely*]. Do as you wish.
EURYMACHUS. Today, then, at noon. But we won't sleep. Such an occasion demands an audience. We'll each go back to our ships and bring fifty soldiers a piece.
PISANDER. Good idea.
ANTINOUS. To the ships!
EURYMACHUS. We bid you farewell, Queen. There's no time to be lost.

[*They bow and start to leave.*]

PISANDER. One moment . . . [*To* AMPHION.] Are you staying here?
AMPHION. I have no vassals to call up. But don't worry, I won't touch the bow.

TELEMACHUS [*belligerently*]. I'll see to that myself!

PISANDER. Good. Let's go. May the Gods reward you, Penelope.

ANTINOUS. And may you inspire your chosen one with strength.

[*He struts out. The rest follow him. Their laughter and boasts of "She'll be mine!" "Mine!" "Yours?" and "You'll never do it!" are heard as they go down the stairs.*]

PENELOPE. Take the slaves away, Nurse. [*Looking at* DIONE.] I won't know until after the contest . . . if I will be free to punish.

EURICLEA. Yes, Lady. [*To the* SLAVE WOMEN.] On with you.

[*They go out Right.*]

AMPHION [*pointing to the door*]. Someone is coming up the stairs.

TELEMACHUS [*looking at the door*]. It's the swineherd and the shepherd.

[*The swineherd,* EUMAEUS, *and the shepherd,* PHILETAS, *enter. They are out of breath and are armed with clubs. They bow.*]

EUMAEUS. Forgive us, Queen. We heard shouts and sounds of fighting.

PHILETAS. We came at once, to see if you needed us.

PENELOPE. My thanks. You may go.

EUMAEUS. We were also looking for the Stranger.

STRANGER. They give me food and shelter. With your leave, I'll go with them.

PENELOPE. You may go. [*The* STRANGER *and his two companions bow and leave.*] Go with them, Telemachus.

TELEMACHUS [*hesitating*]. If I can take the bow.

PENELOPE. Telemachus!

AMPHION [*going between them angrily*]. You insult me? Get out of here at once. [*Short pause.*]

TELEMACHUS. All right, all right . . . I'm satisfied. You'll always be a fool. [*He goes. A pause.*]

PENELOPE [*listens for a moment, then rushes to the bow, takes it down, and holds it out to* AMPHION]. Now try it!

AMPHION. I promised I wouldn't.

PENELOPE [*in anguish*]. And if you lose?

AMPHION. We'll ask the Gods to help us.

PENELOPE. You have to try! This bow must be drawn in a special way . . . [*She tries to remember and makes a vain effort to draw it.*] First one must pull gently, and then . . . hard. But the hand goes here, a little lower than usual . . . and, furthermore . . . Oh, I can't remember! I myself taught Ulysses how to draw it so that he could win me. But I've forgotten! I'm growing old!

AMPHION. I'm glad you've forgotten. I want no advantages.

PENELOPE. Then . . . Don't you love me?

AMPHION [*with deep feeling*]. Don't you see that I couldn't test it here by myself, in front of you. I'd never again be able to look you in the face. Don't you understand?

PENELOPE. I want to . . . Yes, you're right . . . and you're good. But try it! We'll risk everything if you don't try.

[*Smiling,* AMPHION *takes the bow that she holds out to him.* PENELOPE'S *face seems to light up with hope which is suddenly extinguished as she sees* AMPHION *return the bow to its place.*]

AMPHION. I love you, Penelope. But I'll fight for you without advantages . . . [*He goes toward her.*] . . . because I know that that is the way you dreamed of me . . . in there. [*She lowers her head. He takes her hands.*] I'll win the contest. The God of War will not deny me his strength . . . in such a just cause. Pray to him for me. [*He kisses her hands.* PENELOPE, *suddenly, kisses him on the mouth. He tries to embrace her.*]

PENELOPE [*moving away without looking him in the face*]. Go away now. [AMPHION *leaves at Left.* PENELOPE, *deep in thought, touches her lips. She breaks her silence suddenly.*] A great sacrifice! A great sacrifice to the God of War! [*Going out Right.*] Euriclea! We must prepare a great sacrifice to the God of War! . . . And to the God of Love! To the God of Love too! [*Her voice fades away. A long pause. The* STRANGER *enters hurriedly at Left, dragging* TELEMACHUS *by the hand.*]

TELEMACHUS. What are you going to do, Father?

STRANGER. You keep watch. [TELEMACHUS *goes Right and stands guard while the* STRANGER—ULYSSES—*takes down the bow and crosses to the center of the stage.*] In undertakings such as these, my son, it's best not to take any chances. This bow has its secret, but it's also a strong one. I could draw it once, but now I'm old, and . . .

TELEMACHUS. You can still do it. I'm sure of it!

ULYSSES. We'll see. Do you hear anything?

TELEMACHUS. No, no! Go ahead and draw it.

ULYSSES. Well . . . have at it! [*He tries and strains . . . in vain.*]

TELEMACHUS [*surprised*]. Father! [ULYSSES *tries once more but does not manage to draw it the full way. The string snaps out of his fingers with a twang.* TELEMACHUS *is almost in anguish.*] Father! [ULYSSES, *on the third try, draws the bow easily in two movements.*]

ULYSSES [*proudly*]. I can still do it! [*His figure seems to draw itself up. His silhouette is truly that of an avenging archer. He remains in this stance for a moment, his face aglow. His son runs to him and falls at his feet.*]

TELEMACHUS [*full of awe*]. Father!

CURTAIN

ACT THREE

[*It is noon. The curtains at either side of the chamber are drawn. Beyond the balustrade we see the wide blue of the sky and, in the distance, the tops of the walls that surround the courtyard. The door of the chamber is closed, but the door at Left is open. The bow has been removed but the quiver, full of arrows, hangs in its place.*

Standing at the balustrade, PENELOPE *witnesses the test of the bow which is taking place in the courtyard.* TELEMACHUS, *at her side, watches her carefully. Gathered around the balustrade at Right are the five* SLAVE WOMEN. EURICLEA *is sitting on the floor next to the door of the chamber.* ULYSSES *sits Down Left resting his chin in his hands, motionless, gloomy.*]

PENELOPE [*apostrophizing the invisible suitors*]. That's right, grease it! My husband's bow is a strong one. [*To* EURICLEA.] They've warmed it over the fire, Nurse, and now they're rubbing it with grease. Antinous suggested that they temper it that way . . . "just in case it had hardened over the years." They're afraid they'll lose. [*To the courtyard once more.*] Grease it well!

EURICLEA [*sadly*]. Lamb of mine, don't get excited.

PENELOPE [*jeeringly*]. Your hands treat it with respect, don't they? Warm it, grease it, seduce it with pretty words, in case there's a spirit living in it that has an ear for flattery.

TELEMACHUS [*maliciously, after a glance at his father who does not move*]. But just the same, there is one man who'll master it. Isn't that so, Mother?

PENELOPE [*with a cold look*]. Perhaps.

TELEMACHUS [*half threateningly*]. No perhaps about it, Mother. I promise you.

[*She gives him a disdainful look, without understanding him, and turns back to the courtyard.*]

1ST SLAVE. Pisander is going to try!
2ND SLAVE. He doesn't hold the bow well.
1ST SLAVE. What do you know about it?
3RD SLAVE. You can tell just by looking at him. He doesn't know how. He'll lose.
1ST SLAVE. No he won't! He'll win the contest!
4TH SLAVE. That's a lie! Eurymachus will win!
3RD SLAVE. Antinous!
2ND SLAVE. Leocrites!
DIONE. Can't you be quiet? He's starting.

[*They crowd forward.* PISANDER'S *followers burst into cheers.*]

VOICES. Good Luck! Draw well, Pisander! That's it! That's it! That's right!

[*There is a sudden and deep silence.*]

PENELOPE. He's drawing it . . . [TELEMACHUS *also looks on. Suddenly there is a thunder of shouts of "Get out!" and "Out with you!" from the followers of the other suitors.* PENELOPE *sighs with relief.*] He couldn't do it. Nurse! He couldn't do it!

[*The* SLAVE WOMEN *push and shove the* 1ST SLAVE *away, and she stands apart from them, dejected.*]

DIONE. Get away with you and your Pisander!
PENELOPE [*laughing and calling down into the courtyard*]. Pisander, is Ulysses' bow a strong one? It is? Well, what did you think it was? A little reed from the river? It's a man's bow! [*There is a brief pause during which* ULYSSES *looks at her stealthily and is, in turn, furtively observed by* TELEMACHUS.] It's your turn now, Antinous!
3RD SLAVE. Antinous!

[*She jostles the others for a better place. Meanwhile the* 1ST SLAVE *has crossed Down Right and is sitting disconsolately on the first step of level.* ANTINOUS' *followers cheer him on.*]

VOICES. Antinous! Long live our chief! You'll do it Antinous! Show them how strong you are!

PENELOPE. Yes, show me your strength! But don't forget . . even if you do draw the bow, you'll have to shoot an arrow through the twelve rings! [*Intensely, to* EURICLEA.] They'll never do it, Nurse.

EURICLEA. My Queen, don't suffer so. It won't help . . .

PENELOPE. I'm not suffering! I'm happy! [EURICLEA *shakes her head sadly but* PENELOPE *does not see her. Once more, there is a stillness in the courtyard.* PENELOPE *speaks to herself.*] Ha, you can't! You could gorge yourself and drink . . . oh, yes! You could boast and brag about being my favorite! Stealing and insolence came easily, but now you can't draw that bow! You can't! [*Howling.*] You can't!

[*Simultaneously with this, one hears the voices of the men shouting against* ANTINOUS.]

VOICES. Get out, Antinous! Let's have another! Out!

DIONE [*as she pushes the* 3RD SLAVE]. That's it, out! Out with you too! [*The* 3RD SLAVE *joins the* 1ST SLAVE *and sits dejectedly.*]

PENELOPE [*pacing nervously, to* TELEMACHUS]. They can't do it, Son, they're not strong enough. They can't do it, Stranger. Your idea was a good one. Don't you want to see it?

ULYSSES [*under* TELEMACHUS' *gaze*]. It's enough to hear it.

PENELOPE [*who is no longer paying attention to him, turns to* EURICLEA]. They can't do it, Nurse. [*Takes her by the wrists and lifts her up.*] They can't. And I . . . I am happy. Yes, I'm happy!

TELEMACHUS [*from the balustrade where he is once more looking into the courtyard*]. They're a bit shaken . . . no one is taking up the bow.

PENELOPE [*returning to the balustrade*]. Hey, you! Who's next? Are you afraid to try? Do you think it'll bite you like a snake? [*Suddenly frightened.*] No. Not you, no . . . [*Once more reassured and laughing.*] Leocrites stepped forward. Are you really going to try, Leocrites? [*Pointing at him and laughing.*] Look! Leocrites isn't afraid! He's not afraid to be bitten.

VOICES. Good for you, Leocrites! May the Gods help you!

[*The voices encouraging* LEOCRITES *are heard.*]

Pull with all your might!

[PENELOPE'S *laughter is almost hysterical.*]

DIONE. He looks like a boar.

4TH SLAVE. A boar with an ass' head.

2ND SLAVE [*stung*]. Well, he'll win the contest . . . you'll see!

DIONE. Silence!

[*The* 4TH SLAVE *answers the* 2ND SLAVE *with a mocking gesture. They all look down into the court. There is a silence as* LEOCRITES *makes ready to draw. A pause.* ULYSSES *calls his son with a hiss.* EURICLEA *senses this and responds to it with a certain anxiety.*]

ULYSSES [*in a low voice*]. Did you close the palace gates?

TELEMACHUS [*in the same tone*]. Yes, Father. No one will get out.

ULYSSES. And their soldiers?

TELEMACHUS. They're looking at the contest from the postern and they don't know they've been shut off. They won't interfere.

2ND SLAVE. A little more, Leocrites.

[*The others pay no attention.* TELEMACHUS *starts to return to the balustrade but* ULYSSES *holds him back.* EURICLEA *takes a step toward them irresolutely. The* SLAVE WOMEN *Down Right look at them with curiosity.*]

ULYSSES. The weapons?

TELEMACHUS. Eumaeus and Philetas have them behind the door. [*He indicates the door at Left.*] The rest are hidden. [*He returns to the balustrade as shouts of "Out!" and "Out with him!" burst forth and mix with fierce laughter.* DIONE *and the* 4TH SLAVE *join in the laughing.*]

PENELOPE [*laughing*]. Nurse, he fainted! His blood was too fat for him . . . it did him in! [*She crosses to her.*] The calves, the pigs, the bulls that he devoured have done him in. There he was red, drenched in sweat, braying with impotence . . . and . . . [*She laughs as she speaks.*] . . . just then . . . he flopped to the ground like a sheep under the knife. [*She laughs only to stop suddenly, take the nurse by the wrists in a panic.*] Nurse! They're almost done! [*She leaves her on the spot and returns to the balustrade.*]

EURICLEA [*no less upset, trying to hold on to her*]. Lady, say nothing . . .

PENELOPE [*at the balustrade*]. There is still one left.

TELEMACHUS [*by her side, speaking deliberately*]. Two, Mother. [*She looks at him.*] Because they should all try, shouldn't they.

PENELOPE [*upset*]. Why do you talk to me like that?

TELEMACHUS [*nervously*]. I'm trying to run the contest.

PENELOPE. You can't run anything. You're my son.

TELEMACHUS. Mother . . .

PENELOPE [*toward the courtyard*]. It's your turn, Eurymachus. Show me how you'll master the bow. It's strong and supple like Ulysses and, like him too, it won't bend!

[ULYSSES *looks at her surprised.* TELEMACHUS *reacts to the word and looks at his father with a certain fear in his eyes.*]

TELEMACHUS [*insistently*]. Mother . . . Isn't it true that, in spite of everything, you want them all to lose and my father to return? Isn't that it? Say yes, Mother. Say yes. Mother . . .

[*She is staring at the courtyard and is twisting her hands nervously.* ULYSSES' *look of warning seems to paralyze his son who, then, lowers his head. From the courtyard come the cries of* EURYMACHUS' *followers.*]

VOICES. Eurymachus! It's all yours! The Gods protect you! Win Penelope! [*The noise dies down.*]

DIONE [*to the* 2ND SLAVE]. What are you doing here? Didn't your Leocrites just faint? Leave us alone!

2ND SLAVE. I want to see . . .

DIONE [*dragging her by the arm down to the other* SLAVE WOMEN]. Out with you! [*She pushes her violently. Cursing, the* 2ND SLAVE *sits down next to the others.* DIONE *returns to her place. To the* 4TH SLAVE.] And now it's you and I . . . face to face.

4TH SLAVE [*determinedly*]. I'll bet on Eurymachus!

DIONE. And I on Amphion! [*They look into the courtyard.*]

PENELOPE [*unconsciously shaking her head*]. He's picked it up . . . looking at the string . . . No, no, I can't watch it.

TELEMACHUS [*behind her*]. Mother . . .

PENELOPE. No. I don't want . . . I don't want him to draw.

EURICLEA [*softly*]. Be still, lady. You're making it worse.

PENELOPE [*turning upon* ULYSSES]. Why did you ever think of this? I can't stand any more! [ULYSSES *looks at her coldly. She returns to the balustrade.*] I don't want Eurymachus to win! I don't want it! He's a snake . . . a cold, poisonous snake! No, not him! [*Her hands clutch the balustrade as she looks down into the courtyard.*]

ULYSSES. [*to* TELEMACHUS *who has stayed by his side after following his mother down*]. The arrows.

[EURICLEA, *very disturbed, moves a little closer. The* SLAVE WOMEN *down stage also look at them and murmur to each other with a sense of misgiving.*]

TELEMACHUS [*in a tone of entreaty*]. Have pity on her, Father.

ULYSSES [*unmoved*]. The arrows.

TELEMACHUS [*gloomily*]. There they are. [*He points to the quiver.*] They're clean. I inspected them this morning.

[*At this moment* PENELOPE *groans and turns away sobbing convulsively. A confused shouting is heard in the courtyard.* PENELOPE *leans, exhausted, upon* EURICLEA'S *shoulder.* EURICLEA *is not solicitous but seems to bear* PENELOPE'S *weight as though it were fate itself.* TELEMACHUS *runs to the balustrade just as the* 4TH SLAVE *under* DIONE'S *triumphant glance breaks away despondently and joins the other slaves down stage.* PENELOPE *recovers her composure, dries her tears, and, at last, with a gesture of determination returns to the balustrade.*]

PENELOPE [*by tremendous effort, she manages to achieve a bearing and tone of remarkable majesty. She raises her arms*]. Silence! [*The voices in the court die down.*] Listen! You've given me your word to win or lose in fair contest. You've been loyal and true to me, and now I wish to be fair. None of you four was able to shoot an arrow through the rings . . . or, for that matter, so much as draw the bow. [*Short pause.*] Drawing the bow is a difficult test . . . I wish, therefore, to be magnanimous toward the last of my suitors.

TELEMACHUS [*stepping close to her*]. No Mother!

PENELOPE [*keeping him at arm's length*]. I do not show him special favor by this since all of you have tried and failed in what he will have to do.

TELEMACHUS [*looking at* ULYSSES]. As you value your life, Mother, be still!

PENELOPE. Let me remind you of your promise to leave my kingdom in peace. I remind you that this state of affairs ends today. [*Short pause.*] Therefore, it is my wish that the drawing of the bow determine the contest.

TELEMACHUS. Mother, no!

VOICES OF THE SUITORS. No! We won't accept! But Amphion won't win!

PENELOPE [*sarcastically*]. Amphion won't win! Have any of you so much as drawn the bow? You surprise me. Now that you've lost you want no one to win. [*Forcefully.*] What *do* you want then? Do you want to stay here for the rest of your lives? Begin all over again? There are no cattle left. There is nothing left for you . . . or for me!

VOICES OF THE SUITORS. We'll all go! Yes, all of us. Amphion too.

PENELOPE. Do you imagine it will be otherwise? Do you think Amphion is strong enough to draw the bow that conquered you? And if . . . if he did draw it, his superiority would be clear. What difference do the rings make? It's a test of strength not aim. Be noble and generous I beg you . . . for once in your lives! [*Short pause.*] Enough. Let Amphion take his turn. [*She returns from the balustrade with calm only to lose her composure the minute she is out of sight of the courtyard.*] Nurse, they've agreed! They're quiet. They've accepted because they think Amphion will fail. [*Dejectedly.*] And it's true! He'll fail, Nurse, he'll fail.

EURICLEA [*falling in tears at* PENELOPE'S *feet*]. The Furies have heard us, Queen. We've lost.

PENELOPE. Oh, the Furies! You be quiet . . . at once! There's still hope . . . there's still hope! [*She goes to see but doesn't dare.*] No, no I can't watch it.

ULYSSES [*aloud to* TELEMACHUS]. Has he begun?

TELEMACHUS [*approaching him*]. He's just taken up the bow, Stranger.

ULYSSES. Why are there no shouts?

TELEMACHUS. Amphion has no lands or vassals.

[*A silence.*]

DIONE [*suddenly, from the balustrade*]. Amphion! [PENELOPE *turns quickly, her face full of hatred.* TELEMACHUS *also makes an angry gesture and steps off intending to silence her.* ULYSSES *holds him back.*] Grab it firmly! That's right! That's the way! Don't be scared of it, AMPHION! The bow is yours! The Gods are on your side! Slowly . . . ! [PENELOPE *crosses little by little to the right of the chamber and anxiously follows the events that she doesn't dare to look at as* DIONE *sees them for her.*] There's all the strength of Ares in your arms! He's drawing! The bow's giving! More! More! A little more! [*A long pause.* DIONE *screams a half threat, half plea.*] More!! [*A long pause during which:*]

ULYSSES. The bow. [EURICLEA *gets to her feet.*]

TELEMACHUS. Yes, Father. [*He returns to the balustrade. Under the surprised looks of the* SLAVE WOMEN, EURICLEA *approaches* ULYSSES, *who has been getting up slowly, and falls to his feet.*]

EURICLEA. Have pity! [ULYSSES *touches her head and smiles sadly.* DIONE *screams with rage as the courtyard explodes with the shouts of the suitors' men.* PENELOPE *falls to the ground in a faint.*]

TELEMACHUS. I told you you couldn't handle my Father's bow. I told you! But there's still someone to teach you how it's drawn! There's still someone who'll teach you! [*He goes out rapidly at Left and his voice fades away.*]

DIONE [*to herself but looking at the courtyard with an icy calm*]. You deceived me. I took you for something better. [*She turns calmly, her love for* AMPHION *a thing of the past. As she passes* PENELOPE *on the floor, she makes a disdainful gesture.* DIONE *is surprised by the look of fear that she sees on the faces of the* SLAVE WOMEN *as they stare at* ULYSSES *and* EURICLEA. ULYSSES *is standing erect. He is no longer an old man bowed down by the years but a mature and muscular man.* DIONE *joins the other slaves. The group never loses sight of* ULYSSES, *reacting with gestures and murmurs of fear to the ensuing revelation.*]

ULYSSES. Get up. [*He helps* EURICLEA *to her feet and immediately goes to* PENELOPE. *Stopping before her.*] Are you through dreaming, Wife?

PENELOPE [*with an effort, she raises her head and looks at him.*] What did you say?

ULYSSES. You'd do well to remember this scar. You healed it yourself some time ago.

[PENELOPE *looks at the scar but still does not understand. Suddenly she screams, gets to her feet, and looks at* ULYSSES *with horror. Instinctively, she goes to the door of the chamber as if protecting it.*]

PENELOPE. Ulysses!

ULYSSES. Ulysses. [*The* SLAVE WOMEN *cluster together in terror at Right. He moves quickly to Left. When she hears him coming,* EURICLEA *crosses, almost flees, to the* SLAVE WOMEN *who take her in as though she were a possible protector.* ULYSSES *opens wide the door at Left.*] Eumaeus! Philetas! [*They enter immediately. They are wearing short swords at their belts.* ULYSSES *turns to look at* PENELOPE *who, in her fear, has not taken her eyes off of him. The men help him to put on a shoulder strap and sword. Meanwhile*:] Euriclea and the slave women, get out! And don't return 'till I call you. [*They hurry out Right.*]

TELEMACHUS' VOICE [*as he comes up the stairs*]. I'll show you the man who'll teach you! [*He enters with the bow and runs to the balustrade.*] A beggar's the one who'll teach you to draw . . . a beggar! [*The* SUITORS' *vassals make noises in the postern, shouting and pounding against the locked doors.* TELEMACHUS *gives the bow to his father and then runs for the quiver, draws out two arrows, and puts the quiver by the Left arch.* ULYSSES *draws the bow with some effort and, without taking his eyes from* PENELOPE, *lets the string go with a twang.* TELEMACHUS *returns to the balustrade raising the two arrows aloft.*] . . . A beggar named Ulysses! [*He crosses to the quiver.*]

ULYSSES [*to* EUMAEUS *and* PHILETAS]. Close the door! [EUMAEUS *and* PHILETAS *quickly close the door and bolt it. They draw their swords and stand guard. Meanwhile,* ULYSSES *goes to the balustrade and reveals himself. His presence commands an absolute silence. He holds out his hand to* TELEMACHUS *who gives him an arrow.*] The first one is for you, Eurymachus! You're the worst! [*He draws and aims.*]

EURYMACHUS [*full of terror*]. No! . . . No!

[ULYSSES *follows* EURYMACHUS' *flight with his bow. The crowd in the postern shouts deafeningly but* ULYSSES' *voice is heard over them all.*]

ULYSSES. Hunt! Look harder! It's all locked up! [*He shoots and is answered by a scream of agony.*]

TELEMACHUS [*triumphantly as he looks into the courtyard.*] He did a somersault! [*He gives his father another arrow and runs back for more.* ULYSSES *draws immediately.* PENELOPE *approaches.*]

ULYSSES. Now it's your turn, Antinous, you stupid, arrogant beast!

ANTINOUS' VOICE. Come down here and fight like a man!

ULYSSES. I'm not a man, I'm king.

ANTINOUS' VOICE. Come down! Come d . . .

[ULYSSES *shoots and* ANTINOUS' *voice becomes a scream of pain.*]

TELEMACHUS. In the heart!

ULYSSES [*placing another arrow given to him by* TELEMACHUS]. This one's for you, Pisander!

TELEMACHUS. Look at him run! He's picking up the arrows but there's no bow . . . this is the only bow in the palace!

PENELOPE [*behind* ULYSSES, *as if possessed*]. Kill! Kill them!

[ULYSSES *gives her an unfathomable look.*]

ULYSSES [*aiming*]. Pisander! So I was old, and dead, eh? Take this!

PENELOPE [*as though in a trance*]. Kill!

ULYSSES [*preparing to shoot once more*]. Woman, do you really want me to kill?

PENELOPE [*violently*]. Yes, yes!

ULYSSES [*once more calling into the court*]. Leocrites! Don't move! Your time has come. [*He aims.*]

TELEMACHUS. Look at him clawing at the gate. He's trying to squeeze through the bars . . . They're trying to pass him a shield . . . but it won't fit. [*Pause.*] He's stopped squirming. He's frozen with terror. Crush him . . . like a snake.

ULYSSES [*calling into the courtyard*]. What are you looking at? It's no longer Penelope, is it? It's an armed man! It's her husband! It's death! [*He shoots.*]

TELEMACHUS. In the mouth! [*Little by little the noise in the postern dies down.*] Their soldiers are stunned. They don't know what to do. [*Pause. He turns to his father.*] There's only one left, Father.

ULYSSES. One who neither runs nor trembles. The only brave one. [*He holds out his hand for an arrow which* TELEMACHUS *gives to him after a moment of indecision.*]

PENELOPE [*behind him*]. Ulysses . . .

ULYSSES [*turning suddenly and angrily*]. What! [PENELOPE *cannot bring herself to speak. She straightens up and freezes like a statue.* ULYSSES *holds up the arrow.*] This one's yours, Amphion!

AMPHION'S VOICE. It's fair, Ulysses! I'm waiting!

ULYSSES [*gravely*]. I knew your father, Amphion. He was my best friend.

AMPHION'S VOICE. I don't want pity!

ULYSSES. You won't get it. However, you should die like a hero, not a rat. Come, get your arrow. [*He steps back from the balustrade and waits.* TELEMACHUS *follows* AMPHION'S *assent.*]

TELEMACHUS. He's coming up, Father. Quite calm.

[*Pause.* TELEMACHUS *faces front.* ULYSSES *places his arrow. Two knocks are heard at the door. At a signal from* ULYSSES, EUMAEUS *and* PHILETAS *draw the bolt and open the door.* AMPHION *remains outside, invisible, but he and* ULYSSES *look quite fixedly at one another.*]

ULYSSES [*before drawing*]. You know how to die . . . None of the others was worth so much.

AMPHION'S VOICE. I am an orphan and forged in the mill of poverty.

ULYSSES. Too much . . . You're the worst kind of suitor for a man's wife! I have to kill you!

AMPHION. I defended Penelope. But I accept death at your hand, Ulysses. You're killing me because you're already dead. Remember what I'm saying to you. Death is our great dream. To die and go on living is worse. Let me die now. [ULYSSES *draws.*] I thank you for your arrow, Ulysses. Death is the great dream that frees us. [*Short pause.*] . . . And my thanks to you for your dreams, Penelope.

[ULYSSES *shoots. It is as if the arrow had also pierced* PENELOPE. *There is the sound of* AMPHION'S *body as it falls.*]

TELEMACHUS [*looking out*]. He rolled down the stairs.

ULYSSES. Telemachus, go at once and announce my return to all the fighting men of Ithaca. Bring them here and, with their help, put that rabble in the postern under guard. They'll be our hostages and will pay us ransom. The palace must recover its losses. Off with you! [TELEMACHUS *salutes his father and leaves.*] Eumaeus and Philetas, my thanks for your loyalty and your silence. Amphion must be burned tomorrow with all the honors that befit a great chieftain. Take his body [*indicating the courtyard*], dress it in my best armour, and lay it upon the ceremonial stone that he may be mourned tonight. [EUMAEUS *and* PHILETAS *salute and leave.* ULYSSES *steals a glance at* PENELOPE, *who has low-*

ered her head. He crosses Left and calls out.] Euriclea! Bring in the slave women!

[*Pause.* EURICLEA *and the* SLAVE WOMEN *enter at Right. As they enter they kneel and beg for mercy.*]

SLAVE WOMEN [*simultaneously*]. Pity! Have pity on us! Ulysses, our king, have mercy!

ULYSSES. Silence! You who betrayed my wife and my kingdom shall be punished. Hanging isn't enough. [*The laments and entreaties of the* SLAVE WOMEN *become louder.*] First, with those hands that once caressed them, gather up the bleeding corpses down in the courtyard. Carry them to the dunghill and leave them there for crows to feed on. Then come back and wash away the blood from the courtyard. Euriclea, take them away. [EURICLEA *rises and they leave at Left distraught and moaning.* DIONE, *however, has neither wept nor pleaded; when she kneeled it was almost against her will. Pause.* ULYSSES *goes to the quiver and takes an arrow. He turns and faces* PENELOPE, *who is looking at him now, her eyes wide, her bearing full of assurance.*] You too betrayed me, Penelope. [*In a surge of temper he draws the bow and aims.*]

PENELOPE [*very erect*]. Kill me! [*A short pause.* ULYSSES *lowers his bow little by little and, then, sets it down at his side.*]

ULYSSES. I didn't come back to kill you. I came back to care for my kingdom and my wife. I came to prevent many things . . . not to set them loose. [*He approaches her.*] Listen, Penelope, I told you a story that disturbed me . . . the story of a king who was murdered by his wife and her lover. [*Short pause.*] I haven't told you its conclusion. The story does not end there. Their son, Orestes, after sallying out into the world, returned and killed his mother. Yes! He killed his own mother . . . and her lover, his father's assassin.

PENELOPE. You've killed Amphion . . . make me another Clytemnestra.

ULYSSES. Didn't I just tell you I came to avoid all that? First to prevent you from becoming another Clytemnestra and, next, to prevent another Orestes from killing you.

PENELOPE [*horrified*]. What?

ULYSSES. Hadn't you noticed? Telemachus was beginning to hate you because of your love for that . . . dreamer? But I'm here now and my son will not become an Orestes.

PENELOPE. I've been faithful.

ULYSSES [*screaming*]. With your body!

PENELOPE. What more did you want? I was just a girl when you left.

ULYSSES. What difference does that make?

PENELOPE. Why did you leave me?

ULYSSES. Why did you think I wasn't coming back?

PENELOPE. It's been twenty years!

ULYSSES. What of it? We can't put an end to war.

PENELOPE. Oh, can't you? You start them in order to make us suffer the consequences. We want peace, a husband, and children . . . and you give us wars, you thrust us into the danger of adultery and turn our sons into our murderers.

ULYSSES. We also die.

PENELOPE. Death's nothing.

ULYSSES. Must I remind you that this war was caused by a woman?

PENELOPE. That's a lie! It was your lust that brought it on.

ULYSSES. It was Helen . . . a woman. A mad, frivolous, dangerous thing . . . like you . . . who've envied her and set yourself to sterile dreaming and weaving in there instead of caring for the cattle and the vineyards; instead of behaving like a faithful wife who waits for the return of her husband and works to increase his riches while he is away. As for Helen . . . [*Pause.* PENELOPE *advances expectantly.*] I lied to you. There is no Helen, Wife! She doesn't exist!

PENELOPE. Is she dead?

ULYSSES. No. [*Spitting his words.*] But she's old and ugly.

PENELOPE [*lowering her head*]. Not even that is left me.

ULYSSES. That's exactly why I'm telling you. You've been jealous in vain.

[PENELOPE *moves away moaning with pain.* EURICLEA *comes on at Left.*]

EURICLEA. Master . . .

ULYSSES. What do you want?

EURICLEA. The slave women are already washing the courtyard. They beg for mercy.

ULYSSES. And do you, who know what they've done . . . do you plead for them?

EURICLEA. They're just weak women, Ulysses. It wasn't easy to resist the suitors.

ULYSSES. Then they'll be hanged for weakness. [*Pause.*]

EURICLEA. The slave women entreat Your Highnesses' permission to chant the rhapsody you taught them this morning . . . begging in this manner for your forgiveness. [*Short pause.*]

ULYSSES. Whose idea was that? Yours?

EURICLEA. Dione, Sire.

ULYSSES [*after pacing a bit*]. Let them chant. I'll forgive them. [*Short pause.*] But Dione will hang.

EURICLEA. Ulysses, you are just and wise!

ULYSSES. Retire. [*He leads her to the door with a certain deference.*]

EURICLEA [*before going out, with infinite sorrow and conviction in her voice*]. Ulysses, beware of the Furies. [*She leaves. A brief pause.*]

ULYSSES. My order pleased you, didn't it? I can see it in your face. Dione must die because it was she who opened that door last night . . . and because I don't want her to spoil Telemachus. [*Acridly.*] But you were kind to her . . . why?

PENELOPE. I didn't want Telemachus to love her more because I punished her.

ULYSSES. Speak the truth. You did it because of Amphion.

PENELOPE. For Amphion too. He wasn't cruel, and he would never have forgiven cruelty in me.

ULYSSES [*shaking his head*]. You're deceiving yourself. You were kind to her because you enjoyed seeing Amphion disappoint her.

PENELOPE [*examining him, coolly*]. I didn't remember you like this.

ULYSSES. How?

PENELOPE. Niggardly.

ULYSSES. Niggardly but truthful. I don't dream. Now . . . open the chamber!

PENELOPE [*frightened*]. No!

ULYSSES. I'll chop the door down with an axe!

PENELOPE. You animal!

ULYSSES. You . . . dreamer! . . . Dreamer, give me the key!

PENELOPE. And what do you expect to find on the shroud?

ULYSSES. Your soul.

PENELOPE. You can't take my soul by force.

ULYSSES. The key!

PENELOPE. No! [*She draws herself up. They stare at each other for a moment with profound hatred.* ULYSSES, *his fists clenched, advances toward* PENELOPE, *who faces him pale but determined.*]

ULYSSES [*suddenly changing his manner*]. Sh! [*He steps back.* EUMAEUS *enters and looks at them.*]

EUMAEUS. Your commands have been carried out, Ulysses. Amphion's corpse is laid out on the ceremonial stone.

ULYSSES [*gruffly, having perceived the old servant's concern*]. It wasn't necessary for you to report. [EUMAEUS *lowers his head.*] Go now. [EUMAEUS *salutes him and leaves.* PENELOPE, *shaken by* EUMAEUS' *words, looks cautiously at her husband. He stands rigidly with his arms crossed, staring fixedly at her. At last, she can stand it no longer and runs, crying, and falls to her knees at the balustrade, and looks into the courtyard. There is a long pause which is punctuated by sobs from* PENELOPE. ULYSSES *speaks angrily.*] Will you be silent! [PENELOPE *rises slowly and faces him. The noble anger in her face is such that he steps back from her.*]

PENELOPE. Coward.

ULYSSES. What?

PENELOPE. Yes, you, the crafty Ulysses. That's what your craftiness amounts to . . . cowardice . . . nothing more.

ULYSSES. I killed them without risking my life . . . because I had to.

PENELOPE. Because you're a coward!

ULYSSES [*unable to suppress a mounting uncertainty in the presence of her composure*]. Be quiet, woman. I proved myself in the war. And I wasn't afraid to come here and run the risk of being killed by you . . . and that one down there.

PENELOPE. But you hid behind a disguise. Coward!

ULYSSES. In order to find out everything! I'm not afraid of fact.

PENELOPE. But you are afraid to feel and to trust. You didn't dare trust me. You doubted me . . . [*She approaches him.*] . . . and you doubted yourself. [*He lowers his head.*] You think I don't understand? You tried to make me believe that my patience with Dione was due to some hidden rivalry for Amphion . . . that it was some sort of cleverness. Well, I don't understand things like that. I was dreaming then . . . and I could feel the goodness of Amphion! It was something that went through me and possessed me, and made me a better person . . . even toward Dione. I felt it! Something which you, you miserable reasoner, have never known! And now I *know*, I *feel* . . . the reason for your disguise. I feel it in my own disgust for you, in my . . . repugnance. You disguised yourself because you knew you were old, because you were afraid you couldn't please me with your gray hairs and wrinkles!

ULYSSES. Penelope!

PENELOPE. Be quiet! It's my turn to talk now. Now, let me tell you that your cowardice has destroyed everything. Nothing . . . mark what I'm saying . . . nothing had happened between Amphion and myself before your arrival . . . except for my poor solitary dreams. If you had come to me honestly and courageously, and offered me those gray hairs made noble by war and suffering . . . I could have responded in time! In spite of everything, you would have been that courageous man of whom all women dream. The Ulysses I dreamed about here, during those early years . . . and not this sly, hypocritical, cowardly clown . . . disguised as a vile old man who destroyed all my hopes!

ULYSSES [*icily*]. That's not why I disguised myself. I was also afraid of finding you an old woman . . . as I have.

PENELOPE [*picking him up on it*]. You were afraid! [*Pointing to the courtyard.*] He wasn't afraid. That gigantic heart of his, which you destroyed, loved my youth and my beauty! There's only one way you could have beaten him! . . . to have had the courage of your feelings, as he did . . . to have come determined to find the kind and lovely Penelope you left behind. At once I would have found in you the man in my dreams. But . . . oh . . . you aren't that man, you couldn't be, not even by startling me with your cunning or by sweeping my palace clean of those suitors. It's you . . . you alone . . . who've lost. I've won. Because you're right, we are old . . . to one another. But you will never have a woman to remember your youth . . . for you were born old. I will always be young. Young in the lovely memory and dream of Amphion! All that's left to you now is your wife . . . in the eyes of the world, that is. In having me you own nothing, you hear? Nothing! Because he's taken it all with him forever. All you have left is the appearance, the laughable shell of marriage. You're to blame! You are . . . for not speaking in time, and not having been brave . . . ever . . . you are to blame! I despise you. [*She goes back to the balustrade and kneels slowly before the distant corpse worshiping him, as it were, for the last time.*]

ULYSSES. And you love him. I see that . . . [*Gloomily.*] It's all lost. . . . So it is that the Gods work our undoing.

PENELOPE. Don't blame the Gods . . . We work it out ourselves.

ULYSSES. I'll leave. [*Sophistically.*] I'll pretend to fulfill some vow and go off on a pilgrimage.

PENELOPE [*reprovingly*]. Go . . . and go on pretending.

ULYSSES. I will. But I'm king of Ithaca. Our name shall be free of stain and will shine into the future. No one will know of this.

PENELOPE. Go on with your icy speeches! What warmth there is left in that poor corpse is worth more to me.

ULYSSES. It will be cold soon . . . and so will we be, sooner or later. That's why there is still something to be done. That's why I came. I came to . . .

PENELOPE. To what? To shatter my dreams and run away?

ULYSSES. No. I came to . . . [*The chorus of* SLAVE WOMEN *suddenly starts chanting in the courtyard.*] . . . to make certain that this much would survive. [PENELOPE *listens.*]

CHORUS.

How like a rock is the woman of strength
in the absence of her husband.
The Queen, another Ulysses, has defended
her honor of bed and palace.

PENELOPE. I hate you!

ULYSSES. Who cares? . . . This is what will be remembered.

CHORUS.

Penelope, surrounded
by dangers and desires,
lived for Ulysses alone.
Not to fall like Clytemnestra,
she wove and unwove through the years
deceiving her many suitors.
Weaving and embroidering!
She wove her dreams in the cloth . . .
dreams, all of Ulysses!

[PENELOPE *gets up suddenly and runs to open the chamber door.*]

PENELOPE. You can see them! [*Her voice breaks.*] It doesn't matter now. [ULYSSES *approaches the door and looks at his wife who has lowered her head. A long pause.*]

ULYSSES [*closing the door, and shaking his head*]. No one will see them now. They don't exist. You dreamt of Ulysses! That shroud will be burned tomorrow with Amphion's body. Unless you'd prefer to unweave it gradually. . . .

PENELOPE. Burn it.

CHORUS.

> To dream of our loved one while we weave,
> this is the law of the hearth.
> May glory smile upon our queen
> who loved her husband alone.

PENELOPE. A lie!

ULYSSES. In your soul, yes! . . . I'm no longer interested in your soul.

CHORUS.

> Penelope teaches us how to wait,
> so that years may pass as a night.
> Love never ages in our blood.
> Our blood knows how to wait
> for the coming home of the loved one.

PENELOPE [*staring intently at the corpse*]. Wait . . . wait for the day when men will be like you and not like him. A day when they will love with courage . . . and be kind to everyone. When they will no longer make war and desert us for its charms. Yes . . . that day will come sometime. [*To* ULYSSES.] And let me tell you, you dog! You know when it will come? When there are no more Helens in this world . . . *or* Ulysses. But there needs to be a universal promise, a bond of love . . . something only we women dream of . . . at times.

ULYSSES. That bond doesn't exist.

PENELOPE. It does! [*Toward the courtyard.*] You knew it. My thanks, Amphion. And dream of me, dream of me always . . . a good woman. [ULYSSES *takes his bow and throws it over the balustrade.*]

ULYSSES. Let it be burned too. There will be no more contests. [*Dejectedly.*] And now, to try and live . . . while we're dying.

PENELOPE [*crossing down toward the proscenium and stopping as though transfigured, her eyes high and her voice full of infinite sweetness*]. Or to dream that we die . . .

There are no more figures to weave. The chamber of my soul is empty. But I do have something after all . . . [*She sobs.*] Oh, Amphion! . . . You're happy now, my Amphion, and I envy you. The dead are fortunate!

[ULYSSES *sits in silence as the* SLAVE WOMEN *begin again and the curtain falls slowly.*]

CHORUS.

Her name, Penelope the Queen,
a model for all wives to come.
She weaves her household dreams in cloth
and her modesty shines like a gem . . .

CURTAIN

ALFONSO SASTRE

1927–

ALFONSO SASTRE is not widely known outside of Spain, but in his native country he is regarded as one of the most important dramatists writing today. Sastre is a writer of the cities, and in most of his plays he is concerned with dramatizing the difficulty of maintaining one's sense of self within the context of demoralizing social forces. Like so many of his contemporaries in Spain, he is a child of the Civil War and his plays are aflame with his burning indignation over social and political injustice and corruption. For this reason, Spanish censorship practices being what they are, Sastre is what might be called an "underground playwright." His work is known, respected, but practically never produced in Spain. Furthermore, unlike so many of his fellow writers, Sastre is not so much a Spanish writer as he is European. All of his work is tinged with the despair and negation that characterize the main current of the modern theatre. The influences of Pirandello, Shaw, Ibsen, and Strindberg are clearly present, but so, too, strangely enough, is the social optimism of Arthur Miller, the playwright Sastre seems to respect and admire above all others.

DRAMA AND SOCIETY[1]

by Alphonso Sastre

Translated by Leonard C. Pronko

I. Tragedy as an Instrument of Torture

1. The Problem Is Posed. It seems that tragedy is a kind of social sin. The average spectator considers the writer of tragedies, in the best cases, as a sort of sinister mar-joy worthy of criminal persecution, social ostracism, and the most rigorous repression by the censors. It seems we are opposed to the voices of sorrow, death, and catastrophe on the stage. Theatre managers illustrate this evident antipathy for the tragic genre by programing silly light comedies, and musical reviews whose artistic pretensions go no further than an exhibition of nude bodies, and saucy facility of situation, puns, and jokes.

2. Tragedy Is Not an Optimistic Genre. A writer of tragedies went so far as to say—in an effort of social justification—that tragedy is an optimistic genre. This is clearly a defensive formulation, in a world where only an optimistic formula of life is accepted. Of course, tragedy is not an optimistic genre; just as it is not a pessimistic genre either. The writer of tragedies does not believe that all is for the worst, nor that all is for the best. If he really believed that all were for the worst, he would not write. Why should he? But he also realizes that all is not well. And he knows that optimism—that is to say, the form of life which considers that everything is perfect or may easily become perfect—exists only in backward and conformist minds.

[1] *Drama and Society*, by Alfonso Sastre, translated by Leonard C. Pronko, copyright © 1964 by Literary Discoveries, Inc., San Francisco. Printed by permission.

3. Tragedy and Torture. Tragedy is—and we can gain nothing by denying it—a strange artistic mechanism which tortures the spectator and leaves him gravely wounded. The spectator is presented with "fearful" deeds and "pitiful" situations (and we know that Aristotle already told us about fear and pity: it is not a defeatist invention of contemporary authors) with the mysterious and obscure intention that he be made uneasy. With the intention—we might say—of torturing and wounding him. The spectator of *Hinkemann, Strife, Dirty Hands,* or *Death of a Salesman* leaves the theatre literally shattered, undone. A little more, and blood would cover his face, and his eyes be blinded by tears. Tragedy wounds, or at least it reveals, bloody and painful, forgotten wounds.

4. Torture Accepted. The curious, and of course essential, part of this torture which is tragedy is that the spectator submits willingly to it. (Tragedy in effect has never been a required spectacle.) Let us be precise about this torture which is offered by tragedy. The problem will then be posed in exact terms.

Can the spectator of *The Victors* honestly say that he has spent a comfortable evening? It is obvious that he cannot. Nor can the spectator of the film tragedies *Bicycle Thief* and *Shoeshine.* On the contrary, it is likely that such a spectator will say to you, "I left the theatre shattered." And yet he is happy that he went. And when he felt that the tragic action was cutting him painfully, making him shudder, suffer, weep, he did not leave. Glued to his seat, breathing with difficulty, he endured the torture to the end. He declared himself, for some mysterious reason, to be at one with the tragic action, and did not even think of the easy rupture which he could have effected by simply getting up from his seat and going out to the lobby to smoke a cigarette, or—more radically—going home and reading an adventure story. No. He was there to receive the tragic current. He could not move from there. The torture was accepted beforehand. He had gone to see a tragedy. But why? Why does the announcement of a tragedy attract the public? What kind of public does tragedy have?

5. Questions, Questions, Questions. Must we admit that the spectator obtains a particular pleasure from this torture freely accepted? What moves the spectator of tragedy? The "Desire for pain" of which St. Augustine speaks in his *Confessions,* when he tells us of his youthful love for the theatre? Is the spectator of tragedy a masochist? Or is his suffering unreal? Is there true suffering on the stage? And in the house? Might it not be an artistically tempered suffering, a suffering which has lost its strength?

6. *The Reality of Tragic Suffering.* It seems to me that we must revindicate the reality of tragic suffering, and in general of all the passions and emotions which come into play in tragedy. The common criticism which holds that tragic passions are "purged," tempered, artistic, and finally inoffensive —capable, at most, of producing in the spectator an aesthetic emotion—has no foundation in the reality of tragedy. Tragic action is really painful. The drama is the conductor, the line of least resistance, through which the pain and anguish go from the social reality to the heart of the spectator. Through the tragedy the spectator communicates with the anguish of others. The spectator, armored by life for the struggle, dozing, peaceful, with his moral consciousness half asleep, is often invulnerable to the pain of others which rubs against him every day in his work, in the street, in the bar, or the bus. Drama produces in his mind the sudden revelation of the true structures of human suffering. The drama becomes then the conductor between the suffering of the street and the mind of the man. The suffering does not lose strength through the act of communication (if the tragedy is good). It is not a purged suffering. In good tragedies the fearful is real, and truly fearful (and it produces real fear; not a "fear" which is a form of aesthetic emotion), and the pitiful is real, and truly pitiful (and rouses true pity and not an aesthetic emotion; a pity which finds its objective after the curtain has fallen, and finds it in social reality; pity potential and as it were suspended during the presentation of the tragedy). Art has done nothing more than effect a very complicated transfer. Transfer (or if we wish, *mimesis*), but not a purgation (the meaning of *catharsis* is something else).

7. *The Meaning of Tragic Catharsis.* For me the meaning of tragic *catharsis* is to be found not in the transfer from reality to tragedy, but in the effect which the tragedy produces on reality: in an immediate way on the spectator, and through him upon Society.

8. *St. Augustine and Tragedy.* The spectator, when he accepts the tragic torture, is suspect of some kind of masochism (and is not the writer of tragedies perhaps a very special kind of sadist?) and therefore, tragedy may be a form of collective insanity: St. Augustine is not far from

this conception. "Why," asks St. Augustine, "does man like to be made sad when viewing doleful and tragical scenes, which yet he himself would by no means suffer? And yet he wishes, as a spectator, to experience from them a sense of grief, and in this very grief his pleasure consists. What is this but wretched insanity?" St. Augustine later adds the concepts of "misery"—*when it is oneself who suffers*—and "pity"—*when one suffers for another*. "But what kind of pity is it that arises from fictitious and scenic passions? The hearer is not expected to believe," St. Augustine explains, "but merely invited to grieve; and the more he grieves, the more he applauds the actor of these fictions." "According to this," the saint asks, "we also enjoy tears and sorrow?" For St. Augustine, in short, tragedy is a strange madness. The spectator of tragedy is a kind of desperate masochist. He would be incapable of enduring personally the pain which is represented, but he enjoys the representation of the suffering which makes him weep and moves him superficially. This conception views the spectator of tragedy, in the last analysis, as a "false sado-masochist," since he enjoys the (feigned) suffering of the characters and his own (superficial) suffering as a spectator of the tragedy. Tragedy, in these terms, is an abomination which any adult society should cast from its midst. Tragedy would be truly a grave social sin. But the fact is that . . .

9. Tragedy, in Spite of Everything, Is Something Else. Once we have revindicated the reality of tragic suffering—by the conception of drama as a conducting wire which connects and syntonizes (let us use this word taken from the vocabulary of physics: to put into resonance with each other) human suffering with the heart of the spectator—the suspicion of masochism would lead to a graver formulation of "tragic madness." Tragedy would be a dangerous and punishable game of sadists and masochists. Opposed to these suspicions is the conception of tragedy as a form of mortification, and, in the last analysis, as an instrument of moral and social purification. The spectator of tragedy does not seek suffering; he accepts mortification. The spectator of tragedy feels himself deservedly mortified. He accepts the torture in an access of self-punishment. Then, does he feel himself guilty? Yes, tragedy wakens in him a profound feeling of guilt. And so . . . ? He accepts mortification. And then? When the tragedy ends, his spirit has been purified. And then? Then—sometimes—a social revolution. Or at least social improvement. Then, does it turn out that tragedy was something else?

10. A Purely Literary Page about the Real Meaning of Tragedy. Yes, tragedy was something else, and something very different. Tragedy is, precisely, the opposite of a social sin: a social virtue. Although true and happy sinners try, in their self-defensive struggle to eradicate from society this filthy sin which, according to them, tragedy is. (Those happy sinners who are afraid of the truth, and are defending their lives.)

This brief study of tragedy as it relates to the spectator ends with a purely literary page, in which we see a man stopping in the street before a theatre poster. The man is wearing a raincoat—it is raining a bit—and a felt hat. He could be an obscure member of a Chicago "gang," or a humble office worker in Madrid. It is all the same. The poster announces for tonight the presentation of a tragedy. The man, we know not why, has stopped, and is reading: "Seven and eleven o'clock, *Death of a Salesman,* by Arthur Miller." The man goes off. It continues raining. He enters a bar and drinks a glass of wine. He pays and leaves. He pulls up the collar of his raincoat. Night falls. He goes into an old restaurant. He has dinner: soup, an omelet and an orange. He appears to have forgotten that he even saw the theatre poster. But he looks at his watch; and it so happens that he has not forgotten. He pays, leaves a tip and goes back into the street. The theatre is near. He goes to the ticket window—up till now everything has been very easy—and buys a mezzanine seat. He enters the theatre. He makes himself comfortable. The house lights go down. The curtain rises. Against a background of strange music a traveling salesman, old and tired, returns home. The story begins. The man sees, from the beginning, that all this will have to end badly, but he does not know how. He does not know the how of the death, the how of the catastrophe, the how of the desperation and the final anguish. The tragedy becomes more and more intelligible. The salesman is not responsible for what is happening. His wife is not responsible. Neither are the children. No one is exclusively responsible for what is happening. All are innocent. All, at the same time, are guilty. The characters and those who surround them: the invisible men who surround them. The social system? All, even we the spectators—thinks the man—are a little responsible for what is happening to this poor old salesman. The salesman weeps. He wants to die. Because he thinks he is worth more dead than alive. The salesman weeps. The man weeps. He is weeping for the salesman, and for all the salesmen in the world, and for all other men, and because he did not behave as he should have toward someone who is now dead. The man is weeping for himself. At the end, when the family of the salesman is praying before his grave and wondering, quietly, why the salesman did it, why did he kill himself, the man is also praying a bit himself and feels somewhat purified by this viewing of the true structures—but it doesn't occur to him to think of "structures"—of suffering. He goes into the street. Now he is a man ready for something good. Now, yes. Because the man has been moved to help—and he does not know whether St. Augustine thought the opposite—not by intervening in the tragic action which is only a transfer or *mimesis* but in the reality which was transferred or imitated. The man, going homeward, is tranquil, His hands are in his raincoat pockets. His face has become calm, almost handsome. The man thinks that he "must do something"—but he doesn't know what; he will find out—and that "things can't go on this way." Fine. Go home to bed, my friend. Tomorrow . . . The man goes off.

II. An Open Letter on *Death of a Salesman*

I have just read with the greatest attention your criticism of *Death of a Salesman* and, for the first time in my life, I am writing an "open letter" (a very poorly paid literary genre). I must confess that I am impelled to write to you by a desire to put in their proper place several things which seem to me out of place. Your criticism—in short—seems unjust to me. I believe that you center your commentary not on the work itself, but on the reality to which the work bears witness, and it appears that the work consequently seems bad to you for the same reasons that the reality seems bad and impure (the sons who fail their father, etc.). I believe that if in reality "there are many millions of Willy Lomans" and Arthur Miller has succeeded in presenting one of them, the drama is fully justified and successful. For him, as for many modern authors, tragedy is "documentation"—Miller defines it as "balanced documentation"—and *Death of a Salesman* presents us with a rather complete documentation, and apparently an exact one, of Willy Loman. The drama is complete. What must be purified is the reality which the drama attests. There is drama precisely because the reality is impure. If Willy Loman had taught his sons, as you say, "love of his fellows and a sense of honor," and brought them up "in dignity and honesty," speaking to them "of God and of hope," it is possible that there may have been no drama. The terrible part of it is—and the fact that Miller has noticed it is to his credit as a dramatist—that there are millions of men who struggle only to gain comfort and security. Willy Loman, old, abandoned by his clients and his sons, enslaved by the payments on the icebox and the house, dead before everything was finally his, is a purifying sight, and the dramatic recreation of his life represents a cruel criticism of certain forms of human existence which are hopelessly condemned to failure. The author thus situates himself in a great tradition of modern drama. I have said "cruel criticisms," and this is so, even though Miller treats poor Willy Loman with compassion.

All this is in reply to your claim that the interest of the play seems to you "sociological and scarcely artistic." To me it seems that the play has no sociological interest whatsoever. Sociology is a science, and drama has very little to do with science. It has, of course, a social interest, and certainly a human interest; but built upon a solid artistic base. It certainly does not seem to me to be an "amorphous" work. On the contrary, it seems to me that it avoids, with some hesitation, the obvious danger of falling into "confusion and chaos."

Moreover, this is apparently what the public also thinks. Saturday evening, at least, the public—at the risk of missing the last subways and busses—applauded interminably. And I believe it was for reasons other than purely "sociological" ones. We must see here "social emotion," and not "sociological reason."

III. Theatre of Magic and Theatre of Anguish

The obligation of those of us who write for the theatre and of the theatre—and we are few—is, simply, to effect a diagnosis of the symptoms which we find in the "shapeless mass" of works which are produced, which are published, and which our friends read to us. We are interested in knowing what is happening and what is going to happen. We are interested in knowing whether anyone is coming along with us, or whether a difficult and lonely fight awaits us.

Two trends—according to latest observations—seem to stand out, incipient and blurred as yet, in the panorama of the Spanish theatre. On one side, the theatre of magic. On the other, misconstrued, repressed, deformed by the critics, the theatre of anguish. And we are not simply uttering—as do many superficial observers—words, words, words. Theatre of magic and theatre of anguish are terms with an immediate foundation in reality, based upon what Spanish theatres are presenting and the young authors are writing.

In the theatre of magic we see women who come from the sea (sirens)—how many sirens and similar monsters can we count in modern theatre?—phantoms (jesting spirits for the most part, but also some serious, circumspect and rather saddened ghosts), voices of the dead, angels, characters reflected in mirrors, consciences which speak in their own voices, dead people of flesh and blood who give us their impressions (as in the magic act of *Our Town*), objects with strange powers, superstitions which prove true, palmistry, card-reading, magic crystals, men transported to another era "because time does not exist," premonitions founded on the same fact (the idea that "the present, the past and the future coexist" and that "if we see time from above . . ." and that "if we see a river from a bridge . . ."), prophetic visions, mysterious characters who arrive (like messengers from the beyond, or voices of conscience, or I know not what), strange calls, signs—a whole parade of shades, almost always built upon the base of a realistic story (it is a kind of magical realism . . .) and in most cases with some common metaphysical pretensions. This is the "magic" of the modern theatre. This "magic," for some poor souls, exhausts the possibilities of the modern theatre. This type of drama—considered *avant-garde* in Spain until very recently!—is what now seems to be penetrating the professional companies who, weary of the old repertory, wish to perform "modern theatre."

The other trend, what we called "theatre of anguish," is the result of a very different feeling toward the theatre, its meaning and its function. It is the specifically tragic current of the modern theatre, based upon the postulates of realism. It is the theatre which looks upon existence as a fearful temporal wound: time is a tragic reality, and we are, ourselves, that time which is passing; there are no magical or fantastic evasions. It is the theatre in which things appear as they are. This is the current trend fostered by the great "witness dramatists." I am referring to those whose major production—discounting the magical levities to which most theatrical writers have given in—is a testimony of reality. It does not matter that Lenormand wrote several magical works, like *Time Is a Dream* and *The Madwoman of Heaven*, and other phantasmagoric dramas like *Man and His Phantoms*. Lenormand is, fundamentally, the author of *The Failures* and *The Coward*. O'Neill—to use another example—is not a magic author, in spite of *Lazarus Laughed* and his choruses, masks and mysteries. O'Neill is the cruel naturalist of *Strange Interlude*. A magical author is, for example, Maeterlinck. And not only because of that delightful "féerie," *The Bluebird*.

The magic trend has suffered several rude blows in the last few years. Literature founded on "neo-realistic" postulates, "existentialism," and, in general, the entire "socio-realistic" cultural front have fired their pistols straight into the "scatterbrain" of magic, of criminal evasion, and of suicidal and complacent smiles. We are in battle. The bourgeois public—that is to say, the public—asks for magic, evasion and dreams. The happy and confident city gives over most of its theatres to thoughtless and sentimental farces, while there is hunger, misery, and knives are being sharpened. While new kinds of bombs are tried out. While the proletariat the world over—hopelessly—asks for a raise in salary; the budgets for armaments are increased. On some stages we can hear the voice of anguish, and an urgent cry for purification.

And so the theatre continues having two masks. The comic mask has grown magician's whiskers. The tragic usually wears a war helmet, or chews a wad of proletarian tobacco, or wears the tie of a political party. The comic mask wears a degenerate smile. The tragic, a grimace of hunger and pain. Aside from this, things have not changed much.

It must be said that the young Spanish writers—to judge by the latest unpublished plays I have read—seem to follow more easily the magic way than the tragic one. One feels almost abandoned by those of his own generation (and I am not even mentioning the older generation!). They are disgusted by Sartre's tragedies, and note punctually the pleasure caused by the latest farce which has opened in Paris. In the movie theatres there was an "Oh!" of relief at the magical crisis and denouement of *Miracle in Milan*. So much the better—they said—that "neo-realism" has found a way out. That is how things are. Fortunately, there continues to be a public for tragedies.

DEATH THRUST

by ALFONSO SASTRE

1961

DEATH THRUST[1]

A Drama in Two Acts with a Prologue and an Epilogue

Translated by Leonard C. Pronko

CAST OF CHARACTERS

DOCTOR SANCHEZ, *Doctor of the bullring infirmary*
JIMENEZ, *his assistant*
BELTRAN, *police commissioner*
JOSE ALBA, *a bullfighter*
MARCOS, *his manager*
GABRIELA, *Jose's wife*
ALICIA, *a friend of Jose*
RAFAEL PASTOR, *Jose's auxiliary* (*sobresaliente*)
JUAN, *sword carrier for Jose*
A Chambermaid in the hotel
An Employee of the bullring
A Medical aide
A Beggar
Assistants at the bullring
A minor bullfighter at the bullring (*peon de brega*)

SOUND TRACK: Attention is called to the importance of the sound track (wind, rain, thunder, trumpets and drums, ovations, cries of horror, etc.) which is almost the central character of the prologue. This track must have a certain "musical" structure, and help in composing it may be derived from the experiments in "concrete music" and its application to the theatre.

[1] *Death Thrust* by Alfonso Sastre, translated by Leonard C. Pronko, copyright © 1963 by Literary Discoveries, Inc., San Francisco. Reprinted by permission. No performance may take place without a license obtained from Literary Discoveries, Inc.

[*The action takes place in a city like Madrid.*

The Prologue takes place in an anteroom of the bullring infirmary. At the back, a door which opens onto the tunnel leading to the bullring. At the right, the entrance to the operating room. Another door leading to the outside.

The Epilogue requires no setting. It depicts the interior of a tavern, which may be suggested schematically, by lights falling upon the necessary objects, as noted in the text. An amber lantern is prominently displayed.

The rest of the action takes place in the suite of a hotel in which MARCOS *and* JOSE ALBA *are staying. The hallway which leads to the suite is assumed to be at the extreme forestage; at this level, to the extreme right (of the spectator), is the door of the elevator whose movement should be indicated by sounds and the play of lights through the door which has a frosted glass. Downstage left is the door which opens into the suite. The suite, insofar as it is visible to the audience, is made up of an ample living room—in which most of the action takes place—and an area at the rear which is reached by a step and a door suggested in outline. This area is an anteroom which has a door at the rear opening onto a bathroom which we cannot see, and another opening onto the bedroom, likewise invisible. In the living room there is a full-length mirror attached to some piece of furniture, and a sofa downstage with its back facing the audience. In the anteroom there is a mirror which will be used when* JOSE *is dressing. It is a cloudy autumnal day.*]

PROLOGUE

[*A room off the infirmary of the Plaza de Toros. Through the windows a turbid light enters. In the distance, very faintly, we can hear the sound of the crowd. We can hear the noise of rain, which, shortly after the curtain rises, grows heavier.*

DOCTOR SANCHEZ, *an old man of jovial appearance, is setting up a chessgame on the board. When he has finished he hides it in a corner, rubs his hands together, goes toward a small electric coffeemaker and plugs it in. He coughs. He puts his hand to his forehead as though taking his temperature. He opens a cabinet which looks like a first aid cabinet; we can see several bottles of gin and cognac inside. He takes out a tube and takes a pill. At this moment we hear knocking on the outside door. The* DOCTOR *answers immediately.*]

DOCTOR [*energetically*]. Come in, come in.

[*The door opens and* JIMENEZ *enters. He is a young man with an ingenuous, candid expression. His suit is wet and he has turned up the collar of his coat.*]

JIMENEZ. Good afternoon, doctor.
DOCTOR. Good afternoon. Where've you been?
JIMENEZ [*as though apologizing*]. I'm a little late, I know . . .
DOCTOR [*smiles*]. That's not what I mean . . . Your suit's all wet. Is it raining that hard?
JIMENEZ [*nodding*]. It's a real downpour. I got soaking wet just between here and the subway.
DOCTOR. You came in the subway?
JIMENEZ [*taking off his coat in order to put on his white medical jacket*]. What else . . .
DOCTOR. You'll have to buy yourself a car. It's absolutely necessary in this profession.

JIMENEZ. But, how? [*He laughs. Behind the noise of the rain we can hear the trumpet and the drumroll—henceforth the indication "trumpet" will refer to this. The* DOCTOR *makes a face when he hears the trumpet.*]

DOCTOR. So you almost got here late? Can I bawl you out a little? Since you're new, you can do nothing but listen to me. Watch your timing . . . You know the bullfight is the only thing in Spain that starts on time.

JIMENEZ [*smiles*]. I know . . . even though I'm not much of a fan. [*He puts on his white smock.*] On the way, I decided they would probably cancel it this afternoon.

DOCTOR [*he coughs*]. It'll have to rain harder than this . . . When the bullfighters begin to sink knee-deep in the mud they'll begin to think about it. . . . [*A silence.*] Did you intend to see the fight this afternoon? I can't bring myself to go out there today.

JIMENEZ. You're not sick?

DOCTOR. It's nothing. . . . This weather . . . and old age. Plus a slight cold.

JIMENEZ. I'm sorry.

DOCTOR [*smiles*]. I almost didn't come this afternoon.

JIMENEZ [*impressed*]. I . . . I'm grateful to you for coming. It's still a little difficult for me.

DOCTOR. Don't worry. You've already shown you've got nothing to be afraid of. Now all you need is experience. [*A silence.*] So, then? Will you see the fight?

JIMENEZ [*undecided*]. I don't know. . . . I mean . . . What else can you do at the bullring?

DOCTOR [*smiling*]. Several things . . . [*With a mysterious smile.*] The other day you told me you were fond of a certain game.

JIMENEZ. Oh, yes! . . .

DOCTOR [*points, with almost childish eagerness, to the prepared chessboard*]. It was this one, wasn't it?

JIMENEZ [*laughs*]. Yes.

DOCTOR [*watching* JIMENEZ'S *reaction to his words*]. I thought we might play a game . . . if the weather turned bad. . . . Don't feel you have to. Not at all . . .

JIMENEZ [*laughing*]. I'd like to. I'm not interested in getting wet again out there.

DOCTOR. Our little niche out there has a cover over it . . .

JIMENEZ. That doesn't help!

DOCTOR [*breathes with relief*]. As you can see, I knew I could count on you. I had already set up the pieces.

JIMENEZ. And this?

DOCTOR. Coffee. Everything is ready.

JIMENEZ. Thanks . . . for your hospitality.

DOCTOR. You're at home here as much as I am. You were foolish enough to let them place you here. . . . *There, you . . .*

JIMENEZ [*laughing*]. Is it so bad here?

DOCTOR. Not always. . . . Well, anyway, since we're going to spend several hours of our life together, I thought it would be a good idea to . . . become friends.

JIMENEZ. I can see it's not going to be difficult.

DOCTOR. I hope not. [*He sits.*] Last Sunday I got a very good impression of you.

JIMENEZ. You explored me thoroughly, didn't you?

DOCTOR. I did what I could.

[JIMENEZ *has hung his wet coat up on a hanger. Now he sits facing the* DOCTOR, *who is filling his cup with coffee.*]

DOCTOR. Full?

JIMENEZ. No, thanks.

DOCTOR. Afraid of your nerves?

JIMENEZ. No . . . but . . . I'd rather not drink too much. You never know what's going to happen.

DOCTOR. Usually things will go just as they did last time. . . . No unpleasant incidents. . . . [*He hands him a cup.*]

JIMENEZ. But the very worst could also happen . . . That's what you keep thinking about. At least, that's what a beginner thinks about.

DOCTOR. Of course, something . . . well, pretty horrible, could happen. If you don't mind, I'll make the first move. [*He moves a piece.*] The wounds made by a bull's horn, you know the kind I mean . . . they can tear a man's insides to pieces. . . . I've seen bullfighters' bodies literally torn apart . . . from the horns. [*He forgets what he is saying. He is more interested in the move he has just made.*] I warn you I haven't played for a long time. . . . To be honest, I couldn't find anyone to play with. . . . What was I saying? Oh, yes . . . It's frightening, if you start thinking about it.

JIMINEZ. It certainly is. . . . I mean . . . [*He's rather moved. He is about to sip his coffee when the trumpet sounds. He jumps slightly and spills some coffee.*] Oh . . . I'm sorry!

DOCTOR. Doesn't matter. Would you like a drink?

JIMENEZ. Yes, please.

DOCTOR [*showing him the bottles in the "medicine cabinet"*]. Cognac? Gin? That's all I've got.

JIMENEZ. I'd rather have cognac.

DOCTOR. So would I. [*He pours out two glasses and gives one to* JIMENEZ, *who takes it. The rain is getting worse. Wind.*] What weather, huh?

JIMENEZ. I don't see how they can fight in this kind of downpour. [*He moves a piece.*]

DOCTOR. They can't. [*He has a fit of coughing.*]

JIMENEZ [*takes a drink, puts down the glass, and asks smilingly*]. Then what do they do?

DOCTOR. The bull has just gone out. . . . They're looking at it, wondering. [*He moves a piece.*] The assistant makes a few passes to test the bull. Once, again . . . Careful! Back to the safety of the enclosure . . . He breathes a sigh of relief. It's better . . .

JIMENEZ. Isn't that fighting?

DOCTOR. As much fighting as they can do under the circumstances . . . For the rest, they just hold out . . . fulfill their contracts . . . Does that seem like little to you?

JIMENEZ. It's enough.

DOCTOR. They earn their bread as best they can. They kill the bulls they're given. That's their job. [JIMENEZ *is pensive before the chessboard.*] You're thinking about it, eh?

JIMENEZ. The game? No . . . [*He moves a piece.*] I was thinking about the fellow that's out there fighting today. I read an article in the paper. . . . [*Trumpet.*] Of course, you probably pay by the line. . . . They were trying to create a legend of his life. . . . His parents had died in a bombing during the war. . . . An orphan . . . someone took care of him, a distant relative who had been a bombardier . . . He felt guilty about some of the actions he'd participated in . . . something like that . . . Then, studies . . . Did you know he'd been a medical student?

DOCTOR. Yes.

JIMENEZ. He always wears black and gold. . . . That's what the article says. I've never seen him.

DOCTOR. I have.

JIMENEZ. Is he worth it? I mean, as a bullfighter?

DOCTOR. In my opinion, he is; but there are many people who say he isn't.

JIMENEZ. In the subway they were saying this afternoon's fight is a mistake.

DOCTOR [*laughs*]. To face a bull is always a mistake.

JIMENEZ. They meant, for him to take six bulls.

DOCTOR. A terrible mistake.

JIMENEZ. In what way? Because of the risk?

DOCTOR. Because of the show . . . The people want variety . . . No, don't think you've got me in a tight spot . . . it's just that I like to meditate each play. . . . What was I saying? Oh, yes . . . six bulls . . . There used to be bullfighters who were up to that, they say; take on six bulls and vary the plays. But nowadays, of course, no . . . They don't even have the physical strength . . . They can scarcely lift the sword! . . . Haven't you noticed they use a wooden one, so they won't tire themselves out? [*Drinks coffee.*]

JIMENEZ [*smiles*]. I can see that at one time you were quite a fan.

DOCTOR. It was when it used to be a real fiesta brava. . . . Long ago . . . [*He moves a piece and gets up, satisfied with his move.*] Cigarette?

JIMENEZ [*meditating before the chessboard*]. No, thanks.

DOCTOR. I shouldn't smoke, either. [*Opens the "medicine cabinet," gets out a pack of cigarettes, and takes one, lighting it with obvious pleasure. He smokes.*] You were speaking of a legend . . . It's not so much that . . . It's just that the stage director gives it a different twist depending on the needs of the moment. . . .

JIMENEZ [*looking up from the board*]. The stage director? Who's that?

DOCTOR. I'm not letting you concentrate on the game. . . . I'm sorry . . . We're not really playing a formal game. . . . A formal game must be played in absolute silence. . . . I keep running into that difficulty . . . I like to talk too much.

JIMENEZ. We can finish later. I'm interested in what you just said. A stage director? Who is he?

DOCTOR. His name is Juan Marcos. . . . He's the manager of the boy who's fighting today.

JIMENEZ. Juan Marcos? I've never heard of him. [*We hear a clap of thunder in the distance, and darkness seems to invade the room.* JIMENEZ *shudders.*] They'll have to stop it. With this weather, it's a crime . . . [*Wind. The rain is heavier. A pause.*] This Juan Marcos, what kind of man is he?

DOCTOR. Quite a fellow . . . I've known him for some time.

JIMENEZ. He's an impresario?

DOCTOR. Let's call him an agent. He makes a business of launching unknown bullfighters. . . . From starvation to fame! It's sometimes a deadly leap. Do you remember Ricardo Platero?

JIMENEZ. I just know he was a famous bullfighter.

DOCTOR. One of Marcos' creations . . . A few brilliant years, until it all came crashing down around him. Then he discovered this boy, Jose Alba . . . We'll see how long he lasts . . . He'll bring him to ruin just like the others. . . . He tries to make them give more than they've got in them . . .; he gives them nervous disorders. . . . Drives them mad with his promises. They have . . . a terrifying ambition. Sometimes I think he's insane . . . [*Trumpet.*]

JIMENEZ. A strange person, huh?

DOCTOR. Yes . . . You might say that . . . Aren't you going to make a move?

[JIMENEZ *turns back to the board. A pause during which we hear the surrounding noise. Whistles for some badly placed banderillas. The* DOCTOR, *standing near the chessboard, smokes meditatively . . . he speaks absently.*]

DOCTOR. You know what I compare him to?

JIMENEZ. What?

DOCTOR. I mean Marcos . . . It's a meaningless comparison, I know . . . I remember that picture of Saturn devouring one of his children.

[*A clap of thunder in the distance. A slight ovation when the din of the thunder subsides.*]

DOCTOR. A good pair of banderillas. The people appreciate that . . . But it must be almost time . . . [*Trumpet.*] The moment of truth. Good luck, kid.

JIMENEZ [*with a slight shiver*]. This . . . is the worst moment.

DOCTOR [*lightly*]. Yes . . .

JIMENEZ. If I were alone here, it wouldn't be easy.

DOCTOR. That used to happen to me at first, too. Then you get used to it, you'll see.

[JIMENEZ *tries to concentrate on the chessboard. The* DOCTOR *looks at him, smiling benevolently.* JIMENEZ, *slightly trembling, moves a piece. Then the* DOCTOR *sits down facing him, as though he had decided to make it a formal game. Now there is also silence outside.* JIMENEZ *tries to listen to something, with a nervous look. The* DOCTOR *looks up from the board.*]

DOCTOR. What's the matter?
JIMENEZ. This silence.
DOCTOR. It happens sometimes.
JIMENEZ. It's as though the ring were empty.
DOCTOR [*listening*]. On the contrary . . . The people have returned to the bleachers.
JIMENEZ. It seems to have stopped raining.
DOCTOR. Yes. . . .
JIMENEZ. While you're studying the next play, I'm going to take a look.
DOCTOR. Go ahead.
JIMENEZ. Don't you want to? . . .
DOCTOR [*smiling*]. All I want is to checkmate you.
JIMENEZ. I'll be right back.

[*He goes out the door leading to the tunnel. The* DOCTOR *studies his play. There is a spectacular silence. The surrounding noise which till now has been continuous, has completely subsided. The* DOCTOR *now smiles and moves a piece, murmuring.*]

DOCTOR. Check . . . [*Suddenly we hear a collective cry of anguish. The* DOCTOR *rises quickly and crosses to the door leading to the tunnel, through which* JIMENEZ *returns, quite pale.*] What's happened?
JIMENEZ. A goring.

[*Noises. A white-coated aide appears in the door of the operating room.*]

AIDE. A goring, doctor?
DOCTOR. Yes. . . . Is everything ready?
AIDE. Yes, doctor.
DOCTOR [*turning to* JIMENEZ]. How did it happen?
JIMENEZ. It looked to me like he got him in the groin. Just as he was making a pass, the wind blew his cape, leaving him uncovered.
DOCTOR. We'll see . . . Go into the operating room, please.
JIMENEZ. Yes . . .

[*He goes out, followed by the* DOCTOR. *At the same time the attendants arrive, with a minor bullfighter,* (*member of* JOSE's *cuadrilla*), *carrying* JOSE's *body. He is wear-*

ing a suit of black and gold, now torn, and stained with blood and mud. He has passed out, and his arms are hanging limp. They take him into the operating room, helped by the AIDE. *The door is closed. The stage remains empty for a moment. The noise from the outside grows louder, and it becomes apparent that people are trying to enter the room from the tunnel, while a uniformed employee attempts to keep them out.*]

EMPLOYEE [*from outside*]. No one can come in. [*Noises.*] No, absolutely forbidden. Orders of the management.

[*From the bullring we hear a loud ovation. Another, even greater. The door to the operating room opens, and the men who had carried* JOSE'S *body come out. The* AIDE, *from the door of the operating room, points to the door leading to the tunnel.*]

AIDE. Please leave by that door. Don't remain in here.

[*The men, grave and silent, file out while the door of the operating room is again closed. Another loud ovation. A sudden silence. Then a delirium of enthusiasm. A trumpet sounds. More rain once more and a clap of thunder, this time very close. The door of the operating room opens suddenly, and* JIMENEZ, *very agitated, enters. He goes toward the door leading to the tunnel, and calls outside to the uniformed* EMPLOYEE.]

JIMENEZ. Would you come here, please?

EMPLOYEE [*entering the room*]. They're trying to get in.

JIMENEZ. I'll take care of that. Go get Commissioner Beltran and tell him Dr. Sanchez would like to see him. . . . It's urgent.

EMPLOYEE. But what's happened?

JIMENEZ. Quickly. I'll close the door.

EMPLOYEE. Is it serious?

JIMENEZ. Go on, please . . . [*The* EMPLOYEE *exits.* JIMENEZ, *at the door, speaks to the people outside.*] No, no one may come in.

[*He closes the door. He lights a cigarette, as though intending to wait for the* COMMISSIONER *there.* DOCTOR SANCHEZ *comes in from the operating room.*]

JIMENEZ. Is there nothing we can do?

DOCTOR [*gravely*]. Nothing. . . . Have they gone for the Commissioner?

JIMENEZ. Yes.

DOCTOR. What a strange thing.

JIMENEZ. A horrible . . . surprise. Do you mind if I have a drink?

DOCTOR. No, go ahead.

JIMENEZ [*serving himself*]. You want one?

DOCTOR. No.

JIMENEZ [*drinking*]. I'm . . . a little nervous.

DOCTOR. Did the wound shock you?

JIMENEZ. No. It's just . . . that it surprised me and . . . [*He makes a vague gesture.*]

DOCTOR. It surprised me too, of course.

JIMENEZ. What do you think?

DOCTOR. Think? In this kind of case it's beyond me. . . . It's a case for the Commissioner . . . [*Someone knocks authoritatively at the tunnel door.*] Would you open it, please? It must be him.

[JIMENEZ, *who is near the door, opens it.* COMMISSIONER BELTRAN *comes in, closing the door behind him.*]

COMMISSIONER. Good afternoon. What's the matter?

DOCTOR [*shaking hands*]. It's . . . something serious, Commissioner. [*Introducing*] Doctor Jimenez. Commissioner Beltran. [*They shake hands.*]

COMMISSIONER. What's happened?

DOCTOR. This boy, Jose Alba, was dead when he got to the operating room.

COMMISSIONER [*shaking his head*]. I thought it looked like a serious goring.

DOCTOR. It wasn't.

COMMISSIONER. What? What do you mean?

DOCTOR. A scratch on the leg. That's all.

COMMISSIONER. And he's dead?

DOCTOR. Yes.

COMMISSIONER. Explain yourself.

DOCTOR. He was fighting, although he was already seriously wounded.

COMMISSIONER. Wounded? What kind of wound?

DOCTOR. A steel blade . . . in the stomach.

COMMISSIONER. My God! Tell me everything you know.

DOCTOR. He had received temporary treatment before coming to the bullring. There's no doubt about it. A good job, done by a professional, undoubtedly: an intern . . . or a doctor.

COMMISSIONER. And he went out to fight in that condition?

DOCTOR [*nodding*]. He couldn't take it. The jab and the fall . . . the shock . . . brought on the catastrophe: a terrible hemorrhage. . . . If that hadn't happened, he might have lasted to the end. I don't know. Six bulls were too many . . . under such conditions.

COMMISSIONER. When do you think all this might have happened?

DOCTOR. A few hours before the bullfight; perhaps an hour. I don't know. It's a recent wound. [*The* COMMISSIONER *is pensive.*] What do you intend to do?

COMMISSIONER. First of all, to take a look at the body.

DOCTOR. All right. Come this way.

[*At this moment we hear loud pounding on the door leading to the tunnel. The* COMMISSIONER *turns back from the operating room door.*]

DOCTOR. Wait. Let's see who's trying to beat the door in.

[*He opens the door. A man with sharp features, consumed by some strange fever, enters with affected calmness. His eyes seem lustreless. He is very excited, but tries to appear calm. He speaks to the* DOCTOR.]

MARCOS. What's happened? [*The* DOCTOR *does not answer. He doesn't know what to say.*] Is it serious?

DOCTOR. We could do nothing, Marcos.

MARCOS. What do you mean? [*He seems not to have understood. He has a stupid look. The* DOCTOR, JIMENEZ, and *the* COMMISSIONER *observe him. He look distrustfully at the others.*] I wasn't out there. I saw nothing. Suddenly . . . I heard the people shout.

DOCTOR. Since you hadn't come, I thought you weren't at the ring.

MARCOS [*hesitant, as though trying to answer something*]. I came as soon as I could, because . . . I don't know what came over me, but I couldn't stand to watch it this afternoon. [*He speaks evasively without looking at anyone.*] It's the first time that's happened to me. I wanted to go somewhere far away, to wait it out. It was . . . a kind of apprehension. How horrible! [*He is depressed. The* DOCTOR *puts a hand on his shoulder.*]

DOCTOR. Calm yourself . . .

[*The trumpet sounds. This grates on* MARCOS' *nerves; he suddenly shouts, unexpectedly.*]

MARCOS. But, my God, what are they doing? What are they doing? Are they going on? No. They can't! It's all over! This is my fight! Who will they go on with? Be quiet!!

[*He seems on the verge of an attack, as though delirious. The* COMMISSIONER *has approached him, and puts his hand on his shoulder.*]

COMMISSIONER. Listen.
MARCOS [*turning*]. Who are you?
COMMISSIONER [*showing his identification*]. Police.
MARCOS. What do you want with me?
COMMISSIONER. Are you Juan Marcos, the manager of that poor boy in there?
MARCOS. Yes.
COMMISSIONER. Were you with him the past few hours?
MARCOS [*he hesitates, but finally answers resolutely*]. Yes.
COMMISSIONER. Then you're going to answer a few questions for me.

[MARCOS *is about to protest, but restrains himself.*]

MARCOS. Me? Why?
COMMISSIONER. Sit down, please. I don't want you to move from here until you've answered my questions satisfactorily.
MARCOS. No! What are you getting at? You want to arrest me? You can't do that! Now less than ever! I have to see Jose! He's the only thing I had in the world! Let me in!

[*The* COMMISSIONER *makes a gesture of negation to the* DOCTOR.]

DOCTOR [*blocking the door*]. You can't now, Marcos. Calm yourself.
MARCOS. I have to see him . . . [*With a sad tone of reproach.*] Won't you let me in either?
DOCTOR. Not now, Marcos. Please.

[MARCOS *sits down, intimidated. A pause. He looks from one to the other. Finally his gaze remains fixed on that of the* COMMISSIONER.]

MARCOS. All right. Ask anything you want.
COMMISSIONER. What I want to know from you is . . .

[*From outside we hear an immense ovation.* MARCOS *does not listen to the* COMMISSIONER. *Another ovation.* MARCOS *trembles, as though he were listening to some infernal noise.*]

COMMISSIONER. What's the matter?
MARCOS. The fellow . . . out there . . . the replacement . . .
COMMISSIONER What about him?
MARCOS. His name . . . I think his name is Rafael Pastor. What's he doing? [*Another enormous ovation.* MARCOS *covers his ears in anguish.*] My God, what's he doing?

[*The* COMMISSIONER *looks impatient.*]

COMMISSIONER. I think you'd better come with me. If you don't mind?
MARCOS [*seems calmed by the silence which has now fallen. Murmurs*:] No.
COMMISSIONER. Come with me. [*To the* DOCTOR.] I'll be back soon. I'll give orders that no one is to enter. . . . I would like you to stay here . . . until I return.
DOCTOR. Of course, Commissioner.

[*The* COMMISSIONER *goes out the door to the outside.* MARCOS, *downcast, follows him. When he reaches the door, he turns and asks sadly*:]

MARCOS. Can I see him later? Not then . . . either?
DOCTOR. Certainly you can . . .

[MARCOS *goes out. The* DOCTOR *sighs, goes toward the chessboard, is about to knock over the pieces, but something makes him look at* JIMENEZ . . . *he points to the chessboard, and* JIMENEZ *approaches and looks at it gravely. He nods . . . then the* DOCTOR *slowly knocks over the pieces while darkness falls, and on the soundtrack the noise dies down, becoming total only at the moment the lights come on—or the curtain rises—for the first act.*]

ACT ONE

[*Darkness in the suite. A light at the door of the elevator, whose noise we hear. A play of lights, and the noise stops. The door of the elevator opens and* MARCOS *and* JOSE ALBA *enter. Lights come up in the downstage area representing the hallway outside the suite.* MARCOS *leads and* JOSE *follows silently, some distance behind.* MARCOS *opens the door of the suite and enters.* JOSE *stands waiting in the doorway until* MARCOS *has turned on the lights.* MARCOS *opens the venetian blinds and light enters the room; it is the grey light of a cloudy day, a sad light. Then* JOSE *enters the room but does not look at it.*]

MARCOS. You like it?
JOSE. Yes. . . .

[MARCOS *opens the door in the arch at the rear, and in the light which now falls into the anteroom we can see a black and gold bullfighter's suit lying over a chair. A screen hides part of the anteroom.*]

MARCOS. That's the door to the bedroom.
JOSE [*looks inside without interest*]. All right.
MARCOS. I told Juan to hang your clothes in the closet. Everything else is where it belongs. . . . If you want anything . . .
JOSE [*shaking his head*]. Thanks.

[*He notices on a table a kind of ikon or religious triptych, before which there is a light, extinguished now.*]

JOSE [*with a weary smile*]. You never forget it.
MARCOS. Never . . .
JOSE. What is it? A little idol or a mascot? You've never told me what it really means to you.

MARCOS. Don't laugh at it.

JOSE. I'm not laughing. [*He shrugs his shoulders.*]

MARCOS. You think it's superstitious, don't you?

JOSE. No. . . . [*A silence.*]

MARCOS. At our last fight, I saw you going into the chapel. I'm glad.

JOSE. Yes. . . .

MARCOS. You should never forget it. Even if you're not very religious.

JOSE. I think I'm beginning to be . . . And you know when it started?

MARCOS. No . . .

JOSE. When I realized that I was getting rich! [*He laughs.*]

MARCOS. Sometimes you say things . . .

JOSE. Just to say something . . . [*He goes to the window and looks out, worried.*]

MARCOS [*lights a cigarette*]. I thought, later in the afternoon, after the fight . . .

JOSE [*turning*]. What?

MARCOS. . . . We might do something.

JOSE [*sitting down wearily*]. No, count me out. [*He looks very tired.*]

MARCOS. I've reserved a table . . . You need to enjoy yourself a little . . .

JOSE [*with a slight yawn*]. What I need is sleep . . .

MARCOS. All right. Whatever you want.

[JOSE *takes out a cigarette. When he lights it, his hands tremble slightly.* MARCOS *notices.*]

MARCOS. How do you feel?

JOSE [*shrugging his shoulders*]. All right . . .

MARCOS. Tired?

[JOSE *suddenly laughs bitterly.*]

JOSE [*aggressive*]. Would it be so strange if I were?

MARCOS. I didn't say anything. I simply asked a question, that's all.

JOSE. Yes, I am.

MARCOS. What are you trying to do? Make me feel guilty?

JOSE. No. . . .

MARCOS. When the season began I asked you if you felt strong enough for eighty fights. You said yes. I signed you up for them. Many people would like to be in your shoes. Don't forget it.

JOSE. I'm not blaming you for anything. Come on, let's forget it . . . Is it my fault if I'm tired?

MARCOS. I told you to come by plane.

JOSE. No . . . The bulls are enough . . . I can't waste the . . . little courage I've got.

MARCOS [*laughing forcedly*]. You see? That's the way to talk . . . I like to see you that way, in a good mood.

JOSE. You've got a strange idea of a good mood.

MARCOS. Perhaps. [*A silence.* MARCOS *observes* JOSE.] I told them the usual. No one is to come up. Do you agree?

JOSE. Yes.

MARCOS. I'm glad.

JOSE. Why? What were you thinking?

MARCOS. That this time you just might want to see . . . someone.

JOSE. No. . . . [*A silence.* MARCOS *makes up his mind to say it.*]

MARCOS. I'm mentioning it, because she'll probably come.

JOSE. My wife?

MARCOS. Yes.

JOSE. How do you know?

MARCOS. She called here this morning. They told her you hadn't arrived.

JOSE. You think she'll come?

MARCOS. I think so.

JOSE. She knows we're finished.

MARCOS. She may have something else in mind.

JOSE [*upset*]. If she comes, I won't know what to do. No . . . I don't want to see her.

MARCOS. Then authorize me to keep her out.

JOSE. Do whatever you want.

MARCOS. Don't worry, then.

JOSE. I never should have accepted this fight. I told you it was risky to come here. The further away I stay the better.

MARCOS. Then, you're still . . . in love.

JOSE. No, it's not that . . . [*Shakes his head.*] Sometimes I think I didn't do the right thing.

MARCOS. Don't start stirring up old memories.

JOSE [*obsessed*]. You shouldn't have signed me up for this fight.

MARCOS. I couldn't refuse it. Six bulls in a major bullring is . . . a great opportunity.

JOSE. A great opportunity for what?

MARCOS. To be awarded an ear in this ring is important. . . . More important than a hundred smalltown victories. You're ready for this now. That's why I've brought you here. It's a necessary step in your career. Can't you see how I'm leading you, step by step, to real fame?

JOSE [*with an ironic smile*]. I'm not famous enough already? Then what am I?

MARCOS [*takes his hand*]. What are you talking about? [*With enthusiasm.*] This is nothing yet, Jose. I'm taking you to the top, don't you understand? If this afternoon turns out well, you've got America wrapped up. Doesn't that appeal to you? Caracas, Mexico, Lima. Money by the shovelful, then the return to Spain, delirious crowds, shouting for you every afternoon. And we can laugh at everyone who didn't believe in us, everyone who said we were nothing, we were crazy and that you would end up like the others I wanted to raise to the top—who didn't give me all they had. Like Platero, who broke me, brought me nothing but humiliations, till I found you . . . [*His eyes are shining.*] Don't you like the idea? America . . . and all the rest?

JOSE [*moved, his eyes moist, nods*]. Can you take me . . . to the top?

MARCOS. A lot of it depends on you! A lot depends on this afternoon.

[*He is watching the effect of his words.* JOSE *has risen, and looks at himself in a full-length mirror. He contemplates himself complacently. He smiles and turns slowly on his heels.*]

JOSE. Marcos.

MARCOS. What?

JOSE. Sincerely . . .

MARCOS. What?

JOSE. Can you speak sincerely?

MARCOS. Of course. Why?

JOSE. I'd like to ask you something.

MARCOS. Go ahead.

JOSE. It's about myself.

[*He continues watching himself in the mirror, making slow turns like a "salon bullfighter."*]

MARCOS. What is it?

JOSE. You won't be sincere.

MARCOS. All right, then, forget it.

JOSE. Do you really think I'm a great bullfighter? Sincerely?

MARCOS. Well, what do you think?

JOSE. Greater than all the others today?

MARCOS. Undoubtedly.

JOSE [*turning to him*]. And greater than Platero?

MARCOS. Platero had a bad temper . . . We did what we could. Nothing more.

JOSE. Nothing? You talk about him this way now? Other times you hold him up as an example.

MARCOS. He was . . . great . . . but just at the beginning. Then he started letting me down, right away. In a single season I could see him falling, and there was no way to save him. . . . It was after the goring in Barcelona, a blow in the face that disfigured him. There was nothing to be done. . . . But don't think I abandoned him when I saw he was lost. On the contrary . . . I risked a lot on him. . . . Money to the newspapers . . . you can't understand . . . what I went through . . . each afternoon was another shovelful of earth thrown on his grave. . . . In one row he had to leave the ring, protected by the police. . . . One of my bullfighters! . . . What humiliation. But I said nothing to him that night when he broke down and cried. "Marcos, I can't! I'm washed up!" he said; and the scar on his face gave him a sad, ugly look. . . . I gave him one more fight but it was the last.

JOSE. Where is he now?

MARCOS. I don't know. Sometimes he's come to ask me for money . . . a tramp.

JOSE. And did you give it to him?

MARCOS [*evasive*]. Not always . . . It wasn't my fault. . . . He dragged me down with him—to ridicule . . . but not to hunger, because I can't stand hunger. . . . [*with pride*] Leave that for others. . . but to ridicule! [*a silence, with rancour*] I could have killed him! Yes, I could have choked him to death!

JOSE [*after a pause*]. And the others . . . before Platero . . . how were they?

MARCOS. They all had . . . talents . . . But none of them were complete, like you.

JOSE [*after a pause*]. Were they courageous?

MARCOS. Yes, and you are too.

JOSE. We're speaking sincerely now, remember.

MARCOS. You are, . . . sincerely.

JOSE. I'm sick.

MARCOS. Nonsense! It's your imagination.

JOSE. Did you know, it happened to me again?

MARCOS [*alarmed*]. When?

JOSE. Last night.

MARCOS. How?

JOSE. I was in a bar. I fell over backwards, and passed out completely.

MARCOS. You were drunk.

JOSE. No.

MARCOS. You mustn't drink.

JOSE. I hadn't.

MARCOS. Not even one glass. It's bad for you.

JOSE. I know [*a silence*].

MARCOS [*fearfully*]. Did they take you to a doctor? Who was with you?

JOSE. I was alone . . . They didn't take me anywhere. . . . They probably thought I was drunk.

MARCOS. Were you in the same place when you came to?

JOSE. Yes. I drove home.

MARCOS. You drove?

JOSE. Of course.

MARCOS. You shouldn't do that. It's not wise.

JOSE. And getting in a ring with a bull *is*?

MARCOS. In the bullfight you're looking for something. But driving in that condition is a needless risk.

JOSE. I'll have to go back to the doctor.

MARCOS. Why? They know nothing about what's wrong with you.

JOSE. They know that I shouldn't be fighting bulls.

MARCOS. They say that . . . just to say something. Have you ever seen an epileptic? It's something completely different from what happens to you . . . a momentary fainting fit . . . it can't be too serious. But epileptic attacks! I've seen them! I know what they're like.

JOSE. Anyway . . . I think sometimes it would be better to have another examination. A complete examination, if possible.

MARCOS. If that's what you want, of course we'll go. . . . I'll go with you myself. . . . You'll see . . .

[*A silence. Now* JOSE *examines himself in the mirror in a completely different way: the sick man trying to see how he is.*]

JOSE. I measure up, though, don't I? In the ring . . . I measure up.

MARCOS. Of course you do.

JOSE. In spite of . . . everything.

MARCOS. You're strong . . . despite everything.

JOSE. Even with my sickness . . . and what we've decided to call my nerves.

MARCOS. What do you want to call it?

JOSE. By its real name.

MARCOS [*discouraged*]. Not that again.

JOSE [*hard*]. Yes, that again and always!

MARCOS. You like to torture yourself.

JOSE. I'm frightened! How else do you think I can say it? I'm afraid!

MARCOS [*frantic*]. No you're not!

JOSE. I refuse to deny it.

MARCOS. You like to say things that just aren't true.

JOSE. I like the truth.

MARCOS. You're full of complexes, you're twisted. . . . With all you've got, you could be happy. But you'd rather think about what you don't have. . . . If you can't find anything you don't have, you invent it.

JOSE [*smiling, ironically*]. That's psychology, Marcos. Where did you drag that out from?

MARCOS. I didn't learn it at the University, I can tell you . . . can you remember anything you learned?

JOSE. Nothing, fortunately. That's how I keep on living.

MARCOS. You may lack other things, but you don't lack courage.

JOSE [*smiles, enjoying what he's saying, as though it were a kind of self-flagellation*]. You turn white . . . break out in a cold sweat . . . your teeth chatter . . . your knees tremble . . . you feel sick. . . . What's it called?

MARCOS. Don't say it, not even jokingly.

JOSE. Are you ashamed of it?

MARCOS. Any man would be.

JOSE. I'm not ashamed. I'm the one who should be ashamed, isn't that so?

MARCOS. Never say it to anyone.

JOSE. It's bad for publicity, isn't it?

MARCOS. Never say it.

JOSE. They'll see it for themselves. I won't have to tell them.

MARCOS. In the bullring no one can tell. So be quiet.

JOSE. In the bullring . . . by then I'm over it. . . . It's here that I suffer . . . in the hotel rooms, before going to the ring . . . when it's almost time to leave . . . when my black and gold suit is lying there on the chair . . . [*The bells in a nearby church ring.*] What's that?

MARCOS [*not answering*]. There's nothing to worry about despite what you're saying. . . . I go with you, and that's all there is to it. . . . Everyone has his peculiarities. [*The bells continue.*] I know how to talk to you when it happens. Then you get over it and it's as though nothing had ever happened. You leave the hotel smiling. . . . That's the way it's always been.

JOSE. It's before . . .

MARCOS. Before, I calm you, put some sense in your head. They're just foolish ideas you get . . . nerves.

JOSE. That's when I'd like to be far away. But I can't; I'm caught . . . as though I were in a spiderweb. [*He laughs.*] You're the spider, Marcos, a hairy, old spider. . . .

MARCOS [*a forced laugh*]. Is that what I look like? [JOSE *laughs.*] That's how I like to see you—laughing. What I can't stand is to see you in a bad humor, sad and upset.

JOSE. Even if it means I'm laughing at you?

MARCOS. Do whatever you want. [*The bells are still ringing.*]

JOSE. What *is* that?

MARCOS. Church bells. Didn't you see the tower from the window?

[JOSE *goes to the window. He looks out and a grave look of distress comes over his face.*]

JOSE. Have you noticed?

MARCOS. What?

JOSE. The weather.

MARCOS. A little overcast . . . but the sun will come out, you'll see.

JOSE. It's windy.

MARCOS. Not very.

JOSE. There's . . . a strong wind. [*He looks toward the sky, at the clouds, and shivers.*] If it keeps up, I won't be able to do a thing.

MARCOS. The fight's a long time off. Don't worry.

JOSE [*shivering*]. It's not so long now. This wind cuts me to the bone. Gives me . . . a kind of chill.

MARCOS. Get away from the window. . . . [JOSE *moves gloomily away.*] Aren't you going to lie down for a while? It's nothing to . . . but you're going to need all your strength. . . . Go on, lie down. [*He sounds paternal.*] Just lie down . . . and stop thinking about everything . . . You'll feel better then.

JOSE [*who looks terribly tired*]. I'm going to take a bath first . . . it'll relax me. . . . I feel like I've got a slight temperature.

MARCOS. You'll feel all right, you'll see.

[JOSE *crosses upstage into the anteroom and to the bathroom which we cannot see.* MARCOS *closes the door leading to the area. When he is alone, his face takes on a look of fatigue, of worry, as though he had removed a mask. He suddenly looks older. He looks out the window, and an expression of despair comes over his face. He serves himself, at the bar, a large cognac and drinks it avidly. Then he serves another. We hear the noise of the elevator. It has stopped at this floor. The door opens and we see* GABRIELA. *She looks rather hard and aggressive, is dressed very simply. She hesitates a moment, looking toward the audience, as though searching for the number of a door. Then she goes toward the door of the suite. She hesitates a moment before knocking, but does so just as* MARCOS *is drinking his second cognac. He starts, hesitates.*]

MARCOS. Who is it?

[*She does not answer; perhaps she has not heard, or has recognized his voice.* MARCOS, *when he hears no answer, puts down his glass and makes up his mind to open the door. His first impulse, upon seeing who it is, is to close the door immediately, but he does not.*]

MARCOS. Come in . . .

[*He steps aside so that she may come in. She enters, studying the room carefully. He remains near the door.*]

MARCOS. If you're looking for your husband, he's not in.

GABRIELA. They already told me downstairs.

MARCOS. I'm sorry. . . .

GABRIELA. I wanted to find out for myself.

MARCOS. He's gone out. I . . . excuse me, but . . . I'm very busy.

GABRIELA. Where is he?

MARCOS. In . . . He's gone for a drive. He didn't say where.

GABRIELA. I'll wait.

MARCOS. Fine. But he may be gone some time.

GABRIELA. That doesn't matter.

MARCOS. If you have to wait, would you mind waiting downstairs? I have a great deal to do.

GABRIELA [*a cold look at him*]. So much . . . that you can't even give me a moment?

MARCOS [*he is worried, and glances furtively toward the bedroom*]. Of course not. What can I do for you?

GABRIELA. Thank you. [*She looks at him with a rough, mocking smile.*] I still remember the afternoon we met for the first time . . . when Jose introduced us.

MARCOS. I remember it, too.

GABRIELA. You looked nice . . . innocent and kind . . . I remember you kissed my hand with a great deal of ceremony . . . a ceremony I'm not used to, and don't want to be used to! [*She laughs bitterly.*] An inoffensive man, a friend who wanted to do something for Jose . . . full of good will, isn't that right?

MARCOS [*coldly*]. Yes.

GABRIELA. "You've had enough misery . . . from now on . . ." I remember your words. . . . Do you remember that dingy house we lived in?

MARCOS. Yes.

GABRIELA. I still live there.

MARCOS [*with a slight shrug of his shoulders and a gesture indicating that it's not his business*]. What are you trying to get at by telling me this? Speak to Jose . . . if that's what you want. I have nothing to do with it. . . . It's absurd for you to tell me about . . .

GABRIELA [*cutting him off*]. I see his name in the papers. . . . A brilliant career . . . triumphs! His picture with crowds carrying him out of the ring on their shoulders . . . success. . . .

MARCOS. That's right.

GABRIELA. And all, thanks to you . . .

MARCOS [*denying*]. I gave him the dreams . . . and the means. But the rest . . . was his.

GABRIELA. And I owe everything to you too. . . . Everything . . . [*She is moved, weeping.*]

MARCOS. Please.

GABRIELA. All I've lost . . . everything's been lost in this story. But what do you care? How can it matter to you?

MARCOS. Calm yourself . . . I can't take you seriously. . . . You're upset. I haven't had such an influence as you seem to think. He's completely independent, and doesn't let himself be ruled by anyone. . . . Look somewhere else for an explanation of what's happened . . . look in yourself . . . in him . . . I know nothing about it. . . . Everything that's not the profession is outside my territory. . . . Only the professional aspects matter to me . . .

GABRIELA [*bitterly*]. Inoffensive, as always. [*She discretely dries her tears. He answers suddenly, brusquely.*]

MARCOS. I am . . . if I'm left in peace. Otherwise, no. [*His look has grown hard.*]

GABRIELA [*smiles as she notes the change*]. Now we can understand each other. That's what I wanted.

MARCOS. We have nothing to talk about.

GABRIELA. On the contrary. You've seen me cry. [*He shrugs his shoulders.*] That's all the tears there are. There are no more . . . no matter how much I'd like them. Do you know why I've come? [MARCOS *remains silent.*] Don't think it's a romantic gesture . . . the miserable wife . . . alone . . . suffering over her unforgettable love . . . [*sarcastically*]. No, that's not it at all! Don't think that for a moment! How disgusting! [*Transition, calmly.*] I've come to share the spoils of conquest . . . I need more money, that's all. Does it surprise you? Were you expecting something else? Well, there is nothing else! There's nothing left. . . . Nothing. . . . inside me [*cruelly*]. Nothing!

MARCOS [*who has become very grave*]. I have a favor to ask you.

GABRIELA [*laughing*]. Me? A favor?

MARCOS. Why not? [*Uneasily.*] Jose needs his rest today, do you understand? Absolute calm . . . his nerves have been on edge these past few weeks. . . . Nothing serious . . . the doctor said so . . . Nothing at all . . . but he needs . . . a certain amount of care. . . . It would be dangerous today . . . do you understand? . . . to upset his nerves . . . Precisely today when he needs all his strength. . . . Your attitude is understandable . . . completely natural . . . [*His voice becomes almost sweet.*] I'm not blaming you for anything. . . . On the contrary . . . consider me your friend. . . . The situation has been equivocal. . . . Yes, you thought that I . . . but it's not that at all . . . on the contrary . . . you can count . . . try to believe me . . . my friendship . . . my respect . . . even though I don't know all the complexities of your problem. . . .

GABRIELA. Words! I know them already too well.

MARCOS [*making an effort not to reply angrily, he keeps his sweet tone*]. That's not right . . . you're unjust. . . . But we can talk about that too some other time when it's more convenient. . . . What I wanted to ask you is . . . please, postpone this interview until after the fight . . . remember what I've told you. We can't gamble with Jose's life. This isn't the usual bullfight today, do you understand? There are six bulls down there, waiting for him, in the corral of the bullring.

GABRIELA [*looking at him straight in the eyes, murmurs:*] I'm astounded . . .

MARCOS. What?

GABRIELA. By your brazenness.

[MARCOS' *face, which was trying to reflect a complacent smile, suddenly becomes hard, as though he had suddenly turned cold and ashen. He says nothing, but turns away in order to gain time, to control himself. He pours himself a cognac while* GABRIELA, *without moving, continues ferociously.*]

GABRIELA. We can't gamble with Jose's life, can we? And what do you think you're doing? Where is your money coming from? The car you've got at the door of the hotel . . . why the very suit you're wearing? From gambling with Jose's life! Gambling with all their lives! [*She works herself up through her own words.*] You've driven him mad. . . . Why does Jose insist on bulls whose horns haven't been blunted? Why? So they can wound him, tear him apart! He's insane . . . but it's you who's driven him mad . . . with your wild promises . . . what are you trying to do? What do you want? To see him bleed to death in the infirmary of some god-forsaken town? [*A silence.*]

MARCOS [*coldly*]. Are you finished?

GABRIELA. I've just begun. But I'm going to say the rest of it to him, I don't care . . . before the fight . . . I'll tell him.

MARCOS. I'll do my best to stop you. And if I don't, you'll be responsible for what happens.

GABRIELA. Don't try to frighten me. . . . I'm not going to move from the lobby, do you understand?

[*She goes out.* MARCOS *thinks a moment, and finally follows her into the hall.*]

MARCOS. Listen to me.

[*She stops on her way to the elevator.*]

GABRIELA. What do you want, now?

MARCOS [*his tone is now one of humble request. He goes up to her and speaks almost in a whisper*]. Please . . . You can't do this to us . . . I ask you as a personal favor . . .

[*As though she hadn't heard him, she continues to the elevator and pushes the button.* MARCOS *does not follow her, but raises his voice.*]

MARCOS. We have great hopes for today. . . . Try to understand that. . . . It's for all of us, for you too, if you want to ask Jose for what he obviously owes you . . .

[*The elevator has arrived.* GABRIELA *opens the door.* MARCOS *grabs her arm. He is flushed. He grits his teeth, speaks hoarsely.*]

MARCOS. I'm trying to control myself! But I could easily let myself go and do something drastic!

GABRIELA [*challenging him*]. Try!

MARCOS. I think you've probably gotten all that you deserve. Now act according to your conscience.

GABRIELA [*with a cold smile*]. What are you talking about? Do you even know what that word means?

[*She breaks loose and enters the elevator. The noise and lights indicate that it has descended.* MARCOS, *exhausted, returns to the suite. He enters and closes the door. He finishes the cognac in his glass and pours another. With the glass in hand, he goes to the window and looks out, examining the sky anxiously.* JOSE *comes out of the bathroom; he is wearing a bathrobe. In the bedroom he knots the belt, then opens the door and comes down to the living room.* MARCOS, *lost in thought, has not heard him, and jumps when he hears* JOSE'S *voice.*]

JOSE. What's the matter?

MARCOS. Nothing . . .

JOSE. You're beginning to worry . . .

MARCOS. About the weather? No . . . the sun is trying to come out. . . .

JOSE. It's getting darker and darker. It's going to rain . . .

MARCOS. I don't think so.

JOSE. And the wind is just as strong. You can hear it in the inside courtyard.

MARCOS. It's still early.

JOSE. I don't know what we'll do.

MARCOS. Think about something else.

JOSE [*he sits down, puts his head back, and closes his eyes.*] I can't . . .

MARCOS. Lie down a while . . .

JOSE. No. Not now . . .

MARCOS. You feel better now, don't you?

JOSE. Yes. The warm water . . . I feel fine . . .

MARCOS [*is about to move, and staggers a bit*]. I've . . . been drinking a little. [JOSE *looks at him, laughing.*] What are you laughing at?

JOSE. You're more nervous than I am. Are we exchanging roles?

MARCOS [*a forced smile*]. I didn't sleep well last night. Don't pay any attention to me.

JOSE [*sitting up*]. Or is something wrong?

MARCOS [*quickly*]. No. Really, nothing at all.

JOSE. Good. [*He leans his head back again.*] Give me a cigarette.

[MARCOS *solicitously gives him one, and lights it for him.*]

MARCOS. I'm just out of sorts, that's all. That's why I had a couple of drinks. . . . [JOSE *examines him, uncomfortably.*] Why're you looking at me?

JOSE [*examining him slowly*]. You're as tired as all that?

MARCOS. What do you mean?

JOSE. What's happened?

MARCOS. To me? [*He picks up his drink with an attempt at indifference.*]

JOSE. Are you falling apart, too?

MARCOS. Me? Never . . . the man hasn't been born yet who . . .

JOSE. Yes he has. It's the passage of time. [*He smiles.*]

MARCOS. I can't feel it passing.

JOSE. But look at yourself. . . . Your head bent over, almost twisted, and you're standing there, discouraged and drooping, with a drink in your hand . . . like I've never seen you before. . . . [MARCOS, *as though by reflex action, pulls himself up straight.* JOSE *smiles.*] It doesn't matter . . . relax.

MARCOS. You know what I'd like? To meet death . . . vigorously.

JOSE. That's impossible . . . You men who stand on the other side of the fence grow old, go to pot . . . little by little. In the ring it's different. . . . Especially when the bull's defenses are first rate, as I want them to be [*He smiles bitterly.*] . . . as you've *made* me want them to be.

MARCOS. Doesn't it suit you? It's won you a public . . . so? . . . We must return to the pure bullfight, etcetera. . . . It sounds good, doesn't it? Besides, it's true.

JOSE. I don't know what you think. . . . Is there any truth for you?

MARCOS. Truth? [*Pause. Suddenly he speaks, excited.*] Success, that's the only truth. If you don't get that, nothing makes sense. To be right, you have to be successful! I only believe in the truth that brings money with it; that's the truth I'm looking for, the one I find where I look for it. Everything else is lies, disappointment . . . unimportant things . . . all that beggars tell each other while they sit around drinking in the cheap cafes . . . don't you agree?

JOSE. I don't know! [*He looks at* MARCOS, *whose expression is now somber.* JOSE *smiles, mockingly.*] What's the matter with you? You're in a thoughtful mood aren't you?

[*A pause.*]

MARCOS [*finally, hoarsely, without looking at* JOSE]. Someone I loved very much thought differently . . . and he was torn to pieces. [JOSE *seems surprised, as though he had never heard him speaking this way.*] When he fell, they grabbed hold of him and tore him to shreds. Now do you understand?

JOSE. I didn't mean to bring up unhappy memories. I was just talking.

MARCOS. What? [*He seems to come to. He explains in a forced tone.*] I was just talking to hear myself talk, too. Did you think I was serious? [*The phone rings.* MARCOS, *with a nervous, annoyed gesture, picks it up rapidly in order to get it before* JOSE. *Drily:*] Hello. [*Pause.*] No . . . [*Pause.*] Who? [*Pause.*] Wait a moment. [*To* JOSE:] Alicia Puente . . . says she's a friend of yours. . . . [*Angrily*] I told them to cut off the phone calls . . . is she a friend of yours?

JOSE. Yes. . . . But I haven't seen her for years. [*Takes phone.*] Hello, Alicia . . . yes . . . fine . . . how are you? Ah . . . no, I didn't see you . . . [*Pause.*] yes . . . yes . . . [*Pause.*] Let's meet after the bullfight. . . . Here in the hotel, all right? Fine . . . I'm looking forward to seeing you, Alicia . . . bye [*Hangs up, he looks more tranquil now*].

MARCOS. Who is it?

JOSE. A friend, from the University. We were in the same class . . . she's a doctor now . . . lives in this hotel and says she saw me come in this morning.

MARCOS [*with a shadow of resentment*]. What does she want?

JOSE. To see me . . . talk. . . .

MARCOS. That call changed you completely . . . you seem happy now . . . a kind of childish surprise . . . it's strange.

JOSE. I'll be happy to find out about all the others. The ones who finished, and the ones who didn't. . . . What they're doing . . . [MARCOS *takes a drink.*] Are you still drinking?

MARCOS [*caught in the act*]. Now . . . it's for your triumph . . . in a certain way . . . [*He doesn't finish the phrase, makes a strange gesture.*]

JOSE. You've drunk a lot already, haven't you?

MARCOS. No . . . but . . . I think maybe I should take a walk, take care of a few last minute details . . . the newspapers . . . tie up loose ends . . .

JOSE. If you're going out, don't stay long.

MARCOS. Of course not . . . you lock yourself in, you understand? Lie down a while and don't answer the door. The desk clerk apparently didn't understand my instructions, as you can see . . . I'll tell him again when I go down . . . I'll be back soon . . .

[*A poor-looking young man has come into the hallway, fearing that he is being followed, and then searches for the room. He knocks.* MARCOS *freezes when he hears the knock.*]

JOSE. Who can that be?
MARCOS [*unsure*]. I don't know.
JOSE. Open it.
MARCOS. I thought we said . . .
JOSE. Open the door, please. . . . We're not trying to hide, are we? Like a pair of fugitives . . .
MARCOS [*hesitates a moment still, and finally opens. When he sees the boy, he is relieved.*]. What is it?
PASTOR. Good afternoon, Senor Marcos.
MARCOS [*rudely*]. I don't know you . . . excuse me. . . . [*He is about to close the door.*]
PASTOR. My name is Rafael Pastor.
MARCOS. Ah! The auxiliary for this afternoon?
PASTOR. Yes, sir.
MARCOS [*without letting him in*]. What did you want?
PASTOR. To speak with the maestro, if it's possible.
MARCOS. No, I'm afraid you can't now.
PASTOR. It was . . . it was very important.
MARCOS. We can't settle anything for you here. You're a friend of the management, aren't you? They refused the name I suggested, and put your name on the program instead—against my will, and I want you to know it.
PASTOR. I know that. But I'm not a friend of the management. . . . I paid them to let me go out there this afternoon . . . and gave them a recommendation too.
MARCOS. I see . . . I don't know who you are. I don't recognize your name . . . where did you come from? Where have you fought before? Anyway, it doesn't matter. All you have to know how to do is to hold that cape. . . . You'll have nothing else to do today. . . .
PASTOR. If I had to do something more, I'd do it . . . [*Corrects himself.*] I'd try to do it.
MARCOS. What are you looking for? A chance?
PASTOR. Yes . . . I've put all my savings into this. I'd like . . .
MARCOS. For Jose Alba to be gored this afternoon, that would be your big chance. If that's what you're thinking . . .
PASTOR [*vigorously*]. No, that's not it. I came to see the maestro. Couldn't I see him?
MARCOS. Certainly not . . .

JOSE [*who is lying back in an easy chair, his eyes half-closed*]. Who is it?

MARCOS. No one . . .

PASTOR. You're wrong. [*With a decisive gesture, he pushes* MARCOS *aside and enters the room.* JOSE *sits up a bit and looks at him.*] My name is Rafael Pastor. I'm going to be with you in the ring this afternoon.

JOSE. Rafael Pastor . . . yes, I remember now . . . did you want something?

PASTOR [*he looks at* MARCOS, *who is looking at him disdainfully, and then he turns back to* JOSE.] Yes. To speak with you.

JOSE. Sit down, if you'd like.

MARCOS [*to* JOSE]. You can't now . . . !

JOSE [*to* PASTOR]. You just want a minute, don't you?

PASTOR. Yes, sir.

JOSE [*to* MARCOS]. See? Will you be back soon?

MARCOS. I think so . . .

[*We hear rain beating on the window.*]

JOSE. Is it raining now?

MARCOS [*at the window*]. Not much; just sprinkling. . . . That's good. . . . It'll clear the air. That's the best thing that could happen. . . . I'll be right back.

[*He goes out, closing the door. Goes to the elevator and calls it. While he waits, he passes his hand over his eyes. He is distressed.*]

JOSE. Don't you want to sit down?

PASTOR. Yes, sir. Thank you [*He watches* JOSE *intently.*]

JOSE. What are you looking at? [*He smiles.*]

PASTOR. I've never seen you up close . . . like this . . . just the way we are now . . .

[*The elevator has arrived and* MARCOS *enters it and closes the door. The elevator goes down.* JOSE *smiles and adopts a very friendly tone.*]

JOSE. What did you want?

PASTOR. You'll see . . . It's just . . . I had to see you before the fight. I couldn't make up my mind to come here, but finally . . . The desk clerk wouldn't let me by, but I finally got through without his seeing me. I hope you're not angry.

JOSE. What did you have in mind?

PASTOR [*nervously*]. I wanted to . . . to congratulate you for your work this season. . . . I mean it sincerely, from my heart.

JOSE. Thank you . . . from my heart, too.

PASTOR. It's a great honor for me to go into the ring with you this afternoon. An honor . . . and also . . . the chance of my lifetime . . . I've given everything I've got to go into the ring with you.

JOSE [*flattered*]. Do you think it's worth it?

PASTOR. Of course it is! It's more than I dared dream of! To make the great processional entrance into the bullring with you!

JOSE. Do you know the business? Have you killed many bulls?

PASTOR. Yes, many . . . I do everything I can to make myself known, go to all the trial fights . . . I spend all the money I earn that way. I have some friends who help me, who recommend me . . . I don't like to do that, but there's no other way. In Spain that's the only way you can become somebody. . . . I didn't want to . . . I thought that if a person had a real love for it . . . and talent . . . and if he turned out to be really gifted, . . . you understand? I thought nothing else was necessary. . . . But that's not the way things are . . .

JOSE. What kind of work do you do?

PASTOR. I own . . . a tavern, a small tavern. . . . I'm not ashamed to say it. . . . It belonged to my father. . . . My friends in the neighborhood get together there, and encourage me. . . . "You'll arrive someday," they tell me . . . It's on the edge of the city, in the calle de las Acacias. . . . There's an amber lamp at the door. I put that up when I redecorated, after my father died. It's nice . . . but I'm just no good there . . . My mind keeps wandering off. . . . Some people think I'm conceited, that I think I'm somebody. But people who know me well, know that's not true. . . . It's my love for the bullring that just won't let me live without it, it's consuming me. And today, at last! This afternoon! Do you understand what I'm going through? It's something very important for me!

JOSE [*smiles*]. What do you hope to get from this afternoon?

PASTOR. I . . . I don't know!

JOSE. A substitute hardly ever gets to do anything. A bit of capework . . . Is that what you want?

PASTOR. Yes . . . a bit of capework in the major bullring. Even if that's all . . .

JOSE. What more could there be? [*A pause,* PASTOR *looks down.*]

PASTOR. Of course . . . Only if . . . God forbid! . . . I could kill a bull!

JOSE. You've thought of the chance you'd have if something happened to me, haven't you?

PASTOR [*in a very low voice*]. Yes . . . I've even thought of that.

JOSE. . . . of my being gored. [PASTOR *does not answer. He seems ashamed.*]

PASTOR. It's sinful, isn't it?

JOSE. Have you hoped for that? Tell me, sincerely.

PASTOR. No . . . I mean . . . It's not that I hoped for it, it's . . . [*He doesn't know how to say it.*]

JOSE. You would be happy?

[PASTOR *twists his hands in anguish.*]

PASTOR. No! How could anyone hope for something like that? I don't want anything bad to happen to you. . . . Or anyone . . . But I'd . . . I'd like to kill a bull in the major bullring! I've struggled for that . . . for years and years. This afternoon . . . I've got it here . . . I don't know if you understand me.

JOSE [*trying to smile still, but it is a pale smile*]. What have you got here? The bull?

PASTOR. It's just . . . as though I had it here within reach of my hands. One of the six bulls! Just one! I'd know how to handle him! I know I'm a bullfighter! All I need is a chance in front of the press . . . in front of the public . . .! So they can see me!

JOSE [*serious*]. And . . . what do you want from me? [*Now it seems that* JOSE *is enjoying the situation.*] You want me to give you a bull? A slight accident near the end . . . eh? I go to the infirmary and you . . . you take charge of the situation . . . a great kill . . . they give you the ears . . . you're carried around on the shoulders of the crowd . . . through the main entrance . . .

PASTOR [*his eyes are shining*]. I didn't say anything like that. No. How can I explain?

JOSE. Just what do you want? Tell me.

PASTOR. I'm a decent person. I couldn't wish for something bad. No matter what.

JOSE. Then . . .?

PASTOR. Nothing . . . I just wanted to introduce myself to you . . . To let you know I exist, and that I'm there in the calle de las Acacias, not far from the bullring. . . . If you let me trade off with you in the cape work, I'll be very grateful to you . . . And if some day you can do something for me, you know where I am, waiting. Remember it's the bar with the amber light at the door.

JOSE. And I wish you good luck. . . . But not that you get it this afternoon at my expense!

PASTOR. God forbid such a thing!

[*The telephone rings.* JOSE *is frozen by the ring.* PASTOR *discretely retires toward the window and looks at the sky, disturbed.* JOSE *finally decides to answer the phone.*]

JOSE. Hello . . . [*What he hears makes him shudder, as though it were the impact of a voice both feared and expected, tremuously.*] Yes . . . It's me . . . [*With a choked voice.*] I . . . didn't tell them not to let you come up . . . I . . . [*Pause. He closes his eyes and murmurs*] Come up . . . yes, come up . . . please. [*He hangs up. He is pale. He turns to* PASTOR.] I'll see you in the ring. . . . I have lots to do now . . .

PASTOR. And will you forgive me?

JOSE. For what?

PASTOR. For bothering you.

JOSE. It was no bother.

[*He opens the door.* PASTOR *goes out and exits the same way he came in. He hesitates a moment before the elevator, but does not use it.* JOSE *has watched pensively from the door of the suite, while he disappears. Then his eyes turn toward the elevator. He lights, unsteadily, a cigarette. The noise of the elevator which begins to sound makes him shiver. He walks as though hypnotized toward the elevator door. Motionless, before the door, he waits. The door opens, it is* GABRIELA. *They look at each other fixedly, as though surprised to see each other. She still has the hard, shameless expression she had during her conversation with* MARCOS. *Suddenly she bursts into tears, childishly, and seeks refuge in* JOSE's *arms.* JOSE *speaks to her in a deeply moved, choked voice.*]

JOSE. I don't know . . . how things happen the way they do . . .

GABRIELA [*looking at him, through her tears*]. I was . . . so alone . . . I wanted to die . . .

JOSE. Come on . . .

[*He leads her to the suite and closes the door, this time locking it. She has gone to the window and tries to pull herself together. She weeps softly. A pause.*]

GABRIELA. I didn't want to come . . . And then . . . I decided to come, to try to hurt you . . . to hurt you terribly . . . to wound you . . . like bulls never can wound . . deep down, in your soul . . . I was coming to make you bleed slowly, to tell you I was disgusted with our memories . . . that I didn't need you at all . . . that I wouldn't mind seeing you dead . . . or lying there bleeding in the sand of some miserable fifth-rate bullring . . . I was coming to tell you, too . . . that you've betrayed all we loved . . . that my father died there . . . where he'd been for so long . . . and that I haven't had even a note from you . . . That we see you in the papers, along with all the people who've triumphed, and all of us in the neighborhood . . . we spit on your name and no longer recognize the boy who used to play with us . . . children's games, when we used to run through streets . . . and one night . . . something happened that left you alone with me . . . alone in this world . . . And I was coming to tell you . . .

[JOSE *is crying. He kisses her on the lips and embraces her passionately. She too is weeping, and abandons herself in his arms. At this moment, the noise of the elevator announces its arrival. It stops, the door opens; it is* MARCOS. *He comes out, staggering slightly. He does not close the elevator door. He goes toward the door of the suite, but before arriving there he stops. He has a gloomy look, as though he had been drinking more. He lights a cigarette, turns and looks toward the door. With his back to the public, he takes a deep drag on his cigarette. He expulses the smoke. When he turns toward us again, we see his face is disfigured by resentment. He crushes the cigarette in his hand and drops it. He looks at his hand with no sign of pain, although he has probably burned himself; his face is twisted with anguish and rage. The lights have gone down slowly in the suite, so that now we no longer see* JOSE *and* GABRIELA. *Then the curtain falls slowly.*]

ACT TWO

[*The suite. No one in the livingroom or anteroom.* MARCOS *beats on the door. A pause.* JOSE, *wearing the same dressing gown, comes from the bedroom. He is smiling, but his smile changes to a vague look of fear. He opens the door.* MARCOS *looks at him a moment.* JOSE *sustains the look.* MARCOS *passes into the room and* JOSE *closes the door.*]

JOSE. I want to tell you something.
MARCOS [*indifferent*]. I know already.

[*With a lighter he lights the little lamp in front of the triptych. He does it mechanically.*]

JOSE. Then . . .
MARCOS. Where is she? [*He has turned toward* JOSE.]
JOSE [*gesturing toward the bedroom*]. She was . . . you'll see.
MARCOS [*not interested in explanations*]. It doesn't matter . . . [*Without transition he changes the subject.*] I told Juan to come up. All right?
JOSE. Yes. [*A pause.*] Where were you?
MARCOS [*not looking at him*]. They told me your wife had come up, and I thought it would be better not to disturb you. I had a cup of coffee. . . . It's just what I needed. Do you want anything?
JOSE. No. What time is it?
MARCOS. Three-thirty.
JOSE. There's time.
MARCOS. Have you eaten?
JOSE. No.
MARCOS. It's getting late. But have a bite with me if you want.
JOSE. I'm not hungry. As usual.

MARCOS. Why don't you start dressing? There's not all that much time.

JOSE. You're right. [*At the window.*] You still think it's going to change? I think it's going to get worse.

MARCOS. Perhaps . . . what can we do about it! [*Sits down and opens a newspaper.*]

JOSE. What are you reading?

MARCOS. The article about you. It was expensive, but I think it's worth it.

JOSE. Who wrote it? You?

MARCOS. The critic did. I can't write.

JOSE. What does it say?

MARCOS. Expectations . . . six bulls without flagging . . . The bullfight of the year, etc.

JOSE. I'm nervous, Marcos.

MARCOS. Where's Juan? I told him to come up right away.

JOSE [*with a shudder*]. I'm terribly nervous. . . . Each minute that goes by, I feel . . .

MARCOS. That's your problem . . . Mine is to put you in the bullring and charge as much as I can for you. Now it's . . . your moment. Or what did you want? For me to go out there and kill the bulls too?

JOSE. I just want you to put me in the bullring; just as you said. Once I'm there, I don't need you. But now . . .

MARCOS. Now, I'm tired. [*A pause.*]

JOSE. That may be true. But I need you.

MARCOS. Well, here I am.

JOSE. That's what I want, to have you here. What are you trying to do to me?

MARCOS. Nothing.

JOSE. To make me feel like I owe you an explanation?

MARCOS. No.

JOSE. Well, then?

MARCOS. Nothing, I tell you.

JOSE. Marcos, you can't take this attitude! After the bullfight do what ever you want! But now! . . .

MARCOS. I drank quite a bit this morning. I don't feel well.

JOSE [*with a despairing cry, holding on to* MARCOS]. Marcos, don't leave me!

MARCOS. I won't move from here. Let go.

JOSE. Don't leave me now!

MARCOS [*he pulls away from him and goes toward the win-*

dow. He looks out. A pause.]. There'll be no sunshine, I can see that now . . . I'd thought it would be different. . . .

[GABRIELA *comes out of the bedroom. She crosses the anteroom and from the door looks into the livingroom.* MARCOS *turns and looks at her. She wears a vague smile of triumph as she comes down the steps and approaches* JOSE, *as though asking him to embrace her in front of* MARCOS. JOSE *hesitates a moment, and finally embraces her. Then she frees herself from his embrace, and turns toward* MARCOS.]

GABRIELA. We're going to live together again . . . [*A pause.*]

MARCOS [*to* JOSE, *as though* GABRIELA *did not exist*]. I just want to know one thing.

JOSE. What?

MARCOS. If this changes the situation, *our* situation?

JOSE. What do you mean?

MARCOS. I'm talking about our professional plans; that's the only thing that I'm concerned with.

JOSE [*hesitating*]. You'll see, we can . . . talk about all this after the fight.

MARCOS. I want to know now.

JOSE. Well . . . everything will stay the same, of course . . . except . . . we'll have to think some about the business of going to America.

MARCOS [*coldly*]. You don't want to go to America?

JOSE. I just said we'll have to think about it.

MARCOS. You don't want to go! And next season, what do you intend to do? Will you want eighty more bullfights? No, you won't want nearly that many. And you should have ninety, a hundred! Those are my plans! Can I count on you or not? You have to decide!

JOSE [*hesitant*]. Of course you can . . . Only we'll have to look more closely at things. . . . Not just jump into it with our eyes closed. Don't you understand? Be . . . a little prudent.

MARCOS [*shaking his head "no"*]. It's not worth bothering about . . .

JOSE [*now aggressive*]. What's not worth bothering about?

MARCOS. I can't work that way . . . It's not worth the trouble. . . . I'm not made to go after crumbs. . . . I want to aim for the top. If you're not interested in that, then I agree, and let's break the contract. In the situation I'm leaving you in, anyone can book you for a couple of "prudent" bullfights each season. . . . [*Sarcastically.*] Until you grow old and respected, surrounded by your loved ones . . . safe and sound at home.

JOSE. Then what do you want?

MARCOS. Nothing . . . If I can't work, I'll just leave.

[GABRIELA'S *face has grown harder during this scene, and now she breaks in furiously.*]

GABRIELA. I'll tell you what he wants! He wants everything! He wants you to belong to him, body and soul! Yes, that's exactly what he wants, and I don't care how it sounds! He wants you like a woman, more than a woman, because he can't even stand the idea of sharing your life with anyone! That's why he separated us before! He let it go at that! But he'd kill me if he could! He'd strangle our children if we had any. Because he knows all this robs him of part of what he needs to throw into the bullring, to fight the bulls and fill his pockets with money, that money he throws away at night while you're trying to rest, your nerves raw and shattered, caught in a nightmare! Do you know how horrible it was to listen to you at night? It was frightening! And now it'll be worse, and it'll keep on getting worse, till one day there'll be no way out. And that day don't count on him for a thing, Jose. That day you can count on his contempt! That's all he'll have for you then, forgetfulness and contempt! Or haven't you begun to understand that yet?

MARCOS [*furious, looking tensely at* GABRIELA]. Tell your wife to shut up! Tell her!

JOSE. You're hysterical! Be quiet!

GABRIELA. I'm telling the truth! Don't you want to hear the truth?

JOSE. Be quiet, please . . . For my sake. Let me go to the bullfight in peace . . . I need that . . .

GABRIELA. Forgive me . . . Forgive me . . . [*She weeps; a pause.*]

MARCOS [*calm now*]. She's right. I can't do anything with just a little bit. . . . I need a whole man. I can't share him with a woman . . . or with anyone. It sounds ugly, doesn't it? But there've been enough women in my life, so you won't misunderstand. Bulls are that way. . . . You have to give them free men, ready for anything. . . . It's from those men the great figures come. What can come from happy family life? A brilliant diplomat, perhaps. But bullfighters, no! Nor artists either! Nothing important! They're a world apart. Made of other clay, and it's a pity to throw them away.

GABRIELA [*calmly*]. I beg your pardon for everything I said. We'll try to talk things out afterwards, all right? The best way possible . . . We gain nothing by trying to claw each other.

MARCOS [*accepting the truce*]. Exactly. I beg your pardon, also.

JOSE [*moved, in a low voice*]. Thank you . . .

[*A simple-looking man has come to the door. It is* JUAN, *the sword carrier. He knocks at the door.*]

JUAN. May I come in?

MARCOS. Yes, yes, come in.

[JUAN *opens the door, and enters respectfully.*]

JUAN. Good afternoon.

JOSE. Good afternoon, Juan.

JUAN. Are you ready to start dressing, maestro?

JOSE [*with a slight sigh*]. Yes . . . Excuse me . . .

[*He goes to the anteroom.* JUAN *follows him, and during the scenes which follow, proceeds to dress* JOSE. *For this silent scene the actors may use the screen mentioned earlier, and the door to the bedroom, from which* JUAN *may get the cape, cap, etc. In the meantime, in the livingroom, the following scene takes place: when* GABRIELA *and* MARCOS *remain alone there is an uncomfortable silence.* GABRIELA *studies the triptych.*]

GABRIELA. Is this Jose's?

MARCOS. No . . .

GABRIELA. That would have surprised me. Do you think it does any good?

MARCOS. Jose has had only one mishap, a small one. It may mean something.

GABRIELA. You attribute that to the lamp?

MARCOS. It may have helped.

GABRIELA. What do you mean?
MARCOS. The day of the accident I had forgotten to light it.

[GABRIELA *shrugs her shoulders*.]

GABRIELA [*smiles*]. A coincidence, don't you think?
MARCOS. I don't know.
GABRIELA. And that's the only time you forgot?
MARCOS. Once before . . . a long time ago. But since that day, never.
GABRIELA. And nothing had happened before?
MARCOS. No . . .
GABRIELA. It makes me sad to look at it. Almost like something had already happened . . . or were going to happen. It's so dark today, and that little lamp burning there, as though it were the day of the dead or . . . I don't know.
MARCOS. Don't try to put it out.
GABRIELA [*shrugging her shoulders*]. No . . . [A pause.]
MARCOS. This is only a truce. I hope you realize that.
GABRIELA. You're referring to . . .?
MARCOS. I'm referring to speaking with you in this tone. Or even the simple fact of speaking to you at all.
GABRIELA. You don't want to speak with me ever again?
MARCOS. I won't have an opportunity to do so.
GABRIELA. Then, you're going away?
MARCOS. Yes. I turn him back over to you safe and sound. . . . With some money in the bargain; not all he thinks he has, however.
GABRIELA. That's all the same now. The money doesn't matter.
MARCOS [*smiling, ironically*]. When you came this morning, you were talking sincerely. Have you forgotten? Why the change? Have you decided to use other tactics? [*They look at each other with hatred.*]
GABRIELA. You'll never understand me. It's useless.
MARCOS [*now playing it jokingly*]. Then you think you're very complicated, don't you . . . That's no surprise. . . . Lots of women do.
GABRIELA [*angrily*]. Well, I don't! What are you trying to do? Make me angry again? Is that what you want?
MARCOS [*calmly*]. No, please. After the bullfight. [*A pause.*] Are you coming to the ring?
GABRIELA. Today less than ever. [*A pause.*]
MARCOS. And now? What are you going to do?

GABRIELA. I'm going to leave.
MARCOS [*pleased*]. I was going to ask you to do that.
GABRIELA. Jose has already asked me.
MARCOS. I'm glad you're not raising difficulties.
GABRIELA. I'd just like to know why?
MARCOS. Ask him. There are certain things . . . I don't like to talk about.
GABRIELA. What do you mean?
MARCOS. Out of respect for Jose, I ask you not to question me on the subject. [*He says this with affected gravity under which there is—we can see it in his eyes—a mocking irony.*]
GABRIELA. Are you expecting someone, or what's going on?
MARCOS. We're not expecting anyone, and nothing is going on.

[*A chambermaid has entered from the side opposite the elevator. She is pushing a wagon with a cold buffet lunch. She knocks.*]

MAID. Good afternoon.
MARCOS. Just leave it there. Thank you.

[*The* MAID *pushes in the wagon, then leaves, closing the door. She exits by the door facing the elevator.*]

GABRIELA. I'm sure it has to do with one of your orders.
MARCOS. Why?
GABRIELA. Jose asked me in a special way . . . and I recognized the tone. The same one he used to use.
MARCOS. Look at it that way if you want: a technical . . . order. From now till the fight begins we'll have lots of work to do. We've got to make particular . . . preparations. So much so that I'm afraid you shouldn't even stay [*points to the tray*] to have lunch, although I would be very happy . . .
GABRIELA [*tartly*]. I hadn't intended to.
MARCOS. Everything conspires to make my behavior with you seem very improper. I'm sorry.
GABRIELA. It doesn't matter. [*She seems about to leave. She fixes her hair, looking in the mirror.*] The fellow who carries the swords will take me home in the car, Jose said.
MARCOS. Good. Whatever he says.
GABRIELA. I'll be back later. I'll wait for you here.

[MARCOS *hesitates.*]

MARCOS. Here? That's not necessary. . . . We can pick you up at your place.

GABRIELA. Nevertheless, I'll wait for you here.

MARCOS [*laughs harshly*]. What are you thinking? That I'm going to carry him off, despite you? I don't intend to do that. But you might as well know that if he asked me to, that's precisely what we'd do even though you were standing by the luggage waiting for us. Now do whatever you wish!

GABRIELA [*with controlled anger, in her teeth*]. No one but you would ever think of such a thing! . . . No, that's not what I'm worried about, but you wouldn't understand. . . . I'm coming back here because I couldn't stand being alone there at home! I'm coming back here . . . [*She turns her head toward the audience; transition.*] I'm coming back because Sunday is sad . . . because those four walls are stifling me . . . because the house is dark and full of unpleasant memories . . .

[*Pause. She adds, with controlled emotion, while* MARCOS *listens with a strange twisted expression on his face.*]

GABRIELA. I'm coming back here, also, because . . . because this room which will be empty tomorrow and occupied by a stranger . . . an indifferent traveler . . . this room . . . is now a special place for me . . . and I think that what's happened here can never be erased from these walls and no matter how many people pass through here, no matter how much they scrub and clean or change the furniture around, this will always be a place where something important happened . . . something that should make people happy. . . . Something called, . . . I don't know, peace, perhaps! Or reconciliation! Or love! I don't know what name to give it!

[MARCOS *suddenly seems to shake himself out of the painful absentmindedness into which he had fallen. As though reacting, he shrugs his shoulders slightly, and walks toward the door of the anteroom.* GABRIELA, *who is unaware of his presence, is weeping silently.* JUAN *is finishing dressing* JOSE, *who has on his breeches, stockings, shoes, and shirt. . . .* JOSE *is knotting his tie while* JUAN *tightens the tassels on his jacket.*]

MARCOS [*from the door*]. How's it going?

JOSE. Fine.

[MARCOS *returns to the livingroom. A silence. Smiling, he observes* GABRIELA.]

MARCOS. So there were some left after all.
GABRIELA. What?
MARCOS. Tears.
GABRIELA. You can see there were.
MARCOS. You think you've won.
GABRIELA. It doesn't occur to me to think of it in those terms.
MARCOS. They're the correct terms. Let's not be hypocritical.
GABRIELA. Be quiet . . .

[*She has noticed that* JOSE *is coming into the livingroom. At the door, before coming down the steps, he stops a moment and looks somberly at* GABRIELA. *His expression has changed.*]

GABRIELA. Jose . . . you'll be careful, won't you?

[JOSE *does not answer. He comes down toward us. He seems to be another man. His face is now ashen, his eyes sunken.*]

GABRIELA. What's wrong? What's the matter with you, Jose? [*He does not answer. It is as though he has not heard.*] Jose . . . [*She embraces him.*]
MARCOS [*to* JUAN]. Take her wherever she tells you. Come right back.
JUAN. Yes, sir.
MARCOS [*to* GABRIELA]. Please. They're waiting for you.
GABRIELA [*terrified*]. But . . . I can't leave Jose in this condition. . . . What's the matter with him? Is he sick?
MARCOS. It's nothing. All he needs is to be left alone with me. Do you understand now why we asked you to leave? Jose is no longer as . . . as steady as he used to be. But it's nothing! Now leave us alone. . . . Things will go best that way . . . Don't worry. . . . I know how he is in these circumstances. You don't understand these things at all.
GABRIELA. But . . . I've never seen him like this! He's . . .
MARCOS [*with a hard voice*]. I've asked you to leave! Do as I say! You should have gone long ago! [*His tone becomes gentler.*] Please . . .
GABRIELA [*distressed*]. But what's the matter with him?

[MARCOS *no longer answers.*]

JUAN. Shall we go, miss?

GABRIELA [*looks at* JOSE, *who seems not to see her. She whispers:*] Yes . . .

[*She goes out, followed by* JUAN. *They go to the elevator and descend in it, while* MARCOS *somberly locks the suite door.*]

MARCOS [*authoritatively*]. Sit down.

[JOSE, *like an automaton, absentmindedly obeys. He looks about him now, and says, surprised.*]

JOSE. Has she gone?

MARCOS. Your wife? Yes.

JOSE. No. . . . Don't let her go . . . Don't . . . [*He seems frightened. He looks at* MARCOS *with fear.*] What are you going to do with me?

MARCOS What am I going to do? Nothing.

JOSE. I'm afraid.

MARCOS. I'm used to that. It's a humiliation I've had to get used to.

JOSE [*looking at him, horrified*]. I'm frightened . . . of you.

MARCOS [*laughs bitterly*]. Of me? What for?

JOSE. Don't do anything to me, Marcos.

MARCOS. Me?

JOSE. Help me.

MARCOS. To what?

JOSE. To get through it. Without you, I can't.

MARCOS [*irritated*]. Now you remember.

JOSE. I'm . . . alone . . . sick . . . I feel . . . [*Hand to back of neck.*] a pressure here . . . take me to a doctor . . . quick . . . before . . . it's too late.

[MARCOS *hums, distractedly, the rhythm of the finale of* ACT I. *He goes to the window.*]

MARCOS. It's raining. Look. [JOSE *does not hear.*]

JOSE. Alicia Puente . . . that girl . . . She lives in the hotel . . . Call her! I feel sick, very sick . . .

MARCOS. You'll get over it . . . as usual. You'll see. . . . The worst is the rain and the wind. They'll have to cancel the bullfight. So you can find something else to worry about.

JOSE. Something else? But there is nothing else.

MARCOS. Have a drink. You'll feel better.

JOSE. I don't want anything. Just thinking about it makes me feel sick.

MARCOS [*shrugs his shoulders*]. I'm hungry now. [*He sits down facing* JOSE *and eats something. He speaks lightly.*] So you're abandoning me . . . You've made up your mind?

JOSE. You're the one who said . . . that . . . you don't want . . .

MARCOS. All right. You'll have to stand on your own feet then.

[*He cuts something with the knife and eats it.*]

JOSE. We'll talk about that later. But now . . .

MARCOS. Now? Call your wife, if you want.

JOSE. My wife?

MARCOS. She'll help you.

[JOSE *shakes his head despairingly.*]

JOSE. Talk to me like you always do. Tell me . . .

MARCOS. No. [*He continues eating. He looks at* JOSE *with an almost mocking expression.*]

JOSE. Then?

MARCOS. Then, get ready. It's almost time.

JOSE. I'm [*He shudders.*] ready.

MARCOS. If the wind keeps up, be careful.

JOSE. Is it very windy?

MARCOS. Quite.

JOSE. I'm afraid of the wind.

MARCOS. Get your bearings from the flag. Stick to the most sheltered section of the ring. [*Eats.*]

JOSE. You'll be there, as usual?

MARCOS. I'll try to be there. If nothing unforeseen comes up.

JOSE. What could come up?

[MARCOS *has stopped eating. He lights a cigarette.*]

MARCOS. I don't know. Something.

JOSE. You're going to leave me alone?

MARCOS. You don't need me any longer. You know all you need to know.

JOSE. Don't leave the edge of the bullring! I want to feel you're there.

MARCOS. Only if it rains too hard.

JOSE. Even if it rains! Stay there!

MARCOS. Don't be a child, Jose. Leave me in peace.

JOSE [*suddenly shouts*]. Marcos!

MARCOS [*annoyed*]. Don't shout!

JOSE. Marcos, if you treat me this way, I won't be able to leave the hotel! Help me to leave!

MARCOS. Calm yourself. Behave like a man.

JOSE. Then you're going to treat me like that?

MARCOS. That's all I can do for you now. Whatever else you need, look for it in your wife. Kiss her . . . maybe that'll give you strength. I'm tired of treating you with affection . . . I've spoiled you too much; that's what's happened. But that's all over now. You want to make up your own mind? Go ahead, then . . . As far as this afternoon is concerned, be careful. Use everything you've got in the bullring today, you'll need it. They're six-year-old bulls, big as castles, with wide horns. But don't let that frighten you. Put yourself on the bull's terrain; you'll be secure there. And stand up to him! If ever you want to fight again, stand up to those bulls this afternoon. Even if it pours rain! Even if it's a hurricane. Even if the bleachers are emptied! Do you understand? And fight as only you know how! Without adornments; leave the fancy stuff for the end, when the people have already gone mad over what you've done before. . . . With the left hand, calmly. Without breaking the body line. Commanding, controlling the bull to the last . . . and leading gracefully from one pass to the next. . . . Even if the bull jostles you, don't let it show. Let them see all you've got, and finish it off slowly; the chest passes, gentle as though you were signing your name to the series. Again! And again! as though you were never satisfied, and were looking for something in the bull, something you'll never find; growing drunk on the bull. And when you kill, throw yourself desperately on him, as though you wanted to die with the bull, embracing him, and as though it were a miracle to see you alive after the encounter. Is that the way you're going to do it? Are you going out there prepared to do it that way?

JOSE [*weakly*]. I don't feel strong enough. I'm worse than ever. Why are you talking to me this way? You've never done it before. . . . You've always tried to convince me that everything was easy . . . that all I had to do was to open the cape in front of the bull for the whole plaza to thunder applause. . . . Why are you treating me so heartlessly this afternoon? I didn't want to hurt you. [*Transition, gently and sweetly.*] When I saw my wife, I felt something deep down . . . and I realized how much I had been deceiving myself by thinking that it was all over . . . You should understand that. What are you trying to make of me? A bullfighter of iron, with feelings for no one, separated from the world and only made to kill bulls in the ring? I'm no good for that . . . I'm no good. You can see, I just can't do it. . . .

MARCOS. If you can't do it, then retire. That's the least we can expect of you.

JOSE. Maybe I will.

MARCOS. But until you retire, play it with all you've got. If this is going to be your last fight with me, give yourself to it completely. Leave me with a good reputation in the eyes of the public, and in the eyes of the profession. Don't try to humiliate me, to ruin me, as Platero did. . . . If you show cold feet this afternoon, I'll kill you, I swear it! Do you hear? And if you feel the horn ripping your stomach, you hold in your guts as best you can, and kill that bull! And if you fall, even if you can't go on, you get up! You're going to do it that way, even if it means you're carried from the ring dead. Those remains, whatever's left of you, will be a bullfighter—a bullfighter at last, and forever!

[JOSE *has risen. He does not look at* MARCOS.]

MARCOS. All right. Now go get ready. It's getting late.

JOSE. What time is it?

MARCOS. Four o'clock.

JOSE. Already?

MARCOS. A little past.

[*A pause.* JOSE *turns to* MARCOS, *trembling and murmurs:*]

JOSE. Then, have pity on me. . . . Tell me the things you used to tell me. Make me believe that I'm healthy, that this pain in the back of my head is nothing serious, that the bulls will be easy, that the sun will come out, and the weather will be good. . . .

MARCOS. No. I can't.

JOSE [*anguished*]. Tell me!

MARCOS. It's a lie! I'm tired of lying! You're going to fight knee-deep in the mud . . . and against bulls as big as hell itself! Now you know the truth!

JOSE. And you can tell it to me that way? As coldly as that? [MARCOS *shrugs his shoulders.* JOSE *picks up a knife from the table.*] You're blurry . . . I can hardly see you. As though I were going to pass out.

MARCOS [*frightened*]. Drop that!

JOSE [*with a confused smile*]. No.

MARCOS. Drop it, I tell you!

JOSE. As though I were going to faint! [*He takes a step toward* MARCOS, *who is frightened.*]

MARCOS. Drop it, or I'll make you drop it.

JOSE. Go away. Go away, if you don't want me to . . . leave me alone.

MARCOS. I won't leave you. We're going together. I'm going to take you to the bullring.

JOSE. I'm not leaving here.

MARCOS. Have you gone mad?

JOSE. I'm not leaving here!

MARCOS. We'll see about that . . . I'll call the police. . . . They'll take you to the ring by force . . . Don't pretend you're sick now.

JOSE. I *am* . . . Wounded . . . to death . . . I'm . . .

MARCOS. Not yet. . . . This afternoon, with a little bad luck you may fall. . . . But not now . . . What do you want? A certificate? A declaration of unfitness? Look for it in the bullring. A lucky scratch, and you'll have it. . . . But now . . . you have to go down there and face six bulls. Let's go.

[*We hear, like a cry of alarm, the wind whistling in the patio.* JOSE, *deathly pale, looks up—toward what?—with terror.*]

JOSE. Now? [*With a sudden movement he sinks the knife in his own stomach.*] Now? [MARCOS *has turned pale.*] I'd rather not go out now . . . I . . .

MARCOS. What have you done?

[JOSE *is holding the bloody knife in his hand. He lets it fall. He clutches the wound with his hand. He does not fall.*]

JOSE. I'm . . . sick. [*He takes away his hand covered with blood, and looks at it horrified.*] A bad thrust . . . of the horns. I didn't end . . . the pass well . . . No one came to attract the bull away. . . . I . . . alone. . . . [*He seems to be delirious.*] in the middle of the ring. Now it doesn't hurt at all. Not at all!

MARCOS [*looking at him, horrified*]. Jose! Jose! You've gone mad!

JOSE. It's nothing, Marcos. . . . A little accident . . . Now take me away from here. That's all I ask of you.

MARCOS. Lie down here. . . . Wait . . . You're bleeding. . . . [JOSE, *dizzy, lies on the sofa.*] What's her name?

JOSE. Who?

MARCOS. Your friend who lives in the hotel?

JOSE. Alicia . . . Doctor Alicia Puente . . .

MARCOS. We've got to call her . . .

JOSE. Call her, yes . . . Now . . . I'm beginning to feel the pain. I don't want to bleed to death here . . .

[MARCOS *has picked up the phone. Distressed.*]

MARCOS. Give me Miss . . . Doctor Alicia Puente, please. [*Pause, to* JOSE *in despair.*] They think she isn't in. She had an urgent call.

JOSE. I can get down the stairs. Take me to an emergency ward! [*He tries to sit up.*]

MARCOS. Don't move. [*In the telephone.*] Yes . . . Is this Doctor Puente? Excuse me, I'm calling for your friend Jose Alba. . . . the matador . . . He's had a slight accident here in his room . . . A wound . . . Could you come right away, please? He's bleeding badly. . . . In 201 . . . thank you . . . [*Hangs up.*] She's coming right away. Let me see.

[*He leans over* JOSE. *The back of the sofa prevents us from seeing what he is doing*: *uncovering the wound.*]

MARCOS. I don't think it's serious. . . . But no matter whether it is or not, you're through. . . . Our contract is broken, Jose . . . I'll cancel all the contracts we've signed with various managements for the rest of the season. . . . Now are you satisfied? I'm sorry . . . I had placed so many hopes in you. . . . We could have climbed to the top. . . . I hope you're happy in what you're going to do now, Jose . . . I wish you that sincerely, because I've always been and I'll continue to be your friend. I wanted to make you suffer a little, so you'd see . . . how important I am in your life. . . . But I didn't think you'd . . . go so far as this . . .

JOSE [*tries to be cheerful; he seems relieved*]. It's nothing serious, you'll see! And I can keep on. . . . What do you want? For us to go to America? We'll go . . . She'll have to understand.

MARCOS. It doesn't matter. Forget it.

JOSE [*sad*]. Do you really want to break our contract?

MARCOS. It's broken already. . . . You can't put together what's been broken into a thousand pieces, and in the worst way.

JOSE [*sorry*]. I won't know what to do without you . . .

[*As though arriving from another room on the same floor,* ALICIA *approaches and knocks at the door.* MARCOS *hastens to open it.*]

MARCOS. Come in, Please.

[*She approaches* JOSE. *She is carrying a small bag.*]

ALICIA. But Jose . . .

JOSE. Alicia . . .

ALICIA. What happened?

[*She leans over him.* MARCOS *nervously attempts to explain while* ALICIA *works—we cannot see what she is doing—over the wound.*]

MARCOS. A stupid accident. . . . We still don't know how . . . [*He picks up the knife from the floor and holds it up, gripping it.*] I was showing Jose how to meet the upward thrust of the bull's horns . . . a way of withdrawing in the last tenth of a second . . . I don't know who was the clumsy one . . . probably me . . .

JOSE. No . . . It's my fault . . . I wasn't careful . . . You understand? and then . . .

ALICIA. Please, don't talk now. [*She continues working.*]

MARCOS. Is it serious?

ALICIA. No. But it could have been.

MARCOS. Will he be able to get up?

ALICIA. It would be better for him to rest.

MARCOS. He can't go to the bullring?

[ALICIA *dresses the wound while she is talking.*]

ALICIA. No, that would be foolish. . . . I can stop the hemorrhage and dress the wound, but . . . any sudden movement . . . It would be best to move him to the hospital where I work. I have an urgent call to answer now. [*To* JOSE.] I'll send an ambulance, and stop by your room to see you. I think that'll be best. [*She turns to* MARCOS.] Don't you?

[MARCOS *nods his head "yes," in silence.*]

JOSE. Thank you, Alicia. What a strange way to meet again, after all these years!

ALICIA. It's hardly a meeting. But we'll talk later . . . about so many things.

JOSE. I want to ask you . . . [*He makes a gesture of pain.*]

ALICIA. It's nothing. [*She smiles.*] I'm going to hurt you . . . but just a little. [JOSE *moans.*] You see? It was nothing . . . [*She smiles, with an affectionately mocking tone.*] Torero . . . It's funny to think of you as a bullfighter . . . I never imagined . . . that's what you'd turn out to be. . . . [*Continues dressing the wound.*] When I saw you go through the lobby this morning, my heart turned over. . . . None other than Jose Alba . . . I often see your picture in the papers. . . . [JOSE *tries to speak, but* ALICIA *prevents it.*] No, be quiet . . . It'll be better that way. . . . I know you've married. . . . Many of our classmates have married. . . . But, I haven't. I suppose I should begin thinking about it, don't you? Wait a minute . . . no don't move. . . . Just a moment . . . What was I saying? Oh, yes . . . I think I'm happy, but I don't know. . . . It's something I'll have to look into some day. . . . [*Smiles.*] There you are. It's not a fabulous treatment, but it'll do, I think. . . .

JOSE. I want to tell you . . . Wait! [*Like a shout for help.*] Don't go yet. I want to tell you . . . to talk to you . . .

ALICIA [*smiling*]. We'll have time later. . . . Now you must rest. [*She has risen, and closes her bag. To* MARCOS.] Unfortunately I can't take time to chat now. Wait for the ambulance here.

MARCOS. Fine.

ALICIA. Good-bye, Jose [*Smiling.*] "Prognosis, good. He can fight again in five days."

JOSE [*smiling*]. Thanks for everything, Alicia. You see, it was . . . [*He makes a gesture which explains nothing.*]

ALICIA. See you soon.

[MARCOS *accompanies her into the hall. Once outside, he asks.*]

MARCOS. Is it serious?

ALICIA. No, it's nothing. What I told him was true.

MARCOS. Do you think the ambulance is really necessary?

ALICIA. I think it would be . . . wise.

MARCOS. It'll attract so much attention. . . . [*He approaches the elevator and pushes the button.*]

ALICIA. Nevertheless . . . just to be sure . . .

MARCOS. I could take him by car. He can walk, can't he?

ALICIA [*thinking*]. Yes, he can walk. I don't think there's any serious risk in that.

MARCOS. Then, do you authorize me to take him myself?

ALICIA [*hesitates a moment*]. All right. I agree. Take him to the central hospital and ask for me. As soon as I'm through with this visit, I'll go there.

MARCOS. Thank you for everything.

[*The elevator has arrived.* MARCOS *opens the door and* ALICIA *enters. He closes the door and pushes the down button. When he sees the elevator disappear, he breathes a sigh of relief. He returns to the suite and enters. Without looking at* JOSE, *who is watching him, he approaches the window.*]

MARCOS. It's raining hard, and the wind seems to be getting stronger. . . . [JOSE *dares not speak.*] You can get up now.

JOSE. Did she tell you I could?

MARCOS. Yes. We're going.

JOSE. To the hospital? [*A pause.*]

MARCOS. We'll stop by the bullring first.

JOSE. Call them, and tell them I'm wounded.

MARCOS. Are you mad? At this hour?

JOSE. Then what do you intend to do?

MARCOS. People are pouring into the bullring already. We can't provoke a public scandal.

JOSE. Then . . .?

MARCOS. We'll have to trust to the weather.

JOSE. The weather?

MARCOS. We can't cancel the fight. Let the weather do it . . . the rain . . .

JOSE. And if they don't cancel it?

MARCOS. Let's go to the ring. You can look as calm as if you were ready for anything. I'll take care of it. If the rain continues I think I can succeed in . . .

JOSE. And if it doesn't continue?

MARCOS. At the last moment we could tell them. Unless, at that moment, you felt strong enough . . . [*A silence.*]

JOSE [*rises*]. I feel fine now. This is nothing.

[MARCOS *looks at him with a shadow of the old affection.*]

MARCOS. Of course not.

JOSE. I think I could . . .

MARCOS [*smiling slightly*]. It won't be necessary. . . . We'll put in an appearance, and I'll request a cancellation because of the bad weather, and then we can quietly go to the hospital in the car. All right? Just do this for me. It's the last thing I'll ask of you. I don't want to be mixed up in a scandal.

JOSE. Help me. [MARCOS *helps him finish dressing.*] You know? It's going to be like always. I'm over it now . . . I'm going to walk calmly out of the hotel. . . . [*He tries to walk and appears quite steady on his feet.*]

MARCOS. Smiling . . . [JOSE *smiles.*] That's the way I like it. . . . You've got a little, blood there. . . . With the cape . . . [*He indicates that he should cover the bloodstain with his cape.*]

JOSE [*picks up the cape and cap*]. What about Juan? [*He has placed the cape over his arm, hiding the bloodstain.*]

MARCOS. He can meet us at the ring. I'll tell them downstairs. Shall we go?

JOSE. Yes.

[*They go out. When they are outside, the elevator stops at their floor.* GABRIELA *and* JUAN *enter from it.* MARCOS *stiffens with surprise when he sees them.* GABRIELA *goes nervously to* JOSE. *He smiles calmly now.*]

JOSE. We were just leaving. . . . It's time, you know?

[MARCOS *looks coldly at* JUAN. JUAN *tries to excuse himself with a gesture.*]

GABRIELA [*a little relieved by his smile*]. How are you?

JOSE. Fine . . .

GABRIELA. It was nothing serious then? Do you want me to help you?

[*A suspenseful silence.* JOSE'S *and* MARCOS' *eyes meet.* JOSE *lowers his eyes.*]

JOSE [*after a long pause*]. I'm all right . . . really . . .

GABRIELA [*then, throwing herself in his arms*]. I couldn't! I came back because I just couldn't stay there. Forgive me!

JOSE [*with a pale smile*]. Thank you . . .

GABRIELA [*embracing him intensely*]. Be . . . very careful, Jose . . . very careful . . .

[MARCOS *makes a gesture of impatience.*]

MARCOS. Shall we go?

[JOSE, *seeing* MARCOS' *gesture, loosens himself from* GABRIELA'S *embrace, and goes to the elevator, and enters it. Then* MARCOS *and* JUAN *enter it. The door closes, and* GABRIELA *sadly watches it disappear. She goes to the suite and enters. As though surprised, she looks at the objects in the room, as though she were seeing them for the first time. She opens the window and looks out for a moment. When she opens it we can hear the loud noise of the rain. She comes back to the room and stands motionless, as though hypnotized, before the triptych. She picks it up and looks at it curiously, almost fearfully, as though she had thought of blowing out the light but did not quite dare. She puts it down and stands watching the flickering flame. The bells of the nearby church begin to ring and* GABRIELA *feels cold—perhaps because the window is open. She crouches in an armchair and closes her eyes. The bells continue ringing while the curtain falls.*]

EPILOGUE

[*Downstage, an amber lamp. The lights reveal a table in a tavern and the suggestion of a counter with a shelf covered with bottles. Noticeable on one wall are the head of a bull and a poster. The poster is that of the bullfight in which* JOSE ALBA *died. We can read, "Six Bulls," ("Seis toros") and "Jose Alba," and in smaller letters, "auxiliary, Rafael Pastor," ("Sobresaliente de espada."). We can hear the noise of rain. There is a man in a raincoat sitting at a table. The tavernkeeper, whom we recognize as* RAFAEL PASTOR, *approaches the table.*]

PASTOR. What'll you have?

[*The man who had his back to us, turns to* PASTOR *and we recognize* MARCOS; *he seems aged, but is dressed elegantly.*]

MARCOS. A beer.
PASTOR [*recognizes him, surprised*]. But . . . is it you?
MARCOS. You can see for yourself . . .
PASTOR. What are you doing out here?
MARCOS. Why does it surprise you?
PASTOR. I'd heard that because of the . . . death of Alba . . . you'd had some difficulties.
MARCOS. That's all over. It wasn't my fault. The kid insisted on going out there wounded. I couldn't stop him.
PASTOR. Excuse me. I'll get your beer.

[*He goes to get it.* MARCOS *lights a cigar and smokes absently.* PASTOR *brings the beer.*]

PASTOR. Here you are.
MARCOS. Thank you. Would you like to sit down? I've come to talk with you.

PASTOR [*sitting*]. With your permission.

MARCOS. You're at home here, aren't you? Don't ask my permission.

PASTOR. I'm asking permission to sit at your table. . . . What was it?

MARCOS. How are you here? Are you happy?

PASTOR. No . . . No, sir . . . I've had bad luck since then. . . . I don't know what's happened to me. . . .

MARCOS. The afternoon of the accident I thought you'd go places . . . after the riot you caused with the second bull. . . .

PASTOR. I was like a madman. . . . I would have . . . I don't know . . . if they hadn't stopped the bullfight. I've fought again since then, but never had any luck. It's as though suddenly everything was against me. I've almost decided that I irritate other people, and they try to ruin me . . . I've had to come back to the tavern. . . . and I think . . . I think I'll forget the bulls.

MARCOS. What you need is someone to guide you. But not just anyone. Someone . . . special.

PASTOR. I know. Fighting isn't enough. You have to have the right connections.

MARCOS. Someone who can raise you to the top in a single season! That's what you need, Rafael!

PASTOR. Would that . . . be possible?

MARCOS. I'd like to consider it.

PASTOR. Would you take charge of me?

MARCOS. It would depend on whether we could reach an agreement.

PASTOR. What would I have to do? [*Silence.*]

MARCOS [*gestures to the tavern*]. All this is in your way.

PASTOR. The tavern?

MARCOS. Yes . . . You've got a bridge behind you. You can't do anything as a bullfighter that way . . . Burn your bridges . . . You know what I mean?

PASTOR [*trembling*]. Yes.

MARCOS. And what do you think?

[PASTOR'S *face is grave.*]

PASTOR. It . . . belonged to my father. . . . This is where I grew up . . . between these four walls . . .

MARCOS. Give it all up.

PASTOR. That's . . . a lot to ask.
MARCOS. A ridiculous price for what you could achieve.
PASTOR. And if I fail?
MARCOS. You can't! I'll take care of that.
PASTOR [*thoughtful*]. I see . . .
MARCOS. I'd launch you grandly. . . . If you let me, I'd make yours a typical Spanish story. . . . We'd have to talk of hunger, even though you've never suffered from it . . . Hunger and death! The wounds of hunger, that's good for the tourists! We have to slant the bullfight with them in mind. Understand? They're the ones who pay. . . . Without actually lying, we'll manipulate whatever we can get our hands on within your own experience. . . . That's fair . . . This hunger is true, because others are suffering it for you, but you can represent them all. . . . A national, a popular bullfighter! I don't know . . . we could make it up as we go along! You climb up from misery, and tell them that hunger wounds worse than the bulls. Others have said the same thing, people like Espartero, who died in the Madrid ring! And a full length photograph in "Life" magazine. Can you imagine it? Sentimental old ladies weeping over you! Next year's tourist trade! And you, in the photographs, with a desperate, bitter look on your face! A little bit of acting, if you like . . . but a necessary bit . . . these days when you have to keep your head above water, as best you can, in order not to drown with the others! Everything oriented to the outside! Haven't you seen the bleachers? The bullfight is for foreigners! We'll be in Europe and in America, think of that! You can't live isolated! We have to do widerange advertising, American style—you know what that means! Newspaper headlines, movies, television! I've got the money and the organization to do this, and more! They'd come to see you from all over the world! Do you see my plans? What do you say?

[PASTOR *lowers his head.*]

PASTOR. A typical Spanish story . . . [*With repugnance.*] What did you mean by that? Why? It looks like lying to me . . . Is that necessary to reach the top?
MARCOS. Yes, it is.
PASTOR. Then, . . . I'm not your man.
MARCOS. Of course you are! You should jump at the chance.

PASTOR [*shaking his head*]. If you exploit hunger to make money, then that money belongs to the hungry . . . not to us. I'm not so smart, maybe, but that's what I think.

MARCOS. Don't be childish, boy. You'll never get anywhere if you restrict yourself to these senseless ideas.

PASTOR. I had hopes. But I'm losing them.

MARCOS. You'll have them again. Let me help you.

PASTOR. I don't think I could.

MARCOS. You'll see. You know what they call people like you? Romantics . . . We were all romantics at one time or another, when we were young. We all hated to deceive, to lie. Besides, it's not a question of lying now. . . . We just have to tell the truth in a special kind of way, understand? You have to do it that way, if you want to succeed in life. Otherwise you'll end up croaking in some filthy hole. Is that what you want?

PASTOR [*pensive*]. What you're saying may be true. . . . I don't know what you call people like me. But I do know, from what I've seen already, that there are people in this life who live off the misfortunes of others; who earn their living by taking advantage of other people's danger, of other's deaths . . . of the slow wasting away of others. . . . That's a typical Spanish story, too, isn't it? Throw your man into the ring, and watch the bulls yourself from the sidelines, keeping the dead man's money . . . I also know that I'm not that kind; and I'm not saying that you are either, you understand? I'm speaking to you respectfully, without wanting to hurt you. There're lots of things that don't seem right to me, the fact that the world is full of offices and paperwork for example. When I left this tavern, I saw how things were elsewhere, and I came back here. Here I'm behind my counter, and I'm getting used to the idea that this is the best thing that could have happened to me. [*A pause.*] You know who comes here every day? I give him a dish of food so he won't starve to death. . . . A drunken beggar called Ricardo Platero . . . Do you remember him?

MARCOS [*icily*]. Yes.

PASTOR. I often think of Jose Alba, too. It seemed impossible he'd ever die, that morning in his hotel room. All this makes me think, even if I didn't want to. [*A silence.*]

MARCOS. I'm not interested in what you think. I've made you a proposition. What's your answer? [*A silence.*]

PASTOR [*thoughtful*]. When I came back here from the bull-rings, I saw that this is the truth. This. [*He makes a vague gesture to the surrounding tavern.*]

MARCOS. This? What? Your tavern?

PASTOR [*shakes his head*]. The winter beginning, and the work it'll take to get through it . . . The man who has a refuge can take whatever comes to him . . . gorings worse than those caused by bulls, wounds given in the streets, at every corner. I'll light the stove . . . in case anyone wants to shelter himself from the cold here . . . And . . . I'll try to forget that I ever . . . wore a suit of lights.

MARCOS. Then, you've given up everything. [*He rises.*] Here . . . [*He throws a few coins on the table.*] Take it out of that.

PASTOR [*makes no effort to pick up the money. He feels something is slipping out of his hands, and tries to grab hold of it*]. Listen, . . . I don't like people inventing lies about me. That's why I said . . .

MARCOS. We could think about that. There are many ways of . . .

PASTOR. But, still . . . [*He stops.*]

MARCOS. You're still thinking about it? [*A pause.*]

PASTOR. I can't sell my house.

MARCOS. I'm sorry. [*With an indifferent air, he takes a puff on his cigar.*] Look kid, what I need can be found anywhere. I've got lots to choose from. If you can't make up your mind, it's useless to waste time. [*A pause.*]

PASTOR. I can't . . . make up my mind.

MARCOS. There are thousands of people ready to sell anything . . . even their souls . . . for an opportunity like this. You're letting it slip through your fingers. You'll never have this chance again. Throw your suit of lights in the trash can, and put on your white jacket now forever. It fits you better.

[*A silence.* PASTOR'S *face has grown hard now. Unperturbed, he sustains* MARCOS' *look.*]

PASTOR. Good night, sir.

MARCOS. Good night.

PASTOR. Oh, wait a minute! [*He picks up the money from the table.*] It's on the house. [*He holds out the money.*]

MARCOS. No . . . Take out the price of the beer . . . the rest is a tip. Good night.

[*He turns and* PASTOR *stands, not knowing what to do, with the money in his hand. A* BEGGAR *has entered into the lighted zone, and we see his profile. He holds out his hand to* MARCOS, *but the latter passes in front of him without looking at him.* MARCOS *pauses a moment under the amber lamp, then goes out. The* BEGGAR *circles over to the place where* MARCOS *went out, and little by little turns his face towards the public. We can see that it has a horrible scar from a bull wound. His hand is still held out, and he seems to be stupidly surprised that* MARCOS *did not stop for him. With the same dazed, alcoholic attitude he looks now toward the audience in the theatre.* PASTOR, *who had gone out for a moment, is putting a plate of food on the table. He says:*]

PASTOR. He didn't even recognize you . . .

[*The* BEGGAR, *as though not hearing, continues looking at the audience, and now reaches out his hand toward the audience as though in a mute and permanent plea for help.*]

CURTAIN

GREGORIO MARTÍNEZ SIERRA

1881–1947

GREGORIO MARTÍNEZ SIERRA began his dramatic career under the influence and with the help of Jacinto Benavente. He acted in a play of Benavente's in Madrid, wrote several dramas in collaboration with a friend, Rusinol, and finally struck out on his own. Martínez Sierra experimented with a variety of styles, but he was at his best when he wrote *Cradle Song*, the play in this volume.

In this play, as well as in such ingenuous little idylls as *The Kingdom of God* and *The Two Shepherds*, he succeeds by the irresistible force of simple humanity. He delineates characters who are real people with individual eccentricities. They are humble, religious people in uncomplicated situations, contending only with the corrigible faults of their own souls and the inevitable passage of time. Out of this almost unconscious flow of time, Martínez Sierra creates that ancient pathos of things passing, of good people growing old. But Martínez Sierra's characters are not ravaged by time; instead, they mellow with age, their simple lives free of remorse, and even as they proceed toward death we feel their agelessness. There is no philosophic pandemonium here, but rather the transforming power of human love. It is a context which, if we give ourselves over to it, disarms us with its peace and gentleness.

Martínez Sierra avoids sentimentality in these plays through his unfailing feeling for dramatic proportion and a certain ironic sense of humor. The theme of *Cradle Song* is tempting material for a fully orchestrated "tear-jerker"; but he keeps things under control, with the result that we are more conscious of the humaneness of his treatment of the situation than we are of its essential implausibility. Using two acts, he shows Teresa's arrival at the convent as a foundling and her departure eighteen years later to marry. Within this space he reveals the peculiarities of each of the nuns, and also shows their varying relationships to the girl committed to their charge.

Martínez Sierra's later drama is peopled with characters

other than nuns and priests, but these plays do not measure up to his earlier work. (Of all his plays, only *Cradle Song* is still produced.) In his last years he wrote, together with his wife, a number of plays dealing with the emancipation of women. Spain being the country that it was (and still is), these plays were not successful in Spanish theatres; nor were they hailed elsewhere. His career as a playwright is a good illustration of the problems facing the modern Spanish dramatist. Given a repressive theatre it was difficult for a writer of talent to experiment and grow; but Martínez Sierra did so in spite of these conditions and in all of his work we find a dramatic sense of life that still rings true.

AN INTRODUCTION TO THE PLAYS OF G. MARTÍNEZ SIERRA[1]

by John Garrett Underhill

(1922)

PRECOCIOUS in talent, Gregorio Martínez Sierra attended the University in his native Madrid where he came to grief in history, doubtless, as he says, because of a settled aversion to battles. His affinity for formal study was slight. On the other hand, his wife, the former María de la O Lejárraga, whom he married in 1899 when he had just turned eighteen, had early associated herself with the educational system and was already established as a teacher in the public normal schools at the time of their marriage. However, they soon abandoned all thought of academic preferment and turned to literature as a joint career. Actually, Gregorio Martínez Sierra is also the couple's pen name, and the works which have appeared under it are the result of a collaboration which had begun even before their marriage and has continued through all their books and plays ever since.

At seventeen, with the manuscript of his first book, *El poema del trabajo* ("The Song of Labor"), he presented himself to Jacinto Benavente, who furnished an introduction and arranged its publication which took place in 1898. Two series of prose poems, or pastels, as they were called in that day, followed, besides a collection of short stories, *Cuentos breves*, issued independently and attributed to María. In 1900 a novelette, *Almas ausentes*, was awarded the prize in a contest conducted by the *Biblioteca Mignon*. This and other tales of the sort, subsequently appearing separately, have been

[1] Introduction by John Garrett Underhill to *The Plays of G. Martínez Sierra.* Copyright Renewal, 1951, by E. P. Dutton & Co., Inc. Reprinted by permission of E. P. Dutton & Co., Inc.

reprinted in three volumes, *Abril melancólico* ("Melancholy April"), *El diablo se ríe* ("The Devil Laughs"), and *La selva muda* ("The Silent Wood"). The most notable work in the shorter form, however, is contained in *Sol de la tarde*, or "Declining Sun," which established their reputation beyond cavil in 1904. To the same year belongs the first of two novels, "The Humble Truth," while a second and more popular venture in the field of fiction, "Peace" (*Tú eres la paz*), was composed two years later.

In the beginning an intellectual by temperament and a word-painter by inclination, Martínez Sierra may be characterized as an impressionist, well versed in the procedure of the modern French schools. Perhaps the principal personal influence of his formative period was that of the poet Juan Ramón Jiménez, with whom he kept bachelor hall at Madrid. Other associations of these days were likewise predominantly literary, and leaders of the modern movement such as Antonio and Manuel Machado and the Catalan, Santiago Rusiñol, painter of gardens, proved themselves kindred spirits. Under their friendly stimulus, he published a volume of verse, *La casa de la primavera*, a chance excursion into an alien domain, as well as a prose poem upon "Hamlet in the Person of Sarah Bernhardt." With these works his "Dream Theatre" may be coupled, a quartet of symbolic, mystical dialogues with pronounced Maeterlinckian tendencies.

The first decade of the productivity of Martínez Sierra suggests little of the theatre. It was quietistic in feeling, essentially contemplative, a communion with idyllic and elegiac poets. Yet through these days another influence had been active, although less conspicuously, which in the end was to prove decisive. In the year immediately following the publication of "The Song of Labor," the Art Theatre was founded at Madrid by Benavente. The coöperation of the more promising of the younger generation was enlisted, among whom was Martínez Sierra, who played the rôle of Manuel in support of Benavente in the latter's comedy "A Long Farewell" at the opening performance. The ensuing months were months of intimate association with a remarkable mind. "As I listened to him talk, the fundamental laws of the modern theatre were revealed to me, and I have profited by his instruction unceasingly." So, properly, Martínez Sierra had already served an apprenticeship in the theatre before he began to write plays. His début as a playwright was delayed for ten years, and was then made in collaboration with Rusiñol, with whom he composed a comedy entitled *Vida y dulzura*, presented at the Teatro de la Comedia, Madrid, in 1907. This was followed by *Aucells de pas*, also in collaboration with Rusiñol, produced in Catalan at Barcelona in 1908, and, after a further interval of two years, by *Cors de dona*, in Catalan by the same hands. Meanwhile, during the spring of 1909, Martínez Sierra attained his first independent success with the comedy in two acts, *La sombra del padre*, presented at the Lara Theatre, one of the favorite houses of the capital. *El ama de la casa* ("The Mistress of the House"), was acted at the same theatre in 1910, and in 1911 he achieved a definitive and permanent triumph with the production of "The Cradle Song" (*Canción de cuna*). A companion piece, *Los pastores* ("The Two Shepherds"), was brought out in 1913, also at the Lara. As Martínez Sierra's non-dramatic prose becomes most nicely expressive, most pictorial and most imaginative in *Sol de la tarde*, his comedy attains perfection in these beautiful idylls of the religious life. Radiant with the bland charm and luminosity of the Andalusian sketches of the Quinteros, these comedies possess, nevertheless, a quality which is distinctive and personal, at once richer and humanly more significant than the work of any competitors in the *genre*. No other plays convey so convincingly, or with equal grace, the implications of environment as it interprets itself in terms of character, not symbolically nor in any didactic way, but directly and visually so that the ambient becomes the protagonist rather than the individual, and the spirit of the *milieu* is felt to express more clearly than words the fundamentals which condition its life.

"The Cradle Song" has been translated into many languages, and has been played and imitated widely throughout the civilized world. Ten years after the Madrid premiere Augustin Duncan hazarded four special matinees in English at the Times Square Theatre, New York, beginning in February, 1921, without, however, attracting support. A play in two acts was held to be revolutionary by the consensus of experts, and was thought to fall wholly without the purlieus of drama. During the same season a slighter piece, "The Romantic Young Lady" (*Sueño de una noche de agosto*), reached the London stage with Dennis Eadie, achieving a *succès d'estime*. The publication of the plays in translation fortunately attracted general attention, and it was not long before the wisdom of the pioneers had been justified. On November 2, 1926, "The Cradle Song" reappeared at the Fortune Theatre, London, with Miss Gillian Scaife, to be later transferred to the Little Theatre, where it completed a run of 109 performances, while Miss Eva LeGallienne brought her singularly fine and sensitive interpretation to the Civic Repertory Theatre, New York, during the following January, where it has been repeated 125 times. A special company headed by Miss Mary Shaw later traveled throughout the United States. Productions at the Playhouses of Oxford and Liverpool and the Abbey Theatre, Dublin, also deserve mention. Meanwhile "The Romantic Young Lady" was revived at the Neighborhood Playhouse, New York, with Miss Mary Ellis, "The Lover" presented at the Fortune Theatre and on tour through England and Scotland, and "Madame Pepita" at the Playhouse, Oxford and the Festival Theatre, Cambridge. "Love Magic," the first piece by Sierra to be acted in English (Waldorf-Astoria, New York, March 1918), "Poor John," "The Two Shepherds" and "Wife to a Famous Man" are all familiar in the little theatres of Great Britain and America. Finally, during the fall of 1927, Miss Scaife and Mr. Eadie brought "The Kingdom of God" to the Strand Theatre, and the same play, staged and directed by Miss Ethel Barrymore, was chosen to inaugurate the new Ethel Barrymore Theatre in this city in December, 1928.

Martínez Sierra has now written some forty-six original plays which have been acted, in addition to the three composed in collaboration with Rusiñol. He has translated and adapted forty-seven plays, chiefly from the French, English and Catalan, besides making occasional excursions into German. Perhaps the most important translation is a five-volume edition of Maeterlinck. His non-dramatic works occupy thirty-two volumes to which six others of translations must be added. In the intervals of composition, he established and edited *Helios*, a short-lived literary periodical, and founded and directed the *Biblioteca Renacimiento*, one of the most prosperous and progressive publishing houses of the capital. He has also edited a library for the world's classics in translation, and has established a publishing house of his own, the *Biblioteca Estrella*. In 1916 he assumed the management of the Teatro Eslava, Madrid, installing there a stock company, the *Compañía Lírico-Dramática Gregorio Martínez Sierra,* for the presentation of the modern repertory, prominently featuring his own plays. Whether from the point of view of acting or of *mise en scène,* this company must be accounted one of the most complete and satisfying in the peninsular. A Parisian engagement was undertaken successfully in 1925, and the company has since twice visited America, appearing first in a repertory of eighteen plays upon a tour extending from Buenos Aires to New York, terminating at the Forrest Theatre in May, 1927. An admirably printed and illustrated selection of monographs, *Un teatro de arte en España,* records the story of Sierra's tenancy of the Eslava and renders adequate tribute to Catalina Bárcena, the gifted and versatile actress around whom from the beginning the company has been built.

An artist who is subjected continually to the distractions of business, sacrifices with his leisure opportunity for detachment. Already, previous to the production of *Los pastores,* Martínez Sierra had manifested a tendency to approximate the main currents of the modern popular theatre. An improviser of unusual facility, he composed the slightest of musical comedies in *Margot* and *La Tirana*; a charming light opera libretto, *Las golondrinas* ("The Swallows"), based upon an earlier play, *Aucells de pas;* grand opera libretto in *La llama,* and the scenario of a dancing suite with music by Manuel de Falla for the gypsy *bailarina* Pastora Imperio. He remade old comedies, reworked juvenilia, republished forgotten stories, and dramatized his novel *Tú eres la paz* as *Madrigal.* He contrived pantomime. The lesser plays of this miscellaneous epoch become an epitome of the activities of the contemporary Madrid stage, broadened, however, by a thorough cosmopolitanism. They are eclectic, light-hearted, persistently gay, and, upon the more serious side, progressive documents considered from the sociological point of view. As he has grown older, Martínez Sierra has come to be interested not so much in the picturesque, in the life which is about to pass, as it lies inert in the present with all the remoteness of objective art, as he is in the future with its promise of the amelioration of the life which he formerly portrayed. He is an apostle of the new order, which is to be assured in his conception through the dissemination of a wider and more complete knowledge, a more truly international culture and sympathy, a keener social consciousness, and, more precisely and immediately, through the promotion of certain reforms. The more significant of the recent comedies, "The Kingdom of God" and *Esperanza nuestra* ("The Hope That is Ours") are indicative of this development. Although by no means didactic, they are purely social in genesis and in trend. Even his *Don Juan de España*, a re-embodiment of the traditional libertine celebrated by Tirso de Molina and by Zorrilla, is a Don Juan redeemed. Yet Sierra remains essentially a man of the theatre. As a social thinker, his ideas are general, by no chance controversial, rising little beyond a broad humanitarianism, temperately and engagingly expressed. "Letters to the Women of Spain," "Feminism, Femininity and the Spanish Spirit," and "The Modern Woman," all volumes of frankly confessed propaganda, are more effective because they persuade rather than provoke, avoiding partisan commitments or advocacies of any sort. They are quite as dispassionately impersonal as the plays. In these maturer works, as in those of Linares Rivas and Benavente, the modern movement, which during the earlier years of the century had been predominantly intellectual and aesthetic, turns toward the practical and political sphere, and fixes its attention upon results. It is the completion of the cycle which began in 1898.

Thirty years have slipped by since the publication of "The Song of Labor." Martínez Sierra is no longer a young man of promise. Soon he will be counted among the elders whose art has matured and attained its full extension, consolidated and ripened by experience. It is now possible to appraise his accomplishment and to determine with relative certainty his contribution to the contemporary theatre.

In this task, the secrets of a collaboration as intimate as it has been enduring, must of necessity be respected. We have no work avowedly solely by Martínez Sierra. Only one has been acknowledged by his wife as her own. Obviously, the letters and lectures in promotion of feminism are at least in great part by a feminine hand. Beyond question she is responsible for the major share of translation. An increasing proportion of the later output, also, may safely be attributed to her, more especially the collaborations with the poet Marquina and the actor Sassone, carried on during the absence of the Sierra troupe in America. Then "The Cradle Song" is a reminiscence of María's youth in Carabanchel, a town in which her father was convent doctor and where her sister took the veil, the Sister Joanna of the Cross of the play. Her intervention here has been confessed publicly. Yet these facts, though conceded, shed no light upon the basic problem, and provide no data for the identification of individual styles. A study of the earlier poems and stories might seem, indeed, to indicate that the elaboration and the subsequent simplification of the style are predominantly to be credited to Gregorio, while the bulk of actual composition—and to an increasing extent with the passing years—has been done by María.

Like the Quinteros, Sierra is primarily an optimist, a child of the sun. This is fundamental in his theatre and has not escaped the attention of the Spanish humorists:

"Glory to God in the highest,
On earth peace, good will toward men!
All's well with the world, says Martínez Sierra,
And then says it again."

He is not, however, an optimist by virtue of high spirits or uncommon enthusiasms, or because he has found life pleasant and easy, but through his sensitiveness. It is an optimism that is partly aesthetic, partly emotional. His sympathies have led him to hope. He has faith in the human equation, trust in men rather than in measures. The law he esteems very little in face of the gentle wisdom whose increment is sure with the years. Social progress is individual progress and individual progress is spiritual progress whose conquests are recorded first in the heart. This, of course, is no new doctrine, but it is the core of Martínez Sierra's philosophy and the main-spring of his art. In so far as the Church is a liberating and humanizing force he is a Christian, but he is a dissenter from all creeds and doctrines which restrict and inhibit the upward march of man.

Curiously enough, as a playwright, Sierra, for all his tenderness, has little concern with the individual. This is the source of his calm. One of the most sensitive of men, he is also one of the most detached. His drama is expository, chiefly for the reason that the inception of his plays is invariably generic and abstract. They are illustrative each of some general axiom or principle, whether human or social. He is no apostle of personal causes. Every man must be suffered, none the less, to shape his own career—"Live Your Own Life." The old virtues are destined to make way before the advance of the new—"The Two Shepherds." Sometimes, again, he has paused to probe some universal passion or emotion, devotion as in "The Lover," or, as in "The Cradle Song," to echo the cry of the eternal mother instinct which has been stifled and denied. Sometimes, as in "Fragile Rosina," in a sportive mood, he is content to parade mere temperament or an idle trait. Plays like "The Cradle Song" and "The Kingdom of God" are eloquent too, above the plane of feeling, of a social scheme, a new, a better life. The course of the story is the setting forth of the idea, the impelling emotion in all its significant phases, now by direct statement, now through contrast, but, in whatever way it may be effected, the content is plainly implicit in the theme from the beginning to become evident in detail as the action proceeds. For this reason the volitional element, in so far as it passes beyond mere childish caprice, is almost wholly lacking. Sierra draws no villains, creates no supermen, heroically imposing their wills, inherits no complexes, and cherishes small love for the tricks of display. His taste is unfailingly nice. Mystery, however veiled, he abhors, complication of plot, all thrill of situation. He even flees those internal crises of character which are so absorbing to the great dramatists, through whose struggles personality is built up and self-mastery won. These savor always of violence and conflict, no matter how subjective or subtle they may be. They are drama of action, and Sierra's drama is static drama. He is content to sacrifice movement to visual quality, excitement to charm.

Although indubitably theatre of ideas, characteristically and fundamentally this is emotional theatre. It is live and warm. Naturally the spectacular ardors which have been associated time out of mind with the so-called emotional play have been discarded. Yet there is no more skillful purveyor of tears. The feeling is always direct, the presentation transparently clear. The playwright displays the intuitive grace of simple truth. The spectator sees and is persuaded without argument at sight. Life is depicted as a process of adjustment, a pervading harmony which influences the characters and tempers them to its key, so that they are never suffered to become intellectualized. This is the most extraordinary of Sierra's gifts. His men and women remain spontaneously human, unchilled by the ideas in which they have previously been conceived. Standing by themselves, it is true, they betray a tendency to pale and grow thin, because, like the action, they have been born of the theme, and acquire substance and vitality only as they fit into the general plan and merge themselves with the incidents and scenes which reflect their life history. It is an art compact of simplicities, so delicate and frail that it can exist authentically only at propitious moments. Every element must concur in the perfection of the whole. Absolute unity is indispensable. Character must synchronize with theme, dialogue with action, situation with background, until each at last becomes articulate in the other, through every shade of feeling and the concord of smiles and tears. Otherwise the spell is shattered and ceases to be. Comedy and pathos join as one. Sierra's art is a blending of the more tractable emotions, of technical elements and all the ingredients which go to make up a play, that is so complete as not to stop short of interpenetration. To achieve less for him means failure. In the rehearsal of memory, the people of the plays do not recur to the mind, nor the stories, nor any fragments nor striking features, but the atmosphere, the feeling, the impression of the ensembles. The plays live as emotion, pictures.

When posterity comes to assess the fame of Martínez Sierra, the non-dramatic works, despite their undoubted merits, beyond peradventure will be set to one side. Time will ignore, also, as it has already done in large measure, the purely theatrical, occasional pieces contrived to meet the needs of aspiring actors or to tide over the exigencies of importunate companies, including specifically his own. There will remain a body of plays, considerable in bulk, and notable, at least superficially, in variety. A surprising amount of the best work must be assigned to the plays in one-act. Few have wrought more happily in miniature, or have qualified more instinctively in the lesser *genre*. The briefer pieces are without exception deft and tenuous, by their very nature peculiarly congenial to a temperament that is shy and retiring and a method that is tactful and restrained. Sierra's success has been unquestioned in this field. In two acts, he has shown equal facility, profiting in addition by the superior dignity and weight which are corollaries of the larger scale. "The Cradle Song" is Martínez Sierra, the epitome of his virtues and the confutation of his detractors, while into this group fall also the major number of his more serious efforts often, perhaps, only by limitation of subject inferior to those better known. In drama of greater extension and presumably more profound import, prolonged through three or more acts, he has been less impressive. The expository method here becomes treacherous, for either the play or the audience in the end is obliged to move. Confronted by this dilemma, Sierra falls back upon episode, and takes refuge in devices which temporize to sustain the interest, and at best are purely conventional. The most noteworthy of the longer plays such as "The Kingdom of God," are in consequence properly sequences of one-act units, carefully assembled and held together by a common subject or related, it may be, by a single character which runs its course through them all. Still they preserve unity of atmosphere, still they plead unobtrusively their causes and retain the freshness of their visual appeal, but the problem at full length is more complex, position and juxtaposition of incident are not so potent nor so suggestive, while even the most skillfully graduated emotion proves unable except in the rarest instances to dispense with progressive action and a continuous story artfully unrolled. These are multiple dramas, spoken pageants. They are chronicles of the modern stage.

In the history of the theatre, only two names, Ramón de la Cruz and Quiñones de Benavente, both countrymen of Sierra's, have lived as creators of one-act plays. Sierra's title to fame has a broader basis. He has produced the popular masterpiece of the two-act style, already secure as an international classic. He has written also more perfectly than his contemporaries the Spanish realistic comedy of atmosphere, that gently sentimental, placid communion with patience and peace whose quiet falls like a benediction upon a restless world.

THE CRADLE SONG

by GREGORIO MARTÍNEZ SIERRA

1911

THE CRADLE SONG[1]

Comedy in Two Acts

with an Interlude in Verse

Translated by John Garrett Underhill

TO JACINTO BENAVENTE

CAST OF CHARACTERS

SISTER JOANNA OF THE CROSS, *18 years of age.*
TERESA, *aged 18.*
THE PRIORESS, *aged 40.*
THE VICARESS, *aged 40.*
THE MISTRESS OF NOVICES, *aged 36.*
SISTER MARCELLA, *aged 19.*
SISTER MARÍA JESÚS, *aged 19.*
SISTER SAGRARIO, *aged 18.*
SISTER INEZ, *aged 50.*
SISTER TORNERA, *aged 80.*
THE DOCTOR, *aged 60.*
ANTONIO, *aged 25.*
THE POET.
A COUNTRYMAN.
Also a Lay Sister, Two Monitors, and several other Nuns, as desired.

[1] From *The Plays of G. Martínez Sierra.* Translated by John Garrett Underhill.

ACT ONE

[*A room opening upon the cloister of a Convent of Enclosed Dominican Nuns. The walls are tinted soberly; the floor is tiled. Three arches at the rear. In the right wall a large door with a wicket in it, leading to a passage communicating with the exterior. A grilled peephole for looking out. Above the door a bell which may be rung from the street. Beside the door an opening containing a revolving box, or wheel, on which objects may be placed and passed in from the outside without the recipient's being seen, or a view of the interior disclosed. Not far from this wheel, a pine table stands against one of the piers of the cloister. Ancient paintings relieve the walls. Through the arches the cloister garden may be seen, with a well in the middle; also a number of fruit trees, some greenery and a few rose bushes. Beneath the arches, potted flowers—roses, carnations, sweet basil, herb Louisa and balsam apple—together with a number of wooden benches and rush-seated chairs, and three arm chairs.*

As the curtain rises THE PRIORESS *is discovered seated in the largest of the arm chairs, and* THE MISTRESS OF NOVICES *and* THE VICARESS *in the smaller ones, the former on the right, the latter on the left, well to the front. The other* NUNS *are grouped about them, seated also. The novices,* SISTER MARCELLA, SISTER JOANNA OF THE CROSS, SISTER MARÍA JESÚS *and* SISTER SAGRARIO *stand somewhat to the right,* SISTER JOANNA OF THE CROSS *occupying the centre of the stage. The* LAY SISTER *and* SISTER TORNERA *remain standing by the table at the rear.*

It is broad daylight. The scene is one of cheerfulness and animation.]

SISTER SAGRARIO. Yes, do! Do! Do let her read them!

SISTER MARCELLA. Yes, do Mother! Do say yes!

PRIORESS. Very well. You may read them then, since you have written them.

SISTER JOANNA OF THE CROSS. I am very much ashamed.

MISTRESS OF NOVICES. These are the temptations of self-love, my child.

VICARESS. And the first sin in the world was pride.

SISTER JOANNA OF THE CROSS. They are very bad. I know you will all laugh at me.

VICARESS. In that way we shall mortify your vanity.

MISTRESS OF NOVICES. Besides, since we are not at school here, all that our Mother will consider in them will be the intention.

PRIORESS. Begin. And do not be afraid.

SISTER JOANNA OF THE CROSS [*reciting*]. To our Beloved Mother on the day of her Blessed Saint—her birthday:

Most reverend Mother,
On this happy day
Your daughters unite
For your welfare to pray.
We are the sheep
Who under your care
Are seeking out Heaven—
The path that leads there.
On one side the roses,
On the other the thorn,
On the top of the mountain
Jesus of Mary born.
To Jesus we pray
Long years for your life,
And of the Virgin María
Freedom from strife;
And may the years vie
In good with each other,
In holiness and joy,
Our dearly-loved Mother!

[*The nuns applaud and all speak at once.*]

SOME. Good! Very good!

OTHERS. Oh, how pretty!

SISTER TORNERA. They are like the Jewels of the Virgin!

SISTER INEZ [*depreciatively*]. She has copied them out of a book.

SISTER JOANNA OF THE CROSS [*carried away by her triumph*]. Long live our Mother!

ALL [*enthusiastically*]. Long live our Mother!

PRIORESS. Come, you must not flatter me, my children. The verses are very pretty. Many thanks, my daughter. I did not know that we had a poet in the house. You must copy them out for me on a piece of paper, so that I may have them to read.

SISTER JOANNA OF THE CROSS. They are copied already, reverend Mother. If your Reverence will be pleased to accept them . . .

[*She offers her a roll of parchment, tied elaborately with blue ribbons. The verses are written on the parchment and embellished with a border of flowers, doves and hearts, all of which have been painted by hand.*]

PRIORESS [*taking and unrolling the parchment*]. Bless me! What clear writing and what a beautiful border! Can you paint too?

SISTER JOANNA OF THE CROSS. No, reverend Mother. Sister María Jesús copied out the verses, and Sister Sagrario painted the border. Sister Marcella tied the bows.

SISTER MARCELLA. So it is a remembrance from all the novices.

PRIORESS. And all the while I knew nothing about it! The children have learned how to dissimulate very skilfully.

SISTER JOANNA OF THE CROSS. We had permission from Mother Anna St. Francis. She gave us the ribbon and the parchment.

PRIORESS. No wonder, then. So the Mother Mistress of Novices knows also how to keep secrets?

MISTRESS OF NOVICES. Once . . . Only for today. . . .

SISTER JOANNA OF THE CROSS. Today you must forgive everything.

PRIORESS [*smiling*]. The fault is not a grave one.

VICARESS [*acridly*]. Not unless it leads them to pride themselves upon their accomplishments. The blessed mother Santa Teresa de Jesús never permitted her daughters to do fancy work. Evil combats us where we least expect it, and ostentation is not becoming in a heart which has vowed itself to poverty and humility.

MISTRESS OF NOVICES. Glory be to God, Mother Vicaress, but why must your Reverence always be looking for five feet on the cat?

[SISTER MARCELLA *laughs flagrantly*.]

VICARESS. That laugh was most inopportune.

SISTER MARCELLA [*pretending repentance, but still continuing to laugh in spite of herself*]. I beg your pardon, your Reverence, I didn't mean it. This sister has such temptations to laugh, and she can't help it.

VICARESS. Biting your tongue would help it.

SISTER MARCELLA. Don't you believe it, your Reverence. No indeed it wouldn't!

PRIORESS [*thinking it best to intervene*]. Come, you must not answer back, my daughter. Today I wish to punish nobody.

VICARESS [*muttering*]. Nor today, nor never!

PRIORESS [*aroused*]. What does your Reverence mean by that, Mother Vicaress?

VICARESS [*very meekly*]. What we all know, reverend Mother —that the patience of your Reverence is inexhaustible.

PRIORESS. Surely your Reverence is not sorry that it is so?

VICARESS [*belligerently*]. Not upon my account, no. For by the grace of God I am able to fulfil my obligation and accommodate myself to the letter and spirit of our holy rule. But there are those who are otherwise, who, encouraged by leniency, may stumble and even fall . . .

PRIORESS. Has your Reverence anything definite in mind to say? If so, say it.

VICARESS. I have noticed for some time—and the Lord will absolve me of malice—that these "temptations to laugh" of which Sister Marcella speaks, have been abounding in this community; and these, taken with other manifestations of self-indulgence, not any less effervescent, are signs of a certain relaxation of virtue and deportment.

PRIORESS. I hardly think we need trouble ourselves upon that account. Providence has been pleased of late to bring into our fold some tender lambs, and perhaps they do frisk a little sometimes in the pastures of the Lord. But the poor children mean no harm. Am I right in your opinion, Mother Mistress of Novices?

MISTRESS OF NOVICES. You are always right in my opinion, reverend Mother. *Gaudeamus autem in Domino!*

VICARESS. Your Reverences of course know what you are doing. I have complied with my obligation.

[*The bell rings at the entrance.* SISTER TORNERA, *who is an active little old woman, goes up to the grille and looks through it, after first having made a reverence to the* PRIORESS.]

SISTER TORNERA. *Ave Maria Purissima!*

A VOICE [*outside, hoarse and rough*]. Conceived without sin. Is it permitted to speak with the Mother Abbess?

SISTER TORNERA. Say what you have need of, brother.

VOICE. Then here's a present for her from my lady, the mayor's wife, who wishes her happiness, and sends her this present, and she's sorry she can't come herself to tell her; but she can't, and you know the reason . . . [*The* PRIORESS *sighs, lifting up her eyes to heaven, and the others do the same, all sighing in unison.*] And even if she could on that account, she couldn't do it, because she's sick in bed, and you know the reason . . .

SISTER TORNERA. God's will be done! Can the poor woman get no rest? Tell her that we will send her a jar of ointment in the name of the blessed Saint Clara, and say that these poor sisters never forget her in their prayers. They pray every day that the Lord will send her comfort. [*She turns the wheel by the grille, and a basket appears, neatly covered with a white cloth.*] Ah!—and the reverend Mother thanks her for this remembrance. And may God be with you, brother. [*Approaching the others with the basket, which she has taken from the wheel.*] Poor lady! What tribulations our Lord sends into this world upon the cross of matrimony!

PRIORESS. And to her more than anybody. Such a submissive creature, and married to a perfect prodigal!

MISTRESS OF NOVICES. Now that we are on the subject, your Reverences, and have the pot by the handle, so to speak, do your Reverences know that the blasphemies of that man have completely turned his head? You heard the bells of the parish church ringing at noon yesterday? Well, that was because the mayor ordered them to be rung, because in the election at Madrid yesterday the republicans had the majority.

ALL. God bless us. God bless us!

VICARESS. Did the priest give his consent to that?

SISTER INEZ. The priest is another sheep of the same color—he belongs to the same flock, may the Lord forgive me if I lack charity! Didn't your Reverences hear the sacrilege he committed upon our poor chaplain, who is holier than God's bread? Well, he told him that he was more liberal than the mayor, and that the next thing he knew, when he least expected it, he was going to sing the introitus to the mass to the music of the Hymn of Riego!

PRIORESS. Stop! Enough! It is not right to repeat such blasphemies.

MISTRESS OF NOVICES. Yes, calumnies invented by unbelievers, the evil-minded . . .

SISTER INEZ. No such thing! Didn't Father Calixtus tell me himself while he was dressing for mass this morning? We'll have to put a new strip pretty soon down the middle of his chasuble.

PRIORESS. What? Again?

SISTER INEZ. Yes. It's all worn out; it looks terrible. Poor Father Calixtus is so eloquent! Pounding on his chest all the time, he simply tears the silk to pieces.

VICARESS. God's will be done, the man is a saint!

PRIORESS. And all this while we have been forgetting the present from the mayor's wife. Bring it nearer, Sister.

SISTER SAGRARIO. Mercy! What a big basket!

SISTER TORNERA. It's very light, though.

SISTER INEZ. Ha! It's easy to see what sister has a sweet tooth!

SISTER MARÍA JESÚS. As if she didn't like sweets!

[*Aside.*]

SISTER MARCELLA. Now, Sister Inez, what did we see you doing this morning? You know we caught you licking the cake pan yourself.

SISTER INEZ. I? Licking the pan? Your Sister licking the pan? Oh, what a slander! *Jesús!*

PRIORESS. Come, you must not be displeased, Sister Inez; for it was said only in pleasantry. Ah, Sister Marcella! Sister Marcella! Do have a little more circumspection and beg your Sister's pardon.

SISTER MARCELLA [*kneeling before* SISTER INEZ]. Pardon me, Sister, as may God pardon you, and give me your hand to kiss as a penance for having offended you.

PRIORESS. That is the way my children should behave, humbly and with contrition. Sister Inez, give Sister Marcella your hand to kiss, since she begs it of you so humbly.

SISTER MARCELLA [*spitefully, after kissing her hand*]. *Ay!* But what a smell of vanilla you have on your fingers, Sister! Goody! We're going to have cookies for lunch.

[*The others laugh.*]

SISTER INEZ [*irritated, almost in tears*]. Vanilla? God-a-mercy! Vanilla! Look at me! Do my fingers smell of vanilla?

PRIORESS [*imposing silence*]. Surely the devil must be in you, Sister Marcella, and may God forgive you for it! Go and kneel in the corner there with your face to the wall, and make the cross with your arms while you repeat a greater station. May the Lord forgive you for it!

SISTER MARCELLA. Willingly, reverend Mother.

SISTER INEZ [*rubbing her hands under her scapular*]. Too bad! Too bad! *Ay! Ay! Ay!*

SISTER MARCELLA [*aside*]. Old box of bones!

[*She goes and kneels in the corner, right, but keeps smiling and turning her head while she lets herself sink back on her heels, as if not taking the penance too seriously.*]

PRIORESS. You may uncover the basket now, Sister. Let us see what is in it.

SISTER TORNERA. With your permission, reverend Mother. Why! It's a cage!

SISTER SAGRARIO. With a canary in it!

ALL. A canary! A canary! Why, so it is! Let me see! How lovely!

MISTRESS OF NOVICES. Isn't it pretty?

SISTER MARÍA JESÚS. The dear! Isn't it cunning, though?

SISTER JOANNA OF THE CROSS. It looks as if it were made of silk.

SISTER INEZ. I wonder if it can sing?

PRIORESS. Of course it can sing. The mayor's wife would never send us a canary that couldn't sing.

SISTER SAGRARIO. What a beautiful cage! Why, there's a scroll on the front!

MISTRESS OF NOVICES. That isn't a scroll. It has letters on it.

SISTER MARÍA JESÚS. Why, so it has! Look and see what they say.

MISTRESS OF NOVICES. "The Convent of Dominican Nuns!"

SISTER INEZ [*laughing*]. I'd call that a pretty airy convent!

VICARESS. The good woman is holier than God's bread.

PRIORESS. She could not have sent me anything that would have pleased me better. I have always been anxious to have a canary.

SISTER INEZ. The Carmelite Sisters have two lovely canaries, and they say last year on Holy Thursday they hung them in the door of the tomb they have in the church for Easter, and it was like a miracle to hear them sing.

MISTRESS OF NOVICES. Then if ours sings, we can hang him in the church this year, and take the music box away.

PRIORESS. No, for the music box is a present from the chaplain, and he would rightly be offended. We will have the box and the canary there together, and when we wind up the box, it will encourage the bird to sing.

SISTER JOANNA OF THE CROSS. Oh, look at him now—he's taking his bath!

SISTER SAGRARIO. See how he jumps.

PRIORESS. What wonders God performs!

VICARESS. And yet there are misguided creatures who pretend that the world made itself!

SISTER INEZ. Sister Marcella stuck her tongue out at me.

SISTER MARCELLA. Oh, reverend Mother! I did nothing of the kind!

VICARESS. How nothing of the kind? Didn't I see it with my own eyes? And I was struck dumb!

SISTER MARCELLA. I said nothing of the kind . . . as . . . as that I had stuck my tongue out at Sister Inez. I stuck it out because there was a fly on the end of my nose, and since I had my arms out making the cross, I had to frighten him away with something.

SISTER JOANNA OF THE CROSS. Reverend Mother, since this is your Saint's day, won't you please excuse Sister Marcella this time?

SISTER MARÍA JESÚS. Yes, reverend Mother! I am sure she won't do anything that's wrong again.

PRIORESS. Sister Inez is the one who has been offended, and she is the only one who has the right to request her pardon.

NOVICES. She does! She does! You do, don't you, Sister Inez?

SISTER INEZ [*with a wry face*]. Your Reverence will pardon her when your Reverence thinks best.

PRIORESS. Then come here, my erring daughter.—She knows that I pardon her because of the day, and so as not to spoil the pleasure of her sisters.

SISTER MARCELLA. May God reward you, reverend Mother!

PRIORESS. And set your veil straight, for this is the Lord's house, and it looks as if you were going on an excursion. —And now to your cells, every one. (*To the* NOVICES.) What are you whispering about?

SISTER SAGRARIO. We were not whispering, Mother . . . We wanted to ask you something.

SISTER MARÍA JESÚS. And we are afraid to do it.

PRIORESS. Is it as bad as that?

SISTER MARÍA JESÚS. No, it isn't bad. But—

SISTER JOANNA OF THE CROSS. Your Reverence might think so.

PRIORESS. I might? I am not so evil-minded.

SISTER SAGRARIO. I . . . I . . . Our Mother Mistress will tell you.

MISTRESS OF NOVICES. They mean me.—Do you want me to?

NOVICES. Yes! Yes! Do!

MISTRESS OF NOVICES. With God's help I will try. Though I don't know for certain, I think what they want is for your Reverence to give them permission to talk a little, while they are waiting for the beginning of the *fiesta*. Am I right?

NOVICES. Yes! Yes! You are! Do, Mother, do!

SISTER MARCELLA. Long live our Mother!

PRIORESS. Silence! Silence! What? Haven't they had talking enough to-day after the dispensation I allowed them this morning?

VICARESS. The appetite always grows by what it feeds on. It is an unruly monster, and woe to her who gives it rein. If they came under my authority, I would not give them opportunity to make a single slip, for the holy Apostle Saint James has said and well said: "He who saith that he hath not offended by his tongue, lies."

SISTER MARCELLA. Ah, Sister Crucifixion! Don't spoil this holiday for our Mother.

VICARESS. Spoil it, eh? Who pays any attention to what I say in this house?

PRIORESS. Will you promise not to whisper nor offend the Lord with foolish talk?

NOVICES. We promise.

PRIORESS. Then you may talk as much as you like until the hour for prayers.

NOVICES. Thanks, thanks!

[*The bell rings at the entrance twice.*]

SISTER TORNERA. Two rings! The doctor!

PRIORESS. Cover your faces. [*The nuns lower their veils over their faces.*] And pass out through the cloister.

[*The nuns begin to file out slowly and disappear through the cloister.*]

SISTER SAGRARIO [*approaching the* PRIORESS]. This Sister has a felon, reverend Mother.

PRIORESS. Remain then—and you too, Sister María Jesús. [*To* SISTER TORNERA.] Open, Sister.

[THE PRIORESS, SISTER TORNERA, SISTER SAGRARIO *and* SISTER MARÍA JESÚS *remain.* SISTER TORNERA *unchains, unbolts and opens the door. The* DOCTOR *enters. He is about sixty years of age.*]

SISTER TORNERA. *Ave Maria Purissima!*

DOCTOR. Conceived without sin. [*He comes in.*] Good morning, Sister.

SISTER TORNERA. Good morning, Doctor.

DOCTOR. Well, what progress are we making in holiness today?

SISTER TORNERA [*laughing*]. Ho, ho, Doctor!

DOCTOR. Enough! Enough! No doubt, no doubt! [*Discovering the* PRIORESS.] Congratulations, Mother.

PRIORESS. What? A heretic, and yet you remember the days of the saints?

DOCTOR. You are the saint, Mother; you are the saint.

PRIORESS. Ah! You must not scandalize me before my novices.

DOCTOR. Novices? Where, where? I said so when I came in. I smell fresh meat.

PRIORESS. Don José! Don José!

DOCTOR. But I say no more. Come! To work! To work! . . . What is the trouble with these white lambs?

SISTER SAGRARIO. Your handmaid has a felon, Doctor.

DOCTOR. Eh? On the hand? And such a lovely hand! Well, we shall have to lance it, Sister.

SISTER SAGRARIO [*alarmed*]. What? Not now?

DOCTOR. No, tomorrow, Sister. Tomorrow, unless it yields first to a poultice and five *Pater nosters*. Remember, not one less!

SISTER SAGRARIO [*in perfect earnest*]. No, Doctor.

DOCTOR. And this other one, eh?

PRIORESS. Ah, Doctor! She has been giving me a great deal of worry. She falls asleep in the choir; she sighs continually without being able to assign any reason; she cries over nothing whatever; she has no appetite for anything but salads . . .

DOCTOR. How old are you?

SISTER MARÍA JESÚS. Eighteen.

DOCTOR. How long have you been in this holy house?

SISTER MARÍA JESÚS. Two years and a half.

DOCTOR. And how many more do you remain before you come to profession?

SISTER MARÍA JESÚS. Two and a half more, if the Lord should be pleased to grant this unworthy novice grace to become his bride.

DOCTOR. Let me see the face.

PRIORESS. Lift your veil.

[SISTER MARÍA JESÚS *lifts her veil.*]

DOCTOR. Hm! The Lord has not bad taste. A little pale, but well rounded, well rounded.

SISTER TORNERA. Don José! But who ever heard of such a doctor?

DOCTOR. So, we have melancholy then, a constant disposition to sigh, combined with loss of appetite—well, there is nothing else for it, Sister: a cold bath every morning and afterwards a few minutes' exercise in the garden.

SISTER TORNERA [*somewhat scandalized*]. Exercise? Don José!

DOCTOR. Unless we write at once home to her mother to hurry and fetch her and find us a good husband for her.

SISTER MARÍA JESÚS. Oh, Don José! But this Sister has taken her vows to the Church!

DOCTOR. Well, in that case cold water. There is nothing else for it. For melancholy at eighteen, matrimony or cold water.

SISTER SAGRARIO [*summoning her courage*]. You always talk so much about it, Doctor, why don't you get married yourself?

DOCTOR. Because I am sixty, daughter; and it is fifteen years since I have felt melancholy. Besides, whom do you expect me to marry when all the pretty girls go into convents?

PRIORESS. Doctor, doctor! This conversation will become displeasing to me.

DOCTOR. Is this all the walking infirmary?

SISTER TORNERA. Yes, Doctor.

DOCTOR. And the invalid? How is she?

SISTER TORNERA. She is the same to-day, Doctor. Poor Sister Maria of Consolation hasn't closed her eyes all night! Don't you remember? Yesterday she said she felt as if she had a viper gnawing at her vitals? Well, today she has a frog in her throat.

DOCTOR. Goodness gracious! Come, let me see, let me see. What a continual war the devil does wage against these poor sisters!—Long life, Mother, and happy days!

PRIORESS. Long life to you, Doctor. [*To* SISTER TORNERA.] Go with him, Sister, and meanwhile these children will take care of the gate. [SISTER TORNERA *takes a bell from the table and, her veil covering her face, precedes the* DOCTOR *through the cloister, ringing solemnly in warning. They disappear.*] I must repair to the choir; I fear that today I have fallen behind in devotion and prayer.

SISTER MARÍA JESÚS. Will your Reverence give us permission to call the others?

PRIORESS. Yes, call them; but be careful that you commit no frivolity.

[*The* PRIORESS *goes out.*]

SISTER MARÍA JESÚS [*approaching one of the arches of the cloister*]. Sister Marcella! Sister Joanna of the Cross! Pst! Come out! We are watching the grille and we have permission to talk.

[SISTER MARCELLA *and* SISTER JOANNA OF THE CROSS *re-enter.*]

SISTER SAGRARIO. What shall we talk about?

SISTER JOANNA OF THE CROSS. Let Sister Marcella tell us a story.

SISTER MARCELLA. Yes, so that you'll all be shocked.

SISTER MARÍA JESÚS. *Ay!* We are not such hypocrites as that, Sister.

SISTER MARCELLA. Or so that Sister Sagrario can run and tell on us to the Mother Mistress.

SISTER SAGRARIO. Oh, thank you, Sister!

SISTER MARCELLA. It wouldn't be the first time either.

SISTER SAGRARIO. You needn't mind me, Sisters. I am going to sit here in the corner and work, and you can talk about whatever you please. I shan't hear you.

[*She takes a pair of pincers, some beads and a piece of wire out of her pocket, and sitting down in a corner, begins to string a rosary.*]

SISTER JOANNA OF THE CROSS. Oh, come on, Sister! Don't be foolish.

[*They all surround her, and finally she allows herself to be persuaded, after many expressions of protest, like a small child who says "I won't play."*]

SISTER SAGRARIO. Why! If they haven't forgotten the canary!

SISTER MARCELLA. Poor thing! How do you like to be left in this nest of silly women, little fellow? Let's open the cage.

SISTER MARÍA JESÚS. What for?

SISTER MARCELLA. So that he can fly away, silly, if he wants to.

SISTER SAGRARIO. No, no!

SISTER MARÍA JESÚS. Our Mother wouldn't like that.

SISTER MARCELLA. He would like it, though. Come on! [*She opens the door of the cage.*] Fly out, sweetheart! Fly away, the world is yours. You are free!

SISTER JOANNA OF THE CROSS. He doesn't fly out.

SISTER MARÍA JESÚS. He doesn't budge.

SISTER MARCELLA. Stupid, don't you see what a bright, sunny day it is?

SISTER JOANNA OF THE CROSS. They say canaries are born in cages and, see, now he doesn't care to fly away.

SISTER MARÍA JESÚS. He'd rather stay shut up all his life like us nuns.

SISTER MARCELLA. Then you're a great fool, birdie. [*She shuts the door of the cage.*] God made the air for wings and He made wings to fly with. While he might be soaring away above the clouds, he is satisfied to stay here all day shut up in his cage, hopping between two sticks and a leaf of lettuce! What sense is there in a bird? *Ay,* Mother! And what wouldn't I give to be a bird!

SISTER JOANNA OF THE CROSS. Yes! What wouldn't you give to be a bird?

SISTER MARÍA JESÚS. They say that the swallows fly away

every year over the ocean, and nobody knows where they go.

SISTER SAGRARIO. I often dream that I am flying in the night time—that is not flying, but floating—just floating in the air without wings.

SISTER SAGRARIO. I often dream that I am running fast—oh so fast!—and that I am skipping down stairs, without ever touching my feet to the ground, or to the stairs.

SISTER SAGRARIO. Isn't it nice, though? And how disappointed you are when you wake up and find out after all that it isn't so, that it was only a dream!

SISTER MARCELLA. I have dreamed that dream so many times, that now when I wake up, I hardly know whether it is the truth or a dream.

SISTER JOANNA OF THE CROSS. What do you suppose it is that makes you dream the same dream so many times?

SISTER MARCELLA. I don't know, unless it is because it is the things you want to do, and you can't, and so you do them in dreams.

SISTER MARÍA JESÚS. What nice things you want to do!

SISTER SAGRARIO. But then what good would it be if you could do them? For instance, if we had wings like birds, where would we fly?

SISTER MARCELLA. I? I would fly to the end of the world!

SISTER MARÍA JESÚS. I, To the Holy Land, to Mount Calvary!

SISTER JOANNA OF THE CROSS. I would fly to Bethlehem and to the garden of Nazareth, where the Virgin lived with the child.

SISTER SAGRARIO. How do you know that there is a garden at Nazareth?

SISTER JOANNA OF THE CROSS. Of course there's a garden there, with a brook running by it. The song says so:

"The Virgin washed his garments
And hung them on the rose.
The little angels sing
And the water onward flows" . . .

[*Simply*.] There was a garden, too, by our house in the village, with a big rosebush on the border of a brook that ran by it; and I used to kneel beside the brook, and sing that song while I washed my baby brother's clothes, for there were seven of us children, and I was the oldest. [*Feelingly*.] And that's what I miss most! [*Drying her eyes with her hands.*] *Ay*, Mother! And I always cry when I think of that baby boy! But it isn't right, I know . . . He loved me more than he did mother, and the day that they took me away to the Convent, and I left home, he cried—he cried so that he nearly broke his little baby heart!

SISTER MARCELLA. I have a brother and a sister, but they are both older than I am. My sister married two years ago, and now she has a baby. [*With an air of importance.*] She brought him here once to show me.

SISTER JOANNA OF THE CROSS [*interrupting her, greatly interested*]. I remember. He stuck his little hand in through the grille and your sister kissed it. Did you ever think how soft babies' hands are? Whenever I take communion I try to think I am receiving our Lord as a little child, and I take and press him like this to my heart, and then it seems to me that he is so little and so helpless that he can't refuse me anything. And then I think that he is crying, and I pray to the Virgin to come and help me quiet him. And if I wasn't ashamed, because I know you would all laugh at me, I'd croon to him then, and rock him to sleep, and sing him baby songs.

[*The bell rings by the grille.*]

SISTER SAGRARIO. The bell! I wonder who it is?

SISTER JOANNA OF THE CROSS. Better ask. That's why they left us here.

SISTER MARÍA JESÚS. Who'll do it? I won't. I'm afraid.

SISTER SAGRARIO. So am I.

SISTER MARCELLA. You're not usually so bashful, I must say. I'll ask, though I was the last to enter the house. [*Going up to the grille, she says in a timid voice:*] *Ave Maria purissima!* [*A moment's silence.*] No one answers.

SISTER JOANNA OF THE CROSS. Try again. Say it louder.

SISTER MARCELLA [*Raising her voice.*] *Ave Maria purissima!*

SISTER SAGRARIO. Nothing this time, either.

SISTER MARÍA JESÚS [*summoning her courage, in a high-pitched voice.*] *Ave Maria purissima!*

[*Another silence. The Novices look at each other in surprise.*]

SISTER MARCELLA. It is very strange.

SISTER MARÍA JESÚS. It must be spirits.

SISTER SAGRARIO. Oh, I'm afraid!

SISTER JOANNA OF THE CROSS. Nonsense! It's some little boy who has rung the bell on his way home from school, so as to be funny.

SISTER MARÍA JESÚS. Peep through the hole and see if anybody is there.

SISTER MARCELLA [*stooping down to look*]. No, nobody. But it looks as if there was something on the wheel. Yes . . .

SISTER JOANNA OF THE CROSS. Let me see! Yes . . . Can't you turn it? [*She turns the wheel, and a second basket appears, carefully covered with a white cloth like the first.*] A basket!

SISTER SAGRARIO. Another present for our Mother.

SISTER MARÍA JESÚS. Of course it is! And here's a paper tied fast to it.

SISTER JOANNA OF THE CROSS [*reading, but without unfolding the paper*]. "For the Mother Prioress."

SISTER SAGRARIO. Didn't I tell you?

SISTER MARCELLA. Somebody wants to give her a surprise.

SISTER JOANNA OF THE CROSS. I wonder if it's Don Calixtus, the chaplain?

SISTER MARCELLA. Of course it is, child!

SISTER MARÍA JESÚS. Or maybe it's the Doctor.

SISTER JOANNA OF THE CROSS. No. He was just here and he didn't say anything about it.

SISTER SAGRARIO. All the same it might be from him. Maybe he wants to keep it a secret.

SISTER MARÍA JESÚS. Let's take it off the wheel.

SISTER MARCELLA [*lifting and carrying it to the table*]. We'd better put it here by the canary. My! But it's heavy!

SISTER SAGRARIO. I wonder what it is?

SISTER MARCELLA. Let's lift the corner and see.

SISTER MARÍA JESÚS. No, for curiosity is a sin.

SISTER MARCELLA. What of it? Come on! Let's do it. Who will ever know? [*She lifts the corner of the cloth a little and starts back quickly with a sharp cry.*] *Ay!!*

SISTER JOANNA OF THE CROSS [*hurrying to look*]. *Jesús!*

SISTER MARÍA JESÚS. *Ave Maria!* [*Looking too.*]

SISTER SAGRARIO [*following*]. God bless us!

[*The Convent is aroused at the cry of* SISTER MARCELLA. *Presently* THE PRIORESS, THE VICARESS, THE MISTRESS OF NOVICES *and the other* NUNS *enter from different directions.*]

PRIORESS. What is the matter? Who called out?

VICARESS. Who gave that shout?

MISTRESS OF NOVICES. Is anything wrong? [*The four Novices, trembling, stand with their backs to the basket, their bodies hiding it completely.*]

VICARESS. It is easy to see it was Sister Marcella.

PRIORESS. What has happened? Speak! Why are you all standing in a row like statues?

MISTRESS OF NOVICES. Has anything happened to you?

SISTER JOANNA OF THE CROSS. No, reverend Mother, not to us; but—

SISTER MARÍA JESÚS. No, reverend Mother; it's . . .

SISTER MARCELLA. Someone rang the bell by the wheel . . . and we looked . . . and there was nobody there . . . and they left a basket . . . this basket . . . and . . . and your sister had the curiosity to undo it . . .

VICARESS. Naturally, you couldn't do otherwise.

SISTER MARCELLA. And it's . . .

PRIORESS. Well? What is it?

SISTER MARCELLA. It's . . . I . . . I think it would be better for your Reverence to look yourself.

PRIORESS. By all means! Let me see. [*She goes up to the basket and uncovers it.*] *Ave Maria!* [*In a hoarse whisper.*] A baby!

ALL [*variously affected*]. A baby?

[*The* VICARESS, *horrified, crosses herself.*]

PRIORESS [*falling back*]. Your Reverences may see for yourselves.

[*The* NUNS *hurry up to the basket and surround it.*]

VICARESS. *Ave Maria!* How can such an insignificant object be so pink?

MISTRESS OF NOVICES. It's asleep.

SISTER JOANNA OF THE CROSS. See it open its little hands!

SISTER MARÍA JESÚS. Why! It has hair under the edge of its cap!

SISTER SAGRARIO. It is like an angel!

VICARESS. A pretty angel for the Lord to send us.

SISTER JOANNA OF THE CROSS [*as if she had been personally offended*]. *Ay,* Mother Vicaress! You mustn't say that.

PRIORESS [*tenderly*]. Where do you come from, little one?

VICARESS. From some nice place, you may be sure.

PRIORESS. Who can tell, Mother? There is so much poverty in the world, so much distress.

VICARESS. There is so much vice, reverend Mother.

MISTRESS OF NOVICES. You say that there was nobody at the grille?

SISTER MARCELLA. Nobody; no, Mother. The bell rang; we answered . . . but there was nobody there.

SISTER SAGRARIO [*picking up the paper which has fallen on the floor*]. Here is a paper which came with it.

PRIORESS [*taking the paper*]. "For the Mother Prioress."

VICARESS. An appropriate present for your Reverence.

PRIORESS. Yes, it is a letter.

[*She unfolds the paper and begins to read.*]

"Reverend Mother:

Forgive the liberty which a poor woman takes, trusting in your Grace's charity, of leaving at the grille this newborn babe. I, my lady, am one of those they call women of the street, and I assure you I am sorry for it; but this is the world, and you can't turn your back on it, and it costs as much to go down as it does to go up, and that is what I am writing to tell you, my lady. The truth is this little girl hasn't any father, that is to say it is the same as if she didn't have any, and I—who am her mother—I leave her here, although it costs me something to leave her; for although one is what one is, one isn't all bad, and I love her as much as any mother loves her baby, though she is the best lady in the land. But all the same, though she came into this world without being wanted by anyone, she doesn't deserve to be the daughter of the woman she is, above all, my lady, of her father, and I don't want her to have to blush for having been born the way she was, nor for having the mother she has, and to tell it to me to my face, and I pray you by everything you hold dear, my lady, that you will protect her and keep her with you in this holy house, and you won't send her to some orphanage or asylum, for I was brought up there myself, and I know what happens in them, although the sisters are kind—yes, they are—and have pity. And some day, when she grows up and she asks for her mother, you must tell her that the devil has carried her away, and I ask your pardon, for I must never show myself to her, nor see her again, nor give you any care nor trouble, so you can do this good work in peace, if you will do it, for I implore you again, my lady, that you will do it for the memory of your own dear mother, and God will reward you, and she will live in peace, and grow up as

God wills, for what the eyes have not seen the heart cannot understand, my lady."

VICARESS. Bless us! *Ave Maria!*

MISTRESS OF NOVICES. Poor woman!

SISTER JOANNA OF THE CROSS. Baby dear! Darling baby!

VICARESS. What pretty mothers the Lord selects for his children!

PRIORESS. God moves in his own ways, Sister. God moves in his own ways.

SISTER INEZ. Is that all the letter says?

PRIORESS. What more could it say?

[THE DOCTOR *and* SISTER TORNEA *have re-entered during the reading.*]

DOCTOR. Exactly. What more could it say?

PRIORESS. What do you think, Don José?

DOCTOR. I think that somebody has made you a very handsome present.

PRIORESS. But what are we going to do with it? Because I . . . this poor woman . . . she has put this poor creature into our hands, and I would protect her willingly, as she asks, and keep her here with us . . .

NOVICES. Yes, yes, Mother! Do! Do!

MISTRESS OF NOVICES. Silence!

PRIORESS. But I don't know if we can . . . that is, if it is right, if it is according to law . . . for, when we enter this holy rule, we renounce all our rights . . . and to adopt a child legally . . . I don't know whether it can be done. How does it seem to you?

DOCTOR. I agree with you. Legally, you have no right to maternity.

VICARESS. And even if we had, would it be proper for our children to be the offspring of ignominy and sin?

PRIORESS. I would not raise that question, reverend Mother, for the child is not responsible for the sin in which she was born, and her mother, in renouncing her motherhood, has bitterly paid the penalty.

VICARESS. Yes, it didn't cost her much to renounce it.

PRIORESS. Do we know, Mother? Do we know?

VICARESS. We can guess. It is easy enough to go scattering children about the world if all you have to do is leave them to be picked up afterwards by the first person who happens along.

DOCTOR. How easy it is might be a matter for discussion. There are aspects of it which are not so easy.

SISTER SAGRARIO. Oh! She's opened her mouth!

SISTER JOANNA OF THE CROSS. The little angel is hungry.

SISTER MARÍA JESÚS. She's sucking her thumb!

SISTER JOANNA OF THE CROSS. Make her take her thumb out of her mouth. She'll swallow too much and then she'll have a pain.

SISTER SAGRARIO. Don't suck your fingers, baby.

SISTER JOANNA OF THE CROSS. Isn't she good, though? You stop her playing, and she doesn't cry.

PRIORESS. There is another thing we must consider. What are we to do for a nurse?

SISTER JOANNA OF THE CROSS. The gardener's wife has a little boy she is nursing now.

PRIORESS. In that case I hardly think she would care to be responsible for two.

SISTER JOANNA OF THE CROSS. But it won't be any trouble—she's so tiny! Besides, we can help her out with cow's milk and a little pap. The milk will keep on the ice and we can clear it with a dash of tea.

DOCTOR. It is easy to see Sister Joanna of the Cross has had experience with children.

SISTER JOANNA OF THE CROSS. Your handmaid has six little brothers and sisters. Ah, reverend Mother! Give her to me to take care of and then you will see how strong she'll grow up.

VICARESS. Nothing else was needed to complete the demoralization of the Novices. You can see for yourselves how naturally they take to this dissipation.

PRIORESS. I want you to tell me frankly what you think—all of you.

[*All speak at once.*]

MISTRESS OF NOVICES. Your Sister thinks, reverend Mother . . .

SISTER TORNERA. Your handmaid . . .

SISTER INEZ. It seems to me . . .

PRIORESS [*smiling*]. But one at a time.

SISTER TORNERA. It is an angel which the Lord has sent us, and your Sister thinks that we ought to receive her like an angel, with open arms.

MISTRESS OF NOVICES. Of course we ought. Suppose, your Reverences, it hadn't been a little girl, but . . . I don't know

—some poor animal, a dog, a cat, or a dove, like the one which flew in here two years ago and fell wounded in the garden trying to get away from those butchers at the pigeon-traps. Wouldn't we have taken it in? Wouldn't we have cared for it? And wouldn't it have lived happy forever afterward in its cage? And how can we do less for a creature with a soul than for a bird?

SISTER TORNERA. We must have charity.

VICARESS. I am glad the Mother Mistress of Novices has brought up the incident of that bird, for it will absolve me from bringing it up, as it might seem, with some malice. It was against my advice that that creature was received into this house, and afterward we had good reason to regret it, with this one saying "Yes, I caught him!" and that one, "No, I took care of him!" and another "He opens his beak whenever I pass by!" and another, "See him flap his wings! He does it at me!"—vanities, sophistries, deceits all of them, snares of the devil continually! And if all this fuss was about a bird, what will happen to us with a child in the house? This one will have to dress it, that one will have to wash it, another will be boasting, "It is looking at me!" another that it's at her that it googles most . . . There is Sister Joanna of the Cross making faces at it already!

SISTER JOANNA OF THE CROSS. What did your Reverence say?

VICARESS. Dissipation and more dissipation! Your Reverences should remember that when we passed behind these bars, we renounced forever all personal, all selfish affection.

MISTRESS OF NOVICES. Is it selfish to give a poor foundling a little love?

VICARESS. It is for us. Our God is a jealous God. The Scriptures tell us so.

MISTRESS OF NOVICES. Bless us! Mercy me!

VICARESS. And this quite apart from other infractions of our order which such indulgence must involve. For example, your Reverences—and I among the first—take no account of the fact that at this very moment we are transgressing our rule. We are conversing with our faces unveiled in the presence of a man.

PRIORESS. That is true.

DOCTOR. Ladies, as far as I am concerned—Take no account of me. . . .

PRIORESS. No, Doctor, you are of no account. I beg your pardon, Don José; I hardly know what I am saying.—Your

Reverence is right. Cover yourselves—that is, it makes no difference . . . The harm has been done . . . only once. . . . But comply with your consciences . . . [*The* VICARESS *covers her face. The others, hesitating, wait for the* PRIORESS, *who makes a movement to do so, but then desists. The* VICARESS, *when she is covered, cannot see that she has become the victim of the rest.*] But where were we? I confess that my heart prompts me to keep the child.

VICARESS. The Doctor already has told us that we have no right to maternity.

MISTRESS OF NOVICES. But the child is God's child, and she is returning to her father's mansion.

VICARESS. God has other mansions for his abandoned children.

SISTER JOANNA OF THE CROSS. Don't send her to the asylum!

SISTER SAGRARIO. No!

PRIORESS. Her mother entreats us.

VICARESS. Her mother is not her mother. She has abandoned her.

PRIORESS. She has not abandoned her. She has entrusted her to others who seemed worthier to undertake her keeping.

VICARESS. Unholy egotism!

MISTRESS OF NOVICES. Christian heroism!

VICARESS. So? We are coining phrases, are we? Is this a convent, or an illustrated weekly?

MISTRESS OF NOVICES. Life is hard to some people, and thorny.

VICARESS. Yes, and into the details of it, it is not becoming for us to go, since by the grace of God we have been relieved from the temptations and the frailties of the world.

MISTRESS OF NOVICES. All the more, then, we ought to have compassion on those who have fallen and are down.

VICARESS. Compassion? Mush and sentiment!

MISTRESS OF NOVICES. The veil of charity!

PRIORESS. Silence! And let us not begin by rending it, irritating ourselves and aggravating each other.—Don José, I suppose this birth will have to be reported?

DOCTOR. It will, madam. To the Register.

SISTER JOANNA OF THE CROSS. But then they will take her away?

DOCTOR. If nobody wants her. But if you have made up your minds you would like to keep her, I think I can propose a solution.

PRIORESS. A solution that is legal?

DOCTOR. Perfectly. Thanks be to God I am a single man. But,

although I am not a saint, yet I cannot take to myself the credit of having augmented the population of this country by so much as a single soul. I have not a penny, that is true, but like everybody else, I have a couple of family names. They are at the service of this little stranger, if they will be of use to her. She will have no father and no mother—I cannot help that—but she will have an honorable name.

PRIORESS. Do you mean to say?——

DOCTOR. That I am willing to adopt her; exactly—and to entrust her to your care, because my own house . . . The fact is the hands of Doña Cecilia are a little rough for handling these tiny Dresden dolls, and perhaps I might prove a bit testy myself. The neighbors all say that the air grows blue if my coat rubs against me as I walk down the street.

[*All laugh.*]

DOCTOR. Besides I am sure Sister Crucifixion is better equipped for the robing of saints.

VICARESS. Doctor, God help us both!

DOCTOR. Is it agreed?

PRIORESS. God reward you for it! Yes, in spite of everything. We shall notify the Superior immediately. It is not necessary that the child should live in the cloister. She can remain with the gardener's wife until she has grown older, and enter here later when she has the discretion to do so. She has been entrusted to our hands, and it is our duty to take care of her—a duty of conscience.

DOCTOR. If I cannot be of further service, I will go. And I will speak to the Register.

PRIORESS. As you go, be so kind as to ask the gardener's wife to come in. We must see if she will take charge of the child and nurse her. And tell her also to bring with her some of her little boy's clothes.

SISTER JOANNA OF THE CROSS. Yes, for we shall have to make a change immediately.

SISTER SAGRARIO. We shall?

VICARESS. Not a change, but a beginning.

DOCTOR. Good afternoon, ladies.

ALL. Good afternoon, Don José.

[*The* DOCTOR *goes out.*]

[*A pause.*]

PRIORESS. Sisters, may God pardon us if we have acted in this with aught but the greatest purity of motive. I hope and pray that His grace will absolve us of offense, nor find us guilty of having loved too much one of His poor children. The child shall be brought up in the shadow of this house, for we may say that her guardian angel has delivered her at the door. From this hour forth we are all charged with the salvation of her soul. The Lord has entrusted to us an angel and we must return to Him a saint. Watch and pray.

ALL. Watch and pray. We will, reverend Mother.

PRIORESS. And now bring her to me, Sister Joanna of the Cross, for as yet it can scarcely be said that I have seen her. [*Looking at the child.*] Lamb of God! Sleeping as quietly in her basket as if it were a cradle of pure gold! What is it that children see when they are asleep that brings to their faces an expression of such peace?

SISTER JOANNA OF THE CROSS. They see God and the Virgin Mary.

SISTER MARÍA JESÚS. Maybe the angel who watches over them whispers in their ears and tells them about heaven.

PRIORESS. Who can say? But it is a comfort to the soul to see a child asleep.

SISTER MARÍA JESÚS. It makes you want to be a saint, reverend Mother.

SISTER SAGRARIO. Will your Reverence grant me permission to give her a kiss?

SISTER MARÍA JESÚS. Oh, no! For it hasn't been baptized yet, and it is a sin to kiss a heathen!

PRIORESS. She is right. We must send for the Chaplain and have her baptized immediately.

MISTRESS OF NOVICES. What shall we call her?

SISTER INEZ. Teresa, after our beloved Mother.

SISTER TORNERA. María of the Miracles.

SISTER SAGRARIO. Bienvenida.

[*A large bell rings outside.*]

PRIORESS. The summons to the choir! We can decide later. Let us go. [*The* NUNS *file out slowly, looking at the child as they go.*] Remain with her, Sister Joanna of the Cross—you understand children; and wait for the coming of the gardener's wife. Follow the devotions from where you are, and do not let your attention falter.

[*All the* NUNS *go out, except* SISTER JOANNA OF THE CROSS, *who bends over the basket; then sinks on her knees beside it. The choir is heard within, led by a single* NUN *in solo, the responses being made in chorus, in which* SISTER JOANNA OF THE CROSS *joins. While the* NUN *is leading,* SISTER JOANNA OF THE CROSS *talks and plays with the child; then she makes her responses with the others.*]

VOICE WITHIN. *In nomine Patri et Filio et Spiritui Sancto.*

[SISTER JOANNA OF THE CROSS *crosses herself and says with the other* NUNS:]

VOICES WITHIN AND SISTER JOANNA OF THE CROSS. *Amen!*

SISTER JOANNA OF THE CROSS [*to the child*]. Pretty one! Pretty one!

VOICE WITHIN. *Deus in adjutorium meum intende.*

VOICES WITHIN AND SISTER JOANNA OF THE CROSS. *Domine ad adjuvandum me festina.*

SISTER JOANNA OF THE CROSS [*to the child*]. Do you love me, sweetheart? Do you love me?

VOICE WITHIN. *Gloria Patri et Filio et Spiritui Sancto.*

VOICES WITHIN IN CHORUS. *Sicut erat in principio et nunc et semper et insecula seculorum. Amen! Allelulia!*

[*But this time* SISTER JOANNA OF THE CROSS *makes no response. Instead she bends over the basket, embracing the child passionately, oblivious of all else, and says:*]

SISTER JOANNA OF THE CROSS. Little one! Little one! Whom do you love?

INTERLUDE

Spoken by the Poet

You came tonight to listen to a play;
Instead into a convent you made way.
Singular hardihood! Almost profanation!
What will a poet not do to create sensation?
Pardon, good nuns, him who disturbs the rest
And troubles the serene quietude of your nest,
Kindling amid the shades of this chaste bower
The flame of love you have renounced and flower.
Nay! Do not frown because I have said love,
For you must know, chaste brides of God above,
That which you have deemed charity and pity,
The act of mercy, clemency for the pretty,
Unfriended foundling fate has brought along,
Yearning of adoption and the cradle song,
No other is than love's fire, divine and human
Passion ever brooding in the heart of woman.

Ah, love of woman, by whose power we live,
Offend so often—but to see forgive!
Whence do you draw your grace but from above?
Whence simply? Simply from maternal love!
Yes, we are children, woman, in your arms;
Your heart is bread, you soothe our wild alarms,
Like children give us the honey of your breast,
In a cradle always your lover sinks to rest
Although he prostitutes our grovelling flesh.
Mother if lover, mother if sister too,
Mother by pure essence, day long and night through,
Mother if you laugh, or if with us you cry
In the core of being, in fibre and in mesh,

Every woman carries, so God has willed on high,
A baby in her bosom, sleeping eternally!

So being women, you are lovers, nuns;
Despite the ceintured diamond which runs
Across your virgin shields, showing in your lives
How to be mothers without being wives.
And in this child of all, you have poured all
The honey of your souls, and blended all
The fire of the sun, all fragrance and all light,
The first sweet morning kiss, the last good-night,
Till all her being tenderness exhales,
Her heart the home of love and nightingales.
A hundred times a woman but no saint.
The nuns pray in the choir; outside her plaint
A song; her prayer, gay rippling laughter.
Mass and the May morning slip by, she running after
Or dreaming in the garden. The roses smell
So sweetly! No child this for the hermits' cell.
She loves Heaven, but in good company;
And before the altar of the Virgin see
Her with a boy, ruddier than the candle's flame,
Who calls her "Sister," the nuns "Aunt" for name.
A smiling, bashful boy, who soon will grow
To be a strong man, learn to give a blow
And take one, conquer worlds and redress wrong,
Justice in his heart, and on his lips a song!
Sometimes she takes the cat up, calls it "Dear!"
The nuns cross themselves, religiously severe.
"The child is mad," they say. Ah! No such thing!
With her into the convent entered Spring.

This then the simple story. The poet would
Have told it day by day, if well he could,
In shining glory. But the task were vain.
The glory of our daily lives is plain.
For life builds up itself in such a way,
The water runs so clear, so bright the day,
That time is lulled to sleep within these walls.
An age or moment? Which passes? Who recalls?
The wheel turns round, but no one notes the turn.
What matter if the sisters' locks that burn
With gold, in time to silvery gray have paled?

Their hoods conceal it. And the pinks have failed
In the cheeks, and the lilies on the brow.
There are no mirrors. The sisters then as now
May walk in the garden, believe it still is May.

Among these hours which softly slip away,
This timeless time, we shyly pause at that
In which there is most warmth, the concordat
Of youth and incense, breaking of the spring.
The years have passed, the child is ripening.
The curtain rises on a soul in flower,
And a love chapter claims us for an hour.
It is quiet afternoon, quiet breeding;
The nuns are sewing and their sister reading:

ACT TWO

[*Parlor of a Convent.*

At the rear, a grille with a double row of bars. A curtain of dark woolen cloth hangs over the grille and intercepts the view of the outer parlor, to which visitors are admitted. This is without decoration, and may be brightly illuminated at the proper moment from the garden. A number of oil paintings of saints hang upon the walls—all of them very old and showing black stains. With them a carved crucifix or large black wooden cross. A small window furnished with heavy curtains, which, when drawn, shut off the light completely, is cut in the wall of the inner parlor on either side of the grille, high up toward the ceiling. A pine table, a carved arm chair, two other arm chairs, smaller chairs and benches, together with all the materials necessary for sewing.

THE PRIORESS, THE MISTRESS OF NOVICES, SISTERS INEZ *and* TORNERA, SISTER SAGRARIO, SISTER JOANNA OF THE CROSS, SISTER MARCELLA, SISTER MARÍA JESÚS *and the other* NUNS *are discovered upon the rise of the curtain. Only* THE VICARESS *is absent. All are seated, sewing, with the exception of* SISTER MARÍA JESÚS, *who stands in the centre, to the left of* THE PRIORESS'S *chair, reading. A bride's trousseau is spread out upon the table and chairs. It is embroidered elaborately, trimmed with lace and tied with blue silk ribbons. A new trunk stands against the wall on the right, the trays being distributed about the benches and upon the floor.*

Eighteen years have passed. It must be remembered that the NUNS *have changed in appearance, and those who were novices have now professed and have exchanged the white for the black veil.*]

SISTER MARÍA JESÚS [*reading and intoning*]. "The Treasury of Patience, the Meditations of an Afflicted Soul in the presence of its God."

SISTER MARCELLA [*sighing*]. *Ay!*

SISTER MARÍA JESÚS [*reading*]. "First Meditation: The Sorrows of an Unhappy Spirit, Submerged in a Sea of Woe."

[*Outside,* TERESA'S *voice is heard, singing gaily.*]

TERESA. "Come singing and bringing
Flowers from the field,
Flowers from the field,
Sweet gardens, to Mary.
Flowers you must yield
For Love's sanctuary!"

[*The reader stops, and, smiling, glances in the direction of the window through which the voice is heard. The other* NUNS *smile also, complacently.*]

PRIORESS [*with affected severity*]. The child interrupts us continually.

SISTER INEZ. And a day like to-day!

SISTER JOANNA OF THE CROSS [*sympathetically*]. She sings like a lark.

MISTRESS OF NOVICES [*indulgently*]. She is so young!

SISTER MARCELLA. *Ay,* Mother!

PRIORESS. Continue reading, Sister María Jesús.

SISTER MARÍA JESÚS [*reading*]. "The Sorrows of an Unhappy Spirit, Submerged in a Sea of Woe. My God, O my God, save me, for every moment I die! Overwhelmed, I sink in the midst of this terrible storm. Every moment I am buffeted and borne down. I am sucked into the uttermost depths, and there is no health in me!"

TERESA [*singing*].
"From the glory of your brightness,
Radiantly sweet,
O, let me stoop and bend me
To kiss your feet!
Let me stoop and bend me
To kiss your feet!"

[*Again the reader stops. The* NUNS *smile again.*]

PRIORESS. Sister Sagrario, will you step out into the garden and ask the child not to sing? We are reading. [SISTER

SAGRARIO *goes out, right, after making the customary reverence.*] Continue, Sister, continue.

SISTER MARÍA JESÚS [*reading*]. "There is no health in me. I cannot support myself; I cannot resist the shock of the horrible onrushing waves."

TERESA [*singing*].

"You too were happy, Mary,
Happy in his love,
Flowers of love and springtime
That bloom above!"

[*The song is broken off suddenly, as if the* NUN *had arrived and commanded* TERESA *to stop. A moment later, there is a sound of light laughter.*]

PRIORESS. It cannot be helped [*smiling*]. The child was born happy and she will die so. [*To the reader.*] Continue.

SISTER MARCELLA. Ay, Lady of Sorrows!

PRIORESS. But Sister Marcella, my daughter, why do you sigh like this? Are you unwell?

SISTER MARCELLA. No, reverend Mother. But your daughter has temptations to melancholy.

PRIORESS. The Lord protect and keep you. You know how it displeases me to see the shadow of melancholy enter this house.

SISTER MARCELLA [*making a reverence*]. *Ay,* reverend Mother, pardon me and assign me some penance if I sin, but your daughter cannot help it.

PRIORESS. Who was thinking of sin? Go out into the garden and take a little sunshine, daughter; that is what you need.

SISTER MARCELLA. *Ay,* reverend Mother, you don't know what you say! For when your daughter sees the flowers in the garden, and the blue sky so bright above them, and the sun so beautiful overhead, the temptation comes upon her then to sigh more than ever. *Ay!*

PRIORESS. If that is the case, return to your seat and let us pray that it may cease. But do not let me hear you sigh again, for I do not wish to send you to the prison to brighten your spirit with solitude and confinement.

SISTER MARCELLA. As your Reverence desires. [*Returning to her seat.*] *Ay,* my soul!

[THE PRIORESS *raises her eyes to heaven in resignation.*]

A NUN. *Ay*, Blessed Virgin!

ANOTHER. *Ay, Jesús!*

PRIORESS [*somewhat ruffled*]. What? Is this an epidemic? Nothing is wanting now but that we should begin to sigh in chorus. Remember, it is with gladness and thanksgiving that the Lord is to be served *"in hymnis et canticis,"* for the second of the fruits of the Spirit is joy and there is none higher but love, from which it springs.

[*A pause.* SISTER MARÍA JESÚS *reopens the book, and without waiting for the signal from the* PRIORESS, *resumes reading.*]

SISTER MARÍA JESÚS [*reading*]. "I cannot resist the shock of the horrible onrushing waves. They break over me unceasingly; irresistibly they bear me down."

PRIORESS. Close the book, Sister María Jesús, for the blessed father who wrote it, alas, he too was of a melancholy turn of mind!

[SISTER MARÍA JESÚS *closes the book, makes a reverence and sits down to sew.* THE MOTHER VICARESS *appears in the door on the left, accompanied solemnly by two other nuns.*]

VICARESS [*greatly agitated*]. *Ave Maria purissima!*

PRIORESS. Conceived without sin.

VICARESS. Have I permission, reverend Mother?

PRIORESS. Enter and speak [*looking at her*]. If I am not mistaken, your Reverence is greatly disturbed.

VICARESS. You are not mistaken, reverend Mother. No, and I dare affirm it is not for a slight reason. Your Reverence will be judge if this is the time and place to confront with a charge of *ipso facto* a member of this community.

PRIORESS. Speak, if the knowledge of the fault in public will not in itself constitute a scandal and a cause of offense.

VICARESS. In the opinion of your handmaid all cause of scandal will be avoided by looking the offense straight in the face.

PRIORESS. Speak then.

VICARESS [*making a profound inclination*]. I obey. Reverend Mother, while making the round of my inspection of the cells with these two monitors, as your Reverence has been pleased to command . . . [*The two* MONITORS *each make a reverence.*] And coming to the cell of Sister Marcella . . .

[*All the* NUNS *look at* SISTER MARCELLA, *who lowers her eyes.*] I found under the mattress of the bed—in itself a suspicious circumstance and sufficient to constitute a sin—an object which should never be found in the hands of a religious, an object which, to say nothing of the sin against the rule of holy poverty which the private possession and concealment of any property whatever must presuppose, is by its very nature a root of perdition and an origin and source of evil.

PRIORESS. Conclude, Mother, in God's name! For you keep us in suspense. What is this object?

VICARESS. Disclose it, sister [*to one of the* MONITORS].

[*The* MONITOR *makes a reverence, and draws from her sleeve a piece of glass, covered on one side with quick-silver.*]

PRIORESS. A piece of looking-glass.

VICARESS. Exactly, a piece of looking-glass!

[*Horrified silence on the part of the community.*]

PRIORESS. What has Sister Marcella to say to this?

SISTER MARCELLA [*leaving her place and kneeling before the* PRIORESS]. Mother, I confess my guilt and I beseech your pardon.

PRIORESS. Rise. [SISTER MARCELLA *rises.*] Unhappy woman! What was the use of this piece of glass?

VICARESS. To look at herself in it, and amuse herself with the sight of her beauty, thus offending her Maker with pride and vain glory, and the exhibition of her taste.

SISTER MARCELLA [*humbly*]. No, reverend Mother; no!

VICARESS. Or else to dress herself up and fix herself by it, and make faces and grimaces such as they do on the streets in these days. [*The* VICARESS, *who has taken the mirror, looks at herself in it for a moment, then turns it hurriedly away.*]

SISTER MARCELLA. No, reverend Mother.

PRIORESS. For what then?

SISTER MARCELLA. For nothing, reverend Mother.

PRIORESS. What? For nothing?

SISTER MARCELLA. Your daughter means for nothing evil. On the contrary . . .

VICARESS. Ha! Now I suppose we are going to hear that it is a virtue in a religious to have a glass!

SISTER MARCELLA. No, reverend Mother, it is not a virtue. But your Reverences know already that your Sister suffers from temptations to melancholy.

VICARESS. Yes, yes . . .

SISTER MARCELLA. And when they seize upon her too strongly, they put it into her head to climb trees and run along the tops of walls, and jump over the fences in the garden, and to throw herself into the water of the fountain, and since your Sister knows that, in a religious, these . . . these . . .

VICARESS. These extravagances.

SISTER MARCELLA. Are unbecoming, your Sister catches a sunbeam in the mirror and makes it dance among the leaves and across the ceiling of her cell, and over the walls opposite, and so she consoles herself and imagines that it is a butterfly or a bird, and can go whenever it pleaseth.

VICARESS. It can, and stay there.

PRIORESS. For this fault, Sister Marcella . . . [SISTER MARCELLA *kneels.*] which, without being a grave one, yet is more than a little, considered according to the constitution of our rule, I assign you this penance. Tonight, before you retire, you are to repeat four times in your cell the psalm *"Quam dilecta."* Rise, and return to your seat.

[SISTER MARCELLA *obeys, but before seating herself she makes a reverence before each of the* NUNS.]

[*To the Vicaress.*] You may be seated.

[THE VICARESS *and the two* MONITORS *seat themselves: Three light knocks on the door. It is* TERESA *who says:*]

TERESA. *Ave Maria purissima!*

PRIORESS. Conceived without sin.

TERESA. May I come in?

PRIORESS. Come in.

[TERESA *enters. She is eighteen, very pretty, very sunny and very gay, with nothing about her to suggest the mystic or the religious. She is dressed simply in gray and wears a white apron. She has a flower in her hair, which is arranged modestly, and without an excess of curls or ornament.*]

Where are you coming from in such a hurry? You are all out of breath.

TERESA [*speaks always with the greatest simplicity, without affectation or pretense of any sort*]. From dressing the altar of the Virgin.

PRIORESS. Did that put you out of breath?

TERESA. No, Mother. It's because I wanted it to be all in white to-day, and there weren't white flowers enough in the garden, so I had to climb up and cut some branches off the acacia.

MISTRESS OF NOVICES. Did you climb a tree?

TERESA. Yes, I climbed two; there weren't enough blossoms on one.

MISTRESS OF NOVICES. *Jesús!*

VICARESS. *Ave Maria!*

TERESA. I wish you could see the view from the top of the big acacia!

[SISTER MARCELLA'S *eyes open wide with envy.*]

VICARESS. Child, you have put yourself beyond the pale of God's mercy!

SISTER JOANNA OF THE CROSS. You might have fallen! It's too terrible to think of!

TERESA. Fallen? No, Mother. Why, I've climbed it a hundred times!

PRIORESS. Then you must not do it again.

MISTRESS OF NOVICES [*regretfully*]. It is too late to forbid her now.

PRIORESS [*sorrowfully*]. That is true.

SISTER INEZ. It is the last day she will dress the altar.

SISTER JOANNA OF THE CROSS. The very *last!*

TERESA. Ah, Mothers! You mustn't talk like this. Don't be sad.

VICARESS. No, we had better behave like you do, though it doesn't seem possible when you consider the day that it is, and you laughing and carrying on like one possessed!

PRIORESS. The Mother is right. A little more feeling to-day, daughter, a manner more subdued, would not have been out of place.

TERESA. You are right, reverend Mothers—you always are, in the holiness, which like a halo surrounds your reverend heads; but when a girl wants to laugh she wants to laugh, although, as Mother Anna St. Francis says, it may be the solemnest day of her life.

MISTRESS OF NOVICES. It is a solemn day, a very solemn day. You are leaving this house in which you have passed eighteen years, without scarcely so much as taking thought how it was you came to be here. Tomorrow, you will be your own mistress, and you will have upon your conscience the responsibilities of a wife.

VICARESS. Which believe me, are not light. Men are selfish, fickle . . .

TERESA [*timidly*]. Antonio is very good.

VICARESS. However good he may be, he is a man, and men are accustomed to command. They have been from the beginning of the world, and it has affected their character. And since you are very independent yourself, and like to have your own way . . .

TERESA. Yes, I have been spoiled I know; but you will see now how good I will be. It will come out all right.

SISTER JOANNA OF THE CROSS. Do you want to spoil the day for her?

TERESA. No, Mother—no; you won't spoil it, for I am very, very happy. You have all been so good to me!

VICARESS. Nonsense! No such thing.

TERESA. But it isn't nonsense. I know this is God's house, but you might have closed the doors to me, and you have flung them wide open, freely. I have lived here eighteen years and in all this time, to the very moment that I am leaving it, you have never once reminded me that I have lived here on your charity.

SISTER JOANNA OF THE CROSS. Don't say such things!

TERESA. Yes, I must say them. On your charity, on your alms—like a poor beggar and an outcast. I don't mind saying it nor thinking of it, for I have been so happy here—yes, I am happy now—happier than the daughter of a king: for I love you all so much that I want to kiss even the walls and hug the trees, for even the walls and the trees have been kind to me. This has been the Convent of my Heart!

SISTER MARCELLA. It has been your home. If you had only been content always to remain in it!

PRIORESS. We must not talk like this. God moves in His own ways.

MISTRESS OF NOVICES. And in all of them His children may do His service.

VICARESS. The child was not born to be a religious. The things of the world appeal to her too strongly.

TERESA. It is true. The world appeals to me—poor me! It

seems to me sometimes as if everybody loved me, as if everything was calling to me everywhere to come. I have been so happy in this house, and yet, all the time, I have been thinking how great the world was, how wonderful! Whenever I have gone out into the street, how my heart leaped! I felt as if I were going to fly, it was so light! My brain was in a whirl. Then I was so glad to come back again into this house, it felt so good, as if you were all taking me up once more into your arms, as if I had fallen to sleep in them again and was warm, folded beneath the shelter of the everlasting wings.

VICARESS. The wings of your good angel, who stood waiting at the door—stood waiting till you came.

PRIORESS. Why should he have to wait? Her good angel always has gone with her, and surely there never has been a time when he has had to turn away his face. Am I right, daughter?

TERESA. You are, Mother. [*Sincerely*.]

SISTER JOANNA OF THE CROSS. They needn't have asked her that!

SISTER MARÍA JESÚS [*rising*]. Here are the bows for the corset covers. Do you want them pinned or sewed?

SISTER INEZ. Sewed, I say.

SISTER MARÍA JESÚS. Down the middle?

MISTRESS OF NOVICES. Of course, down the middle.

SISTER MARÍA JESÚS. The reason I asked was because in the pattern they are all fastened down the side.

MISTRESS OF NOVICES [*bending over to examine the fashion plates with* SISTER INEZ *and* SISTER MARÍA JESÚS]. Yes. Don't you see? She is right.

SISTER INEZ. That's funny! But they are pretty that way.

MISTRESS OF NOVICES. I say it's absurd.

SISTER MARÍA JESÚS. What do you think, Mother Crucifixion?

VICARESS. Don't ask me; I don't think. I neither understand nor wish to understand these things—pomp and vanity, artifices of the devil, who, they tell me, is very well acquainted with the dressmakers of Paris, and takes part in their designs and encourages their abbreviations. Take it away, take that paper out of my sight, for it never should have entered this holy house!

SISTER MARCELLA. *Ay,* but we have to know the fashions, Mother!

VICARESS. The fashions! The fashions! Go to hell and you will find the fashions! Any other place would be too far behind.

SISTER MARÍA JESÚS. But you don't want the child to be married, do you, in the dress of the year of the ark?

VICARESS. A pure heart and an upright spirit are what she should be married in, and if that is the case, no one is going to notice whether she has one bow more or less.

SISTER MARCELLA. They say men pay a great deal of attention to such things, Mother Crucifixion.

SISTER MARÍA JESÚS. And we must render unto Caesar the things which are Caesar's, and unto God the things which are God's.

VICARESS. So! We have philosophers, have we, in the house?

SISTER INEZ. Hand me the scissors, if you will. I want to cut off these ends.

SISTER JOANNA OF THE CROSS. I think now everything is ready to put in the trunk.

PRIORESS. Yes, for the carriage will be waiting.

[TERESA *kneels on the floor beside the trunk. The* NUNS *hand her the various articles of the trousseau, which they remove from the benches and the table.*]

SISTER INEZ. Here are the chemises.

SISTER MARCELLA. And the lace petticoats.

SISTER JOANNA OF THE CROSS. Put them in the other tray, so they won't get wrinkled.

SISTER INEZ. Lord of Mercy! What a tuck!— What bungler ran this tuck?

MISTRESS OF NOVICES. You must not say anything against the sister who ran it, Sister; say it would look better if it were redampened and ironed.

TERESA. But it looks splendid; really it does! Give it to me! Here—let me have them. This is too much trouble for you to take.

PRIORESS. Have you everything?

SISTER MARCELLA. The handkerchiefs?

SISTER JOANNA OF THE CROSS. The dressing-jackets?

VICARESS. Here is some edging that was left over, embroidered by hand. You had better put it in the trunk in case of accident.

MISTRESS OF NOVICES. And the patterns—you might need them.

SISTER INEZ. Here is a sachet, my child. It is filled with thyme and lavender and has lime peel in it. It will give a fresh scent to your clothes.

SISTER MARCELLA. She'll have real perfumes soon enough.

SISTER MARÍA JESÚS. Yes, expensive ones.

SISTER INEZ. They may be more expensive, but they won't be any better—I can tell you that; for these are plants that God has made, and they smell sweetly, and of a good conscience. I have them in all the presses in the sacristy, and it is a joy to smell them when you go up the steps to the altar.

TERESA. I think we have everything.

PRIORESS. Yes, everything. Now turn the key. Does it lock securely? [TERESA *gets up*.] And hang the key around your neck with the rosaries, for we have fastened it on a ribbon for you. Take care you don't lose it. The lock is an English one, and not every key will open it.

TERESA. Yes, Mother.

VICARESS. It will be a miracle if she has it tomorrow.

SISTER JOANNA OF THE CROSS. She will settle down soon under the responsibilities of a wife.

MISTRESS OF NOVICES. Well? Are you satisfied?

TERESA. Satisfied is too little, Mother. It does not express it. I don't deserve what you have done for me.

VICARESS. Yes, you do; you deserve it. And you might as well tell the truth as a falsehood. You have a good heart; you are a sensible girl. When you said what you did, you were thinking of your clothes; but you need have no scruples. Everything that you take away with you from this house, and more too, you have earned by your labor. That is the truth and you know it. Maybe we have taught you here how to sew and embroider, but you have worked for us in the convent, and outside of it. You owe us nothing. Besides, you had two hundred and fifty pesetas from the doctor to buy the material. Here . . . [*producing a paper from under her scapular*] is the account of the way they have been spent, so you can see for yourself and answer for it, since delicacy will not permit that we should be asked how it was used.

TERESA [*embarrassed and confused*]. What do you mean? Why, Mother Crucifixion!

VICARESS. That is all there is to it. You will find the account is correct.

[TERESA *takes the paper and having folded it, puts it in her dress.*]

PRIORESS [*to the* NUNS *who have been working*]. You may remove the table and gather up these things.

TERESA. No, Mother—let me do it. I will pick up everything.

[*The* PRIORESS *makes a sign and all the* NUNS *rise and leave the room, except only herself, the* VICARESS, *the* MISTRESS OF NOVICES, *and* SISTER JOANNA OF THE CROSS.]

PRIORESS [*to* TERESA]. What time do you go?

TERESA. My father is coming for me at five, but . . . Antonio has asked me . . . before I go . . . to say that he would like to see you all and thank you, and tell you how happy and grateful he is to you for the little girl you have brought up.

PRIORESS. We shall be very glad to see him.

VICARESS. Glad or not glad, no matter; it is our obligation. He cannot expect to carry her off like a thief in the night, and have no woman ask a question.

TERESA. I will call you when he comes.

[*The* PRIORESS, *the* VICARESS *and the* MISTRESS OF NOVICES *go out.* TERESA *and* SISTER JOANNA OF THE CROSS *remain behind picking up and arranging the papers, patterns and scraps that have been left on the seats or about the floor. They say nothing but presently* TERESA *throws herself on her knees before the* NUN.]

TERESA. Sister Joanna of the Cross!

SISTER JOANNA OF THE CROSS. What do you want, my child?

TERESA. Now that we are alone, bless me while there is no one here to see—no, not one—for you are my mother, more than all the rest!

SISTER JOANNA OF THE CROSS. Get up. [TERESA *gets up.*] Don't talk like that! We are all equal in God's house.

TERESA. But in my heart you are the first. You mustn't be angry at what I say. How can I help it? Is it my fault, though I have struggled against it all my life, that I have come to love you so?

SISTER JOANNA OF THE CROSS. Yes, you have struggled. You have been wilful . . . [*Then seeking at once to excuse her.*] But it was because you were strong and well. When a child is silent and keeps to herself in a corner, it is a sign that she is sick or thinking of some evil. But you . . .

TERESA. *Ay,* Mother! Where do you suppose that I came from?

SISTER JOANNA OF THE CROSS. From Heaven, my daughter, as all of us have come.

TERESA. Do you really think that we have all come from Heaven?

SISTER JOANNA OF THE CROSS. At least you have come from Heaven to me. You say that I am your mother more than the rest; I don't know—it may be. But I know that for years you have been all my happiness and joy.

TERESA. Mother!

SISTER JOANNA OF THE CROSS. I was so glad to hear you laugh and see you run about the cloisters! It was absurd, but I always felt—not now, for you are grown-up now—but for years I always felt as if you must be I, myself, scampering and playing. For I was just your age now, a little more or less, when you came into the Convent. And it seemed to me as if I was a child again and had just begun to live. You were so little, so busy—yes, you were—but I was busy too, if you only knew, before I entered here, at home in our house in the village. I was always singing and dancing, although we were very poor. My mother went out every day to wash in the river or to do housework—she had so many children!—and I was always carrying one about in my arms. And when I entered here, as I could do, thanks to some good ladies, who collected the money for my dowry—God reward them for it—although I had a real vocation, I was sorrowful and homesick thinking of my little brothers and sisters! How I used to cry in the dark corners, and I never dared to say a word! Then the Mother told me that if my melancholy didn't leave me she would be obliged to send me home. And then you came and I forgot everything! That is why I say you came to me from Heaven. And I don't want you to think I am angry, or ashamed—or that it has ever given me a moment's pain to have loved you.

TERESA. Is that the reason that you scold me so?

SISTER JOANNA OF THE CROSS. When have I ever scolded you?

TERESA. Oh, so many times! But no matter. I always tell Antonio, Sister Joanna of the Cross is my mother. She is my mother, my real mother! So now he always calls you mother whenever he speaks of you.

SISTER JOANNA OF THE CROSS. My daughter, will you be happy with him?

TERESA. Of course! I am sure I will. He is so good, he is so happy! He says he doesn't know where it is all his happiness comes from, because his father, who is dead now, was more mournful than a willow, and his mother, poor lady, whenever anything happened to her that was good, burst right out crying. How do you suppose it was she ever managed to have such a boy? It must be that sad mothers have happy children. How does it seem to you?

SISTER JOANNA OF THE CROSS. How do I know?

TERESA. It must be that way. The first boy I have is going to be—what is the solemnest thing in the world? No, the first is going to be an architect, like his father; but the second can be a missionary, and go to China if he wants to, and convert the heathen. Just think what it would be to have a son who was a saint! I shouldn't have to be so humble in heaven, then, should I? I should have influence. And here you are all the time, Sister Joanna of the Cross, praying for me and preparing miracles. So you see I have a good start already.

SISTER JOANNA OF THE CROSS. How you do love to talk!

TERESA. Isn't it foolish, Mother? Don't I? Listen! When you were little didn't you ever want to be a boy? I did. I used to cry because I thought then that I could have been anything I wanted to be—this, that, I didn't care what it was—Captain-General, Archbishop, yes, Pope, even! Or something else. It used to make me mad to think that because I was a girl I couldn't even be an acolyte. But now, since—well, since I love Antonio, and he loves me, I don't care; it doesn't make any difference any more, because if I am poor and know nothing, he is wise and strong; and if I am foolish and of no account, he is, oh, of so much worth! And if I have to stay behind at home and hide myself in the corner, he can go out into the world and mount, oh, so high—wherever a man can go—and instead of making me envious, it makes me so happy! Ah, Sister Joanna of the Cross, when she truly loves a man, how humble it makes a girl!

SISTER JOANNA OF THE CROSS. Do you really love him so?

TERESA. More than life itself! And that is all too little. Maybe it's a sin, but I can tell you. Do you believe that we will meet in Heaven the persons we have loved on earth? Because if I don't meet him there and I can't go on loving him always just the same as I do now, no, more than I do now . . .

SISTER JOANNA OF THE CROSS [*interrupting*]. Hush! Peace! You mustn't say such things. It is a sin.

TERESA. *Ay*, Sister Joanna of the Cross! How sweet it is to be in love!

SISTER JOANNA OF THE CROSS. But he . . . he . . . Does he love you too, so much?

TERESA. Yes, he loves me. How much, I don't know; but it doesn't make any matter. What makes me happy is that I love him. You needn't think that sometimes—very seldom though—I haven't been afraid that perhaps some day he might stop loving me. It used to make me sad. But if I had ever thought that some day I could stop loving him . . . No, it would be better to die first; for then, what would be the good of life?

SISTER JOANNA OF THE CROSS. Ah, my child! To continue in God's love!

TERESA. Do you know how I would like to spend my life? All of it? Sitting on the ground at his feet, looking up into his eyes, just listening to him talk. You don't know how he can talk. He knows everything—everything that there is to know in the world, and he tells you such things! The things that you always have known yourself, in your heart, and you couldn't find out how to say them. Even when he doesn't say anything, if he should be speaking some language which you didn't understand, it is wonderful . . . his voice . . . I don't know how to explain it, but it is his voice—a voice that seems as if it had been talking to you ever since the day you were born! You don't hear it only with your ears, but with your whole body. It's like the air which you see and breathe and taste, and which smells so sweetly in the garden beneath the tree of paradise. Ah, Mother! The first day that he said to me "Teresa"—you see what a simple thing it was, my name, Teresa—why, it seemed to me as if nobody ever had called me by my name before, as if I never had heard it, and when he went away, I ran up and down the street saying to myself "Teresa, Teresa, Teresa!" under my breath, without knowing what I was doing, as if I walked on air!

SISTER JOANNA OF THE CROSS. You frighten me, my child.

TERESA. Do I? Why?

SISTER JOANNA OF THE CROSS. Because you love him so. For earthly love . . . I mean . . . it seems to me it is like a flower, that we find by the side of the road—a little brightness that God grants us to help us pass through life, for we are weak and frail; a drop of honey spread upon our bread each day, which we should receive gladly, but with trembling, and keeping our hearts whole, daughter, for it will surely pass away.

TERESA. It cannot pass away!

SISTER JOANNA OF THE CROSS. It may; and then what will be left to your soul, if you have set your all on this delight, and it has passed away?

TERESA [*humbly*]. You mustn't be angry with me, Mother. No! Look at me! It isn't wrong, I know. Loving him, I . . . he is so good, he is so good . . . and good, it cannot pass away!

SISTER JOANNA OF THE CROSS. Is he a good Christian?

TERESA. He is good, Sister.

SISTER JOANNA OF THE CROSS. But does he fear God?

TERESA. One day he said to me: "I love you because you know how to pray." Don't you see? And another time: "I feel a devotion toward you as toward some holy thing." He! Devotion! To me! And whenever I think of that, it seems to me as if I was just growing better, as if all at once I was capable of everything there was to do or suffer in the world—so as to have him always feel that way!

SISTER JOANNA OF THE CROSS. I hear someone in the parlor. Draw the curtains.

[TERESA, *pulling the cord, draws the curtains over the windows, shutting off the light. The fore part of the stage remains in shadow, but the outer parlor is brightly illuminated.* ANTONIO *has entered and may be seen through the crack where the curtains join. He is twenty-five years of age, well-built, manly and sensitive of feature. He remains alone and his footsteps may be heard on the boards as he paces nervously up and down.*]

TERESA [*in a low voice, going up to the* NUN]. Yes. It is he.

SISTER JOANNA OF THE CROSS. [*Seizing her hand.*] Ah! How tall he is!

TERESA. Yes, he is tall. Doesn't he look splendid though?

SISTER JOANNA OF THE CROSS. Yes, he does. Has he golden hair?

TERESA. No, it's the light; his hair is dark brown, and his eyes are between violet and blue. It's too bad you can't see them. They are so beautiful! When he talks, they sparkle.

SISTER JOANNA OF THE CROSS. How old is he?

TERESA. Just twenty-five.

[ANTONIO *crosses from one side to the other, and continues to pace back and forth.*]

SISTER JOANNA OF THE CROSS. He seems to be of a very active disposition.

TERESA. That is because he is impatient. Shall I speak to him and tell him you are here?

SISTER JOANNA OF THE CROSS [*falling back*]. No!

TERESA. Why not? He loves you dearly. [*In a low voice, going up to the grille.*] Good afternoon, Antonio.

ANTONIO [*looking about from one side to the other*]. Teresa? Where are you?

TERESA [*laughing*]. Here, boy, here; behind the grille. It is easy to see you are not accustomed to calling on nuns.

ANTONIO. Can't you run back the curtain?

TERESA. No, because I am not alone. Can't you guess who is with me? My mother.

ANTONIO. Sister Joanna of the Cross?

TERESA [*to the* NUN, *delighted because he has guessed it*]. There! Do you see? [*To* ANTONIO.] Sister Joanna of the Cross—exactly. We have been watching you through the grille, and she says that she thinks you are a very handsome young man.

SISTER JOANNA OF THE CROSS. Goodness gracious! You mustn't pay any attention to what she says.

TERESA. Don't be angry, Mother. I think so myself.

ANTONIO. You never told me that before.

TERESA. That is because in here, where you can't see me, I'm not so embarrassed to tell you. Listen! We have to send in word now that you are here; but I want you to tell my mother something first, for if you stand there like a blockhead without opening your mouth, I am going to be very much ashamed, after all the time I have spent in singing your praises.

ANTONIO. What do you want me to tell her?

TERESA. What you have in your heart.

ANTONIO. But I don't know whether it is proper to tell it to a religious, although it is in my heart, for I love her dearly.

TERESA. Ah! I tell her that a million times a day.

ANTONIO. Then let us tell her together two million; because I must say to you, Madam, that it is impossible to know Teresa and not to love you.

TERESA. What a treasure is this mother of mine!

SISTER JOANNA OF THE CROSS. For shame, my child! [*Blushing, to* ANTONIO.] I also have a great affection for you, sir, for this child has been teaching me to love you. She is a little blind perhaps, and trusting, for that is natural. She knows nothing of the world, and we—how were we to teach her? And now you are going to take her far away; but don't take her heart away from us, sir, and break ours, when we let her hand go.

ANTONIO. Madam, I swear to you now that I shall always kneel in reverence before the tenderness and virtue which you have planted in her soul.

TERESA. I told you that he was very good, Mother.

SISTER JOANNA OF THE CROSS. May God make you both very happy. And may God remain with you, for his handmaid must go now and seek the Mother.

ANTONIO. But you are coming back?

SISTER JOANNA OF THE CROSS. With the sisters . . . Yes, I think so. Good-bye. I have been so happy to know you.

[SISTER JOANNA OF THE CROSS *goes out, greatly moved.* TERESA *remains standing by the grille until the* NUN *has disappeared, without speaking a word.*]

ANTONIO. Now you can draw back the curtain.

TERESA. Yes, a little. [*She runs back the curtain a little way.*] But it won't do you any good, because you won't be able to see me. Do you really like my mother? Do you really? Why are you so silent? What are you thinking about?

ANTONIO. I don't know; it is very strange. Since I have come into this room, since I have heard your mother speak, and have heard you, behind this grille, without knowing for certain where you were in the dark, I have been almost afraid to love you. But ah—how I do love you!

TERESA. I like that better.

ANTONIO. Teresa!

TERESA. What is it?

ANTONIO. Will you never forget, will you carry with you always wherever you go, this peace and this calm?

TERESA. With you, Antonio?

ANTONIO. Yes, into the world, beyond these walls; for in the world we make so much useless noise. And you—I see it now—you are the mistress of peace and of calm.

TERESA [*laughing*]. I the mistress of calm? As if I hadn't been a little flyaway all my life, without an idea in my head! Mother Crucifixion says that since I was passed in on the wheel there hasn't been one moment in this house of what the rules call "profound calm." I know I don't talk much when I am with you—we have been together such a little while, and it has been all too short to listen to you; but you will see when I grow bolder and am not afraid. You will have to put cotton in your ears then. Ah, Antonio! Only think, we are going to have all our lives to be together and listen to each other talk and tell each other things—that is, all our lives for you to tell me things, because I . . . you will find out soon enough. Tell me really, truly, Antonio: aren't you going to be awfully ashamed to have such an ignorant wife?

ANTONIO. Ignorant or learned?

TERESA. I? Learned? In what?

ANTONIO. In a science which I did not know, and which you have taught to me.

TERESA. You are joking.

ANTONIO. I am in earnest. Until I met you, I knew nothing; I did not even know myself.

TERESA. Pshaw!

ANTONIO. You mustn't laugh. Did it ever seem to you, Teresa, that our soul was like a palace?

TERESA. Of course it is! It is like a castle. Santa Teresa says so: The soul is like a castle—the interior of a castle, all made of one diamond above and below. And it has seven courts, and in the last is stored a great treasure . . .

ANTONIO. Then in the innermost chamber of my soul was stored the love I have for you, and if you had not come and opened the door yourself, and helped me to find it, I should have passed all my life in ignorance, without knowing anything was there.

TERESA. Don't repeat such heresies!

ANTONIO. Is it a heresy—the love I bear for you? No, it is a religion—the only one for me! My girl! Seven courts, you say? Then with a great effort I had passed into the first and I was running here and there aimlessly, and you don't know what horrible things I found—everywhere I stumbled on. They were my own traits. I was cold, selfish, proud, without trust or faith, without other ambitions than material desires—to pass through life easily and well, to be the first in my own petty world, incapable of sacrifice, of abnegation, of compassion, of disinterested love.

TERESA. No! No! You were no such thing.

ANTONIO. But I lived as if I were! What difference did it make? But then one day I heard your voice, and summoned by you, I again searched through the castle, and in the other courts I began to find—ah! under how many cobwebs, all covered-up with dust—humility and devotion, warmth of heart, pity and faith in so many holy things. And then I found my honor, self-respect and sympathy with my fellow man, in which we live, Teresa, for without it nothing else is life, and I began to be a man when I first loved you. For in these things you are the master, and I have learned them all from you!

TERESA. Hush! They are coming.

[TERESA *falls back from the grille, after first drawing the curtains again. The* NUNS *in single file enter silently, the youngest first, followed at last by the* MISTRESS OF NOVICES, *the* VICARESS *and the* PRIORESS. *The* PRIORESS *seats herself in the arm-chair at the left of the grille; the* VICARESS *and the* MISTRESS OF NOVICES *in two other chairs at the right. The remaining* NUNS *stand or are seated round about.* TERESA *supports herself with her hand on the back of the* PRIORESS'S *chair.* SISTER JOANNA OF THE CROSS *approaches her and takes her by the other hand. There is absolute silence as the* NUNS *enter and find their places. They look at each other with expectant attention, and some nod and smile among themselves. When they are seated, there follows an interval of further silence.*]

PRIORESS. *Ave Maria purissima!* [ANTONIO, *somewhat embarrassed, and endeavoring vainly to penetrate the darkness behind the grille, does not answer. The* PRIORESS, *after waiting a moment, turns her head and smiles indulgently at the community.*] Good afternoon, young man.

ANTONIO. Good afternoon, Madam—or Madams—for behind the mystery of this screen, it is impossible for me to see whether I am speaking with one or with many.

[*The* NUNS *smile quietly and discreetly.*]

PRIORESS [*in a low voice*]. Run back the curtain, Sister Inez. [*The Sister runs back the curtain.*] You are speaking with the entire community, which takes great pleasure in knowing you.

ANTONIO. Ladies, the pleasure and the honor are mine, and

they are much greater than you will be ready to imagine.

SISTER INEZ. Bless us! But isn't he a polite and polished talker?

SISTER TORNERA. Keep still! I want to hear what he has to say.

ANTONIO. For a long time I have desired greatly to visit you. Teresa knows it, and she must have told it to you.

PRIORESS. That is true. She has indeed. And we have greatly appreciated your desire.

ANTONIO. But the first time I was in this place it was Advent and the second it was Lent; and both times Teresa informed me that it was impossible for me to see you.

VICARESS. Clearly. In seasons of penitence we receive no visitors.

ANTONIO. But now it is May and past Easter time.

MISTRESS OF NOVICES. How well acquainted he is with the calendar! Surely you must be very devout, sir.

ANTONIO. I am, Madam—very; but chiefly in the worship of certain saints who as yet are not on the altars.

SISTER INEZ. What a nice compliment! Saints, did he say? [*Laughing.*] He *is* a polished talker.

ANTONIO. Ladies, after a hundred years they will be lighting candles to you, and invoking you in prayers, and in gratitude they will be bringing you thank offerings of crutches and wooden legs.

SISTER TORNERA [*laughing*]. Does he think we are going to be the patrons of rheumatism?

MISTRESS OF NOVICES. After a hundred years? You are giving us a century of Purgatory.

ANTONIO. No, Madam, by all that is holy! I am giving you a century of life, and entrance thereafter directly into the choir of seraphim.

PRIORESS. I fear you speak frivolously, Señor Don Antonio.

ANTONIO. Madam, I was never more earnest in my life. Whenever I think of death, you have no idea of the peace which enters my soul. I remember how many saintly white hands will be stretched down to me to help me into Paradise—for I suppose that you will be able to exercise a little influence on behalf of one of the family.

SISTER SAGRARIO [*laughing*]. One of the family?

VICARESS. Certainly. We are all God's children.

ANTONIO. But I shall be so in a double sense; first, in my own birthright, and then as your son-in-law, who are his brides.

VICARESS. Ah! It is not meet to jest about holy things.

ANTONIO. Madam, you are right. And you will pardon me

all the inconsequences which I have said, for I swear to you that they have been nothing but nervousness and fear.

MISTRESS OF NOVICES. You are not afraid of us?

ANTONIO. I am, Madam, very—because of the respect and admiration in which I hold you all. I came here more disturbed than I ever have been before in my whole life. I do not know whether I should thank you, or whether I should beg your pardon.

PRIORESS. Beg our pardon?

ANTONIO. Yes, because I fear that I am not worthy of the treasure which you are entrusting to me.

PRIORESS. We know already through the doctor that you are an honorable young man.

MISTRESS OF NOVICES. And the love which our daughter bears you is our guarantee. Surely the Lord would not permit His child, brought up in His fear, to throw herself away upon an evil man.

ANTONIO. I am not evil, no; but I am a man, and you, ladies, with all the great piety of your souls, have been nurturing a flower for the skies. When I first knew her, my heart whispered to me that I had met a saint. She was a miracle. When I first dared to speak to her, there came over me a fear and a trembling that were out of the course of nature; and when I told her that I loved her, my heart stopped, and bade me to fall on my knees, and now that I have come here to beg my happiness of you, I don't know what I can promise you in token of my gratitude, nor how I can give you thanks enough for the great honor which you do me.

VICARESS. It may be you are speaking more truly than you think, Señor Don Antonio.

MISTRESS OF NOVICES. Why, Mother!

VICARESS. No, let me speak. For he has said well. The girl is not one of those worldly creatures who take to their husbands a great store of physical beauty. That is certain. You cannot call her ugly, but it is the most that can be said. Nor does she bring with her any dower. She is poorer than the poor. But she carries in her heart a treasure, the only one which we have been able to give her, which is more priceless than silver or gold, and that is the fear of God. For this, sir, you must be answerable to us, and we ask you your word now, that you will always respect it in her and in her children, if you should have any, if it should be God's holy will.

ANTONIO. Teresa shall always be the absolute mistress of her conscience and of my house, and my children shall ever be that which she desires. I pledge my word.

PRIORESS. You will never have reason to regret it, for she is a good and prudent girl.

VICARESS. And not hypocritical, for, although, as you have said, we have nurtured her for the skies, we have never permitted ourselves to believe that she was to reach them through the cloister.

SISTER MARÍA JESÚS. Do you mean to take her very far away?

ANTONIO. Yes, Madam. That is to say, there is no longer in the world either far or near. We sail next week. I am going to America as the resident director of a firm of architects.

PRIORESS. Yes, we know already.

ANTONIO. That is the reason for this haste. I do not wish to go alone.

SISTER TORNERA. Aren't you afraid the child will be seasick? They say you do get a terrible shaking-up upon the sea.

SISTER MARÍA JESÚS. You must promise us to take good care of her.

SISTER INEZ. If she gets overheated never let her drink cold water. She is very pig-headed about that.

SISTER MARCELLA. But you mustn't forget that she is accustomed to cold baths.

SISTER INEZ. If she takes cold or gets a cough, make her drink a glass of hot milk with a teaspoonful of hot rum in it, with plenty of sugar, for that's the only thing that will make her sweat.

TERESA. I think perhaps I had better attend to these matters myself, Sister.

SISTER INEZ. Yes, you'd be a pretty one to attend to them! Don't you mind what she says, Señor Don Antonio, for she is spoiled utterly. If you don't give her medicines and force the spoon down her throat, she might be dying for all you'd know, but she'd never ask for them herself.

PRIORESS. We had better not confuse him with too many recommendations. Surely he knows the more important precautions already.

ANTONIO [*smiling*]. Perhaps it would be better if you wrote them out for me on a piece of paper.

SISTER TORNERA. A good idea. [*Laughing.*] If we began where does he think we'd leave off?

SISTER SAGRARIO. How many days will you be on the ship?

ANTONIO. Two weeks.

SISTER MARCELLA. Mercy! What an age! Suppose there should be a storm?

MISTRESS OF NOVICES. It will be at least two weeks more before we can get letters back.

ANTONIO. We will telegraph when we arrive and we will send you a message from the middle of the ocean, so that you will hear from us the same day.

SISTER INEZ. Mother of God! Can they send messages now from the middle of the ocean? How do the words come?

TERESA. Flying through the air, like birds.

SISTER INEZ. What will men invent next? When your handmaid was in the world, they came by a wire, and yet it seemed the work of the devil.

ANTONIO. I should not advise you, Madam, to believe that the devil is ever very far away from these inventions.

SISTER INEZ. Whether he is or not, when the telegram comes it will be safest to sprinkle it with holy water.

PRIORESS. Ah, Sister Inez, you are so simple! Don't you see that the young man is only joking?

VICARESS. It is five o'clock—the hour we were to expect your father.

ANTONIO. I do not wish to molest you further.

PRIORESS. You do not molest us, but we must close the parlor at five.

ANTONIO. You will pardon me if I commit a terrible breach of etiquette, but I should like to ask you one favor before I go.

PRIORESS. If it is in our power to grant . . .

ANTONIO. Although, as it seems, you have run back a curtain, yet the mystery of this screen still remains a mystery to me, a poor sinner, inscrutable as before; and I should be sorry to go away without having seen you face to face. Is it too much to ask?

PRIORESS. For us this is a day of giving. Draw back the curtains, Teresa.

[TERESA *draws back the curtain from one window, a* NUN *that from the other, lighting up the room.*]

ANTONIO [*bowing*]. Ladies! . . .

VICARESS. Well? How does the vision appear to you?

ANTONIO. I shall never forget it as long as I live.

PRIORESS. Then may God go with you, and may you live a thousand years. [*Taking* TERESA *by the hand.*] Here is her hand. See, we give her to you with a great love, and may you make her happy.

ANTONIO. I answer for her happiness with my life.

PRIORESS. And may God go with you.

MISTRESS OF NOVICES. Teresa will give you from us two scapularies, the remembrances of a nun. They are not worth anything, but they have lain beside the reliquary of our father, the blessed Saint Dominic. Keep them in memory of this day.

ANTONIO. I shall treasure them, ladies, from this hour. And I pray you, remember me always in your prayers.

VICARESS. And upon your part do not forget to pray with them from time to time, for although it lies within the province of everyone to help our souls along the way to heaven, yet we must take the first steps ourselves. And may God go with you.

ALL. God go with you.

ANTONIO. Ladies! . . . [*He retires and disappears. A* NUN *draws the curtain over the grille. Then a moment's silence. Some of the* NUNS *sigh and say:*]

NUNS. Ah, Lord! Good Lord! May it be God's holy will! [*The bell by the door rings twice.*]

VICARESS. I thought so—your father.

[TERESA *stands in the midst of the group of* NUNS, *bewildered, looking from one to the other, greatly moved.* SISTER TORNERA *goes to open the door.*]

PRIORESS. Ask him to come in.

[*The* DOCTOR *enters on the arm of* SISTER TORNERA. *He is now very old, but neither decrepit nor cast down.*]

DOCTOR. Good afternoon, ladies; good afternoon, daughter.

TERESA [*kissing his hand*]. Good afternoon, father.

DOCTOR. The whole assembly—the parting, eh? Well, did you see the young man? [*The* NUNS *do not answer.*] A fine fellow, isn't he? He is waiting outside. We have an hour in the coach before we arrive at the station, so you had better get ready now, daughter. [TERESA *goes out with* SISTER JOANNA OF THE CROSS.] Ah! The trunk? Good! Carry it to the door. The boys outside will take care of it.

[*Two* NUNS *lift the trunk and carry it out by the door on the right.*] There, that is done. [*He seats himself in the* PRIORESS's *chair.*] Well, how are we to-day?

PRIORESS. You see, Doctor.

MISTRESS OF NOVICES. Who would ever have believed it eighteen years ago?

DOCTOR. Eighteen years? We are growing old, Mother. We are growing old.

PRIORESS. That is not the worst of it.

SISTER INEZ. How old are you now, Doctor?

DOCTOR. Seventy-eight, Sister.

SISTER INEZ. No one would ever think it.

DOCTOR [*attempting a witticism so as to cheer up the* NUNS]. That is because I am preserved in sanctity, like a fly in thick syrup. [*But none of the* NUNS *laughs.*] A little mournful to-day, eh?

SISTER MARCELLA. What else did you expect?

SISTER SAGRARIO. She is not even going to be married in our chapel.

DOCTOR. No, his mother is old and sick, and naturally she wants him to be with her, so they must be married in her house.

PRIORESS. Naturally. Poor woman! [*A pause.*]

MISTRESS OF NOVICES. She is going so far away!

DOCTOR. But she will come back, Mother. She will come back.

PRIORESS. She knows nothing of the world.

DOCTOR. There is no cause to be alarmed. He is an honorable man.

VICARESS. Yes, he seems to be one.

[TERESA *and* SISTER JOANNA OF THE CROSS *re-enter. It is plain that they have both been crying.* TERESA, *wearing a mantilla, and with her coat on, carries a shawl over her arm for use as a wrap on the voyage. She stops in the middle of the room and stands still, not daring to say good-bye.*]

DOCTOR. Well? Are we ready now?

TERESA. Yes . . . Now . . .

DOCTOR. Then say good-bye. It is late. We must be going, daughter.

PRIORESS. Yes, you must not delay.

TERESA [*throwing herself on her knees before the* PRIORESS *and kissing her scapular*]. Mother!

PRIORESS. Rise, my daughter, rise.

TERESA. Bless me, Mother! Bless me!

PRIORESS. May God bless you; so. Rise. [*As* TERESA *rises, the* NUN *embraces her.*]

TERESA. Mother! I don't know what to say to you . . . I don't know how to leave you . . . but you must forgive me all the wrong I have ever done in all these years. I have been foolish, wilful. I have made so much trouble for you all. You must forgive me. I would like to do something great, something splendid for you all. But—but may God reward you! May God reward you! God reward you! [*She bursts into tears.*]

PRIORESS. My daughter, come! You must not cry. You must not allow yourself to be afflicted so.

TERESA. I am not afflicted, Mother; but . . . it's . . . Mother, I can never forget you! You must pray for me, pray for me! And you must never forget me!

PRIORESS. Ah, no, my child! Never! We will pray God to help you, and to be with you, and you must pray to Him for guidance and for counsel always, whenever you are troubled or perplexed in anything. For the liberty which they enjoy in the world is like a sword in the hands of a child, and life at best is hard, and bitter oftentimes.

MISTRESS OF NOVICES. Be thankful that your heart is well steeled to resist all the temptations that may come. Is it not, my daughter?

TERESA. It is, Mother.

PRIORESS. Will you promise always to be reverent and good?

TERESA. Yes! Yes, Mother!

VICARESS. Remember that your obligation is greater than that of others, because you have come forth from God's own house.

TERESA. Yes! Yes, Mother!

PRIORESS. Remember all the blessings He has showered upon you from the cradle; remember that your whole life has been as a miracle, that you have lived here as few have ever lived, that you have been brought up as few have ever been brought up, like the Holy Virgin herself, in the very temple of the Lord.

MISTRESS OF NOVICES. As He was to the Evangelist, so God has been to you a father and a mother, more than to any other living thing.

PRIORESS. Remember that you are the rose of His garden and the grain of incense upon His altar.

TERESA. Yes! Mother, yes! I will! . . . I will remember all . . . all . . . all . . .

MISTRESS OF NOVICES. And do not forget each day to make an examination of your soul.

TERESA. No, Mother.

SISTER JOANNA OF THE CROSS. And write often.

TERESA. Yes, Mother.

DOCTOR. It is time to go, Teresa.

TERESA [*throwing herself suddenly into his arms*]. Oh, father! Promise me never to leave them! Never abandon them!

DOCTOR. Child of my heart! Ah, may they never abandon me! —for this is my house. For more than forty years I have been coming here day by day, hour by hour, and now there is nobody within these walls who is older than I. I have no children. I have had my loves—yes, a moment's flame—but it was so long ago! I have forgotten them. And these Sisters, who have been mothers to you, have been daughters to me; and now, when I come, they no longer even cover their faces before me. Why should they? It seems to me as if I had seen them born. And in this house [*Greatly moved.*] I should like to die, so that they might close my eyes, and say a prayer for me when life itself has closed!

MISTRESS OF NOVICES. Who is thinking of dying, Doctor?

PRIORESS. It is time to go.

TERESA [*looking from one to the other*]. Aren't you going to embrace me?

[*The* NUNS, *after hesitating and glancing a moment doubtfully at the* MOTHER PRIORESS, *embrace* TERESA *in turn, in perfect silence. Only* SISTER JOANNA OF THE CROSS, *taking her into her arms, says:*]

SISTER JOANNA OF THE CROSS. My child!

PRIORESS. May you find what you seek in the world, daughter, for so we hope and so we pray to God. But if it should not be so, remember, this is your Convent.

TERESA. Thanks . . . thanks . . . [*Sobbing*].

DOCTOR. Come, daughter, come . . .

[*The* DOCTOR *and* TERESA *go to the door, but* TERESA *turns when she reaches the threshold and embraces* SISTER JOANNA OF THE CROSS, *passionately. Then she disappears.* SISTER JOANNA OF THE CROSS *rests her head against the grille, her back to the others, and weeps silently. A pause. The bells of the coach are heard outside as it drives away.*]

MISTRESS OF NOVICES. They are going now.

[*The chapel bell rings summoning the* NUNS *to choir.*]

PRIORESS. The summons to the choir.
MISTRESS OF NOVICES. Come, Sisters! Let us go there.

[*All make ready to go out sadly. The* VICARESS, *sensing the situation, to her mind demoralizing, feels it to be her duty to provide a remedy. She, too, is greatly moved, but making a supreme effort to control herself, says in a voice which she in vain endeavors to make appear calm, but which is choked in utterance by tears:*]

VICARESS. One moment. I have observed of late . . . that some . . . in the prayer . . . have not been marking sufficiently the pauses in the middle of the lines, while on the other hand, they drag out the last words interminably Be careful of this, for your Reverences know that the beauty of the office lies in rightly marking the pauses, and in avoiding undue emphasis on the end of the phrase. Let us go there.

[*The* NUNS *file out slowly.* SISTER JOANNA OF THE CROSS, *unnoticed, remains alone. With a cry, she falls upon her knees beside an empty chair.*]

FEDERICO GARCÍA LORCA

1899–1936

Federico García Lorca gained his first success as a poet. He was a modern-day troubadour who loved to recite his own works, which, as a result, often were well known to his friends long before their publication. He reached the peak of his popularity when his *Gypsy Romances* was published in 1928. After that, Lorca turned his attention solely to the theatre (he had been writing poetic puppet plays since 1920), but he never ceased being the poet. His brother, Francisco, writing in the introduction to the first English edition of the tragedies, insists that "any interpretation of his [Lorca's] theatre made from a viewpoint other than a poetic one will lead to wrong conclusions." In all his later plays Lorca used metaphors taken from nature, varying rhythms of language and musical sound, brightly contrasting colors, and many songs and dances to transform the experiences of Andalusian life into a poetry of the theatre.

The theme in all of Lorca's work is frustration, and the center of the dramatic conflict in his mature plays is to be found in the frustrations of women, who he believed were the bearers of all passion and the source of every form of earthly creativity. On the surface this frustration emerges primarily in sexual terms, but finally the world of Lorca's theatre is ruled by the power of death. In his tragedies he ties up and twists the strands of people's passions so tightly that only the "tiny knife, the tiny golden knife" of death can probe the center of the conflict. Like all Spaniards, Lorca understood and felt life only through death. Death is man's mentor, his companion, and his greatest achievement. And perhaps Lorca's own premature death in the Spanish Civil War may be the fullest embodiment of the meaning of his plays. That death deprived the modern theatre of one of its greatest artists just as he was reaching full maturity.

THE AUTHORITY OF THE THEATRE[1]

Translated by A. E. Sloman

MY DEAR FRIENDS: Some time ago I made a solemn promise to refuse every kind of tribute, banquet, or celebration which might be made in my honor, first, because I know that each of them drives another nail into our literary coffin, and second, because I have found that there is nothing more depressing than a formal speech made in our honor, and nothing sadder than organized applause, however sincere.

Besides, between ourselves, I hold that banquets and scrolls bring bad luck upon the one who receives them, bad luck springing from the relief of his friends who think: "Now we have done our duty by him."

A banquet is a gathering of professional people who eat with us, and where we find thrown together every kind of person who likes us least.

Rather than do honor to poets and dramatists, I should prepare challenges and attacks, in which we should be told roundly and passionately: "Are you afraid of doing this?" "Are you incapable of expressing a person's anguish at the sea?" "Daren't you show the despair of soldiers who hate war?"

Necessity and struggle, grounded on a critical love, temper the artist's soul, which easy flattery makes effeminate and destroys. The theatres are full of deceiving sirens, garlanded with hothouse roses, and the public is content, and applauds dummy hearts and superficial dialogue; but the dramatic poet who wishes to save himself from oblivion must not forget the open fields with their wild roses, fields moistened by the dawn

[1] Originally published under the title, "The Prophecy of Lorca" by Federico García Lorca, translated by Albert E. Sloman. Copyright 1950 by the Estate of Federico García Lorca and by *Theatre Arts Magazine*. Reprinted by permission of the Estate of Federico García Lorca.

where peasants toil, and the pigeon, wounded by a mysterious hunter, which is dying amongst the rushes with no one to hear its grief.

Shunning sirens, flattery, and congratulations, I have accepted nothing in my honor, on the occasion of the first night of *Yerma*; but it has been the greatest pleasure of my short life as a writer to learn that the theatre world of Madrid was asking the great Margarita Xirgu, an actress with an impeccable artistic career, luminary of the Spanish theatre, and admirable interpreter of the part of Yerma, together with the company which so brilliantly supports her, for a special production.

For the interest and attention in a notable theatrical endeavor which this implies, I wish, now that we are all together, to give to you my deepest and sincerest thanks. I am not speaking tonight as an author, nor as a poet, nor as a simple student of the rich panorama of man's life, but as an ardent lover of the theatre of social action. The theatre is one of the most useful and expressive instruments for a country's edification, the barometer which registers its greatness or its decline. A theatre which in every branch, from tragedy to vaudeville, is sensitive and well oriented, can in a few years change the sensibility of a people, and a broken-down theatre, where wings have given way to cloven hoofs, can coarsen and benumb a whole nation.

The theatre is a school of weeping and of laughter, a rostrum where men are free to expose old and equivocal standards of conduct, and explain with living examples the eternal norms of the heart and feelings of man.

A nation which does not help and does not encourage its theatre is, if not dead, dying; just as the theatre which does not feel the social pulse, the historical pulse, the drama of its people, and catch the genuine color of its landscape and of its spirit, with laughter or with tears, has no right to call itself a theatre, but an amusement hall, or a place for doing that dreadful thing known as "killing time." I am referring to no one, and I want to offend no one; I am not speaking of actual fact, but of a problem that has yet to be solved.

Every day, my friends, I hear about the crisis in the theatre, and I feel always that the defect is not one before our eyes, but deep down in its very nature; it is not a defect of the flower we have before us, of a play, that is, but deeply rooted; in short, a defect of organization. Whilst actors and authors are in the hands of managements that are completely commercial, free, without either literary or state control of any kind, managements devoid of all judgment and offering no kind of safeguard, actors, authors, and the whole theatre will sink lower every day, beyond all hope of salvation.

The delightful light theatre of revue, vaudeville, and farce, forms of which I am a keen spectator, could maintain and even save itself; but plays in verse, the historical play, and the so-called Spanish *zarzuela*, will suffer more and more setbacks, because they are forms which make great demands and which admit of real innovations, and there is neither the authority nor the spirit of sacrifice to impose them on a public which has to be overruled from above, and often contradicted and attacked. The theatre must impose itself on the public, not the public on the theatre. To do this, authors and actors must, whatever the cost, again assume great authority, because the theatre-going public is like a school child; it reveres the stern, severe teacher who demands justice and sees justice done; and puts pins on the chairs of the timid and flattering ones who neither teach themselves nor allow anyone else to teach.

The public can be taught—I say public, of course, not people—it can be taught; for, some years ago, I saw Debussy and Ravel howled down, and I have been present since at loud ovations given by a public of ordinary people to the very works which were earlier rejected. These authors were imposed by the high judgment of authority, superior to that of the ordinary public, just as were Wedekind in Germany and Pirandello in Italy, and so many others.

This has to be done for the good of the theatre and for the glory and status of its interpreters. Dignity must be maintained, in the conviction that such dignity will be amply repaid. To do otherwise is to tremble behind the flies, and kill the fantasies, imagination, and charm of the theatre, which is always, always an art, and will always be a lofty art, even though there may have been a time when everything which pleased was labeled art, so that the tone was lowered, poetry destroyed, and the stage itself a refuge for thieves.

Art above all else. A most noble art, and you, my actor friends, artists above all else. Artists from head to foot, since through love and vocation you have risen to the make-believe and pitiful world of the boards. Artists by occupation and by preoccupation. From the smallest theatre to the most eminent, the word "Art" should be written in auditoriums and dressing rooms, for if not we shall have to write the word "Commerce" or some other that I dare not say. And distinction, discipline, and sacrifice and love.

I don't want to lecture you, because I should be the one receiving a lecture. My words are dictated by enthusiasm and conviction. I labor under no delusion. As a good Andalusian I can think coolly, because I come of an ancient stock. I know that truth does not lie with him who says, "Today, today, today," eating his bread close to the hearth, but with him who watches calmly at a distance the first light of dawn in the country.

I know that those people who say, "Now, now, now," with their eyes fixed on the small jaws of the box office are not right, but those who say, "Tomorrow, tomorrow, tomorrow," and feel the approach of the new life which is hovering over the world.

THE LOVE OF DON PERLIMPLÍN AND BELISA IN THE GARDEN

by FEDERICO GARCÍA LORCA

1931

THE LOVE OF DON PERLIMPLÍN AND BELISA IN THE GARDEN[1]

An Erotic Lace-Paper Valentine in Four Scenes
Chamber Version

Translated by James Graham-Lujan
and Richard L. O'Connell

CAST OF CHARACTERS

DON PERLIMPLÍN
BELISA
MARCOLFA
MOTHER OF BELISA
FIRST SPRITE
SECOND SPRITE

[1] From *Five Plays: Comedies & Tragicomedies,* of Federico García Lorca. Translated by James Graham-Lujan and Richard L. O'Connell.

PROLOGUE

[*House of* DON PERLIMPLÍN. *Green walls; chairs and furniture painted black. At the rear, a deep window with balcony through which* BELISA'S *balcony may be seen. A sonata is heard.* PERLIMPLÍN *wears a green cassock and a white wig full of curls.* MARCOLFA, *the servant, wears the classic striped dress.*]

PERLIMPLÍN. Yes?
MARCOLFA. Yes.
PERLIMPLÍN. But why "yes"?
MARCOLFA. Just because yes.
PERLIMPLÍN. And if I should say no?
MARCOLFA [*acidly*]. No?
PERLIMPLÍN. No.
MARCOLFA. Tell me, Master, the reason for that "no."
PERLIMPLÍN. You tell me, you persevering domestic, the reasons for that "yes."

[*Pause.*]

MARCOLFA. Twenty and twenty are forty . . .
PERLIMPLÍN [*listening*]. Proceed.
MARCOLFA. And ten, fifty.
PERLIMPLÍN. Go ahead.
MARCOLFA. At fifty years one is no longer a child.
PERLIMPLÍN. Of course!
MARCOLFA. I may die any minute.
PERLIMPLÍN. Good Lord!
MARCOLA [*weeping*]. And what will happen to you all alone in the world?
PERLIMPLÍN. What will happen?
MARCOLFA. That's why you have to marry.
PERLIMPLÍN [*distracted*]. Yes?
MARCOLFA [*sternly*]. Yes.

PERLIMPLÍN [*miserably*]. But Marcolfa . . . why "yes"? When I was a child a woman strangled her husband. He was a shoemaker. I can't forget it. I've always said I wouldn't marry. My books are enough for me. What good will marriage do me?

MARCOLFA. Marriage holds great charms, Master. It isn't what it appears on the outside. It's full of hidden things . . . things which it would not be becoming for a servant to mention. You see that . . .

PERLIMPLÍN. That what?

MARCOLFA. That I have blushed.

[*Pause. A piano is heard.*]

VOICE OF BELISA [*within, singing*].

Ah love, ah love.
Tight in my thighs imprisoned
There swims like a fish the sun.
Warm water in the rushes.
Ah love.
Morning cock, the night is going!
Don't let it vanish, no!

MARCOLFA. My master will see the reason I have.

PERLIMPLÍN [*scratching his head*]. She sings prettily.

MARCOLFA. She is the woman for my master. The fair Belisa.

PERLIMPLÍN. Belisa . . . but wouldn't it be better . . .?

MARCOLFA. No. Now come. [*She takes him by the hand and goes toward the balcony.*] Say, "Belisa."

PERLIMPLÍN. Belisa . . .

MARCOLFA. Louder.

PERLIMPLÍN. Belisa!

[*The balcony of the house opposite opens and* BELISA *appears, resplendent in her loveliness. She is half naked.*

BELISA. Who calls?

[MARCOLFA *hides behind the window curtains.*]

MARCOLFA. Answer!

PERLIMPLÍN [*trembling*]. I was calling.

BELISA. Yes?

PERLIMPLÍN. Yes.

BELISA. But why, "yes"?

PERLIMPLÍN. Just because yes.

BELISA. And if I should say no?

PERLIMPLÍN. I would be sorry, because . . . we have decided that I want to marry.

BELISA [*laughs*]. Marry whom?

PERLIMPÍN. You.

BELISA [*serious*]. But . . . [*Calling.*] Mamá! Mamá-á-á!

MARCOLFA. This is going well.

[*Enter the* MOTHER *wearing a great eighteenth-century wig full of birds, ribbons and glass beads.*]

BELISA. Don Perlimpín wants to marry me. What must I do?

MOTHER. The very best of afternoons to you, my charming little neighbor. I always said to my poor little girl that you have the grace and elegance of that great lady who was your mother, whom I did not have the pleasure of knowing.

PERLIMPLÍN. Thank you.

MARCOLFA [*furiously, from behind the curtain*]. I have decided that we are going . . .

PERLIMPLÍN. We have decided that we are going . . .

MOTHER. To contract matrimony. Is that not so?

PERLIMPLÍN. That is so.

BELISA. But, Mamá, what about me?

MOTHER. You are agreeable, naturally. Don Perlimplín is a fascinating husband.

PERLIMPLÍN. I hope to be one, madam.

MARCOLFA [*calling to* DON PERLIMPLÍN]. This is almost settled.

PERLIMPLÍN. Do you think so?

[*They whisper together.*]

MOTHER [*to Belisa*]. Don Perlimplín has many lands. On these are many geese and sheep. The sheep are taken to market. At the market they give money for them. Money produces beauty . . . and beauty is sought after by all men.

PERLIMPLÍN. Then . . .

MOTHER. Ever so thrilled . . . Belisa . . . go inside. It isn't well for a maiden to hear certain conversations.

BELISA. Until later.

[*She leaves.*]

MOTHER. She is a lily. You've seen her face? [*Lowering her voice.*] But if you should see further! Just like sugar. But, pardon. I need not call these things to the attention of a person as modern and competent as you. . . .

PERLIMPLÍN. Yes?

MOTHER. Why, yes. I said it without irony.

PERLIMPLÍN. I don't know how to express our gratitude.

MOTHER. Oh, "our gratitude." What extraordinary delicacy! The gratitude of your heart and your self . . . I have sensed it. I have sensed it . . . in spite of the fact that it is twenty years since I have had relations with a man.

MARCOLFA [*aside*]. The wedding.

PERLIMPLÍN. The wedding . . .

MOTHER. Whenever you wish. Though . . . [*She brings out a handkerchief and weeps.*] . . . to every mother . . . until later! [*Leaves.*]

MARCOLFA. At last!

PERLIMPLÍN. Oh, Marcolfa, Marcolfa! Into what world are you going to thrust me?

MARCOLFA. Into the world of matrimony.

PERLIMPLÍN. And if I should be frank, I would say that I feel thirsty. Why don't you bring me some water?

[MARCOLFA *approaches him and whispers in his ear.*]

Who could believe it?

[*The piano is heard. The stage is in darkness.* BELISA *opens the curtains of her balcony, almost naked, singing languidly.*]

BELISA.

Ah love, ah love.
Tight in my warm thighs imprisoned,
There swims like a fish the sun.

MARCOLFA. Beautiful maiden.

PERLIMPLÍN. Like sugar . . . white inside. Will she be capable of strangling me?

MARCOLFA. Woman is weak if frightened in time.

BELISA.

Ah love, ah love.
Morning cock, the night is going!
Don't let it vanish, no!

PERLIMPLÍN. What does she mean, Marcolfa? What does she mean?

[MARCOLFA *laughs.*]

What is happening to me? What is it?

[*The piano goes on playing. Past the balcony flies a band of black paper birds.*]

CURTAIN

Scene 1

[DON PERLIMPLÍN'S *room. At the center there is a great bed topped by a canopy with plume ornaments. In the back wall there are six doors. The first one on the right serves as entrance and exit for* DON PERLIMPLÍN. *It is the wedding night.* MARCOLFA, *with a candelabrum in her hand, speaks at the first door on the left side.*]

MARCOLFA. Good night.
BELISA [*offstage*]. Good night, Marcolfa.

[DON PERLIMPLÍN *enters, magnificently dressed.*]

MARCOLFA. May my master have a good wedding night.
PERLIMPLÍN. Good night, Marcolfa. [MARCOLFA *leaves.* PERLIMPLÍN *tiptoes toward the room in front and looks from the door.*] Belisa, in all that froth of lace you look like a wave, and you give me the same fear of the sea that I had as a child. Since you came from the church my house is full of secret whispers, and the water grows warm by itself in the glasses. Oh! Perlimplín . . . Where are you, Perlimplín?

[*Leaves on tiptoe.* BELISA *appears, dressed in a great sleeping garment adorned with lace. She wears an enormous headdress which launches cascades of needlework and lace down to her feet. Her hair is loose and her arms bare.*]

BELISA. The maid perfumed this room with thyme and not with mint as I ordered . . . [*Goes toward the bed.*] Nor did she put on the fine linen which Marcolfa has. [*At this moment there is a soft music of guitars.* BELISA *crosses her hands over her breast.*] Ah! Whoever seeks me ardently will find me. My thirst is never quenched, just as the thirst of the gargoyles who spurt water in the fountains is never quenched. [*The music continues.*] Oh, what music! Heavens, what music! Like the soft warm downy feathers of a swan! Oh! Is it I? Or is it the music?

[*She throws a great cape of red velvet over her shoulders and walks about the room. The music is silent and five whistles are heard.*]

BELISA. Five of them!

[PERLIMPLÍN *appears.*]

PERLIMPLÍN. Do I disturb you?
BELISA. How could that be possible?
PERLIMPLÍN. Are you sleepy?
BELISA [*ironically*]. Sleepy?
PERLIMPLÍN. The night has become a little chilly.

[*Rubs his hands. Pause.*]

BELISA [*with decision*]. Perlimplín.
PERLIMPLÍN [*trembling*]. What do you want?
BELISA [*vaguely*]. It's a pretty name, "Perlimplín."
PERLIMPLÍN. Yours is prettier, Belisa.
BELISA [*laughing*]. Oh! Thank you!

[*Short pause.*]

PERLIMPLÍN. I wanted to tell you something.
BELISA. And that is?
PERLIMPLÍN. I have been late in deciding . . . but . . .
BELISA. Say it.
PERLIMPLÍN. Belisa, I love you.
BELISA. Oh, you little gentleman! That's your duty.
PERLIMPLÍN. Yes?
BELISA. Yes.
PERLIMPLÍN. But why "yes"?
BELISA [*coyly*]. Because.
PERLIMPLÍN. No.
BELISA. Perlimplín!
PERLIMPLÍN. No, Belisa, before I married you, I didn't love you.
BELISA [*jokingly*]. What are you saying?
PERLIMPLÍN. I married . . . for whatever reason, but I didn't love you. I couldn't have imagined your body until I saw it through the keyhole when you were putting on your

wedding dress. And then it was that I felt love come to me. Then! Like the deep thrust of a lancet in my throat.
BELISA [*intrigued*]. But, the other women?
PERLIMPLÍN. What women?
BELISA. Those you knew before.
PERLIMPLÍN. But are there other women?
BELISA [*getting up*]. You astonish me!
PERLIMPLÍN. The first to be astonished was I.

[*Pause. The five whistles are heard.*]

What's that?
BELISA. The clock.
PERLIMPLÍN. Is it five?
BELISA. Bedtime.
PERLIMPLÍN. Do I have your permission to remove my coat?
BELISA. Of course, [*yawning*] little husband. And put out the light, if that is your wish.

[PERLIMPLÍN *puts out the light.*]

PERLIMPLÍN [*in a low voice*]. Belisa.
BELISA [*loudly*]. What, child?
PERLIMPLÍN [*whispering*]. I've put the light out.
BELISA [*jokingly*]. I see that.
PERLIMPLÍN [*in a much lower voice*]. Belisa . . .
BELISA [*in a loud voice*]. What, enchanter?
PERLIMPLÍN. I adore you!

[*The five whistles are heard much louder and the bed is uncovered. Two* SPRITES, *entering from opposite sides of the stage, run a curtain of misty gray. The theater is left in darkness. Flutes sound with a sweet, sleepy tone. The* SPRITES *should be two children. They sit on the prompt box facing the audience.*]

FIRST SPRITE. And how goes it with you in this tiny darkness?
SECOND SPRITE. Neither well nor badly, little friend.
FIRST SPRITE. Here we are.
SECOND SPRITE. And how do you like it? It's always nice to cover other people's failings . . .
FIRST SPRITE. And then to let the audience take care of uncovering them.
SECOND SPRITE. Because if things are not covered up with all possible precautions . . .

FIRST SPRITE. They would never be discovered.

SECOND SPRITE. And without this covering and uncovering . . .

FIRST SPRITE. What would the poor people do?

SECOND SPRITE [*looking at the curtain*]. There must not even be a slit.

FIRST SPRITE. For the slits of today are darkness tomorrow.

[*They laugh.*]

SECOND SPRITE. When things are quite evident . . .

FIRST SPRITE. Man figures that he has no need to discover them . . . in them secrets he already knew.

SECOND SPRITE. And he goes to dark things to discover them . . . in them secrets he already knew.

FIRST SPRITE. But that's what we're here for. We Sprites!

SECOND SPRITE. Did you know Perlimplín?

FIRST SPRITE. Since he was a child.

SECOND SPRITE. And Belisa?

FIRST SPRITE. Very well. Her room exhaled such intense perfume that I once fell asleep and awoke between her cat's claws.

[*They laugh.*]

SECOND SPRITE. This affair was . . .

FIRST SPRITE. Oh, of course!

SECOND SPRITE. All the world thought so.

FIRST SPRITE. And the gossip must have turned then to more mysterious things.

SECOND SPRITE. That's why our efficient and most sociable screen should not be opened yet.

FIRST SPRITE. No, don't let them find out.

SECOND SPRITE. The soul of Perlimplín, tiny and frightened like a newborn duckling, becomes enriched and sublime at these moments.

[*They laugh.*]

FIRST SPRITE. The audience is impatient.

SECOND SPRITE. And with reason. Shall we go?

FIRST SPRITE. Let's go. I feel a fresh breeze on my back already.

SECOND SPRITE. Five cool camellias of the dawn have opened in the walls of the bedroom.

FIRST SPRITE. Five balconies upon the city.

[*They rise and throw on some great blue hoods.*]

SECOND SPRITE. Don Perlimplín, do we help or hinder you?

FIRST SPRITE. Help: because it is not fair to place before the eyes of the audience the misfortune of a good man.

SECOND SPRITE. That's true, little friend, for it's not the same to say: "I have seen," as "It is said."

FIRST SPRITE. Tomorrow the whole world will know about it.

SECOND SPRITE. And that's what we wish.

FIRST SPRITE. One word of gossip and the whole world knows.

SECOND SPRITE. Sh . . .

[*Flutes begin to sound.*]

FIRST SPRITE. Shall we go through this tiny darkness?

SECOND SPRITE. Let us go now, little friend.

FIRST SPRITE. Now?

SECOND SPRITE. Now.

[*They open the curtain.* DON PERLIMPLÍN *appears on the bed, with two enormous gilded horns.* BELISA *is at his side. The five balconies at the back of the stage are wide open, and through them the white light of dawn enters.*]

PERLIMPLÍN [*awakening*]. Belisa! Belisa! Answer me!

BELISA [*pretending to awaken*]. Perlimplinpinito . . . what do you want?

PERLIMPLÍN. Tell me quickly.

BELISA. What do you want me to tell you? I fell asleep long before you did.

PERLIMPLÍN [*leaps from the bed. He has on his cassock*]. Why are the balconies open?

BELISA. Because this night the wind has blown as never before.

PERLIMPLÍN. Why do the balconies have five ladders that reach to the ground?

BELISA. Because that is the custom in my mother's country.

PERLIMPLÍN. And whose are those five hats which I see under the balconies?

BELISA [*leaping from the bed*]. The little drunkards who come and go. Perlimplinillo! Love!

[PERLIMPLÍN *looks at her, staring stupefied.*]

PERLIMPLÍN. Belisa! Belisa! And why not? You explain everything so well. I am satisfied. Why couldn't it have been like that?

BELISA [*coyly*]. I'm not a little fibber.

PERLIMPLÍN. And I love you more every minute!

BELISA. That's the way I like it.

PERLIMPLÍN. For the first time in my life I am happy! [*He approaches and embraces her, but, in that instant, turns brusquely from her.*] Belisa, who has kissed you? Don't lie, for I know!

BELISA [*gathering her hair and throwing it over her shoulder*]. Of course you know! What a playful little husband I have! [*In a low voice.*] You! You have kissed me!

PERLIMPLÍN. Yes. I have kissed you . . . but . . . if someone else had kissed you . . . if someone else had kissed you . . . do you love me?

BELISA [*lifting a naked arm*]. Yes, little Perlimplín.

PERLIMPLÍN. Then, what do I care? [*He turns and embraces her.*] Are you Belisa?

BELISA [*coyly, and in a low voice*]. Yes! Yes! Yes!

PERLIMPLÍN. It almost seems like a dream!

BELISA [*recovering*]. Look, Perlimplín, close the balconies because before long people will be getting up.

PERLIMPLÍN. What for? Since we have both slept enough, we shall see the dawn. Don't you like that?

BELISA. Yes, but . . .

[*She sits on the bed.*]

PERLIMPLÍN. I have never seen the sunrise.

[BELISA, *exhausted, falls on the pillows of the bed.*]

It is a spectacle which . . . this may seem an untruth . . . thrills me! Don't you like it? [*Goes toward the bed.*] Belisa, are you asleep?

BELISA [*in her dreams*]. Yes.

[PERLIMPLÍN *tiptoes over and covers her with the red cape. An intense golden light enters through the balconies. Bands of paper birds cross them amidst the ringing of the morning bells.* PERLIMPLÍN *has seated himself on the edge of the bed.*]

PERLIMPLÍN.

Love, love
that here lies wounded.
So wounded by love's going;
so wounded,
dying of love.

Tell every one that it was just
the nightingale.
A surgeon's knife with four sharp edges;
the bleeding throat—forgetfulness.
Take me by the hands, my love,
for I come quite badly wounded,
so wounded by love's going.
So wounded!
Dying of love!

CURTAIN

Scene 2

[PERLIMPLÍN'S *dining room. The perspectives are deliciously wrong. All the objects on the table are painted as in a primitive Last Supper.*]

PERLIMPLÍN. Then you will do as I say?
MARCOLFA [*crying*]. Don't worry, master.
PERLIMPLÍN. Marcolfa, why do you keep on crying?
MARCOLFA. Your Grace knows. On your wedding night five men entered your bedroom through the balconies. Five! Representatives of the five races of the earth. The European, with his beard—the Indian—the Negro—the Yellow Man—and the American. And you unaware of it all.
PERLIMPLÍN. That is of no importance.
MARCOLFA. Just imagine: yesterday I saw her with another one.
PERLIMPLÍN [*intrigued*]. Really?
MARCOLFA. And she didn't even hide from me.
PERLIMPLÍN. But I am happy, Marcolfa.
MARCOLFA. The master astonishes me.
PERLIMPLÍN. You have no idea how happy I am. I have learned many things and above all I can imagine many others.
MARCOLFA. My master loves her too much.
PERLIMPLÍN. Not as much as she deserves.
MARCOLFA. Here she comes.
PERLIMPLÍN. Please leave.

[MARCOLFA *leaves and* PERLIMPLÍN *hides in a corner. Enter* BELISA *dressed in a red dress of eighteenth-century style. The skirt, at the back, is slit, allowing silk stockings to be seen. She wears huge earrings and a red hat trimmed with big ostrich plumes.*]

BELISA. Again I have failed to see him. In my walk through the park they were all behind me except him. His skin must be dark, and his kisses must perfume and burn at the same time—like saffron and cloves. Sometimes he passes underneath my balconies and moves his hand slowly in a greeting that makes my breasts tremble.

PERLIMPLÍN. Ahem!

BELISA [*turning*]. Oh! What a fright you gave me.

PERLIMPLÍN [*approaching her affectionately*]. I observe you were speaking to yourself.

BELISA [*distastefully*]. Go away!

PERLIMPLÍN. Shall we take a walk?

BELISA. No.

PERLIMPLÍN. Shall we go to the confectioner's?

BELISA. I said No!

PERLIMPLÍN. Pardon.

[*A letter rolled about a stone falls through the balcony.* PERLIMPLÍN *picks it up.*]

BELISA. Give that to me.

PERLIMPLÍN. Why?

BELISA. Because it's for me.

PERLIMPLÍN [*jokingly*]. And who told you that?

BELISA. Perlimplín! Don't read it!

PERLIMPLÍN [*jokingly severe*]. What are you trying to say?

BELISA [*weeping*]. Give me that letter!

PERLIMPLÍN [*approaching her*]. Poor Belisa! Because I understand your feelings I give you this paper which means so much to you. [BELISA *takes the note and hides it in her bosom.*] I can see things. And even though it wounds me deeply, I understand you live in a drama.

BELISA [*tenderly*]. Perlimplín!

PERLIMPLÍN. I know that you are faithful to me, and that you will continue to be so.

BELISA [*fondly*]. I've never known any man other than my Perlimplinillo.

PERLIMPLÍN. That's why I want to help you as any good husband should when his wife is a model of virtue. . . . Look. [*He closes the door and adopts a mysterious air.*] I know everything! I realized immediately. You are young and I am old . . . What can we do about it! But I understand perfectly. [*Pause. In a low voice.*] Has he come by here today?

BELISA. Twice.

PERLIMPLÍN. And has he signaled to you?

BELISA. Yes . . . but in a manner that's a little disdainful . . . and that hurts me!

PERLIMPLÍN. Don't be afraid. Two weeks ago I saw that young man for the first time. I can tell you with all sincerity that his beauty dazzled me. I have never seen another man in whom manliness and delicacy meet in a more harmonious fashion. Without knowing why, I thought of you.

BELISA. I haven't seen his face . . . but . . .

PERLIMPLÍN. Don't be afraid to speak to me. I know you love him . . . and I love you now as if I were your father. I am far from that foolishness; therefore . . .

BELISA. He writes me letters.

PERLIMPLÍN. I know that.

BELISA. But he doesn't let me see him.

PERLIMPLÍN. That's strange.

BELISA. And it even seems . . . as though he scorns me.

PERLIMPLÍN. How innocent you are!

BELISA. But there's no doubt he loves me as I wish. . . .

PERLIMPLÍN [*intrigued*]. How is that?

BELISA. The letters I have received from other men . . . and which I didn't answer because I had my little husband, spoke to me of ideal lands—of dreams and wounded hearts. But these letters from him . . . they . . .

PERLIMPLÍN. Speak without fear.

BELISA. They speak about me . . . about my body . . .

PERLIMPLÍN [*stroking her hair*]. About your body!

BELISA. "What do I want your soul for?" he tells me. "The soul is the patrimony of the weak, of crippled heroes and sickly people. Beautiful souls are at death's door, leaning upon whitest hairs and lean hands. Belisa, it is not your soul that I desire, but your white and soft trembling body."

PERLIMPLÍN. Who could that beautiful youth be?

BELISA. No one knows.

PERLIMPLÍN [*inquisitive*]. No one?

BELISA. I have asked all my friends.

PERLIMPLÍN [*inscrutably and decisively*]. And if I should tell you I know him?

BELISA. Is that possible?

PERLIMPÍN. Wait. [*Goes to the balcony.*] Here he is.

BELISA [*running*]. Yes?

PERLIMPLÍN. He has just turned the corner.

BELISA [*choked*]. Oh!

PERLIMPLÍN. Since I am an old man, I want to sacrifice myself for you. This that I do no one ever did before. But I am already beyond the world and the ridiculous morals of its people. Good-by.

BELISA. Where are you going?

PERLIMPLÍN [*at the door, grandiosely*]. Later you will know everything. Later.

CURTAIN

Scene 3

[*A grove of cypresses and orange trees. When the curtain rises,* MARCOLFA *and* PERLIMPLÍN *appear in the garden.*]

MARCOLFA. Is it time yet?

PERLIMPLÍN. No, it isn't time yet.

MARCOLFA. But what has my master thought?

PERLIMPLÍN. Everything he hadn't thought before.

MARCOLFA [*weeping*]. It's my fault!

PERLIMPLÍN. Oh, if you only knew what gratitude there is in my heart for you!

MARCOLFA. Before this, everything went smoothly. In the morning, I would take my master his coffee and milk and grapes. . . .

PERLIMPLÍN. Yes . . . the grapes! The grapes! But . . . I? It seems to me that a hundred years have passed. Before, I could not think of the extraordinary things the world holds. I was merely on the threshold. On the other hand . . . today! Belisa's love has given me a precious wealth that I ignored before . . . don't you see? Now I can close my eyes and . . . I can see what I want. For example, my mother, when she was visited by the elves. Oh, you know how elves are . . . tiny. It's marvelous! They can dance upon my little finger.

MARCOLFA. Yes, yes, the elves, the elves, but . . . how about this other?

PERLIMPLÍN. The other? Ah! [*With satisfaction.*] What did you tell my wife?

MARCOLFA. Even though I'm not very good at these things, I told her what the master had instructed me to say . . . that that young man . . . would come tonight at ten o'clock sharp to the garden, wrapped, as usual, in his red cape.

PERPLIMPLÍN. And she?

MARCOLFA. She became as red as a geranium, put her hands to her heart, and kissed her lovely braids passionately.

PERLIMPLÍN [*enthusiastic*]. So she got red as a geranium, eh? And, what did she say?

MARCOLFA. She just sighed; that's all. But, oh! such a sigh!

PERLIMPLÍN. Oh, yes! As no woman ever sighed before! Isn't that so?

MARCOLFA. Her love must border on madness.

PERLIMPLÍN [*vibrantly*]. That's it! What I need is for her to love that youth more than her own body. And there is no doubt that she loves him.

MARCOLFA [*weeping*]. It frightens me to hear you . . . but how is it possible? Don Perlimplín, how is it possible that you yourself should encourage your wife in the worst of sins?

PERLIMPLÍN. Because Perlimplín has no honor and wants to amuse himself! Now do you see? Tonight the new and unknown lover of my lady Belisa will come. What should I do but sing? [*Singing.*] Don Perlimplín has no honor! Has no honor!

MARCOLFA. Let my master know that from this moment on I consider myself dismissed from his service. We servants also have a sense of shame.

PERLIMPLÍN. Oh, innocent Marcolfa! Tomorrow you will be as free as a bird. Wait until tomorrow. Now go and perform your duty. You will do what I have told you?

MARCOLFA [*leaving, drying her tears*]. What else is there for me to do? What else?

PERLIMPLÍN. Good, that's how I like it.

[*A sweet serenade begins to sound.* DON PERLIMPLÍN *hides behind some rosebushes.*]

VOICES.

Upon the banks of the river
the passing night has paused to bathe.
The passing night has paused to bathe.
And on the breasts of Belisa
the flowers languish of their love.
The flowers languish of their love.

PERLIMPLÍN.

The flowers languish of their love.

VOICES.

The naked night stands there singing,
singing on the bridge of March.

Singing on the bridge of March.
Belisa, too, bathes her body
with briny water and spikenard.
With briny water and spikenard.

PERLIMPLÍN.
The flowers languish of their love!

VOICES.
The night of anise and silver
on all the roofs glows and shines.
On all the roofs glows and shines.
The silver of streams and of mirrors
and anise white of your thighs.
And anise white of your thighs.

PERLIMPLÍN. The flowers languish of their love!

[BELISA *appears in the garden splendidly dressed. The moon lights the stage.*]

BELISA. What voices fill with sweet harmony the air of this fragment of the night? I have felt your warmth and your weight, delicious youth of my soul. Oh! The branches are moving . . .

[*A man dressed in a red cape appears and crosses the garden cautiously.*]

BELISA. Sh! Here! Here!

[*The man signals with his hand that he will return immediately.*]

Oh! Yes . . . come back my love! Like a jasmine floating and without roots, the sky will fall over my moistening shoulders. Night! My night of mint and lapis lazuli . . .

[PERLIMPLÍN *appears.*]

PERLIMPLÍN [*surprised*]. What are you doing here?
BELISA. I was walking.
PERLIMPLÍN. Only that?
BELISA. In the clear night.
PERLIMPLÍN [*severely*]. What were you doing here?
BELISA [*surprised*]. Don't you know?
PERLIMPLÍN. I don't know anything.
BELISA. You sent me the message.
PERLIMPLÍN [*with ardent desire*]. Belisa . . . are you still waiting for him?

BELISA. With more ardor than ever.

PERLIMPLÍN [*severely*]. Why?

BELISA. Because I love him.

PERLIMPLÍN. Well, he will come.

BELISA. The perfume of his flesh passes beyond his clothes. I love him! Perlimplín, I love him! It seems to me that I am another woman!

PERLIMPLÍN. That is my triumph.

BELISA. What triumph?

PERLIMPLÍN. The trumph of my imagination.

BELISA. It's true that you helped me love him.

PERLIMPLÍN. As now I will help you mourn him.

BELISA [*puzzled*]. Perlimplín! What are you saying?

[*The clock sounds ten. A nightingale sings.*]

PERLIMPLÍN. It is the hour.

BELISA. He should be here this instant.

PERLIMPLÍN. He's leaping the walls of my garden.

BELISA. Wrapped in his red cape.

PERLIMPLÍN [*drawing a dagger*]. Red as his blood.

BELISA [*holding him*]. What are you going to do?

PERLIMPLÍN [*embracing her*]. Belisa, do you love him?

BELISA [*forcefully*]. Yes!

PERLIMPLÍN. Well, since you love him so much, I don't want him ever to leave you. And in order that he should be completely yours, it has come to me that the best thing would be to stick this dagger in his gallant heart. Would you like that?

BELISA. For God's sake, Perlimplín!

PERLIMPLÍN. Then, dead, you will be able to caress him in your bed—so handsome and well groomed—without the fear that he should cease to love you. He will love you with the infinite love of the dead, and I will be free of this dark little nightmare of your magnificent body. [*Embracing her.*] Your body . . . that I will never decipher! [*Looking into the garden.*] Look where he comes. Let go, Belisa. Let go! [*He exits running.*]

BELISA [*desperately*]. Marcolfa! Bring me the sword from the dining room; I am going to run my husband's throat through. [*Calling.*]

Don Perlimplín
Evil husband!
If you kill him,
I'll kill you!

[*A man wrapped in a large red cape appears among the branches. He is wounded and stumbling.*]

BELISA. My love! . . . Who has wounded you in the breast?

[*The man hides his face in his cape. The cape must be enormous and cover him to the feet. She embraces him.*]

Who opened your veins so that you fill my garden with blood? Love, let me look at your face for an instant. Oh! Who has killed you . . . Who?

PERLIMPLÍN [*uncovering himself.*] Your husband has just killed me with this emerald dagger. [*He shows the dagger stuck in his chest.*]

BELISA [*frightened*]. Perlimplín!

PERLIMPLÍN. He ran away through the fields and you will never see him again. He killed me because he knew I loved you as no one else. . . . While he wounded me he shouted: "Belisa has a soul now!" Come near. [*He has stretched out on the bench.*]

BELISA. Why is this? And you are truly wounded.

PERLIMPLÍN. Perlimplín killed me. . . . Ah, Don Perlimplín! Youngish old man, manikin without strength, you couldn't enjoy the body of Belisa . . . the body of Belisa was for younger muscles and warm lips. . . . I, on the other hand, loved your body only . . . your body! But he has killed me . . . with this glowing branch of precious stones.

BELISA. What have you done?

PERLIMPLÍN [*near death*]. Don't you understand? I am my soul and you are your body. Allow me this last moment, since you have loved me so much, to die embracing it.

[BELISA, *half naked, draws near and embraces him.*]

BELISA. Yes . . . but the young man? Why have you deceived me?

PERLIMPLÍN. The young man?

[*Closes his eyes. The stage is left in magical light.* MARCOLFA *enters.*]

MARCOLFA. Madam . . .

BELISA [*weeping*]. Don Perlimplín is dead!

MARCOLFA. I knew it! Now his shroud will be the youthful red suit in which he used to walk under his own balconies.

BELISA [*weeping*]. I never thought he was so devious.

MARCOLFA. You have found out too late. I shall make him a crown of flowers like the noonday sun.

BELISA [*confused, as if in another world*]. Perlimplín, what have you done, Perlimplín?

MARCOLFA. Belisa, now you are another woman. You are dressed in the most glorious blood of my master.

BELISA. But who was this man? Who was he?

MARCOLFA. The beautiful adolescent whose face you never will see.

BELISA. Yes, yes, Marcolfa—I love him—I love him with all the strength of my flesh and my soul—but where is the young man in the red cape? Dear God, where is he?

MARCOLFA. Don Perlimplín, sleep peacefully. . . . Do you hear? Don Perlimplín. . . . Do you hear her?

[*The bells sound.*]

CURTAIN

THE WRITERS AND THEIR PLAYS

BENAVENTE, JACINTO—1866–1954 (publication dates) *Señora Ama,* 1908; *The Bonds of Interest,* 1915; *The Smile of Mona Lisa,* 1915; *The Evil Doers of Good,* 1917; *His Widow's Husband,* 1917; *La Malquerida* (also known as *The Passion Flower*), 1917; *No Smoking,* 1917; *The Governor's Wife,* 1918; *The Prince Who Learned Everything Out of Books,* 1918; *Saturday Night,* 1918; *Autumnal Roses,* 1919; *Princess Bebé,* 1919; *A Good Marriage,* 1922; *In the Place of Don Juan* (also known as *Another's Nest*), 1922; *In the Clouds,* 1923; *The Truth,* 1923; *Field of Ermine,* 1924; *A Lady,* 1924; *Lecciones de buen amor,* 1924; *The Magic of an Hour,* 1924; *The School for Princesses,* 1924; *Pepa Doncel,* 1928; *At Close Range,* 1936; *Brute Force,* 1936 (*Opera: Gente Conocida,* 1896); *The Witches' Sabbath,* 1901.

MARTÍNEZ SIERRA, GREGORIO—1881–1947 (publication dates) *La Sombra del Padre,* 1909; *El Ama de la Casa,* 1910; *Sólo para Mujeres,* 1913; *Amanecer,* 1915; *The Cradle Song,* 1917; *Love Magic,* 1917; *The Lover,* 1917; *Madame Pepita,* 1917; *Poor John,* 1917; *The Theatre of Dreams,* 1918; *The Kingdom of God,* 1922; *The Romantic Young Lady,* 1922; *The Two Shepherds,* 1922; *Wife to a Famous Man,* 1922; *Idyll,* 1926; *Holy Night,* 1928; *Let Us Be Happy,* 1929; *A Lily Among Thorns,* 1930; *The Forgotten Song,* 1936. Also, these librettos: *Las Golondinas,* 1912; *La Llama,* 1918.

LORCA, FEDERICO GARCÍA—1899–1936 (completion dates) *The Spell of the Butterfly,* 1920; *The Girl Who Waters the Sweet Basil Flower* and the *Inquisitive Prince,* 1923; *Mariana Pineda,* 1927; *Chimera,* 1928; *The Lass, the Sailor, and the Student,* 1928; *Buster Keaton's Constitutional,* 1928; *The Puppet Farce of Don Cristóbal,* 1930; *The Shoemaker's Prodigious Wife,* 1930; *The Love of Don Perlimplín and Belisa in the Garden,* 1931; *If Five Years Pass,* 1931; *The Public,* 1931; *Blood Wedding,* 1933; *Yerma,* 1934; *The Tragicomedy of Don Cristóbal,* 1934; *The House of Bernarda Alba,* 1936.

BUERO VALLEJO, ANTONIO—1916– (publication dates, except as noted) *Historia de una escalera,* 1949; *Hoy es Fiesta,* 1956; *Las Meninas,* 1960; *In the Burning Darkness* (unpublished, unproduced, undated); *The Dream Weaver,* 1964.

SASTRE, ALFONSO—1926– (completion dates) *Cargo of Dreams,* 1949; *Uranium 235,* 1949; *Pathetic Prologue,* 1949; *The Condemned Squad,* 1953; *The Gag,* 1954; *Anna Kleiber,* 1955; *The Blood of God,* 1955; *Everyman's Bread,* 1955; *The Raven,* 1958; *Death in the Neighborhood,* 1959; *The Assault of Night,* 1959; *Sad Are the Eyes of William Tell,* 1960; *Red Earth,* 1960; *Death Thrust,* 1961; *In the Net,* 1961; *Death Has Sounded,* 1962.

SELECTED BIBLIOGRAPHY

GENERAL

BRENAN, GERALD *The Literature of the Spanish People,* New York, 1957.

CHANDLER, FRANK *Modern Continental Playwrights,* New York, 1931.

GASSNER, JOHN *Masters of the Drama,* New York, 1940.

TURRELL, C. A. *Contemporary Spanish Dramatists,* Boston, 1919.

BENAVENTE

BELL, A. F. G. *Contemporary Spanish Literature,* New York, 1925.

ONIS, F. DE "Jacinto Benavente," *North American Review,* March, 1923, Vol. 217.

STARKIE, WALTER *Jacinto Benavente,* London, 1924.

MARTÍNEZ SIERRA

HATCHER, HARLAN *Modern Continental Dramas,* New York, 1941.

UNDERHILL, JOHN GARRETT *The Plays of G. Martínez Sierra,* New York, 1938.

WARREN, L. A. *Modern Spanish Literature,* New York, 1929.

LORCA

BAREA, ARTURO *Lorca: The Poet and His People,* London, 1944.

DURAN, MANUEL (ed.) *Lorca: A Collection of Critical Essays,* Englewood Cliffs, New Jersey, 1962.

HONIG, EDWIN *García Lorca,* New York, 1951.

LIMA, ROBERT *The Theatre of García Lorca,* New York, 1963.

SALINAS, PEDRO "Lorca and the Poetry of Death," *The Theatre in the Twentieth Century,* edited by Robert W. Corrigan, New York, 1962.

BUERO VALLEJO

BUERO VALLEJO, ANTONIO "Commentario," *Colección Teatro,* Madrid, 1951.

CASTELLANO, JUAN R. "Un nuevo comediografo español: A Buero Vallejo," *Hispania,* Madrid, March, 1954.

CASTELLANO, JUAN R. Introduction to *En la ardiente Oscuridad,* New York, 1954.

SANCHEZ, JOSE Introduction to *Historia de una escalera,* New York, 1955.

SASTRE

DECOSTER, CYRUS "Alfonso Sastre," *Tulane Drama Review,* Vol. V, No. 2, 1960.

PRONKO, LEONARD "The Revolutionary Theatre of Alfonso Sastre," *Tulane Drama Review,* Vol. V, No. 2, 1960.

SASTRE, ALFONSO "Drama and Society," *Tulane Drama Review,* Vol. V, No. 2, 1960.